MAKING THE SOVIET INTE

Making the Soviet Intelligentsia explores the formation of educated elites in Russian and Ukrainian universities during the early Cold War. In the postwar period, universities emerged as training grounds for the military-industrial complex, showcases of Soviet cultural and economic accomplishments, and valued tools in international cultural diplomacy. However, these fêted Soviet institutions also generated conflicts about the place of intellectuals and higher learning under socialism. Disruptive party initiatives in higher education – from the xenophobia and anti-Semitic campaigns of late Stalinism to the rewriting of history and the opening of the USSR to the outside world under Khrushchev – encouraged students and professors to interpret their commitments as intellectuals in the Soviet system in varied and sometimes contradictory ways. In the process, the social construct of intelligentsia took on divisive social, political, and national meanings for educated society in the postwar Soviet state.

BENJAMIN TROMLY is Associate Professor in the Department of History at the University of Puget Sound, where he teaches Modern European History.

NEW STUDIES IN EUROPEAN HISTORY

Edited by

PETER BALDWIN, University of California, Los Angeles
CHRISTOPHER CLARK, University of Cambridge
JAMES B. COLLINS, Georgetown University
MIA RODRÍGUEZ-SALGADO, London School of Economics and Political
Science
LYNDAL ROPER, University of Oxford
TIMOTHY SNYDER, Yale University

The aim of this series in early modern and modern European history is to publish
outstanding works of research, addressed to important themes across a wide geographical range, from southern and central Europe, to Scandinavia and Russia,
from the time of the Renaissance to the present. As it develops, the series will
comprise focused works of wide contextual range and intellectual ambition.

A full list of titles published in the series can be found at:
www.cambridge.org/newstudiesineuropeanhistory

MAKING THE SOVIET INTELLIGENTSIA: UNIVERSITIES AND INTELLECTUAL LIFE UNDER STALIN AND KHRUSHCHEV

BENJAMIN TROMLY

CAMBRIDGE
UNIVERSITY PRESS

CAMBRIDGE
UNIVERSITY PRESS

University Printing House, Cambridge CB2 8BS, United Kingdom

Cambridge University Press is part of the University of Cambridge.

It furthers the University's mission by disseminating knowledge in the pursuit of education, learning and research at the highest international levels of excellence.

www.cambridge.org
Information on this title: www.cambridge.org/9781107595347

First published 2014
First paperback edition 2015

A catalogue record for this publication is available from the British Library

Library of Congress Cataloguing in Publication data
Tromly, Benjamin, 1976–
Making the Soviet intelligentsia : universities and intellectual life under
Stalin and Khrushchev / Benjamin Tromly.
pages cm. – (New studies in European history)
ISBN 978-1-107-03110-4 (hardback)
1. Universities and colleges – Soviet Union – History.   2. Higher education
and state – Soviet Union – History.   3. Soviet Union – Intellectual life –
1917–1970.   4. Intellectuals – Soviet Union – History.   I. Title.
LA837.T76   2013
378.47–dc23
2013021429

ISBN 978-1-107-03110-4 Hardback
ISBN 978-1-107-59534-7 Paperback

To Katya, Fred, and Annette, with much love

Contents

Acknowledgments

This project would not have been possible without substantial time spent in Russia and Ukraine over a ten-year period. While at Harvard University, the Fulbright-Hays DDRA program and the International Research and Exchanges Board funded a year of research. I am also indebted to the Davis Center for Russian and Eurasian Studies, which provided support for several research trips and a postdoctoral fellowship. The Harvard Ukrainian Research Institute also provided very generous funding for my research. University of Puget Sound facilitated my final research trip for the project.

This book, which began as a doctoral dissertation, has occupied a decade of my life. The people and institutions that have made it possible are many. My thanks go above all to my graduate advisor Terry Martin, who challenged me to address major issues, to question my evidence, and to reflect critically on my own work – even while providing the supporting hand that is sorely needed by any graduate student. My committee members Timothy Colton, Alison Frank, and Eric Lohr provided invaluable feedback on the project during its formative period. Though not serving in this capacity, Loren Graham, Serhii Plokhii, and Roman Szporluk also provided guidance and intellectual inspiration. I am particularly grateful to my undergraduate advisor Daniel Kaiser, who first sparked my interest in Russian history years ago and has remained an inspiring figure and a friend over the years.

Beyond this group of advisors, many scholars have enriched my project by reading drafts of work at various stages or by discussing my ideas less formally. With the certainty that the list is incomplete, I would like to thank John Connelly, Anne Gorsuch, Steven Lovell, Benjamin Nathans, Lewis Siegelbaum, Liz Wood, Serhy Yekelchyk, and Denise Youngblood for their insights and suggestions over the years. The Russian and East European History Workshop at Harvard was a lively and critical sounding board for the project at various stages, and I am grateful to the people I have learned from in this forum over the years, including Misha Akulov, Mark Baker,

David Brandenberger, Patrice Dabrowski, David Engerman, Michael Gordin, Sofiya Grachova, Karl Hall, Kelly O'Neill, John Ondrovcik, Maya Peterson, Sean Pollock, Timothy Snyder, Eren Tasar, and Helena Toth. I am grateful to several scholars who have helped me with practical support, including tracking down sources and interview subjects: Laurent Coumel, Juliane Fürst, Thomas Krüger, Donald Raleigh, William Risch, and Kelly Smith. I have benefitted from interacting with scholars during my research trips in Russia and Ukraine: Alan Barenberg, Timothy Johnston, Matthew Light, Rosa Magnusdottir, Jeffrey Mankoff, Kristin Roth-Ey, and Jenny Smith. My colleagues at University of Puget Sound have offered valuable advice and moral support while I recast my project as a manuscript. It goes without saying that I alone am responsible for any errors of facts and judgment.

I have benefitted from the kind assistance of countless people in Russia and Ukraine. Elena Zubkova offered some fruitful suggestions at a very early stage of my research, while Heorhii Kasianov and Iurii Shapoval in Kyiv, Gennadii Kuzovkin in Moscow, and Anatolii Avrus in Saratov, directed me to interview subjects and sources. I thank the staff of the archives I worked in (listed in my bibliography), and particularly Galina Mikhailovna Tokareva at the Russian State Archive of Socio-Political History and Natalia Oleksiivna Tkachenko at the State Archive of Kyiv Oblast'. I am grateful to the people who have helped to provide accommodation for me during research trips, and particularly Oksana Mykhed and her family in Kyiv and Ksenia Borisovna in Saratov.

Most of all, I am very indebted to the forty-four people who agreed to be interviewed for this project in Cambridge, Massachusetts, Kyiv, Moscow, Saratov, and St. Petersburg. Within this diverse and fascinating group of individuals, Viktor Seleznev in Saratov, Aleksandr Lavut, Sergei Litvinenko, and Vladimir Tikhomirov in Moscow, and Mikhail Beletskii and Les' Taniuk in Kyiv deserve special thanks for providing me with hard-to-obtain written sources. This book could not have been written without the willingness of these individuals to engage in the difficult project of remembering their distant pasts. Compiling and analyzing their memories and insights has proven a most rewarding and fruitful component of this project.

My family has been a constant support for this project. The Peshkovs in St. Petersburg provided a much-needed home away from home and a support network in Seattle, while Luke, Stephanie, and Henry have cheered me on from Canada. My children Maxim and Sasha are considerably younger than my book, but they have helped me too (unfortunately, Maxim's Darth Vadar illustrations did not make it into this volume).

Fred and Annette Tromly proved to be dedicated proofreaders as well as wonderful parents. Most of all, Katya Peshkova has seen me through the excitement and travails of this project and receives my everlasting gratitude for this (and much else).

A part of Chapter 7 of this book appeared as "An Unlikely National Revival: Soviet Higher Learning and the Ukrainian 'Sixtiers,' 1953–1964" in *Russian Review*, vol. 68, no. 4 (2008): 607–22. Reworked text from "The Rise and Decline of Soviet Patriotism: University Students in Khrushchev-Era Russia and Ukraine," published in *Nationalities Papers*, vol. 37, no. 3 (2009): 299–326, appears in Chapter 7 of this book.

Abbreviations

DAK	Derzhavnyi arkhiv mista Kyiva
DAKO	Derzhavnyi arkhiv Kyivs'koi oblasti
DRZ	Dom Russkogo zarubezh'ia imeni Aleksandra Solzhenitsyna
GANISO	Gosudarstvennyi arkhiv noveishei istorii Saratovskoi oblasti
GARF	Gosudarstvennyi arkhiv Rossiiskoi federatsii
GASO	Gosudarstvennyi arkhiv Saratovskoi oblasti
HIA	Hoover Institution Archives
KDU	T. H. Shevchenko Kyiv State University
KGB	Committee for State Security
Komsomol	All-Union Leninist Communist Youth League (in Ukraine, Leninist Communist Youth League of Ukraine)
MGB	Ministry for State Security (1946–54)
MGU	M. V. Lomonosov Moscow State University of the Order of Lenin and the Order of the Red Banner of Labor
MVO	Ministry of Higher Education
NITS "Memorial" SPb	Nauchno-informatsionnyi tsentr "Memorial" v Sankt-Peterburge
RGANI	Rossiiskii gosudarstvennyi arkhiv noveishei istorii
RGASPI	Rossiiskii gosudarstvennyi arkhiv sotsial'no-politicheskoi istorii
RGASPI-M	Rossiiskii gosudarstvennyi arkhiv sotsial'no-politicheskoi istorii – molodezhnyi arkhiv
RLE/RL, HIA	Radio Free Europe / Radio Liberty corporate records, Hoover Institution Archives

RSFSR	Russian Soviet Federative Socialist Republic
SGU	N.G. Chernyshevskii Saratov State University
TsAOPIM	Tsentral'nyi arkhiv obshchestvenno-politicheskoi istorii Moskvy
TsDAHOU	Tsentral'nyi derzhavnyi arkhiv hromads'kykh ob'iednan' Ukrainy
TsDAVO	Tsentral'nyi derzhavnyi arkhiv vyshchykh orhaniv vlady ta upravlinnia Ukrainy
TsDNA	Tsentr dokumentatsii "Narodnyi arkhiv"
TsK	Central Committee
TsMAM	Tsentral'nyi munitsipal'nyi arkhiv Moskvy
VIET	Voprosy istorii estestvoznaniia i tekhniki
VVSh	Vestnik vysshei shkoly

Introduction

A tourist visiting the Soviet Union in the 1950s would likely be shown a university as part of a standardized tour. Often housed in neoclassical buildings and surrounded by parks and monuments, universities occupied a prominent place in the Soviet cityscape. In Moscow, the spectacle was particularly grand. In addition to its eighteenth-century buildings across the street from the Kremlin, Moscow University received a massive complex of buildings on the Lenin Hills overlooking the capital, which opened with much fanfare in 1953.[1] The "palace of science," as it was dubbed in the press, was a state-of-the-art campus replete with modern laboratories, a twenty-two-floor elevator, and massive dormitories that offered each student a separate room – an unimaginable luxury for a generation that had grown up in cramped communal apartments. MGU's tower on the skyline of the capital was a symbol of the place that learning and culture held in Soviet socialism.

The Soviet university might have seemed both a familiar and foreign setting to the hypothetical visitor. The early Cold War saw the ascendancy of the university on both sides of the Iron Curtain as states proved eager to harness the potential of higher education for national defense and economic development. But the perceptive tourist – and later historian – might ponder what it meant for universities to occupy such a prominent place in state socialism's self-image. Despite the massive letters reading "Science to the Toilers" adorning the entrance to the main building of MGU, the scene inside the university would hardly suggest communist radicalism. On the contrary, telltale signs of academic hierarchy were on display within it: crowds of students parting in the hallways for august professors and lecture halls resounding with the voices of lecturers and the scratching of pens – all drowning out the hushed but animated discussions in the back rows. Moreover, the tourist would gain the impression that historical traditions were taken very seriously in the Soviet university. Soviet higher education

---

[1] "Velikaia zabota o Sovetskoi nauke," *Moskovskii universitet*, 29 August 1953: 1.

establishments carried honorific names drawn not only from party leaders like Stalin and A. A. Zhdanov but also from historical figures tied to a specific institution: Moscow University was named after the eighteenth-century scientist M. V. Lomonosov credited with founding it. Pride in connections to a pre-revolutionary past seemed unlikely in a state predicated on transforming the world.

The official aggrandizement of Soviet universities might appear a puzzle to the perceptive observer for another reason. In Europe and North America, the university is often thought of as an institution devoted to impartial learning as its own end, and therefore as one unencumbered by transient considerations of politics and narrow utility. As an historian of education has quipped, "the distinguishing value of the university is its apparent uselessness."[2] If this notion remains controversial in the West – some criticize universities for failing to live up to the ideal of an ivory tower, while others blame them for trying – it seemed positively aberrant against the backdrop of Soviet realities. For the founders of the Soviet state, learning could hold no value outside of the struggle to build the communist future; Vladimir Lenin held that "the very term 'apolitical' or 'non-political' education is a piece of bourgeois hypocrisy, nothing but humbuggery practiced on the masses . . ."[3] The use of Gulag labor to build the Lenin Hills campus is a fitting illustration of the political foundations of Soviet higher learning. With its historical ties and focus on non-applied knowledge, the university appeared an unlikely symbol of the postwar Soviet order.

The relationship between palaces of science and the state and society that surrounded them is the subject of this book. It focuses on one essential product of universities – students – in order to explore relationships among learning, identity, and society in the postwar Soviet Union. Universities served multiple purposes for the Soviet state during the early postwar period, understood here as one encompassing the sub-periods of late Stalinism (1945–53) and the first post-Stalin decade dominated by Nikita Khrushchev (1953–64). They were training grounds for the military-industrial complex, showcases of Soviet cultural and economic accomplishments, and, especially after Stalin's death, valued tools in international cultural diplomacy. Yet despite their ascendancy in the Soviet order, universities occupied a decidedly awkward position within it. The universities'

[2] Frank M. Turner, "Newman's University and Ours," in John Henry Newman, *The Idea of a University* (New Haven, CT: Yale University Press, 1996), 291.
[3] Vladimir Lenin, *Collected Works,* 4th English edn., 45 vols. (Moscow: Progress Publishers, 1965), vol. 31, 340–41.

pursuit of disinterested knowledge could appear as apolitical insularity, while their prestige and venerable dignity sometimes struck outsiders as a mask for social entitlement. The real and imagined faces of the universities made campus politics a tumultuous affair. This was especially clear with regard to the students the universities trained, people who would one day constitute the country's intellectual elite of scientists, researchers, teachers, and industrial specialists. The fêted national institutions rarely seemed to fit the mold policymakers set for them, in part because the students themselves emerged from the palace on the hill with changed self-conceptions and ambitions.

Little of this was foreseen when the Stalinist state embarked on massive expansion of higher learning after a crippling war. In 1960, there were 2,396,100 higher education students, almost three times the number in the USSR on the eve of World War II.[4] As the postwar educated strata mushroomed in numbers and grew in visibility, the question of where they would fit in the Soviet project became a critical one for all involved: party and state bureaucrats, professors, and the young specialists-in-the-making with their families. Shaping this postwar intellectual stratum proved a difficult endeavor for the Soviet system, in part because it dredged up longstanding and complicated questions about the life of the mind under Soviet socialism. Looming over postwar higher learning from the start was "intelligentsia," a term describing thinkers as a social group that had deep roots in Russian and Soviet history.

Imagining the Soviet intelligentsia

What is the intelligentsia? Although this is a question posed perennially in modern Russian and Soviet history, clear answers to it have rarely been forthcoming among scholars. In part, the word suffers from a malady common to many terms in heavy use among historians like "class" and "nation" – "intelligentsia" is heavily colored by ideological affinities and methodological presumptions. This problem is compounded by the very contours of Soviet history; fast-changing ideas about what intelligentsia should mean ensured that the term would carry myriad associations in any given period, let alone across a longer time span. The nineteenth-century origins of the concept, however, seem relatively clear. Few would contest that many educated Russians under the Tsarist regime showed

---

[4] S. V. Volkov, *Intellektual'nyi sloi v sovetskom obshchestve* (St. Petersburg: Fond "Razvitie," Institut nauchnoi informatsii po obshchestvennym naukam RAN, 1999), 28, 31.

passionate, and sometimes fanatical commitments to truth, progress, and equality or that "intelligentsia" was the mantle for self-identification along such lines. Of course, intellectuals the world over have claimed to represent the public interest, but it was only in underdeveloped and authoritarian Russia – and elsewhere in Eastern Europe in an ethnic nationalist mold – that intellectuals constituted a separate social stratum with its own cultural codes, what Isaiah Berlin called a "secular priesthood."[5] The Bolsheviks came to power armed with deep hostility toward the pre-revolutionary intelligentsia from which their leaders had emerged and a determination to replace it with one drawn from the people – that is, until the arrival of communism would make the concentration of knowledge in a distinct part of society unnecessary.[6]

In one of many drastic reversals of the Stalin period, a social category that had been relegated to the dustbin of history experienced an unexpected revival. In 1936, the dictator declared that a reformed and loyal "toiling intelligentsia" had emerged, a "stratum" (*prosloika*) with a rightful place in socialist society alongside the workers and collective farmers.[7] While perhaps dubious in its Marxist credentials, Stalin's re-establishment of intelligentsia as a social category was both constitutive and reflective of the social system that took shape in the 1930s. By legitimizing the place of educated professionals under socialism in doctrinal terms, Stalin's "toiling intelligentsia" signaled a wider integration of educated elites in the Soviet order. It solidified the career trajectories of the *vydvizhentsy* or "promotion candidates," young workers and peasants rushed through higher education to take up professional occupations (and who would come to provide a crucial basis of social support for the Stalin regime).[8] Just as importantly, the "toiling intelligentsia" provided the possibility of rehabilitation to the remaining representatives of the pre-revolutionary educated stratum, people

---

[5] Entry points to the voluminous literature on the Russian intelligentsia are Richard Pipes (ed.), *The Russian Intelligentsia* (New York: Columbia University Press, 1961) and Isaiah Berlin, *Russian Thinkers* (New York: Viking Press, 1978). On the troubled relationship of Russian intellectuals to the ethnic nation, see Nathaniel Knight, "Was the Intelligentsia Part of the Nation? Visions of Society in Post-Emancipation Russia," *Kritika*, 7 (2006): 733–58. For comparison to the Polish case, see Alexander Gella, "The Life and Death of the Polish Intelligentsia," *Slavic Review*, 30 (1971): 1–27.

[6] On early conceptions of the intelligentsia and higher learning, see Igal Halfin, *From Darkness to Light: Class, Consciousness, and Salvation in Revolutionary Russia* (University of Pittsburgh Press, 2000) and Michael David-Fox, *Revolution of the Mind: Higher Learning among the Bolsheviks, 1918–1929* (Ithaca, NY: Cornell University Press, 1997).

[7] I. V. Stalin, "O proekte konstitutsii soiuza SSSR," in Robert H. McNeal (ed.), *Sochineniia*, 3 vols. (Stanford, CA: The Hoover Institution on War, Revolution, and Peace, Stanford University), vol. 1, 142–46.

[8] Sheila Fitzpatrick, "Stalin and the Making of a New Elite," in *The Cultural Front: Power and Culture in Revolutionary Russia* (Ithaca, NY: Cornell University Press, 1992), 149–82.

who had been considered class enemies or marginalized as "bourgeois specialists" in the preceding years. Of course, such assimilation came at a price: the Stalinist system made professional thinkers of all sorts more dependent on state power and agendas than ever before. Relentless demands from above for unquestioning service and "party-mindedness" accompanied state-employed intellectuals' newfound prominence and (relative) social privilege. Indeed, the very construct of the "toiling intelligentsia" underscored intellectuals' reliance on serving the state, as it defined membership in the group according to formal educational achievement and occupational criteria (the performance of "mental labor"), both of which the party-state monopolized.[9]

Whatever its ideological or social limitations, the Stalinist reworking of an old notion created new possibilities for the emergence of a distinctly Soviet intelligentsia. In fact, Soviet intellectuals – understood broadly as producers and consumers of highly specialized and abstract ideas – always had a sense of purpose and social standing, one that eluded the Stalinist vision of an army of obedient state servants. Three broad aspects of the Stalinist project complicated the idea and reality of a "toiling intelligentsia." First, intellectuals were agents in communism's core agenda of creating a modern social order and overcoming Russian "backwardness," a commitment Bolshevism inherited from the pre-revolutionary Russian intelligentsia.[10] If society is subject to human design through rational intervention, holders of knowledge should, at least in theory, be society's teachers.[11] Reflecting this consideration, the life of the mind was a vital part of socialist "culture," which in the Soviet understanding was a "missionary ideal," "a standard of civilization to be met, not a descriptive or relativistic term."[12] According to official

---

[9] The standard Russian dictionary from 1989 follows this understanding, defining "intelligentsia" as "people of mental labor who possess education and special knowledge in different spheres of science, technology and culture; the societal stratum of people who engage in such labor." S. I. Ozhegov, *Slovar' russkogo iazyka: okolo 57,000 slov* (Moscow: Russkii iazyk, 1989), 251.

[10] Works that place modernity at the center of analysis of Stalinism include Stephen Kotkin, *Magnetic Mountain: Stalinism as a Civilization* (Berkeley: University of California Press, 1995) and David L. Hoffmann, *Stalinist Values: The Cultural Norms of Soviet Modernity, 1917–1941* (Ithaca, NY: Cornell University Press, 2003).

[11] Zygmunt Bauman, "Legislators and Interpreters: Culture as the Ideology of Intellectuals," in Chris Jenks (ed.), *Culture: Critical Concepts in Sociology* (New York: Routledge, 2002), 316–36. Indeed, Lenin's hatred of the old intelligentsia sat uncomfortably with his belief that the proletariat would need to build on culture inherited from the bourgeois past. See Neil Harding, *Lenin's Political Thought: Theory and Practice in the Democratic and Socialist Revolutions* (Chicago: Haymarket Books, 2009), 638–50.

[12] Stephen Lovell, *The Russian Reading Revolution: Print Culture in the Soviet and Post-Soviet Eras* (New York: St. Martin's Press, 2000), 19. Throughout this book, I use "culture" in this specifically Soviet definition in order to avoid applying other meanings of the word to the Soviet case anachronistically.

policies and pronouncements, intellectuals were the carriers of "culture" and exemplars of "culturedness" (*kul'turnost'*), the core attributes of the modern subject such as reason, discipline, personal cultivation, and fluency in a commonly agreed-upon body of knowledge.[13] A core mission of the Soviet project was to create the most modern and cultured society in the world – something one scholar has called "Socialist Realist mass culturalization" – and the intellectuals were to be at the forefront of it.[14]

Changing ideas about history were another aspect of Stalinism that infused new life into the intelligentsia. In the 1930s, the Stalinist party-state rehabilitated aspects of the pre-revolutionary past, part of a broader trend toward traditionalism, conservatism, and social inequality that has (controversially) been dubbed the "Great Retreat." While the term might be misleading – no thought of historical regression entered official calculations in the 1930s – the developments it characterizes were of lasting importance for Soviet history, and perhaps for educated society most of all.[15] The veneration of a (selective) canon of "progressive" writers, artists, and scholars from the pre-revolutionary period constituted a pillar of Soviet culture.[16] Nowhere was the echo of the old intellectual class clearer than in higher education, which took on a decidedly more traditional character under Stalin. Class quotas in admissions disappeared, traditional models of learning replaced experimental methods in the classroom, and comprehensive universities – previously attacked as preserves of class privilege – re-emerged, staffed in part by representatives of the non-communist professoriate.[17] Far from eschewing their historical roots, universities actively cultivated them: the MGU newspaper appealed to

---

[13] Important studies of *kul'turnost'* are Catriona Kelly, *Refining Russia: Advice Literature, Polite Culture, and Gender from Catherine to Yeltsin* (Oxford University Press, 2001) and Vadim Volkov, "The Concept of Kul'turnost': Notes on the Soviet Civilizing Process," in Sheila Fitzpatrick (ed.), *Stalinism: New Directions* (London: Routledge, 1999), 212–13. For Soviet intellectuals' particular connection to *kul'turnost'*, see Timo Vihavainen, *The Inner Adversary: The Struggle against Philistinism as the Moral Mission of the Russian Intelligentsia* (Washington, DC: New Academia Publishing, 2006).

[14] Svetlana Boym, *Common Places: Mythologies of Everyday Life in Russia* (Cambridge, MA: Harvard University Press, 1994), 105.

[15] For the terms of debate, see David L. Hoffmann, "Was There a 'Great Retreat' from Soviet Socialism? Stalinist Culture Reconsidered," *Kritika*, 5 (2004): 651–74 and Matthew E. Lenoe, "In Defense of Timasheff's Great Retreat," ibid.: 721–30.

[16] For the rehabilitation of Tsarist-era figures and traditions, see Kevin M. F. Platt and David Brandenberger, *Epic Revisionism: Russian History and Literature as Stalinist Propaganda* (Madison: University of Wisconsin Press, 2006) and Karen Petrone, *Life Has Become More Joyous, Comrades: Celebrations in the Time of Stalin* (Bloomington: Indiana University Press, 2000), esp. 113–48. For the Ukrainian question within historicized Stalin-era discourse, see Serhy Yekelchyk, *Stalin's Empire of Memory: Russian–Ukrainian Relations in the Soviet Historical Imagination* (University of Toronto Press, 2004).

[17] Sheila Fitzpatrick, "Professors and Soviet Power," in *The Cultural Front*, 37–64. See also Michael David-Fox, "The Assault on the Universities and the Dynamics of Stalin's 'Great Break,' 1928–1932,"

postwar students to become "continuers of the traditions" of pre-revolutionary thinkers (and former students) such as Belinskii, Griboedov, Lermontov, and Herzen.[18] Not surprisingly, young college-educated Soviet citizens before and after the war imagined themselves as continuers of the Russian intelligentsia tradition – unaware, perhaps, that they had abandoned much of its distinctive ideals of intellectual introspection and political opposition.[19]

A third factor that shaped the situation of postwar intellectuals was the Cold War. Technological developments and, most of all, the race to acquire an atomic weapon encouraged Stalin to grant scientific workers and other highly trained educated elites a new position of material privilege that was particularly impressive against the backdrop of universal deprivation of the early postwar years.[20] Heavy funding of the military-industrial complex created desirable new careers in science and spurred rapid expansion of the higher education institutions that provided access to them. As the ranks of educated society grew, the notion that intellectual affairs were integral to the future of the country became entrenched. In particular, the postwar years saw the consolidation of an officially sanctioned cult of science in Soviet society; the scientist who perfected the world and uncovered the secrets of the universe became "hero and idol" in the postwar Soviet imagination.[21]

These different facets of Stalinism – the valorization of *kul'turnost'*, the turn to the past, and the exigencies of the Cold War – formed the basis for the postwar intelligentsia as a distinct social phenomenon. In the postwar conditions, the meanings and imaginative associations of "intelligentsia" shifted. For increasing numbers of Soviet citizens, intelligentsia appeared much more than a mass of toilers with diplomas as the formal Stalinist definition would have it. Rather, it was an "imagined community" defined by its close connection to culture and the enlightening mission of the Soviet

---

in Michael David-Fox and György Péteri (eds.), *Academia in Upheaval: Origins, Transfers, and Transformations of the Communist Academic Regime in Russia and East Central Europe* (Westport, CT: Bergin and Garvey, 2000), 73–104.

[18] N. Obolenskaia, "Osushestvilas' zavetnaia mechta," *Moskovskii universitet*, 9 September 1957: 2 and S. Kozlova, "Poet-demokrat (k 75 – letiiu so dnia smerti N. A. Nekrasova)," *Stalinets*, 10 January 1953: 2.

[19] Yuri Slezkine, *The Jewish Century* (Princeton University Press, 2004), 256–57, 280–81.

[20] N. L. Krementsov, *Stalinist Science* (Princeton University Press, 1997), 98–105.

[21] Mark Kuchment, "Bridging the Two Cultures: The Emergence of Scientific Prose," in Loren R. Graham (ed.), *Science and the Soviet Social Order* (Cambridge, MA: Harvard University Press, 1990), 335. Different treatments of mass science in the USSR include Asif A. Siddiqi, *The Red Rockets' Glare: Spaceflight and the Soviet Imagination, 1857–1957* (Cambridge University Press, 2010), 301–13, and Paul R. Josephson, "Rockets, Reactors, and Soviet Culture," in Graham (ed.), *Science and the Soviet Social Order*, 168–94. For the emergence of popular science in the prewar period, see James T. Andrews, *Science for the Masses: The Bolshevik State, Public Science, and the Popular Imagination in Soviet Russia, 1917–1934* (College Station, TX: Texas A & M University Press, 2003).

state. Moreover, building on the longstanding association between learning and civilized values in Soviet discourses of *kul'turnost'*, the postwar Soviet construct of intelligentsia took on overtones of moral behavior: an *intelligentnyi* (intellectually refined) person was also a good one, or at least had a duty to be.[22]

Rather than being a merely etymological issue, the resurgence of intelligentsia signaled – and, to some degree, affected – social realities in the postwar Soviet Union. The valorization of the figure of the *intelligent* as an agent of enlightenment and civilization distinguished intellectual life in the USSR from that of non-socialist twentieth-century societies. In the capitalist West, intellectuals are often understood as a class apart, divided from the "laity" by the esoteric and lofty nature of their pursuits and by their seemingly inherent proclivity to question power structures.[23] In contrast, Soviet intellectuals – provided, of course, that they were able and willing to pursue knowledge under the aegis of the state – could be confident that their work was part of an overarching mission to civilize society and thereby to contribute to communist construction. As Czesław Miłosz argued, by structuring society on a system of abstract thought and enabling its articulators, Soviet-style socialism made intellectuals feel like they belonged.[24]

The ways that Soviet intelligentsia ideals shaped political and social practices in the USSR remain understudied. Rather, the tendency has been to simplify the issue by defining intelligentsia as a well-defined social group with clear traits of either a social or political nature. The first direction, to see intelligentsia as a "new class" specific to socialism, is understandable: given its ties to cultural superiority and refined values, the postwar intelligentsia was inevitably entangled in social hierarchies. Without a doubt, the early postwar years saw a sharp rise in the material privilege of the highly trained intellectual professions, including "scientific workers" in both higher education and research positions.[25] Along with improved standards of living came hereditary continuity. The Stalin-era professional strata – both the old holdovers and the many more

---

[22] The place of moral concerns in intellectual life is discussed in Philip Boobbyer, *Conscience, Dissent and Reform in Soviet Russia* (London and New York: Routledge, 2005). My account differs in depicting the moral language of the intelligentsia in a neutral rather than normative sense.
[23] Cf. Edward Shils, "The Intellectuals and the Powers: Some Perspectives for Comparative Analysis," *Comparative Studies in Society and History*, 1 (1958): 5–22.
[24] Czesław Miłosz, *The Captive Mind* (New York: Vintage International, 1981), 9.
[25] On privileges and perks in Soviet educated society, see Kirill Tomoff, *Creative Union: The Professional Organization of Soviet Composers, 1939–1953* (Ithaca, NY: Cornell University Press, 2006), 215–67 and M. R. Zezina, *Sovetskaia khudozhestvennaia intelligentsiia i vlast' v 1950–60-e gody* (Moscow: Dialog MGU, 1999), 57–66.

newcomers – reproduced their social position by passing on educational achievement to their children, taking advantage of the end of forced social mobility. In this sense, the educational system in the USSR, as in other modern countries, helped to cement social hierarchies. Indeed, *kul'turnost'* functioned as a form of what Pierre Bourdieu calls "cultural capital," the inherited markers of intellect and social bearing that contribute to social inequality, particularly through their impact on educational systems.[26]

Despite its deep connections to socio-economic divisions, however, the Soviet intelligentsia was not a social class as scholars have sometimes posited.[27] Rather, intelligentsia should be understood as a status group in the Weberian sense. Two considerations make the conceptual distinction between status and class important in this context. First, membership in the intelligentsia emerged from the "social honor" derived from a particular style of life, not from an economic position *per se*.[28] Becoming a Soviet *intelligent* meant abiding by a set of social codes that demonstrated ethical consciousness, concern for transcendent ideas, and distaste for banal and selfish ("petty-bourgeois") concerns.[29] A prime example of the everyday and habituated component of intelligentsia was the reverent attitude to books in educated circles; it was mandatory for a true *intelligent* to have a novel on his or her bedside table, one of the group's self-proclaimed members recently explained.[30] And while the intelligentsia lifestyle marked it off from other social groups, it also – like any other status marker – relied on the values of Soviet society as a whole. Indeed, party-state elites also made "claims to culture" by keeping classical literature on their bookshelves next to their collection of agitprop materials, even if only for show.[31]

[26] Pierre Bourdieu, *The State Nobility: Elite Schools in the Field of Power*, trans. Lauretta C. Clough (Stanford University Press, 1996), 5–6.

[27] For an overview of neo-Marxist approaches, see Ivan Szelenyi and Bill Martin, "The Three Waves of New Class Theories," *Theory and Society*, 17 (1988): 645–67. Some studies approach the intelligentsia as social elite without following the Marxist methodology of "new class" theories. See Mervyn Matthews, *Class and Society in Soviet Russia* (New York: Walker, 1972) and L. G. Churchward, *The Soviet Intelligentsia: An Essay on the Social Structure and Roles of Soviet Intellectuals during the 1960s* (London and Boston: Routledge and Kegan Paul, 1973). See also Eric J. Duskin, *Stalinist Reconstruction and the Confirmation of a New Elite, 1945–1953* (Houndmills, Basingstoke and New York: Palgrave, 2001).

[28] On the category of status, see Max Weber, "Class, Status, Party," in H. H. Gerth and C. Wright Mills (eds.), *From Max Weber: Essays in Sociology* (New York: Oxford University Press, 1958), 180–95.

[29] Boym, *Common Places*, 71–73.

[30] Vladimir Shlapentokh, "A Sociological Portrait of a Russian Intelligent: My Friend Felix Raskolnikov," *Johnson's Russian List*, no. 85 (1 May 2008), www.cdi.org/russia/johnson/2008-85-40. cfm (accessed 22 March 2009). On intellectuals' internalization of the "Russian reading myth," see Lovell, *The Russian Reading Revolution*.

[31] Mikhail Voslensky, *Nomenklatura: The Soviet Ruling Class*, trans. Eric Mosbacher (London: Bodley Head, 1984), 221.

This example leads to a second consideration: the intelligentsia's prestige as bearers of enlightenment and "culturedness" did not reinforce the hierarchies of wealth and power in Soviet society as directly as Bourdieu's class-based model would suggest. For instance, sociological studies of occupational prestige in the Soviet context, conducted among both students in the USSR and postwar Soviet émigrés, show the unique appeal of careers in learning in mature Soviet society. Soviet citizens held careers in research and teaching at the post-secondary level in greater esteem than administrative posts that yielded higher levels of privilege and power. Likewise, they saw second-tier educated ("mass intelligentsia") professions such as teaching in schools as more prestigious than better-paid but less education-based positions in production.[32] In short, being a Soviet intellectual was an end in itself, even if the path to its attainment – formal learning and engagement in ideas – flowed seamlessly into broader socio-economic divisions.

The alternative tradition of assigning a political essence to the Soviet intelligentsia is influential in recent writing in both the West and the post-Soviet space. In the usual presentation, the "intelligentsia" is characterized as the "liberal intelligentsia," a group defined by a civic, moral, or political agenda in implicit or explicit opposition to the authoritarian state.[33] A correlate of this approach is to connect the postwar intelligentsia to its pre-revolutionary Russian antecedent. Thus a recent comprehensive overview presents postwar intellectuals as reconstituting the traditions of championing social justice and freedom that had defined the intelligentsia under the Tsars; invoking the protagonist from Boris Pasternak's novel about the Russian Revolution, the study dubs them "Zhivago's children."[34]

Defining intelligentsia as a group defined by political strivings falls short on several counts. Most obviously, it imposes on the period a specific definition of intelligentsia that was far from universal among educated elites

[32] See Michael Swafford, "Perceptions of Social Status in the USSR," in James R. Millar (ed.), *Politics, Work, and Daily Life in the USSR: A Survey of Former Soviet Citizens* (Cambridge University Press, 1987), 292–98. A major study of displaced Soviet citizens after World War II, which focused on the interwar years, yielded similar results. See Alex Inkeles and Raymond A. Bauer, *The Soviet Citizen: Daily Life in a Totalitarian Society* (New York: Atheneum, 1968), 76–79.

[33] This view, long influential in Western historiography, has been particularly marked in émigré and post-Soviet historical writing. See Elena Zubkova, *Obshchestvo i reformy* (Moscow: Rossiia molodaia, 1993); Iu. Z. Danyliuk and Oleh Bazhan, *Opozytsiia v Ukraini: druha polovyna 50-kh–80-ti rr. XX st.* (Kyiv: Ridnyi krai, 2000) and Vladimir Shlapentokh, *Soviet Intellectuals and Political Power: The Post-Stalin Era* (Princeton University Press, 1990).

[34] Vladislav Zubok, *Zhivago's Children: The Last Russian Intelligentsia* (Cambridge, MA: Belknap Press, 2009). A fruitful *longue durée* perspective on the intelligentsia – albeit one that also underestimates differences in historical context – focuses on the social expectations of intellectuals in both the Tsarist and Soviet periods and the inability or unwillingness of political power to satisfy them. See Marshall S. Shatz, *Soviet Dissent in Historical Perspective* (Cambridge University Press, 1980).

at the time; work by linguists shows that "intelligentsia" was most often used in the period to denote a group defined by civilized behavior and refinement rather than by a civic or oppositional agenda.[35] In a broader sense, understanding intelligentsia in political (or proto-political) terms oversimplifies the historical record by obfuscating the tight integration of highly educated professionals – such as scientists, artists, and professors – into the postwar power structure through party membership and increased material perquisites.[36] Indeed, there is a strong element of myth-making involved in historical writing in this vein. Scholars too often internalize the self-perceptions of members of the intelligentsia by depicting "intelligentsia" as the progressive and moral compass of society – an approach that makes for a history driven by slippery normative concepts such as conscience and intellectual integrity.[37]

Linking Soviet intellectuals to their pre-revolutionary predecessors likewise threatens to obscure important historical contexts. Soviet intellectuals who came of age after the war were, on the whole, far more reconciled to the existing system and far less socially isolated than their Tsarist-era predecessors had been.[38] To be sure, some postwar intellectuals would come to see themselves as "spiritual heirs" of the old intelligentsia. In an influential memoir of the period, Liudmila Alekseeva recalls that she and her Muscovite friends in the 1950s wanted to "recapture" the "intellectual and spiritual exaltation" of the old intelligentsia, but were not attracted to its radical impulse to transform society.[39] In other words, the act of affiliation was not as natural or direct as a filial metaphor would suggest. Most importantly, Alekseeva's account of her affinity for old-regime landmarks

[35] Iu. A. Bel'chikov, "K istorii slov intelligentsia, intelligent," in M. V. Liapon et al. (eds.), *Filologicheskii sbornik: k 100-letiiu so dnia rozhdeniia akademika V. V. Vinogradova* (Moscow: Institut russkogo iazyka im. V. V. Vinogradova, 1995), 69.

[36] See Dietrich Beyrau, *Intelligenz und Dissens: die russischen Bildungsschichten in der Sowjetunion 1917–1985* (Göttingen: Vandenhoeck and Ruprecht, 1993), 262–63.

[37] Ironically, some studies which do not explicitly employ intelligentsia as a category of analysis interpret Soviet history from this social group's point of view, for instance by condemning the Soviet "middle strata" for a lack of culture (*meshchanstvo*) or by presenting the experiences of select groups of highly educated citizens as representative of entire generations of the Soviet people. For the first approach, see Vera S. Dunham, *In Stalin's Time: Middleclass Values in Soviet Fiction*, enlarged and updated edn. (Durham, NC: Duke University Press, 1990). The second tendency is exemplified by Alexei Yurchak, *Everything Was Forever, until It Was No More: The Last Soviet Generation* (Princeton University Press, 2006).

[38] In fact, Zubok's awareness of these differences between intelligentsias works against the central narrative of his informative book. See *Zhivago's Children*, 116, 120, 130, 162, 192, 208.

[39] Ludmila Alexeyeva and Paul Goldberg, *The Thaw Generation: Coming of Age in the Post-Stalin Era* (Boston: Little, Brown, 1990), 97, 4. An account of the appropriations of the old intelligentsia tradition by Soviet dissidenters is Jay Bergman, "Soviet Dissidents on the Russian Intelligentsia, 1956–1985: The Search for a Usable Past," *Russian Review*, 51 (1992): 16–35.

was entirely in line with the cult of the old intelligentsia, or at least the official rendition of it, that Soviet higher learning actively propagated.

Seeking to anchor intelligentsia in a neutral framework, this book presents it as an historically constructed set of identifications and ideas – or, to employ an overused term, an imagined community – rather than a collectivity with clear borders that acted with one will. Approaching the Soviet intelligentsia in this way does not mean ignoring the question of how Soviet subjects confronted and internalized official ideology. It does, how-ever, involve stressing the contingent and ambiguous ways that ideology functioned within Soviet educated society. In the account offered here, higher learning helped to entrench the Soviet intelligentsia by calling upon educated specialists to see themselves as bearers of state-sanctioned models of enlightenment and culture. However, young people could interpret and act upon the intelligentsia in different ways. Even students critical of Soviet institutions or practices – an important aspect of postwar university life – retained strong traces of the worldview that the Soviet order and the university most of all inculcated in them: a commitment to fundamental learning as a way of life, the belief that intellectual culture would civilize the Soviet system, and a predisposition toward idealism instead of narrow material goals. Yet while stressing the Soviet nature of the intelligentsia, the study does not follow an influential literature that reads conformity and dissent in terms of a single model of "Soviet subjecthood."[40] Rather, it attempts a less totalizing approach by stressing both the specific social context in which interactions with official ideology occurred as well as their frequently open-ended and even unpredictable nature.

The postwar university milieu

The universities themselves – as institutions, as social spaces, and as sym-bols – appear as crucial historical actors in this framework. At first glance, higher learning appears a remarkably monolithic pillar of Soviet society. Soon after the Russian Revolution the Bolsheviks uprooted both the uni-versities' hard-won autonomy – including its student corporation – along with many of the scholars and students who had defended it from the

---

[40] See Jochen Hellbeck, "Fashioning the Stalinist Soul: The Diary of Stepan Podlubnyi (1931–1939)," *Jahrbücher für Geschichte Osteuropas*, 44 (1996): 344–73 and Serguei A. Oushakine, "The Terrifying Mimicry of Samizdat," *Public Culture*, 13 (2001): 191–214. A recent study of Soviet postwar youth culture draws on this approach while questioning its applicability for understanding the naïve commitments of postwar youth. See Juliane Fürst, *Stalin's Last Generation: Soviet Post-War Youth and the Emergence of Mature Socialism* (Oxford University Press, 2010), 336–39.

Introduction 13

encroachments of the Tsarist state.[41] In the following decades, a distinct Soviet model of higher education emerged that fused universities to the state more thoroughly than had ever been attempted in Russia or anywhere else. Its goals were as ambitious as the Soviet project itself: to produce a stratum of highly qualified specialists that would internalize the "ideology of the gift" central to Stalinism – the commitment to serve the state selflessly as repayment for its benevolence.[42]

Three interrelated features characterized the Stalinist dispensation in higher learning. The first trait was subordination to the state, or the universities' position as "appendages of the state apparatus and line items in the state plan."[43] Decision-making in matters large and small – appointment of administrators and faculty members, the defense of dissertations, and even the content of lectures – fell under the control of central Communist Party and ministerial bureaucracies. The second feature, professionalization, followed from the first. The overriding mission of Soviet higher learning was the production of cadres needed for the planned economy, and courses of study were defined in terms of students' future occupational roles.[44] A superabundance of political controls constituted a third trait of higher learning in the USSR. Administrators wielded total power over faculty, and official statutes likened rectors to factory directors by granting them "undivided rule." In universities as in all Soviet institutions, "party-state dualism" cemented, and also sometimes undercut, this hierarchy. The Communist Party's extensive recruitment efforts within higher education – roughly half of the professoriate, graduate students, and other personnel held full or partial membership along with a smaller group of undergraduate students – provided a crucial channel through which political priorities shaped everyday practices on the ground.[45] During the Stalin years, party organizations along with the Ministry for State Security screened faculty, students, and applicants to higher learning

[41] See James C. McClelland, "Bolshevik Approaches to Higher Education, 1917–1921," *Slavic Review*, 30 (1971): 829 and Peter Konecny, *Builders and Deserters: Students, State, and Community in Leningrad, 1917–1941* (Montreal and Ithaca: McGill-Queen's University Press, 1999), 51–53. See also Stuart Finkel, *On the Ideological Front: The Russian Intelligentsia and the Making of the Soviet Public Sphere* (New Haven, CT: Yale University Press, 2007), 40–66.
[42] Jeffrey Brooks, *Thank You, Comrade Stalin! Soviet Public Culture from Revolution to Cold War* (Princeton University Press, 1999).
[43] John Connelly, *Captive University: The Sovietization of East German, Czech and Polish Higher Education, 1945–1956* (Chapel Hill, NC: University of North Carolina Press, 2000), 19.
[44] See the articulation of this idea in I. Ia. Braslavskii, "Voprosy vysshei shkoly v bol'shoi sovetskoi entsiklopedii," *VVSh*, no. 7 (1952): 55.
[45] For the sake of simplicity and clarity, I use the terms "professors" and "professoriate" to designate all instructors in higher learning, including professors proper and teaching staff of lower rank. On party recruitment, see Mervyn Matthews, *Education in the Soviet Union: Policies and Institutions since Stalin* (London and Boston: Allen & Unwin, 1982), 113–15.

for signs of ideological weakness. In 1951, party officials at SGU reported that they held compromising political information – about past arrests, suspicious social origins in "non-toiling elements," evidence of strong religious beliefs, or time spent in Axis prisoner-of-war camps – about over a full quarter of the university's teaching staff.[46] Political oversight of students was just as extensive. Nearly universal membership in the Komsomol brought student behavior under close scrutiny, as did a system of periodic "character references" or certificates of ideological health; both ensured that running afoul of university authorities could harm one's career – or worse.

Structures of power in the Soviet universities were not, however, as simple as organizational charts would suggest. Universities had a specific profile within the occupationally oriented Soviet system of higher learning: furthering knowledge in the academic disciplines and training cutting-edge future scholars.[47] They also gained in prestige, size, and resources in the postwar years, as training scientists for the military-industrial complex became a matter of top strategic priority.[48] The rigid structures of Soviet higher education ill-fitted the universities as academic powerhouses and showcase institutions. For instance, top-down diktat and standardization were hard to impose on academic communities devoted to generating fundamental knowledge in sometimes rapidly developing fields.[49] Even elaborate political controls took on a more flexible dynamic in the postwar universities, as patterns of recruitment to university administrative posts showed. In the early Cold War, scientific credentials became as important as party service as criteria for filling leadership posts in the universities. Party-state bureaucrats appointed as rector and deans "men of science" (and they were most often men), scholars with academic titles in the hard sciences with administrative experience in higher education or research institutions. Illustrative of the shifting priorities was the contrast between the first postwar rector of MGU and his successor appointed in 1951. The historian I. S. Galkin was a former railroad worker and Civil War veteran promoted to leading positions in higher education during

[46] GANISO f. 594, op. 2, d. 1890, l. 236.

[47] In the postwar period, approximately 10 percent of all the higher education students in the USSR studied in universities. The rest were enrolled in various kinds of institutions called "institutes" or "special schools" (*uchilishche*) which offered more applied learning. "Higher education establishment" (*vysshee uchebnoe zavedenie*) was the blanket term for all higher educational institutions; I use "colleges" as a convenient English shorthand. See Nicholas De Witt, *Education and Professional Employment in the USSR* (Washington, DC: National Science Foundation, 1961), 210, 231–32.

[48] A. I. Avrus, *Istoriia rossiiskikh universitetov: kurs lektsii* (Saratov: Kollezdh, 1998), 100–102.

[49] For instance, the Soviet government granted several universities "individual academic plans" that allowed some reprieve from central mandates in curricular planning. Ibid., 101.

the Great Terror; I. G. Petrovskii was an influential mathematician serving as the academician-secretary of the Division of Physics and Mathematics of the Academy of Sciences at the time of his appointment. Petrovskii had never joined the Communist Party, perhaps because of his suspect lineage in the pre-revolutionary merchant class.[50]

The drift toward an academically driven administration did not mean that universities gained a degree of autonomy. Petrovskii's lack of party status was the clear exception for directors of higher education establishments, as the frequent questioning of his ideological credentials among the party cells in the university indirectly suggested; in any case, he was flanked by deputies recruited from leading party activists.[51] More fundamentally, party controls guaranteed that research and instruction would be infused with Marxism-Leninism, a state of affairs that many scholars believed was only natural given that doctrine's scientific nature. Predominant in the universities was what Slava Gerovitch calls a "cultural medium" of Soviet science, a single language of intellectual exchange that blurred the line between ideological concepts and ostensibly non-ideological science.[52] Nevertheless, the academic profile of the universities gave their inner workings an incipient dualistic character. While party organizations handled sensitive ideological questions and strove to uphold "party-mindedness" (*partiinost'*) in all matters, academic authorities functioned with a degree of agency in matters of research and instruction that often struck party officials as excessive. This should not be surprising. Universities in other authoritarian state projects have shown some ability to uphold a sense of academic integrity.[53] More importantly, all systems of higher education are resistant to change, meaning that any institution or set of institutions at a specific moment in history is an amalgam of sometimes contradictory elements originating from different historical periods.[54] Despite the thorough transformation of higher learning and much else under Stalin, traces of pre-Stalin Russian academic life – such as a commitment to basic

[50] E. V. Il'chenko (ed.), *Akademik I. G. Petrovskii – rektor Moskovskogo universiteta* (Moscow: Izdatel'stvo Moskovskogo universiteta, 2001), 31–38.

[51] More typical were the rectors of KDU and SGU in the period, I. T. Shvets' (1955–1972) and R. V. Mertslin (1950–1965), who both had extensive party experience. See "Roman Viktorovich Mertslin (1903–1971)," "D. I. Mendeleyev Russian Chemical Society, Saratov Regional Branch," www.chem.saratov.ru/conf/physchemanalysis/mertslinrus.html (accessed 25 May 2011).

[52] Slava Gerovitch, *From Newspeak to Cyberspeak: A History of Soviet Cybernetics* (Cambridge, MA: MIT Press, 2002), 11–50.

[53] For accounts of universities in other authoritarian regimes, see John Connelly and Michael Grüttner (eds.), *Universities under Dictatorship* (University Park, PA: Pennsylvania State University Press, 2005).

[54] Fritz K. Ringer, *Education and Society in Modern Europe* (Bloomington: Indiana University Press, 1979).

research, a hierarchical system of research schools, and the *aspiration* to a measure of academic autonomy – survived into the postwar era, albeit sometimes in an inchoate form.

Students were well positioned to appreciate the universities' awkward position within Soviet ideological and political structures. Rather than being an abstract matter, the ways that universities alternatively implemented and evaded Soviet higher learning's standard package of subordination to the state, professionalism, and political control were a matter of great importance to postwar undergraduates. As this book will show, classroom experiences and particularly interactions with professors sometimes presented students with different models of authority than the peer-dominated and collectivist Komsomol sphere. Students also witnessed different approaches to the link between education and the economy in the universities; while told to see higher learning as a straight path to a single profession, they also observed the universities' commitment to offering relatively broad and theoretical courses of study with altogether less clear career applications.[55] Even ideological control in the universities fluctuated with the universities' intellectual and social contexts. Students sat through dogmatic lectures on the History of the Communist Party, but they sometimes gained quite different intellectual experiences, for instance by attending special seminars in specific subfields (the work of Lev Tolstoi or number theory, for instance) taught by leading authorities on the topic. As both lived experience and symbols, then, universities seemed to present students with seemingly contrasting relationships to higher learning, with knowledge appearing alternatively partisan and universal, applied and pure, or a matter of state policy and of professorial prerogative. In short, the postwar universities offered students different ways of understanding just what kind of intelligentsia they might become. The regime had built the palace of science on the hill and now discovered that it offered a plethora of vantage points on self and society.

Sources, methodology, and focus

Higher learning presents a rich context for examining intelligentsia and the ways it shaped social identities (although far from the only one): the place of learning in society had to be negotiated in institutions tasked with producing highly trained specialists for the future. To be sure, students were only *intelligenty* in formation by definition. However, students in any society are

---

[55] Compare E. Turkovskaia, "Kem budut rabotat' nashi vypuskniki," *Stalinets*, 7 June 1951: 4 and "Nash universitet," ibid.: 1.

shaped by perceptions of the society they are preparing to enter; as one scholar puts it, undergraduate students undergo a process of "anticipatory social-ization" that is every bit as meaningful as their formal studies.[56] In sum, what follows is not a study of "the intelligentsia," higher learning, or youth culture *per se*. Rather, the focus is on the spaces where these forces intersected.

The study addresses a diversity of postwar collegiate experiences by drawing on primary research on universities in three cities: the all-union capital of Moscow (MGU), the Ukrainian capital of Kyiv (KDU), and the provincial center of Saratov on the Volga River (SGU). A visitor to the three cities in the early postwar period would encounter sharply different urban environments in the bustling and well-provisioned Moscow, war-torn Kyiv, and the hungry provincial town of Saratov.[57] The three institutions in question were also starkly dissimilar, a product of their different places in a strictly hierarchical system of higher learning. The most obvious contrast was that of size; in 1955, there were 15,544 students enrolled in MGU, a far cry from the figures of 5,754 and 3,410 in KDU and SGU, respectively.[58] Academic stature and material resources were glaringly unequal in these three institutions. MGU housed whole research institutes and recruited renowned scholars as faculty, taking advantage of its proximity to the All-Union Academy of Sciences where researchers were concentrated; its counterparts not only in Saratov but also in the republic capital of Kyiv seemed decidedly "provincial" institutions to contemporaries.[59] The same cultural-geographical pecking order held with regard to the institutions' contacts with the outside world. Professors and students in Moscow and (to a lesser extent) Kyiv enjoyed rare opportunities to meet foreigners thanks to academic exchanges which brought graduate and undergraduate students from the socialist world and then, beginning in the mid-1950s, from developing and capitalist countries as well. In contrast, Saratov was made a city entirely

[56] Frank A. Pinner, "Student Trade Unionism in France, Belgium, and Holland: Anticipatory Socialization and Role Seeking," *Sociology of Education*, 37 (1964): 177–99.
[57] Portraits of these cities include Timothy J. Colton, *Moscow: Governing the Socialist Metropolis* (Cambridge, MA: Belknap Press of Harvard University Press, 1995), 249–380; Serhy Yekelchyk, "The Civic Duty to Hate: Stalinist Citizenship as Political Practice and Civic Emotion (Kiev, 1943–53)," *Kritika*, 7 (2006): 529–56 and Donald J. Raleigh, *Soviet Baby Boomers: An Oral History of Russia's Cold War Generation* (Oxford University Press, 2012).
[58] Nicholas De Witt, *Education and Professional Employment in the USSR* (Washington, DC: National Science Foundation, 1961), 210. These figures do not include enrollments through the universities' Correspondence and Evening Study Divisions.
[59] Indirectly, the institutional history of SGU confirmed the top-heavy nature of the university system. By all accounts, its postwar stature as the leading university of the lower Volga region owed much to the fact that it had been unified for a time with Leningrad University, which had been evacuated to Saratov during the war. See V. A. Artisevich, *Odinakovykh sudeb ne byvaet: vospominaniia* (Saratov: Izdatel'stvo Saratovskogo universiteta, 2009), 106–15.

"closed" to foreign nationals from 1955 because of its military-industrial profile.

Comparison of these institutions will show how university education participated in the hierarchies of culture and social station that characterized the Soviet intelligentsia and the postwar USSR more generally. The Russian and Soviet trope of "the provinces" as cultural backwaters is surely a stereotype – but it was also a self-fulfilling prophecy given the centralization of material resources and the cultural marginalization of the periphery in Stalin-era mass culture.[60] Nevertheless, the stark differences among these institutions make all the more important a fundamental trait they shared. In both the capitals and the provinces, Russia and Ukraine, universities constituted multivalent social spaces in which students and professors could locate and construct divergent ideas about the Soviet intelligentsia.[61]

A diverse source base is necessary to reconstruct postwar collegiate life and the identities that emerged within it. Archival documents produced at high bureaucratic levels of the Soviet system – party and state bodies concerned with oversight at central and regional levels – provide information on the implementation of policies but offer only inconsistent and selective glimpses of the university environment. A better sense of postwar university life emerges from the internal documentation of the university administrations as well as that of the party, Komsomol, and labor union organizations that claimed large parts of the university communities as members. Of course, these documents are also colored by the political and bureaucratic interests of their authors.[62] Material from CIA-funded Radio Liberty, predominantly reports from exchange students to the USSR and defectors from it, similarly bears the imprint of political agendas.[63]

---

[60] For a masterful treatment of geography in Stalinist culture, see James Von Geldern, "The Centre and the Periphery: Cultural and Social Geography in the Mass Culture of the 1930s," in Ronald G. Suny (ed.), *The Structure of Soviet History: Essays and Documents* (New York: Oxford University Press, 2002), 177–88.

[61] The connection between identity and spaces has been a fruitful line of research in recent years. Cf. Mark Bassin et al. (eds.), *Space, Place, and Power in Modern Russia: Essays in the New Spatial History* (DeKalb: Northern Illinois University Press, 2010).

[62] This book draws on my research in twelve Russian and Ukrainian state archives in Moscow, Kyiv, and Saratov, as well as on publications from the period. See the selected bibliography for a complete list of archival resources consulted.

[63] In its first years until 1959, the station was called Radio Liberation, reflecting its connection to US plans of rolling back communism in the period. Richard H. Cummings, *Cold War Radio: The Dangerous History of American Broadcasting in Europe, 1950–1989* (Jefferson, NC: McFarland & Co., 2009), 26–28. Chapter 7 discusses the specific context of the student exchanges which are the focus of many Radio Liberty materials used here. Radio Liberty's Audience Research Department, which generated the sources used in this book, is discussed in Simo Mikkonen, "Stealing the Monopoly of Knowledge? Soviet Reactions to Cold War Broadcasting," *Kritika*, 11 (2010): 771–805.

Providing a counterpoint to official perspectives is an extensive memoir literature as well as the forty-nine oral history interviews I conducted with people who were students during the period under investigation.[64] Such personal sources give a sense of the concerns of everyday people and help to contextualize a sometimes fragmentary and incomplete archival source base. They also came with their own difficulties. As I was dependent on social contacts and word-of-mouth to find interview subjects, the data is not necessarily representative of postwar students at specific institutions, let alone the student body of Soviet universities as a whole. A more serious dilemma was memory's tendency to erode and restructure experience. An unavoidable problem for practitioners of oral history, it would seem to be particularly pronounced in the Soviet context. The past is always a different country, but this was true in a literal sense for elderly Russian and Ukrainian citizens remembering their adolescence in the postwar Soviet Union. Interviews yielded a welter of cross-cutting narratives and structures of meaning: post-Soviet nostalgia, an idealization of youth that was pronounced in Soviet times, the effort to situate one's experiences either as part of a rebellious intelligentsia or in opposition to it – all narratives, no doubt, influenced by the challenge of presenting one's past to a North American.[65] Seen from another vantage point, however, the sheer multiplicity of perspectives on display convinced me that authentic voices from the past – and, no less important, widely held assumptions about it – did indeed find expression in the interviews I conducted.[66]

Recreating postwar university life in some detail provides a perspective from which to re-examine major questions in postwar Soviet history. The dominant construct for understanding the early postwar period is seasonal: late Stalinism was a cold winter and the Khrushchev years provided a much-needed, if uneven, "Thaw." Like all others, this narrative draws attention to some parts of history – the crimes of Stalinism and the efforts to overcome them – at the expense of others. Historians have recently called into question the scheme's tidy division into Stalinism and post-Stalinism, instead

---

[64] I conducted these interviews during research trips to Moscow and Saratov in 2003 and 2004 and Kyiv and St. Petersburg in 2005. The bibliography provides information on my interviews and explains my practice of assigning pseudonyms to my interview subjects.

[65] For a discussion of oral history in the Soviet context, see Donald J. Raleigh (ed.), *Russia's Sputnik Generation: Soviet Baby Boomers Talk about their Lives* (Bloomington: Indiana University Press, 2006), 1–23.

[66] For an overview of the way oral historians have evaluated evidence and particularly their emphasis on exploring "subjective and collective meaning" in "narrative structures people employ to describe the past," see Anna Green and Kathleen Troup, *The Houses of History: A Critical Reader in Twentieth-Century History and Theory* (New York University Press, 1999), 230–38.

exploring what united the two periods. Late Stalinism saw the rise of many quintessentially "Thaw" phenomena such as reformist impulses in different segments of Soviet society and the emergence of a clearer distinction between private and public spheres in everyday life.[67] Likewise, the supposedly clean break of 1953 has also been placed in doubt by a new literature on the Khrushchev period that shows how efforts at "de-Stalinization" ran up against ongoing ideological commitments while sparking new controversies in their own right.[68] The emerging literature suggests that Soviet rule both before and after Stalin's death faced similar dilemmas, not the least of which was how to maintain a sense of revolutionary momentum in society while grappling with the consequences of devastating war and the geopolitical order of the Cold War.

A more fundamental problem with the narrative of Stalinist winter and Khrushchev Thaw, however, is that it reflects the viewpoint of one set of historical actors: reformist intellectuals. Derived from a novel of the time, the Thaw metaphor encapsulates a contemporaneous belief held by a part of educated society: that the Stalin period was a moral cataclysm that had to be addressed by honest talk, intellectual freedom, and soul-searching.[69] Proponents of a "Thaw" saw themselves as central to the entire affair: it was up to the intelligentsia to lead the process of moral salvation from Stalinism, as only they possessed the knowledge and culture – and therefore the "universal moral Truth" – needed for the task.[70] However clear some found this moral imperative at the time – and however compelling an approach it has proven to historians writing decades later – it cannot serve as the basis for an all-encompassing narrative for the period. The Thaw metaphor universalizes a reading of Soviet history that was not shared by all intellectuals, let alone Soviet society as a whole. Even the quintessential Thaw phenomena – literary discussions, independent analysis of the Stalinist past, and engagement with the new cultural horizons presented by the opening of the country to the outside world – were more contested

---

[67] A useful overview of this trend in the literature is offered in Juliane Fürst, "Introduction," in Juliane Fürst (ed.), *Late Stalinist Russia: Society between Reconstruction and Reinvention* (London: Routledge, 2006), 13–15.

[68] Miriam Dobson, *Khrushchev's Cold Summer: Gulag Returnees, Crime, and the Fate of Reform after Stalin* (Ithaca, NY: Cornell University Press, 2009) and Polly Jones, "From Stalinism to Post-Stalinism: De-Mythologising Stalin, 1953–56," in Harold Shukman (ed.), *Redefining Stalinism* (London and Portland, OR: Frank Cass, 2003), 127–48.

[69] On the history of the term, see Stephen Bittner, *The Many Lives of Khrushchev's Thaw: Experience and Memory in Moscow's Arbat* (Ithaca, NY: Cornell University Press, 2008), 2–19.

[70] This quotation is from a valuable insider's perspective on the mentality of Thaw intellectuals. See Petr Vail' and Aleksandr Genis, *60-e: mir sovetskogo cheloveka* (Moscow: "Novoe literaturnoe obozrenie," 1996), 162.

and unpredictable in nature than the Thaw metaphor suggests with its invoking of a clear shift in epochs. In large part, this was because the Thaw project of addressing the Stalinist past through intellectual and cultural activities remained entangled with the thorny question of the Soviet intelligentsia. While reformers appropriated the social construct of intelligentsia as a touchstone for understanding the Stalin era and what came after, they discovered that the former frequently raised its own questions rather than providing a clear basis for social identity or political action.[71]

In pursuing this theme, the book focuses on episodes in which university politics brought the intelligentsia and the identities that went along with it into focus. Its first part presents postwar universities as environments particularly conducive to thinking about the intelligentsia. Chapter 1 presents student collectives and interactions with professors as particularly meaningful elements of the university student experience. Student collectivism created a socially cohesive student body, one that supported but sometimes also disrupted the hyper-regimented environment of the universities. Meanwhile, the universities' academic worlds – and particularly the experiences they offered of studying under professors of pre-Stalin vintage – provided students with opportunities to imagine themselves as intellectuals in novel ways. Continuing to explore the multifarious functions which university education served, Chapter 2 treats the universities' place in postwar social hierarchies by exploring their elite status in the early Cold War and the social tensions that came with it.

The second part of the book explores late Stalinism and its immediate aftermath in the universities, pointing to the ways that political ruptures in Soviet intellectual and political life called into question the category of intelligentsia. Chapter 3 examines Stalin's chauvinistic political campaigns that enveloped university life with the onset of the Cold War. The anti-intellectual tone of the regime, it argues, created significant backlash against the new patriotic talk – an outcome that was particularly evident among Jewish students given the conflation of "intellectual" and "Jew." The focus of Chapter 4 is the experience of late Stalinist scientific entanglements in the universities, and particularly the divisive ways that party involvement in biology and physics played out in student politics. Both this chapter and the next explore early efforts to grapple with the Stalinist order after the dictator's death in 1953. Chapter 5 explores student politics in the wake of Khrushchev's denunciation of Stalin in 1956, arguing that student protests of

---

[71] This perspective builds on a recent account that stresses the divided nature of the past for the intellectual life of the period. Bittner, *The Many Lives of Khrushchev's Thaw*.

that pivotal year constituted radicalized interpretations of the longstanding and commonly accepted idea of the Soviet intellectual's cultural mission.

Part III turns to the period of Khrushchev's ascendance from 1957 to 1964, arguing that it continued the dynamic whereby central policies and university social settings created confusion about the meaning of the Soviet intelligentsia. Chapter 6 explores Khrushchev's quixotic efforts to transform the Stalin-era intelligentsia by drawing on early Bolshevik precedents of social engineering and labor training in higher learning. Chapter 7 examines the heyday of the "Khrushchev Thaw," which this study treats as a project of overcoming the perceived flaws of post-Stalinist realities through intelligentsia culture. Focusing on the politics of the arts and the growing exposure of university communities to the West, it demonstrates that the cultural-social elitism inherent in the intelligentsia construct complicated the Thaw agenda of saving socialism through culture. Chapter 8 extends analysis of the unlikely permutations of intelligentsia in the period by discussing how student movements of ethnic nationalism in Kyiv and Moscow emerged from the university milieu and drew on the Thaw and the broader cultural mission of Soviet intellectuals. By the end of the Khrushchev years, party overseers discovered to their evident surprise that the system's showcase universities had produced a new kind of educated society that clung to the status granted to it and sometimes employed it in unwanted ways. This outcome was indicative of a broader ambiguity surrounding the place of learning and its practitioners in Soviet communism that would plague the USSR until its demise.

PART I

Universities and postwar Soviet society

CHAPTER I

Youth and timelessness in the palaces of science

Anna Aleksandrovna Verbovskaia remembers her years of study at MGU from 1946 to 1951 fondly. In a recent interview, she commented that she and her classmates enjoyed a rich social life. She remembered excursions out of the city, going to the theater, and parties that were very tame compared to the usual fare of undergraduates, she noted with pride: Verbovskaia played piano, her friends danced and sang. They were very patriotic as "that was after the war," she added simply; she saw her future in romantic terms as a school-teacher who would serve the country humbly by bringing children "morality and science." Right before graduation in 1951, her mother, a Jewish doctor, was arrested as an enemy of the people as part of an anti-Semitic terror wave that would culminate in the Doctors' Plot two years later. Verbovskaia stumbled from one state agency to another, telling indifferent bureaucrats that they had made a mistake and that her mother, a devout communist, could not possibly have conspired against the state. Verbovskaia soon fell under suspicion herself, as did all relatives of "enemies of the people." Well aware of the dark cloud that had gathered over her, she broke off all contact with her friends and stopped picking up the phone. Remarkably, Verbovskaia told the story as an isolated dark chapter in an otherwise happy life. Never arrested herself, Verbovskaia was even allowed to finish her degree: the organs of state security were impressed by her record as a youth activist and motivated student, she posits. When her mother was freed and rehabilitated in 1954, Verbovskaia continued her envisioned career path by taking up work as a teacher of Marxism-Leninism. She did not hold any grudges against her classmates; she still kept up with them, she added.[1]

Verbovskaia's account is sharply discordant with common understand-ings of postwar Stalinism, a period recalled in Soviet educated society – and later analyzed by historians – as one dominated by oppressive ideological offensives and state terror. Certainly, Verbovskaia's attempt to underplay

---

[1] Interview with A. A. Verbovskaia, Moscow, 2004.

the long-term consequences of her time of troubles was representative of personal strategies of coping with trauma and loss in Soviet history.[2] Nevertheless, Verbovskaia's testimony shows that the oppressive political sphere was not the only or even the paramount experience of postwar students – even, it would seem, for one of its victims. Rather, the dominant tenor of postwar student life was social integration and, despite the tumult of Stalinist rule, contentedness.

As my interview with Verbovskaia suggests, university life took its meaning against the backdrop of the devastating war from which the country had just emerged. To grasp the importance of the war for postwar student life it is sufficient to trace the different trajectories of students enrolled in Soviet higher education in 1941, when the Axis invasion of the USSR commenced. Thousands of students fought in the Red Army while others found themselves under Nazi Occupation; in either case, they faced an environment of mass violence from which one was lucky to emerge alive.[3] If survival was much more likely for students who avoided both outcomes, their wartime experiences were extremely trying all the same. Students and others who were evacuated from the Nazi advance to the interior of the country had to settle in unfamiliar places, usually in conditions of hunger and scarcity dire even by interwar Soviet standards.[4] Even non-conscripted "locals" in unoccupied areas suffered tremendous hardship; in Saratov, students of the severely depopulated wartime higher education system heard lectures in unheated rooms and spent most of their time building anti-tank ditches, laying gas pipes, tending to the wounded, and working at garden plots that provided an urgently needed source of food.[5]

Higher education provided a scarred younger generation with a sense of normalcy after the war. Yet postwar students' sense of social belonging was a product of more than a general postwar dispensation. It also had much to do with the specific nature of student experiences within the universities, and particularly the sense of vitality and social belonging that many felt. A young Muscovite writer conveyed the excitement and even exaltation many felt in

[2] See Catherine Merridale, *Night of Stone: Death and Memory in Twentieth Century Russia* (New York: Viking, 2001).
[3] Karel C. Berkhoff, *Harvest of Despair: Life and Death in Ukraine under Nazi Rule* (Cambridge, MA: Belknap Press of Harvard University Press, 2004).
[4] See Rebecca Manley, *To the Tashkent Station: Evacuation and Survival in the Soviet Union at War* (Ithaca, NY: Cornell University Press, 2009).
[5] Two memoir accounts provide a detailed picture of everyday life in wartime Saratov. O. B. Sirotnina, *Zhizn' vopreki, ili ia schastlivyi chelovek: vospominaniia* (Saratov: Izdatel'stvo Saratovskogo universiteta, 2009), 74–82; V. A. Artisevich, *Odinakovykh sudeb ne byvaet: vospominaniia* (Saratov: Izdatel'stvo Saratovskogo universiteta, 2009), 81–105.

the university environment; being a student at MGU was akin to "swallowing the clean air of youth, health, fervor, work, lyricism, and cleverness."[6] Two specific features of postwar university life in both the capitals and the provinces made it seem easy to breathe there. First, higher education immersed young people in a tight-knit world of peer interaction, one that gained its particular coloration from the Soviet system of institutionalized youth collectives. Second, some students entered meaningful communities of learning through contact with the faculty, imbibing an ethos of commitment to science and culture that was particularly prominent in the universities. Youth collectivism and the world of the professoriate made the universities distinct social spaces in postwar society, institutions that struck some outside observers as being oddly self-contained despite tight control from above. Above all, they created a postwar student body with a set of common practices and values, a faint echo of the far more oppositional Tsarist-era student estate that the Bolsheviks had dismantled decades before.[7]

The secret lives of student collectives

In 1952 the seventeen-year-old Muscovite T. P. Mazur recorded in her diary her mixed feelings about graduating from school and beginning her new existence as a college student. While sad that the "sweet years of childhood" were passing, she was enthralled by the "new difficulties and new wonders" awaiting her as a young adult deciding her own path for the first time.[8] Mazur's diary breaks off before her enrollment in Moscow University months later, but we might guess that the transition to studenthood was as pronounced as she imagined. As Mazur's ruminations convey, student-hood in the USSR, as elsewhere, constituted a move – emotional, symbolic, and sometimes geographical – from the family to a new social environment dominated by peer interaction and unfamiliar academic hierarchies. For students, identities emerge at the intersection of old and new social worlds. To be sure, students bring into college the weighty baggage of values and attitudes that they have accumulated before it. But they often define themselves in ways that reflect their collegiate environment and the myriad traditions and models of behavior that it passes down across student

---

[6] Mark Shcheglov et al., *Studencheskie tetradi* (Moscow: Izdatel'stvo "Sovetskaia Rossiia," 1973), 26.
[7] Susan Morrissey, *Heralds of Revolution: Russian Students and the Mythology of Radicalism* (Oxford University Press, 1998); Samuel D. Kassow, *Students, Professors, and the State in Tsarist Russia* (Berkeley: University of California Press, 1989), esp. 49–140, and Daniel R. Brower, *Training the Nihilists: Education and Radicalism in Tsarist Russia* (Ithaca, NY: Cornell University Press, 1975), 108–25.
[8] Entry for 2 September 1952 in TsDNA f. 314, op. 1, d. 25.

generations.[9] "Student culture" in this sense became a particularly important international phenomenon after World War II, as the rapid expansion
of higher learning assembled young people in larger and more volatile
conglomerations than ever before.[10]

The social re-formation which is a part of any higher education system
took on distinctive forms in the Soviet context. Everyday life in higher
education establishments was built on institutionalized collectives (*kollektivy*)
that structured the classroom, dormitory life, and extra-curricular activities.
As conceptualized by the doyen of Stalinist pedagogy Anton Makarenko,
collectivist organization was a means of creating socialist citizens. Officially
constructed social groups would create a collective opinion – alternatively
harnessing or suppressing individual interests in the process – and direct it
toward solving common, "socially useful" problems.[11] The essential building
blocks for this centralization of social interaction were the "mass organizations," the Communist Party and its various subordinate institutions that had
local cells in every institution in the country. For the majority of students who
did not hold party membership, the key purveyor of the regime's collectivist
agenda was Komsomol. In the postwar years, the Communist Youth League
completed its long transformation from a revolutionary vanguard to an
organization devoted to patriotic training for all Soviet young people, one
to which it was virtually mandatory for students to belong – and to which
students would have to answer if they expected to complete their studies.[12]

Komsomol's virtual monopoly on student affairs was not the only reason
for the remarkably collectivist tenor of Soviet student life. In higher education,
the grassroots cells or primary organizations of Komsomol were one part of a
broader organizational system that cemented "collectives" as crucial structures
of the student milieu. The essential unit for forming collectives was the
"academic group," a unit of roughly twenty to twenty-five students enrolled
in the same department and sometimes also the disciplinary sub-department
(*kafedra*).[13] Given the specialization of curricula in the USSR, the members of

---

[9] A classic exploration of the theme for the United States is Helen Lefkowitz Horowitz, *Campus Life:
Undergraduate Cultures from the End of the Eighteenth Century to the Present* (New York: A. A. Knopf,
distributed by Random House, 1987).

[10] Jeremi Suri, *Power and Protest: Global Revolution and the Rise of Détente* (Cambridge, MA: Harvard
University Press, 2003), 92–96.

[11] James Bowen, *Soviet Education: Anton Makarenko and the Years of Experiment* (Madison: University of
Wisconsin Press, 1965), 82.

[12] By 1952, 82 percent of higher education students belonged to the organization. See the report of the
Division for Work with Students of the Komsomol TsK. RGASPI-M f. 1, op. 46, d. 143, l. 23.

[13] The place of academic groups in the universities is virtually unexplored outside of Peter Konecny,
Builders and Deserters: Students, State, and Community in Leningrad, 1917–1941 (Montreal and Ithaca:

academic groups spent countless hours at lectures and seminars together. Rubbing shoulders in the classroom, however, was just the tip of the iceberg. The Soviet higher learning system made the academic groups, subdivisions created by administrative convenience, into consolidated social organisms that would envelop all aspects of their members' lives. The academic groups doubled as primary cells of the Komsomol and trade unions, meaning that their members spent time together in extra-curricular settings such as meetings, social events, and weekend labor projects. The out-of-town students eligible for space in the cramped dormitories usually found themselves living with classmates from their academic groups as well.

The collectives were designed to harness the total energies of the students for party-defined agendas. They would encourage "communist morals, friendship, and comradely mutual-help," for instance through arrangements in which stronger students tutored their less talented peers. When friendly assistance fell short, however, the collectives would take on a policing function and "rebuff egoism, rudeness, and dishonest behavior in private life, insincerity and cheat sheets."[14] To enforce this mutual control among the student body, administrators in higher education emphasized the joint responsibility of the academic groups by presenting specific students' flaws – whether academic woes, violations of public order, infractions of moral principles, or something else altogether – as failures of the collective. In this sense, collective social forms, while shaping the student body in a spirit of self-improvement, also had a fundamentally coercive nature. By eradicating the boundary between the public and the private – one which was highly tenuous in Soviet society in any case – student collectives isolated loners and individualists.[15]

In the eyes of many students, however, the collectives were much more than institutions for enforcing collective discipline. On the contrary, the collective organization of the universities exerted powerful integrative pressures on the student body, assuring that youthful solidarity, what MGU graduate Raisa Gorbacheva later called "comradeship," dominated social interaction.[16] Spending much of their time in a contained social network,

---

McGill-Queen's University Press, 1999), 160, 163–65. An earlier and more ideologically driven form of collectivism in higher learning is explored in Michael David-Fox, *Revolution of the Mind: Higher Learning among the Bolsheviks, 1918–1929* (Ithaca, NY: Cornell University Press, 1997), 82–104.

[14] V. Volokonskii, "Komsomol'skaia gruppa," *Komsomol'skaia rabota v vuze* (Moscow: Molodaia gvardiia, 1953), 37–44.

[15] An edited volume that presents the overlapping of public and private spheres in Soviet society from different angles is Lewis H. Siegelbaum (ed.), *Borders of Socialism: Private Spheres of Soviet Russia* (New York: Palgrave Macmillan, 2006).

[16] Raisa Maksimovna Gorbacheva and G. V. Priakhin, *I Hope: Reminiscences and Reflections* (New York: HarperCollins Publishers, 1991), 48.

students developed powerful feelings of loyalty and mutual responsibility toward it. Iu. V. Gaponov remembers that his academic group in the MGU Physics Department served as a touchstone for almost every part of daily life: studying in the library, conspiring to get ahead in the lines at the cafeteria, discussing academic difficulties at Komsomol meetings, and celebrating holidays as well as its members' birthdays. In his recollection, the students even "walked around in a compact cluster, organized and in love with the group."[17] Part of the appeal of this tight-knit friendship group stemmed from the role it played in easing the transition of youth into the disorienting new world of the university. This integrative function was particularly important for first-year students from outside the city like G. I. Iskrova, a previously self-confident teenager from the town of Dubrovitsy in Moscow Province who became "confused and timid" in MGU with its "skyscraper with high-speed elevators."[18]

   Like many social structures in the Soviet Union, student comradeship found its wellspring in survival skills as much as personal affinities. Postwar dormitories were cramped and dilapidated; in one student dormitory in postwar Kyiv, inhabitants of a room could fit in it at the same time only if they were all lying down.[19] Little wonder that getting by in the dormitories meant finding "a common language with everyone, all the time," as the MGU alumnus B. V. Simonov recalled.[20] The academic groups were also necessary institutions for many students living outside the dormitory, including both youth from the city who continued to live with their parents and out-of-towners forced to rent out "corners" of apartments in the depleted housing stock of the postwar cities.[21] The poverty of postwar students – dire even against the backdrop of near-universal material deprivation in the postwar years – also encouraged collective habits. As a Leningrad University student recalled, the monthly state stipend that most students received would pay for only one meal in the cafeteria per day, which would leave one hungry an hour later.[22] Hunger was a particularly stark reality for students from outside the city who could not rely on support from home. It also plagued those who spent their monthly stipend on theater tickets, stipend-day drinking binges, or any number of

[17] Iu. V. Gaponov, "Otryvki iz nenapisannogo: 'iznachalie'," *VIET*, no. 1 (2001): 224.
[18] These words come from a collection of alumni memoirs, A. D. Belova et al. (eds.), *My – matematiki s leninskikh gor* (Moscow: Fortuna Limited, 2003), 28.
[19] TsDAHOU f. 7, op. 6, d. 2241, l. 13.   [20] Interview with B. V. Simonov, Moscow, 2004.
[21] In war-torn Ukraine, a full 45,000 students lived in rooms or "corners" of private apartments in 1953. TsDAHOU f. 1, op. 71, spr. 105, ark. 194.
[22] Boris Vail', *Osobo opasnyi* (London: Overseas Publications Interchange, 1980), 106–7.

tantalizing attractions of the big city. Strategies of student comradely help evolved to tide such hapless souls over until the next miserly stipend in such forms as monetary loans, a sack of potatoes earned from part-time work in a state farm, shared meat pies sent from home, or even fish stolen from a biology laboratory.[23] While student "communes" that pooled student property and organized communal kitchens sometimes resulted in scandals, the impulse behind them was genuine.[24] The mixture of affection and practicality the collectives inspired – one which historians have identified in many kinds of social relationships in the USSR – surely accounted for much of their influence in the student milieu.[25]

The rich associational world of the universities also transformed the students. By socializing newly enrolled students into common norms, the collective created a group consciousness that dulled previous identities. Of course, the universities were not separated from broader tensions of Soviet society, particularly those surrounding wealth. In 1954, the SGU Komsomol Committee heard the case of Kudriashova, who was accused of skipping classes for a month and taking up with a married man. A classmate Matasova took the floor to announce that her peer's behavior was a result of entitlement; Kudriashova, she alleged, had been spoiled by her parents and also by teachers who had "picked out the children of well-to-do parents" for preferential treatment.[26] Especially stark was the social gap between students of urban and rural backgrounds. S. A. Dybenko arrived at KDU from a village and found that his urban peers were not only "more developed, better read, better prepared" but were also "imposing, intelligentsia-like (*intelligentnye*)."[27] Cultured behavior was an unequally distributed entity in the Soviet context, and some students could lay better claim to it – and hence to belonging in the university, the most cultured of Soviet institutions – than others.

These social divisions were pervasive, but the postwar university milieu worked to soften them.[28] Rural and provincial students sought to overcome their feelings of inferiority through rigorous study, as Mikhail Gorbachev remembered of his own student years.[29] The severe work habits of provincials

[23] Vladimir Pozner, *Parting with Illusions: The Extraordinary Life and Controversial Views of the Soviet Union's Leading Commentator* (New York: Atlantic Monthly Press, 1990), 114.
[24] N. T. Bakaev, *Na mekhmat kto popal . . . Ivan, ne pomniashii rodstvo i potomok Chingis-Khan* (Moscow: Knizhnyi dom "Moskovskii Universitet," 2000), 5.
[25] For a succinct discussion of personal relationships such as *blat* (informal exchanges) and patronage networks, see Sheila Fitzpatrick, *Everyday Stalinism: Ordinary Life in Extraordinary Times: Soviet Russia in the 1930s* (New York: Oxford University Press, 2000), 62–65, 109–14.
[26] GANISO f. 3234, op. 13, d. 51, l. 123.   [27] Interview with S. A. Dybenko, Kyiv, 2005.
[28] The place of universities in postwar social hierarchies is discussed in Chapter 2.
[29] Mikhail Sergeevich Gorbachev, *Memoirs* (New York: Doubleday, 1996), 42.

might pay off; Dybenko in Kyiv claims that he and other rural youth like him – all hard-working and no-nonsense types in his account – achieved the academic level of their urban classmates within a few years and then started to surpass them.[30] Provincial and rural students also sought to overcome subtler markers of cultivation by spending their free time devouring novels or frequenting theaters, museums, and conservatories – all in a search for self-improvement as much as entertainment.[31] On the opposite side of the class spectrum, children from elite backgrounds, well-represented in Kyiv and particularly Moscow, tried not to draw attention to their privileged backgrounds. The MGU history student E. F. Nikiforova reported that she found out about the lofty social origins of two of her friends – the son of an academician and the daughter of a member of the party TsK of Uzbekistan – only years after graduation. As she put it, "they did not stick out in any way," and no one talked about their family backgrounds.[32] Even Stalin's daughter Svetlana "behaved very modestly" in the opinion of a classmate, and once tried to hide from the security guards who escorted her through the halls of MGU.[33]

The student norms of unity and equality were essentially localist in character as they found manifestation in the small worlds of the collective. At the same time, they helped to produce a consciousness of students as a social group. In fact, postwar students seemed to recover something of the social cohesion of students in the Russian Empire, even if very little of their corporate identity and oppositional mindset. One sign of this broader consciousness was the students' lexicon, sometimes of pre-revolutionary origin, which conveyed the familiar sights and situations of university life in colorful ways: a scholar who focused on superficialities was "a remover of foam," a pointless lecture was "water," and a student who improvised answers during an oral examination "grabbed something from the ceiling."[34] Students also developed an elaborate culture of self-written songs, consisting of tales of adventure or unrequited love, all of which gave them an implicit marker of distinction from the surrounding society.[35] To be sure, student slang and songs differed among institutes across the country.

---

[30] Interview with S. A. Dybenko, Kyiv, 2005.
[31] Such a determined imbibing of culture found expression in letters sent home by a Moscow student who was nicknamed "village girl" by the boys in her academic group. G. I. Iskrova, "Vybrala matematiku," in Belova et al. (eds.), *My – matematiki s Leninskikh gor*, 29–33.
[32] Interview with E. F. Nikiforova, Moscow, 2004.
[33] This was related by her classmate A. A. Verbovskaia. Interview, Moscow, 2004.
[34] Nils Åke Nilsson, "Soviet Student Slang," *Scando-Slavica*, 6 (1960): 113–23.
[35] See Ludmila Alexeyeva and Paul Goldberg, *The Thaw Generation: Coming of Age in the post-Stalin Era* (Boston: Little, Brown, 1990), 30 and Mark Shcheglov, *Na poldoroge: slovo o russkoi literature* (Moscow: Progress-Pleiada, 2001), 257–58.

Even students at a single institution saw themselves in different ways according to their courses of study: math students thought they were the smartest, for instance, while geologists and geographers who undertook long summer expeditions prided themselves on being rugged travelers and even a bit uncouth.[36] Such diversity, however, masked more striking unity in patterns of behavior and forms of interaction. Reflecting this reality, after the war the pre-revolutionary word *studenchestvo* came back into circulation to describe higher education students as a "social-demographic group" characterized by a "defined social position, role and status."[37]

Fossils of a former age

The academic sphere of lectures, assignments, and examinations was a social world that contrasted with the seemingly limitless embrace of the student collectives. To be sure, the collectives intervened in academic affairs routinely: Komsomol assigned the best students to tutor their weaker classmates, the elected student "elders" took lecture attendance, and students who ignored their studies might be dragged over the coals by their comrades at a meeting of the primary Komsomol cell. Nevertheless, the academic process did not fit neatly into the mindset of collective agency and responsibility that was so pronounced in many areas of collegiate life. Ever since the Stalinist Great Retreat, Soviet higher learning relied on a traditional pedagogical regime based on lectures, disciplined individual study, and evaluation through state examinations. In practical terms, this meant that academic work and evaluation were individualistic in nature, regardless of the efforts of administrators to enforce collective discipline in this sphere.

The classroom also presented students with a different model of place and time. Although tied to communist rhetoric, the collectives were inward-looking and particularistic social networks. They were also by their very nature transient, as generations of students flowed in and out of the universities. In contrast, the academic sphere presented students with universal truths packaged in a transcendent mission: the enlightenment of the masses and the creation of a modern society.[38] Indeed, the academic world was seemingly timeless; higher learning, according to official pronouncements, led to the communist future and stemmed from a hallowed

---

[36] V. D. Berestov, "Shef (glava iz knigi vospominanii)," *Etnograficheskoe obozrenie*, no. 1 (1997): 63.
[37] See the entry by B. I. Barsukov and V. M. Orel in *Bol'shaia sovetskaia entsiklopedia*, 3rd edn., 30 vols. (1969–78), at *Yandex slovari*, www.slovari.yandex.ru (accessed 3 June 2011).
[38] For a common articulation of this idea, see I. I. Petrovskii, "Zabota I. V. Stalina o sovetskoi v shkole," *VVSh*, no. 3 (1953): 24–25.

past. The universities drove home the idea that students were following in the footsteps of great thinkers of the past, even as they were building the future. First-year MGU student E. Maikov immediately sensed "a feeling that we became a part of a great cultural center of Russia and the world which our teachers told us about with unexpected details, reminding us that Belinskii and Lermontov, Herzen and Ogarev, Turgenev and Chekhov had all studied here."[39] MGU held particular historical resonance in the popular imagination, but other universities, in Ukraine as well as Russia, made a similar impression on first-year students. A former student explained that veneration of KDU as a "temple of science" was common to "us, the guys who came there from the village."[40] The recurrence of such religious metaphors in popular discourse confirms the extent to which the cult of science had penetrated student minds.

The overwhelming initial impression of the university was only deepened by contact with the professoriate – and particularly with a specific part of it. As late as 1958, a foreign observer noted the "extraordinary prominence and influence" in the Soviet intellectual world of elderly scholars, individuals who had come of age before the Stalinist system had transformed the universities in the 1930s. Such "aging symbols of the past – complete, down to their redingotes, pince-nez, and small Van Dyke beards" – still occupied the "major chairs in Russian universities."[41] Pre-Stalin or simply "old professors," defined roughly as those who had earned an academic degree in the mid-1920s or before, had an impact on postwar students that was greater than their relatively small and steadily diminishing numbers would suggest.[42] The seniority of these figures in the academic hierarchy paralleled their privileged place in the student imagination. In oral history sources and memoirs, former students regularly mention their respect for

---

[39] Here he refers to prominent figures in the accepted Soviet intellectual canon: the literary critic V. G. Belinskii, the fiction writers M. Iu. Lermontov, A. P. Chekhov, and I. S. Turgenev, and the radical writers A. I. Herzen and N. P. Ogarev. See the reminiscences in V. V. Voevodin (ed.), *Neuzheli iubilei? Ne veriu!* (Moscow: NIVTs MGU, 2004), 25. See also N. V. Motroshilova, "Pamiati professora," *Voprosy filosofii*, no. 5 (1988): 67–70.

[40] Interview with S. A. Dybenko, Kyiv, 2005.

[41] Leopold H. Haimson, "Three Generations of the Soviet Intelligentsia," in Howard W. Winger (ed.), *Iron Curtains and Scholarship. The Exchange of Knowledge in a Divided World: Papers Presented before the Twenty-third Annual Conference of the Graduate Library School of the University of Chicago, July 7–9, 1958* (University of Chicago, Graduate Library School, 1958), 31.

[42] As of 1947, 11.1 percent of the teacher cadres in Soviet higher education establishments had graduated from universities before 1918, with another 4.2 percent receiving their undergraduate degrees from 1918 to 1923. S. V. Volkov, *Intellektual'nyi sloi v sovetskom obshchestve* (St. Petersburg: Fond "Razvitie," Institut nauchnoi informatsii po obshchestvennym naukam RAN, 1999), 77.

the "old Russian professorate," "the brilliant galaxy of Russian scholars of the old school" that had trained them in the postwar years.[43]

The old professors earned students' adulation by what they represented as much as who they were (or how they taught). Sage-like, worldly, and charmingly absent-minded, they appeared as the living embodiment of the universities in their most idealized manifestation. Most of all, the old professors were living representatives of the intelligentsia tradition that was mythologized in the world of higher learning. At the MGU Philology Department, S. M. Bondi (b. 1891) was so carried away by Pushkin that he recited poems during students' oral examinations; S. I. Radtsig (b. 1882) impressed lecture halls with his "singing voice and very appearance."[44] At the same time, old professors carried themselves with a sense of self-assured dignity that seemed other-worldly to students raised on the folklore of revolution and shaped by the immediate upheavals of total war. A. F. Sergeev, who was at the MGU Mechanics and Mathematics Department from 1947 to 1952, recalled that the older professors were marked by their "intelligentsia way of interacting" (*intelligentnye otnosheniia*). When Sergeev introduced himself as "Sasha" – the diminutive form of Aleksandr – the mathematics professor A. G. Kurosh scolded him with the words, "at my seminar there are no Sashas and Mashas."[45]

It was telling that Kurosh set stringent rules for his research seminar. The "special seminars" were a curricular form specific to the universities in which professors taught specific topics outside of the formal curriculum to select groups of ambitious students.[46] University seminars had a rich history in Russian higher education, particularly as mechanisms for creating and maintaining "schools" of research that passed through the generations. After the conservative turn in Stalinist higher education, seminars which were clear continuations of pre-revolutionary research schools reappeared in the universities.[47] For postwar youth, joining a research seminar could be a

[43] These are the words of the political scientist and advisor to several Soviet leaders Georgi Arbatov in his *The System: An Insider's Life in Soviet Politics* (New York: Random House, 1993), 33.

[44] See the alumni memoirs of the MGU Philology Department in A. L. Nalepin (ed.), *Filologicheskii fakul'tet MGU, 1950–1955: zhizn' iubileinogo vypuska: vospominaniia, dokumenty, materialy* (Moscow: Rossiiskii fond kul'tury "Rossiiskii arkhiv," 2003), 37, 115, 65.

[45] Interview with A. F. Sergeev, Moscow, 2003.

[46] On seminars at MGU, see "O napravlenii nauchnoi raboty v universitetakh (s seminara rektorov)," *VVSh*, no. 2 (1955): 6–7. On the functioning of this system in Saratov, see "Kogo gotoviat fakul'tety universiteta," *Stalinets*, 7 June 1952: 1.

[47] On seminars and research schools in theoretical physics, see Karl Hall, "The Schooling of Lev Landau: The European Context of Postrevolutionary Soviet Theoretical Physics," *Osiris*, 23 (2008): 233. For schools of historical research that crossed the 1917 divide, see V. M. Paneiakh, *Tvorchestvo i sud'ba istorika: Boris Aleksandrovich Romanov* (St. Petersburg: DBulanin, 2000), 159–63.

rich and even transformative experience. In their subject matter, research focus, and personalized tenor, the seminars fell outside the Soviet higher education's usual fare of standardized curricula, rote learning, and mass lectures. Most importantly, participation in the seminars was the path to becoming the protégé of a respected professor and, by extension, a member of a scholarly community – a fact shown by an extensive genre of alumni accolades for seminar leaders (who often became graduate advisors as well).[48] In this sense, the seminars offered a model of community that contrasted with the world of the collectives, where solidarity and equality reigned supreme. Above all, contact with the venerable professors offered students the opportunity to imagine themselves as *intelligenty* in ways that distinguished them from the typical Sashas and Mashas that Soviet higher learning churned out.

Looking back across 1991, some alumni of the postwar universities were tempted to stress the un-Sovietness of the old professors, presenting them as representatives of a superior "old science that had no Marxism in it," as one MGU alumnus described the specialist in medieval Slavic literature N. K. Gudzii.[49] A vision of pre-revolutionary professors as a group of closeted oppositionists, however, is highly misleading. After the Bolsheviks had overrun the overwhelmingly anti-Bolshevik universities in the revolutionary period, it became clear that communists and some of the old-regime academics had much in common: a belief in the transformative power of science and learning and their necessity for the modernization of Russia.[50] Stressing the inherently anti-Soviet nature of the old professors also ignores the multifarious nature of the academic milieu of the Stalin era, which allowed non-Marxist scholars to make peace with the regime and even thrive under it.[51] By reviving traditional educational practices, rehabilitating the Russian past, and raising the social status of state-employed professional thinkers, the Great Retreat of the 1930s offered professors tied to the pre-revolutionary universities weighty reasons to cooperate with the regime. A poignant symbol of the plausibility of compromise with

---

[48] See for instance A. N. Bogomolov and T. L. Kandelaki, *Leonid Samuilovich Leibenzon* (Moscow: Nauka, 1991), 122. See also historian S. S. Dmitriev's recollections of his best students. "Iz dnevnikov Sergeia Sergeevicha Dmitrieva," *Otechestvennaia istoriia*, no. 3 (2000): 163–64.

[49] Nalepin (ed.), *Filologicheskii fakul'tet MGU*, 24.

[50] Christopher Read, *Culture and Power in Revolutionary Russia: The Intelligentsia and the Transition from Tsarism to Communism* (Houndmills, Basingstoke: Macmillan, 1990), 76–83 and Stuart Finkel, *On the Ideological Front: The Russian Intelligentsia and the Making of the Soviet Public Sphere* (New Haven, CT: Yale University Press, 2007).

[51] Sheila Fitzpatrick, "Professors and Soviet Power," in *The Cultural Front: Power and Culture in Revolutionary Russia* (Ithaca, NY: Cornell University Press, 1992), 37–64.

communism was a regular column in the journal of the higher education ministry entitled "Outstanding Pedagogues of the School of the Homeland" that memorialized recently deceased professors and historical figures with only passing reference to their ideological positions.[52]

The old professors were different nonetheless. In however muted a form, they bore the imprint of the freer intellectual climate that had prevailed before the onset of Stalinism at the end of the 1920s. Some members of the older generation maintained a connection to what James C. McClelland has called the "academic ideology" of the pre-revolutionary professoriate: the belief that pursuing pure science was the path to civilization and social progress and therefore needed to be protected from political agendas.[53] To be sure, the Bolsheviks constrained this impulse by immersing scholars in tightly controlled institutions and establishing the state as the arbiter of scientific utility. Nevertheless, as Douglas Weiner has shown, some Soviet-era academics and professors maintained the conviction that science held a "redemptive mission" that was not reducible to state mandates, and, insofar as possible, sought to exercise a degree of intellectual autonomy.[54] Pursuing such an agenda was much more feasible in the natural and physical sciences, which were more resistant to intervention from non-specialists than other disciplines. But there can be no doubt that some elderly professors in all disciplines retained something of the pre-revolutionary cult of science. The student favorite Gudzii (mentioned above) was a case in point. Although he had shown his reliability to officialdom as dean of the MGU Philology Department during the Great Patriotic War, Gudzii was overheard complaining about Russian xenophobia in scholarship during Stalin's final years.[55] Of course, students knew little of the political views of their professors, and this was especially true of the elderly faculty who, regardless of their specific life trajectories, remembered well the regime's hostility toward the bourgeois and "former" people during the early Soviet period.[56] Nevertheless, the accolades of countless alumni leave no doubt that Gudzii

---

[52] Cf. "Viktor L'vovich Kirpichev," *VVSh*, no. 6 (1952): 59–63.

[53] James C. McClelland, *Autocrats and Academics: Education, Culture, and Society in Tsarist Russia* (University of Chicago Press, 1979), 60, 68–70.

[54] For an important discussion of the old academic intelligentsia's survival in the Stalin era, see Douglas R. Weiner, *A Little Corner of Freedom: Russian Nature Protection from Stalin to Gorbachev* (Berkeley: University of California Press, 1999), esp. 27–29.

[55] RGASPI f. 17, op. 32, d. 337, ll. 154–55. On Gudzii's authority in the university, see R. A. Kovnator, *Nikolai Kallinikovich Gudzii: k 70-letiiu so dnia rozhdeniia i 45-letiiu nauchno-pedagogicheskoi deiatel'nosti* (Moscow: Izdatel'stvo Moskovskogo universiteta, 1957), 1–3.

[56] For one account of the psychological baggage carried by older-generation professors, see R. Sh. Ganelin, *Sovetskie istoriki: o chem oni govorili mezhdu soboi: stranitsy vospominanii o 1940-kh–1970-kh godakh* (St. Petersburg: "Nestor-Istoriia," 2004), 12–13, 44–46.

and others like him trained their students to exercise some degree of critical thinking, in the process eschewing the a priori labels that so pervaded academic discourse in the USSR and especially in the social sciences and humanities.[57]

Studying under holdovers from the old intelligentsia, students could imagine their relationship to culture in new ways. In official prescriptions, *kul'turnost'* was a sanitized concept indicating modern and civilized behavior: self-discipline, sobriety, and practical knowledge.[58] A social world dominated by the offshoots of the old academic intelligentsia represented a specifically intellectual version of "culturedness," one that stressed broad erudition and the pursuit of pure learning as a moral and progressive calling. This reading of culture had a tenuous place in Soviet ideological discourse, despite the celebration of the universities' intellectual traditions. Accordingly, the old professors who so clearly embodied the intelligentsia would agitate young minds in unpredictable ways during the chaotic ideological campaigns of late Stalinism, as Chapter 3 will show.

Student collectives and structures of power

Two factors, then, shaped the university student experience and set it apart from other social settings during late Stalinism: student collectivism and the intellectual environment facilitated, in part, by the old professors. Far from being strictly social or cultural phenomena, both of these specificities of the university milieu influenced relationships of power on the ground. The critical context for student politics was Komsomol, the organization with a virtual monopoly over youth activities in the USSR. Komsomol projected central political power into the social worlds of everyday citizens, in large part by providing the institutional space for student collectives to operate. Critical to this task was the *aktiv*, the body of citizen activists holding positions in Komsomol or affiliated institutions (such as the trade unions) along with student party members. The *aktiv*, which made up approximately 10 to 15 percent of the student body in any higher education establishment, was a bridge between communist power and the student masses. It provided the immediate face of party power to the broad mass of rank-and-file Komsomols by conveying its decisions, providing discipline in the ranks, and performing a range of activities to support the latest party campaigns.

---

[57] Vladimir Lakshin, "Professor Gudzii," in *Golosa i litsa* (Moscow: Geleos, 2004), 6–9.
[58] Catriona Kelly, "Kul'turnost' in the Soviet Union: Ideal and Reality," in Geoffrey A. Hosking and Robert Service (eds.), *Reinterpreting Russia* (London: Arnold, 1999), 198–214.

Official Soviet pronouncements holding up activists as a cohesive group of disciplined and selfless communists contained a dose of wishful thinking. In reality, youth activists in higher learning were a diverse lot. It is conceptually useful to divide the youth *aktiv* in higher education into ideal-type categories of "responsible cadres" and "lower activists." The first group, secretaries of the Komsomol committees at both all-university and department level, was a class apart from the student masses. Formally elected by the Komsomol rank-and-file but in fact "recommended" by party overseers, the responsible cadres were trusted individuals who frequently held party membership.[59] Further emphasizing their strategic stature – and, implicitly, their distance from the students – was the fact that top Youth League activists in the colleges were often junior faculty members and graduate students who were sometimes actually too old to belong to the organization in the first place.[60] Material incentives played a large role in recruiting top activists in the colleges. Some responsible cadres received salaries for their work, and even those who did not enjoyed a host of virtually institutionalized perquisites: preferential access to student fellowships (particularly the lucrative "Stalin" and later "Lenin prizes"), favorable treatment in the treacherous system of mandatory job distribution at the end of one's studies, the opportunity to pursue a career in the party, and (particularly in the Khrushchev period) rare and coveted opportunities for foreign travel. These privileges helped to bind the activists to the party, but they might also have been a necessity for recruitment to the *aktiv* and retention in it. Belonging to the *aktiv* meant endless bureaucratic drudgery and relenting pressure from above to answer for students' academic performance, moral rectitude, political loyalty, and public volunteerism. These crushing responsibilities made high turnover among Komsomol activists in higher education establishments a constant concern for leaders in Moscow.[61]

Alumni and latter-day scholars have viewed youth activists as cynical conformists and time-servers.[62] It is broadly true that the idealism and dynamism in the ranks of Komsomol had been deteriorating ever since

---

[59] See a rare complaint about the gerrymandered elections to Komsomol organizations by a Saratov activist in 1953. GANISO f. 3234, op. 13, d. 30, l. 5.

[60] RGASPI-M f. 1, op. 46, d. 143, l. 23.   [61] Ibid., l. 8.

[62] For the view that "playing the system" was the central motivation for postwar activists – though not the only one – see Juliane Fürst, *Stalin's Last Generation: Soviet Post-War Youth and the Emergence of Mature Socialism* (Oxford University Press, 2010), 309–20.

it became a mass organization in the 1930s.[63] Yet the view of activists as a detached body of careerists – one that would become widespread during the Brezhnev era – is ill-suited to the first postwar years, when victory in the war and the hostilities of the Cold War created deep reserves of patriotic feeling from which Komsomol could draw. This was especially clear in the area of student "public work," the wide range of extra-curricular activities students pursued under the auspices of Komsomol and, to a lesser extent, trade union organizations. Many of the activities involved seemed dreary and demoralizing to the rank-and-file Komsomols: a student sent to an apartment block to agitate citizens to vote in the single-candidate elections to the Soviets remembers beginning by "sluggishly talking about the successes of the USSR"; the voters responded by "questioning how big the successes could be when we don't have this or that and someone can't get a pension," but took pity on him and promised to vote anyway.[64] For some activists, however, public work appeared as a litmus test for patriotic feeling, something which seemed all the more necessary given the increasingly static and routine nature of Komsomol affairs. As the top Komsomol official in SGU complained in 1951, public work assignments – which all members were supposed to perform – were "given only to those who ask for it."[65] A dynamic core of Komsomol activists formed something like a club of the elect – ironically, a situation, as the SGU official suggested, that only deepened the apathy of the rank-and-file.

The militancy and discipline of the upper echelons of the *aktiv* also benefitted from the influx of veterans of World War II into the universities. Granted privileged access to higher learning in the immediate postwar years, veterans, sometimes still in uniform, had a large presence in the postwar colleges and a dominant hold on the party and Komsomol *aktiv*.[66] The returning servicemen's high levels of party membership explained their participation in public bodies, and so too did their prestige within the university communities, a fact demonstrated by the actions of one non-veteran student in Baku who "rented" a war medal from an impoverished veteran to wear in his institute.[67] Party leaders in higher education hoped

---

[63] For Komsomol militancy in the 1920s, see Anne E. Gorsuch, *Youth in Revolutionary Russia: Enthusiasts, Bohemians, Delinquents* (Bloomington: Indiana University Press, 2000), 80–95.

[64] Interview with D. F. Sergeev, Moscow, 2004.

[65] Interview with D. F. Rozental', Moscow, 2004; GANISO f. 3234, op. 13, d. 15, l. 10.

[66] At a 1950 KDU party conference, a full 208 of the 250 delegates had fought in the war. Of the delegates overall, 136 were students. DAKO f. 158, op. 3 spr. 96, ark. 239–40. Mark Edele, "Soviet Veterans as an Entitlement Group, 1945–1955," *Slavic Review*, 65 (2006): 122–26.

[67] G. Kh. Shakhnazarov, *S vozhdiami i bez nikh* (Moscow: "Vagrius," 2001), 42.

that the veterans would follow in the footsteps of the "promotees" (*vydviz-hentsy*) of the 1930s in their dedication to the party and singularity of purpose. The comparison had some merit. Evgenii Plimak, a student-veteran, recounts his efforts to bring the orthodoxy and discipline of the army to MGU, for instance by providing a teacher with a list of students who had failed to keep detailed notes on the *Short Course of the History of the Communist Party of the Soviet Union (Bolsheviks)*.[68] In many cases, however, the *frontoviki* fell short of the party's expectations. Confident of their contributions to socialism, veterans sometimes disregarded the pliant atti-tude demanded of them in the Soviet higher education system; Plimak, for instance, would soon lock horns with administrators at the Philosophy Department over its disorganized curriculum.[69] Indeed, not even the veterans' fealty to ideological orthodoxies could be taken for granted.[70] It is indisputable, though, that veterans constituted the raw social material from which the responsible cadres replenished their ranks; indeed, prefer-ential access to graduate school meant that they would retain leading positions in university administrations and party organizations for decades to come.[71]

If the responsible cadres were not a disciplined army imposing their will on their classmates, this was much more the case of the lower activists who composed the majority of the university *aktiv*. The lowest rung of the *aktiv* were the so-called leadership "triangles" in the academic groups that consisted of a Komsomol organizer (*komsorg*), union organizer (*proforg*), and academic monitor or *starosta* (responsible for reporting classmates' attendance informa-tion to the dean's office). Activists in the groups – and, to some extent, their immediate superiors at the departmental level – lacked the responsible cadres' power and privileges, but also their close subordination to party power. In sharp contrast to the rigged elections for responsible cadres, students often had some freedom of action in selecting the leadership triangle in their academic groups. The efforts of responsible cadres to support their own throughout the *aktiv* did not extinguish this element of direct democracy at the lowest rungs

[68] E. G. Plimak, *Na voine i posle voiny: zapiski veterana* (Moscow: Izdatel'stvo "Ves' mir," 2005), 77.
[69] Ibid. and A. N. Iakovlev, *Omut' pamiati* (Moscow: "Vagrius," 2000), 48.
[70] Mark Edele has explored cases of veterans tried for counter-revolutionary crimes to show that no simple political portrait of the group is possible. Mark Edele, "More Than Just Stalinists: The Political Sentiments of Victors, 1945–1953," in Juliane Fürst (ed.), *Late Stalinist Russia: Society between Reconstruction and Reinvention* (London and New York: Routledge, 2006), 167–91. For an example from the memoir literature, see Aleksandr Bovin, *XX vek kak zhizn'* (Moscow: Zakharov, 2003), 31–32.
[71] For this pattern, and the long-term influence of veterans in leadership positions in MGU generally, see B. N. Rudakov, *Mnogo let proneslos' ... o veteranakh Moskovskogo universiteta* (Moscow: Izdatel'stvo MGU, 1995), 56–59, 66, 81–85, 93–99, 100–103.

of the Communist Youth League.[72] As a result, group-level elections often worked to dull the Komsomol's all-consuming demands on the time and energy of the rank-and-file members. As a member of the KDU Party Committee complained in 1952, primary Komsomol cells regularly rejected incumbent *komsorgi* who had proven excessively "demanding and fault-finding" toward their comrades, instead choosing classmates who were "neither fish nor fowl," meaning those who would not go out of their way to impose a harsh disciplinary regime on the group.[73]

The dependence of activists on their peers shaped the everyday activities of Komsomol at the grassroots level. For lower-level activists, the student norm of social solidarity competed with and sometimes outweighed obligations to distant power-holders. For instance, many Komsomol organizers were decidedly listless in carrying out the monotonous and formal "political instruction activities" entrusted to them, such as conducting officially mandated discussions on canned themes: "live, work and study as comrade Stalin teaches," "on the moral makeup of the Soviet student," or "outstanding study is your duty, Komsomol member."[74] Such events rarely interested student audiences, which not infrequently would read novels, chat, or catch up on homework while the hapless *komsorg* recited party resolutions or press materials verbatim, shamefacedly avoiding eye contact with his or her peers.[75] And while forced to report to superior bodies in Komsomol and the party, many activists pursued paths of dissimulation, padding reports with mention of pro forma activities. A 1952 investigation conducted by the Komsomol TsK instructors revealed that many group organizers at Kazan' University limited their work to collecting students' grades in Marxism-Leninism, Political Economy, and Philosophy for edifying public display in the hallways.[76]

The foot-dragging and formalism of Komsomol affairs stemmed primarily from the organization's endemic over-centralization and stifling political orthodoxy (incidentally, factors that have also dampened the enthusiasm of youth activists in other monopolistic state youth organizations in modern Europe).[77] But the weakness of the primary cells in the university Komsomol organizations also reflected the specific social setting of higher education. The

[72] In September 1953, the SGU Komsomol Committee instructed department-level activists to influence elections in the groups by "nominating the most active" cadres. GANISO f. 3234, op. 13, d. 31, l. 92.
[73] DAK f. 1246, op. 5, d. 153, l. 170b.
[74] E. B. Khlebutin, "Aktivnyi organizator vospitaniia molodezhi," *VVSh*, no. 5 (1953): 35.
[75] DAKO f. 158, op. 5, d. 101, l. 12.
[76] See the document from January 1952 in RGASPI-M f. 1, op. 46, d. 145, ll. 2–4.
[77] Bureaucratic ossification is a common theme in literature on youth in so-called totalitarian states. Cf. Detlev Peukert, *Inside Nazi Germany: Conformity, Opposition and Racism in Everyday Life* (New Haven, CT: Yale University Press, 1987), 145–54.

influence of student solidarity on the functioning of Komsomol was particularly pronounced in the organization's handling of disciplinary cases against its members. In addition to being "conveyor belts" for party policy, Komsomol imposed a disciplinary regime on its membership, one that was carefully overseen in the colleges by party organizations, administrators, and representatives of the security organs. Komsomol's role was to punish its members for misdeeds ranging from routine inner-organizational infractions such as non-participation in league-led activities to far more serious violations such as "immoral acts" or "politically unworthy behavior" – charges that could lead to expulsion from the university and a damaging and permanent blot on one's labor records, if not arrest.[78]

Subordinate to the arbitrary oversight of party comrades and exceedingly unsystematic in procedural terms, the Youth League cells were anything but impartial courts for the countless postwar students who appeared as defendants before them. Yet Komsomol disciplinary cases were not always arbitrary exercises in top-down control. Rather, they often revealed the dual identities of the activists as representatives of the party-state and members of the student milieu. In both the capitals and the provinces, the student collectives in the academic groups – and, therefore, the Komsomol cells that were virtually coterminous with them – were marked by a distinctive ethical code of mutual toleration. As SGU alumnus P. R. Krastins recalled, no one in his group "ever brought anyone else down and they all defended each other."[79] This norm of solidarity often blunted administrators' efforts to impose strict controls on student behavior. This was particularly clear in the organization's policing of everyday goings-on in the dormitories; in many cases, the unwillingness of low-level activists to incriminate their peers left university leaders in a state of ignorance about student fights, drunken and rowdy behavior, or even young people with no connection to the university staying illegally in their friends' rooms.[80] As a leading SGU activist complained, the stubborn silence of the students about infractions by their classmates meant that Komsomol committees could only rely on the eyes and ears of "tried-and-true comrades," or the activists themselves, while the mass of students "remained to the side" of the organization.[81]

---

[78] *Ustav vsesoiuznogo leninskogo kommunisticheskogo soiuza molodezhi* (Moscow: Molodaia gvardiia, 1957), 6–8.
[79] Interview with P. R. Krastins, Saratov, 2004.
[80] See complaints made in 1953 by the head of the SGU Union Committee (*profkom*) Ponomarchuk in GANISO f. 3234, op. 13, d. 17, l. 68.
[81] See the comments of activist Akindinov during a 1954 discussion of Komsomol work among third-year students at the Physics Department. Ibid., d. 51, l. 42.

Party organizations decried this student solidarity as "false comradeship," a reactionary placing of personal interests above public ones. This indictment might contain a grain of truth, but it ignores an important circumstance: group cover-ups and refusals to act as whistleblowers were the obverse side of the collective habits of the student body which the regime itself had inculcated. In disciplinary hearings, the responsible cadres who made up the university-wide Komsomol committees frequently solicited input from a defendant's *komsorg*, classmates, and roommates as a way of gauging the "opinion of the collective." Not surprisingly, these character witnesses often presented their accused classmates in a positive light, sometimes drawing on the language of Soviet collectivism for the purpose.[82] Bazavluk, a Komsomol secretary at the SGU Geology Department, argued that two students accused of fighting in the dormitories would be better served by "principled criticism" from their comrades in the collective than by administrative action from above.[83] Of course, leading activists or administrators could easily reject such interjections as biased. Nevertheless, Bazavluk's attempt to limit the punishment of a classmate to the confines of the collective showed the potential for collectivist structures to fragment structures of power in the student milieu. Like it or not, university leaders had to concede that student social solidarity was a structuring reality of Komsomol in higher learning.

Komsomols as cultured subjects

The emphasis on cultured behavior and *intelligentnost'* in university life provided another critical backdrop to the functioning of Komsomol. The Komsomol and the classroom constituted different social worlds for students, and the two could easily come into friction. The Youth League's mandate of creating communists through extra-curricular mobilization had tremendous potential to disrupt the academic process; in a broader sense, the model of the militant and self-sacrificing Komsomol member sometimes proved difficult to reconcile with notions of intellectual culture that university study inspired.[84] For their part, many professors saw Komsomol work as a needless distraction from science. A. G. Kurosh, the mathematician noted above for his old-world manners, wrote to the rector of MGU in 1952 bemoaning that the excessive

---

[82] For an analysis of the instrumental use of Bolshevik discourse, see Stephen Kotkin, *Magnetic Mountain: Stalinism as a Civilization* (Berkeley: University of California Press, 1995), 198–237.

[83] The Komsomol Committee's hearing of the case is in GANISO f. 3234, op. 13, d. 51, ll. 3–6.

[84] For conflict between Komsomol and professors in the interwar period, see Sheila Fitzpatrick, "The Soft Line on Culture and its Enemies," in *The Cultural Front: Power and Culture in Revolutionary Russia* (Ithaca, NY: Cornell University Press, 1992), 98, 102–3.

burdening of students with "social assignments" – activists reported spending up to 30 hours a week on various Komsomol-related activities – made independent research next to impossible and even, more generally, "deprived the majority of students of the possibility to read and think."[85] For Kurosh and others, the profile of the university as a training ground for researchers dictated a loosening of the stringent political demands made on Soviet youth. Most of all, some professors, and particularly those of pre-Stalin vintage, resisted being drawn into explicitly ideological work with the students. For instance, sometimes faculty members avoided serving as "agitators," ideological curators attached to student groups, despite heavy party pressure. After Stalin's death, when the risk of doing so had declined, a few faculty members openly articulated their opposition to being co-opted for such work. In October 1956, the influential 76-year-old MGU geography professor N. N. Baranskii opined at a faculty meeting that overseeing students' ideological beliefs was a task better suited for priests – "there are still some left," he added – than professors.[86]

Wary survivors of Stalinism, old professors were generally careful not to convey such attitudes to students. Nevertheless, the incomplete absorption of the professoriate into the party sphere was apparent to some students. While Komsomol activities were a matter of pride to many patriotic postwar activists, students who saw themselves as scholars-in-training might become skeptical of the organization's relentless demands on their loyalties, time, and bodies. When she enrolled at the MGU History Department in 1950, G. S. Tolmacheva was a Komsomol activist captivated with a romantic vision of working as a rural schoolteacher. After a few years of study under her newfound mentor, Professor P. A. Zaionchkovskii, she resigned as Komsomol secretary of her course – a move that Zaionchkovskii met with the words, "finally you ended these stupidities and you are doing what's important."[87] While Tolmacheva's transformation from activist to detached scholar was a dramatic one, she was not alone in privileging the life of the

---

[85] See the results of a commission headed by Kurosh charged with studying the "time budgets" of students. TsMAM f. 1609, op. 2, d. 345, ll. 3–8.

[86] See the October 1956 general meeting of professors on ideological questions at TsMAM f. 1609, op. 2, d. 415, ll. 34–39.

[87] In Russian, *zanimaetes' delom*. Interview with G. S. Tolmacheva, Moscow, January 2004. Zaionchkovskii belonged to the Moscow historical school that sought to place "facts and not tendentious schemes at the center of research," one of its adherents explained. L. G. Zakharova et al. (eds.), *P. A. Zaionchkovskii 1904–1983 gg.: Stat'i, publikatsii, i vospominaniia o nem* (Moscow: ROSSPEN, 1998), 102. For Zaionchkovskii's influence on American exchange students in the USSR years later, see David C. Engerman, *Know Your Enemy: The Rise and Fall of America's Soviet Experts* (Oxford University Press, 2009), 177–79.

mind over political activism. In 1952, a former activist Svishchev at Kazan' University rebuffed pressure to participate in Komsomol activities on the grounds that "in general one should study and not do public work."[88] While Svishchev drew the ire of party authorities with these words, the late Stalinist party-state leadership actually came to adopt a less categorical version of his assertion: Komsomol's busybodiness was detracting from higher education's core objectives. A 1952 Komsomol TsK plenary meeting declared that diligent study was the students' main duty and cautioned student activists against burdening their classmates with time-consuming activities.[89] So concerned was the regime with producing competent specialists that it was willing to restrict the main agency responsible for ensuring their ideological soundness – a reflection of the high priority of science in the context of the early Cold War.

If the academic purpose of the universities constrained Komsomol, the relationship between the two was hardly a zero-sum game. On the contrary, the Komsomol sphere itself provided some outlets for intellectual expression through its cultural activities. Higher education immersed students in Soviet culture in countless ways, all in order to prepare them for the all-important task of enlightening the Soviet masses. Concerts, plays, student "amateur arts" performances, lectures, and films were regular activities in the dormitories and other campus venues such as MGU's "Home of Culture."[90] In fact, Komsomol organizations themselves not only carried out political surveillance and indoctrination but also organized trips to museums and theaters to raise students' cultural level. Though generally tightly controlled, these activities ingrained in students the notion that they were participants in the noble enterprise of building culture. At the same time, they provided an outlet for students to pursue their intellectual preoccupations within the Komsomol-dominated public sphere in the universities.

One permitted channel for student culture was the *kapustnik* (literally, "cabbage festival"), an amateur dramatic and musical production put on by students at departmental and course-level social events. The inside jokes and university-specific satire that dominated these ritualized performances provided students with a sense of social cohesion while offering an acceptable

[88] This is from a January 1952 Komsomol TsK report on the state of the organization's work in Kazan' University. RGASPI-M f. 1, op. 46, d. 145, l. 19.

[89] *O rabote komsomol'skykh organizatsii vysshykh uchebnykh zavedenii: postanovlenie IX plenuma TsK VLKSM* (Moscow: Izdatel'stvo TsK VLKSM Molodaia gvardiia, 1952). Predictably for Komsomol, enforcement of this resolution was largely focused on disciplinary measures aiming to improve academic success. RGASPI-M f. 1, op. 46, d. 131, ll. 1–3.

[90] RGASPI-M f. 1, op. 46, d. 228, ll. 103–25.

channel for (some) unspeakable thoughts.[91] The *kapustniki* also provided a forum for students to demonstrate their erudition and cleverness. At MGU, Vladimir Lakshin brought down the house at the New Year *kapustnik* by wearing a fake moustache and "brilliantly imitating" the professor G. N. Pospelov. Mimicking his professor's convoluted sociological language, Lakshin made the "solemn proclamation" that "Gogol's 'Nose' is not an organ for smelling, but an organ of social self-confirmation."[92] In taking his professor to task so cleverly, Lakshin, who would later become a major figure in the Khrushchev Thaw as an editor of the liberal journal *Novyi mir* (New World), established his reputation as "merry, witty, sociable, and mischievous" – in short, a model student. No doubt because of such episodes, party and Komsomol leaders fretted periodically that the *kapustniki* and other "mass cultural work" in the universities was "for the most part a form of entertainment for the students and not a means of character formation."[93] However, the light satire that students brandished was largely acceptable to authorities in the universities, as seen in Pospelov's unwillingness to seek retribution against Lakshin during oral examinations.

The acceptability of mild criticism like Lakshin's in the university environment raised awkward questions. Could intellectual refinement become a self-serving obsession rather than a means to the end of building socialism? If so, how much student culture was too much of a good thing? The problem of what to make of students' intellectualized rendition of *kul'turnost'* befuddled party and Komsomol bureaucrats in higher education. University Komsomol organizations had a reputation for laxity and ideological incorrectness in the wider Komsomol elite, and some high-ranking party and Komsomol officials seemed unsure of themselves when they set foot in the colleges. According to his superiors in the Ukrainian Komsomol apparat, a secretary of the Chernihiv Province Komsomol Committee avoided work in the sphere of education, "explaining this by his fear of the higher education establishments."[94]

Though surely exaggerated, such suspicion of student life as falling outside the norms of the Soviet community had some basis in realities on the ground. The centrality of culture-building in university life gave rise to various manifestations of independent student activism which typically appeared suspicious to communist overseers. In the late 1940s, a group of students at

[91] On satire as an idiom in Soviet culture more broadly, see "Introduction," in Andrew Horton (ed.), *Inside Soviet Film Satire: Laughter with a Lash* (Cambridge University Press, 1993), 1–13.
[92] See the recollections of Lakshin's classmates in Nalepin (ed.), *Filologicheskii fakul'tet MGU, 1950–1955*, 55–56.
[93] RGASPI-M f. 1, op. 46, d. 127, l. 166.   [94] TsDAHOU f. 7, op. 6, spr. 2241, ark. 29.

the SGU Philology Department created a wall newspaper entitled "The Militant Organ of Komsomol Satire," commonly known by its acronym BOKS. The medium of the wall newspaper, an amateurish handwritten publication placed on display for public edification, conformed to usual Soviet practices. So too was its ostensible purpose. Subordinated to the department's Komsomol organization, the paper exposed everyday misdeeds and oversights they witnessed, such as a student who never showed up for class or the difficulty of getting an appointment with the dean.

The spirit and substance of BOKS, however, was anything but conventional. The paper's initiators thought of themselves as literary innovators and social critics. Writing years later, a participant depicted the paper's appeal as "absolutely creative work in a circle of talented and atypical people: poets, artists, dreamers, and a writing brotherhood." At their all-night meetings in advance of a new issue, the students would engage in a creative free-for-all, "making a clamor, singing, and rolling around from laughter."[95] Perhaps inspired by the crowds of students who gathered in the hallways to read each issue of BOKS, the students became increasingly reckless by criticizing university authorities – incompetent teachers, rigid administrators – with stinging wit.[96] They devoted an entire issue to goading the department's overbearing Komsomol secretary Gubanova; a poem ostensibly written in her honor read: "You are grandiose like a tall building | Even Lysenko himself is hardly smarter than you | You are desired like state loans | And incomprehensible like the Korean War."[97] They took special pleasure in mocking the heavily censored university newspaper, *Stalinets*. When the latter published what one of the students later called "the half-literate verses of one Komsomol activist and philologist," BOKS reprinted the poem in its entirety under the heading "selected works of local authors." The *Stalinets* editors were bewildered and asked why BOKS had singled out the work, "a poem like any other," for criticism – only to find the poem again reprinted in BOKS under the heading, "a poem like any other."[98]

The paper's criticisms brought it under the scrutiny of the university's party authorities. In 1951 *Stalinets* criticized BOKS for its personal attacks and for placing "form above content."[99] However, the fact that the students

[95] Lia Ivanova, *Iz moego proshlogo: ocherki-razmyshleniia* (Saratov, 2003), 9.
[96] Interview with P. R. Krastins, Saratov, 2004.
[97] Viktor Seleznev, *Kto vybiraet svobodu. Saratov: khronika inakomysliia, 1920–1980-e gody* (Borisoglebsk: "Poliarnaia zvezda," 2010), 64.
[98] Interview with D. Ye. Prokhvatilov, Saratov, 2004.
[99] E. Bochkarev, "Za boevuiu Komsomol'skuiu satiru," *Stalinets*, 18 September 1951: 2. Participants later stated that they were in danger of political repression, a claim that cannot be confirmed by the documents I have located. Viktor Seleznev, "Saratov: khronika inakomysliia" (unpublished manuscript), 9.

emerged from this episode unscathed suggests that party authorities saw the paper as an irritant or perhaps even as a healthy initiative gone too far rather than as ideological heresy. The publication's embrace of public intellectualism, not to mention its willingness to question authority, was far from usual practice in the universities. Yet the episode shows the tendency for the culture-creating mission of higher learning to produce unwanted side effects. Encouraging students and youth in general to become exemplars of culture and "the best educated people in the world," the party was shocked to discover a byproduct of their efforts: intellectually confident students who decided that they knew better than their superiors.[100]

Already in the late Stalin period, this dynamic produced more politically threatening manifestations than BOKS. Indeed, a politicized reading of the role of the intellectual was visible in some of the "anti-Soviet groups" among students that the security organs uncovered in the late Stalin period. To be sure, the political labels imposed on students by the Ministry for State Security were often spurious; merely socializing as an informal group might draw suspicion in the hyper-policed universities, while the evidence used to prosecute cases of youthful sedition was often doctored using brutal interrogation methods.[101] Nonetheless, memoir literature confirms that some of these repressed groups had genuinely oppositional or otherwise radical agendas. Some late Stalin groups produced underground publications that embraced fresh and provocative cultural trends, such as the Cheliabinsk literary almanac "Snow Wine," which experimented with mysticism, eroticism, and aestheticism.[102] Oppositional student groups of a different ilk engaged in socialist critiques of Stalinism, often romantically emulating episodes of revolutionary history with party programs, oaths, and hymns.[103]

Regardless of their agenda and the degree to which they rejected Soviet ideological mandates, student groups repressed by the late Stalinist Soviet security forces reflected the distinct milieu of postwar higher learning, where the prestige of bookish learning, the daily reality of intellectual exploration and opportunities for informal youth socializing met. Indeed, such groups tended to emerge at the interstices of academic life, when

---

[100] H. G. Friese, "Student Life in a Soviet University," in George L. Kline (ed.), *Soviet Education* (New York: Columbia University Press, 1957), 54–55.

[101] On such methodological difficulties, see Hiroaki Kuromiya, "'Political Youth Opposition in Late Stalinism': Evidence and Conjecture," *Europe-Asia Studies*, 55 (2003): 631–38.

[102] Elena Zubkova (ed.), *Sovetskaia zhizn', 1945–1953* (Moscow: ROSSPEN, 2003), 332–54.

[103] Juliane Fürst, "Prisoners of the Soviet Self? Political Youth Opposition in Late Stalinism," *Europe-Asia Studies*, 54 (2002): 353–75.

motivated students established common intellectual interests outside the
classroom.[104] As with BOKS, students who explored ideas together independently of college authorities engaged in intellectual self-fashioning,
understood broadly as a purposeful process of forming one's own identities.[105] Ivan Dziuba, later a leader of the young Ukrainian intellectuals,
spent his student years at the Stalino (later renamed Donetsk) Pedagogical
Institute under late Stalinism crusading for intelligentsia culture through his
work as a Komsomol activist. Inspired by the radical writers Pisarev and
Maiakovskii, Dziuba kept a workbook entitled "the exposure of philistinism" (*razoblachenie meshchanstva*) in which he excoriated his peers for their
indifference, selfishness, and following of empty external conventions at the
expense of "inner culturedness." His Komsomol career came to an end
when he found signs of philistinism in the institute's party committee,
which he accused of squandering funds earmarked for building dormitories
and of corrupt admission practices.[106] In such cases, yesterday's conforming
schoolchildren discovered that they could become satirists of university life,
high-minded poets, or Marxist theorists. However few in number, the very
existence of such self-styled *intelligenty* was testimony to the distinct social
and cultural environment produced in the universities and the complexity
of the intelligentsia ideals they conveyed.

The discovery of youth opposition groups in Stalin's final years has shat-
tered an older consensus that presented Soviet students – and more broadly
society as a whole in the late Stalin period – as being both too conformist
and too terrified by Soviet power to engage in the Soviet public sphere in a
meaningful way.[107] During the height of Stalin's power and the onset of the
Cold War, scattered groups of young people penned revolutionary programs and undertook cultural experiments every bit as radical as the more
publically expressed and better-known independent student activism of the
post-Stalin years. Despite these pockets of radicalism, however, the typical

[104] V. I. Belkin, "Protiv Stalina pri Staline (zametki uchastnika i ochevidtsa): Pis'mo A. Zhigulinu," in
I. A. Mazus (ed.), *"Poka svobodoiu gorim . . ." (o molodezhnom antistalinskom dvizhenii kontsa 40-kh–
nachala 50-kh godov)* (Moscow: Nezavisimoe izdatel'stvo "Pik," 2004), 14–37 and Anatolii Zhigulin,
Chernye kamni: avtobiograficheskaia povest' (Moscow: "Sovremennik," 1990).
[105] For a masterful treatment of self-fashioning and intelligentsia in a different historical context, see
Laurie Manchester, "Harbingers of Modernity, Bearers of Tradition: Popovichi as a Model
Intelligentsia Self in Revolutionary Russia," *Jahrbücher für Geschichte Osteuropas*, 20 (2002): 321–44.
[106] Ivan Dziuba and M. H. Zhulyns'kyi, *Spohady i rozdumy na finishnii priamii* (Kyiv: Vydavnytstvo
"Krynytsia," 2004), 57–76.
[107] Cf. the classic textbook on the Soviet period. Geoffrey A. Hosking, *The First Socialist Society: A
History of the Soviet Union from Within*, 2nd edn. (Cambridge, MA: Harvard University Press,
1992), 403.

experience of late Stalinist university life was one of social cohesion and exalted optimism. Moreover, students who deviated from this norm, like those associated with BOKS, frequently derived much of their confidence from the university environment and the opportunities it provided for internalizing and indeed reinterpreting the state-sanctioned model of *kul'turnost'*.

This contented majority of students, however, was hardly a mass of standardized Soviet subjects, if such a thing indeed existed anywhere. The universities actively shaped the young people that passed through them in growing numbers in the period, giving rise to a student social group with common traits and interests. Ostensibly pillars of party power, student collectives also served to integrate young people into academic communities, creating a kind of social solidarity which sometimes worked against party controls. At the same time, the ongoing influence of pre-Stalin intellectuals in the universities fed the imaginations of students who took seriously the cultural mission associated with their elite education and future careers; in some cases, it also provided a counterpoint to the dogmatism of Soviet higher learning. Indeed, the collectivism and intellectual atmosphere of the postwar universities made the student a distinct type in postwar mass consciousness. As a Komsomol report bemoaned, literary works of the 1950s constantly depicted students as easygoing, witty, and clever rather than principled and disciplined.[108]

The distinctive qualities of postwar university life might be taken as part of a more complex post-Stalin society that was emerging in embryo after the war, a view that corresponds to a growing literature exploring the continuities in ideas and aspirations across the 1953 divide.[109] Complicating this idea of a nascent civil society, however, was the fact that the specific traits of the postwar students emerged in close association with state institutions and policies. Student social solidarity, for instance, was a modified strain of wider collectivist tenor of Soviet society, while the remaking of some postwar youth as *intelligenty* reflected the Soviet ideal of *kul'turnost'*, the mythologization of the old intelligentsia, and the promotion of university learning for the Cold War. Indeed, far from being a force for political opposition or social instability, the postwar *studenchestvo* was integrated into late Stalinist society to a high degree. Higher education promised postwar youth a great many things: the possibility of a comfortable career performing mental labor, a rooted social identity in the student environment, and,

---

[108] RGASPI-M f. 1, op. 46, d. 246, ll. 37–41.   [109] See the Introduction on this trend in the literature.

not least, the opportunity to become enlighteners in the mold of the elderly professoriate – a particularly important goal for young people accustomed to the idea that life without a great cause was not worth living. Against the backdrop of a hyper-politicized, hungry, and exploited society, the material, social, and ideological goods that the universities had to offer were especially enticing.

In retrospect, the ideological ambiguities of Soviet higher learning appear glaring. The universities had divided temporal associations as institutions tied to both the Soviet future and Russian (and sometimes non-Russian) past. Especially fraught was the celebration within universities of the old intelligentsia in a party-state that explicitly rejected several of its defining characteristics, notably value-free science and humanistic introspection. Even the quintessentially Soviet collectives were Janus-faced institutions: while generating strong loyalty among students, they also made sure that those who did not accept its mandates – loners, contrarians, or cranks – would often find themselves isolated in the postwar universities. Yet most students did not linger on these contradictions: the universities were too resplendent, the causes involved were too worthy, and the psychological costs of dredging up doubts were too high.

Ironically, the comfortable and dynamic world of the postwar universities proved unacceptable to the party-state that had created it.[110] Postwar reconstruction and the Cold War created the context for the party-state to patronize higher learning and the scientific workers who controlled it. However, the same historical situation also made Stalin's relationship to educated society explosive and frequently antagonistic, as the party struggled to mold institutions and mindsets for a new period of geopolitical and ideological conflict. In Stalin's final years, students and professors would find their beloved institutions jolted from the outside and divided from within by questions about privilege, academic authority, and how to define insiders and outsiders in the Soviet project.

---

[110] For a discussion of the indirect consequences of state policies on social change under Stalin, see Mark Edele, "Soviet Society, Social Structure, and Everyday Life: Major Frameworks Reconsidered," *Kritika*, 8 (2007): 349–73.

CHAPTER 2

The university in the Soviet social imagination

Vadim Belov and Sergei Palavin were best friends at the Moscow Pedagogical Institute, but they were polar opposites. Vadim was hard-working, morally upright, and heavily engaged in the affairs of the academic group; Sergei was lazy, self-centered, and dismissive of the opinion of the collective. They also saw society differently; Vadim had a social conscience, and found fulfillment in tutoring workers at a nearby factory. In contrast, Sergei looked down on his classmates as intellectual "small fry," maligning a talented classmate and former worker as "uncultured" and likening him to "cod liver oil" (a symbol of backward peasant ways). Vadim planned to utilize his training by becoming a schoolteacher, but Sergei thought that teaching was for people with limited creative abilities and instead thought himself cut out for a "learned profession." In the end, the two friends came into conflict when Belov criticized Palavin at a Komsomol meeting for moral transgressions (abandoning a pregnant girlfriend) and careerism (seeking to cheat on exams), an intervention that allowed the collective to return Palavin to the correct path of moral uprightness and humility.[1]

The plot of Iurii Trifonov's 1952 novel *Students* had all the features of the didactic socialist realist novel: the positive hero who develops revolutionary consciousness, the tidy division of characters according to their relationship to the party. Trifonov's novel nevertheless offers a telling portrayal of postwar students – indeed, one that resonated among student readers at the time.[2] Although he was the novel's lost soul deviating from true consciousness, the character of Palavin might well have struck readers as

[1] Iu. V. Trifonov, *Students: A Novel* (Moscow: Foreign Languages Publishing House, 1953), 11, 76, 79, 120, 245, 409.

[2] A. G. Bocharov, "Vstrechi s Iuriem Trifonovym: vospominaniia," *Literaturnoe obozrenie*, nos. 1–2 (1994): 80–85 and Josephine Woll, *Invented Truth: Soviet Reality and the Literary Imagination of Iurii Trifonov* (Durham, NC: Duke University Press, 1991), 18. On socialist realism and Soviet realities, see Thomas Lahusen, *How Life Writes the Book: Real Socialism and Socialist Realism in Stalin's Russia* (Ithaca, NY: Cornell University Press, 1997).

particularly emblematic of postwar student life. Palavin was in his element in college in a way that the plodding and unexceptional Vadim Belov was not. At one point, he seeks to energize student research at the institute (albeit demagogically) by criticizing the inactive Student Scientific Society. And if Sergei was an unhealthy egoist, his individualism found expression in ways that postwar Soviet citizens associated with belonging to the intelligentsia: cultural refinement and academic ambition. In other words, Trifonov depicted his misled youth as a smug insider at home in the academic milieu.

The fictional Sergei Palavin was representative of social problems that plagued postwar higher learning. Like Trifonov, some observers of postwar higher learning saw disturbing signs of elitism among postwar students, in the universities in particular. It seemed that many students resembled Palavin in looking askance at workers and collective farmers in their midst, in hiding lazy work habits behind intellectual self-confidence, and in seeking cushy careers in research instead of entering the mass professions like secondary school teaching for which the state had trained them. While no doubt exaggerated by the utopian standards Soviet rulers made of their subjects, such fears of social elitism had a basis in social realities of the time. Before the war, Stalin had abandoned social class in admissions criteria to higher education on the grounds that hostile social divisions were a thing of the past and the intelligentsia was now fused to the workers and peasants. By the early postwar years, however, Stalin's new intelligentsia had taken on a life of its own, as educated elites reproduced themselves by passing educational achievement from one generation to the next.

This chapter explores the uncertain connections of universities to social hierarchies in the first postwar decade. After the war, the student bodies in the universities were dominated by urban middle-strata elements, and some young people followed the fictional Palavin by making claims to the cultured style of life that would mark the Soviet *intelligent*. The universities' special character as the domain of intelligentsia privilege had deep-seated origins in the academic focus of their courses of study – at least relative to the vocationally oriented institutes that predominated in Soviet higher education – as well as their prestige as centers of culture in the early Cold War. Yet the Soviet order could never reconcile itself with the universities' social role as preserves of middle-strata, status-conscious intellectuals. As socialist institutions and cogs of the planned economy, the universities were saddled with external agendas which worked against their social function of making the Soviet intelligentsia into a hereditary stratum. Indeed, the relationship of universities to Soviet society as a whole was unfixed, a fact that emerges with particular clarity by examining policies and practices tied to the beginning and ending of the student experience: admissions and postgraduate employment. Pressure to train young people they might not otherwise have admitted – and to block the entrance of others – reminded university communities of their dependence on outside political forces of various kinds. Meanwhile, the mandate to train specialists in the "mass intelligentsia" professions Palavin haughtily rejected exposed the disconnect between the status of the universities and the logic of the planned economy. The contention surrounding both admissions and employment reflected the divided nature of the universities' social roles and, more broadly, the ambiguous identity of the intelligentsia of the future that they were tasked with producing.

Postwar dreams

In 1953, a student at the MGU Biology and Soil Science Department, Iurii Korablev, wrote an article in the university newspaper about his experiences. Korablev had been a partisan in occupied territory during the Great Patriotic War. During long days hiding from the enemy in the forest, he had dreamt about becoming a student after the war (in fact, he even tried to keep up with his studies as a partisan). Now Korablev's "dream had come true": he was a student of the best institute of higher learning in the entire Soviet Union.[3]

Korablev's article fell into a distinct genre of university newspaper articles that chronicled students' happiness and gratitude for their lot. Highly formulaic, such stories probably reflected an effort to "speak Bolshevik" rather than offering an objective picture of the life trajectories they described.[4] Nevertheless, articles like Korablev's also reflected fundamental aspects of postwar higher learning. For young people scarred by war, college education was part of a Soviet postwar dream. In addition to being a potent symbol of peacetime existence as Chapter 1 mentioned, higher learning was a way of getting ahead in the USSR in social and economic terms. Given the near-monopoly of the state on employment, a higher education diploma was a ticket to a professional career, meaning, above all, an escape from manual labor.[5] Given the state's tight control over population movement through

---

[3] Iu. Korablev, "Osushestvlennaia mechta," *Moskovskii universitet*, 1 September 1953: 3.
[4] Stephen Kotkin, *Magnetic Mountain: Stalinism as a Civilization* (Berkeley: University of California Press, 1995), 198–237.
[5] Sheila Fitzpatrick, "Postwar Soviet Society: The Return to Normalcy, 1945–1953," in Susan J. Linz (ed.), *The Impact of World War II on the Soviet Union* (Totowa, NJ: Rowman & Allanheld, 1985), 129–56.

internal passport and registration restrictions, higher education was also one of precious few paths for geographical mobility from the poverty-stricken small towns and villages to the more comfortable big cities. Finally, for male teenagers, gaining admission to higher education promised an easy route to fulfill mandatory military service; most postwar institutes had campus military departments that offered a relatively undemanding system of training students as reserve officers.[6]

Korablev's article also suggests the specific appeal of universities for postwar Soviet society. Universities enjoyed tremendous prestige in the postwar years among Soviet citizens, old and young alike. Comparative literature on higher education offers a framework for explaining the special lure of university education for Soviet society. In any system of higher learning, young people decide on specific institutions and courses of study based on a range of social and cultural factors, including the prestige of occupations to which they provide access, the image or "social character" of specific institutions, and the benefits or costs of associating oneself with the social groups traditionally linked to one kind of institution or another.[7] All these considerations proved important for Soviet universities, which simultaneously provided gateways to desired careers, carried distinction as focal points of Soviet culture, and granted a basis for young people and their families to associate themselves with the intelligentsia as a status group.

The universities' appeal stemmed above all from their function as centers for training specialists in the physical sciences. The early Cold War saw the massive expansion of Soviet science, driven in large part by postwar rearmament projects that drew on scientific discoveries in several fields.[8] To be sure, careers in science had the reputation of being materially advantageous and comfortable in comparison to work in production. But the young people who flooded the science departments of the universities as well as other more specialized scientific colleges also gained inspiration from a distinctly Soviet cult of science, a faith in transforming nature and improving humanity through scientific knowledge. A Saratov student explained that he had enrolled in physics because he saw the possibility of "the application of physical methods in almost all branches of the economy and science," and an MGU student concurred that "the most relevant field was physics, as it

[6] Julian Cooper, "The Military and Higher Education in the USSR," *Annals of the American Academy of Political and Social Science*, 502 (1989): 112.

[7] See Fritz K. Ringer, *Education and Society in Modern Europe* (Bloomington: Indiana University Press, 1979), 8–9.

[8] V. M. Zubok, *A Failed Empire: The Soviet Union in the Cold War from Stalin to Gorbachev* (Chapel Hill: University of North Carolina Press, 2007), 130–32.

seemed that physicists would solve everything."[9] For many young people, visions of a scientifically organized society had a patriotic bent, as they were a way of following Stalin's postwar slogan ("teaching") that "our science must surpass the accomplishments of science beyond Soviet borders."[10]

Another factor drawing youth to the universities was the particular prestige of the institutions themselves. The romance of the universities derived from their idealized image as unequaled centers of learning and all that came with it: culture, progress, and tradition.[11] When asked why he applied to MGU, one interview subject answered, "this was obvious, it was a cherished desire, as we all understood that MGU is the best educational institution in the country," in which it was "remarkably honorable and prestigious" to study.[12] Its reputation spread beyond youth: L. I. Arkhipova's uncle in Omsk recommended that she apply to MGU in order to "live under communism for five years."[13] An indication of the particular reputation of universities – and not just the loudly fêted MGU – was the fierce competition for admission to all university disciplines, including the humanities and social sciences which opened the door, for the most part, to less attractive career paths than the hard sciences.[14] Admission to universities became increasingly competitive after the war, and failure to gain admission was a serious matter, as one could only apply to a single college per year and higher education was the primary way to avoid full military service. Nevertheless, some young people applied to the universities for years on end, unwilling to enroll in less prestigious institutions like the Pedagogical Institutes that offered roughly similar courses of study. Expressing this obsession with the university was the young Valerii Shevchuk from Zhytomyr, who understood that getting admitted to KDU would be a challenge but saw failure as a cultural death warrant; "I will drown in the sea of the mundane and disappear," he lamented.[15] For Shevchuk and many

[9] G. Shvedov, "Moia budushchaia professiia," *Stalinets*, 23 April 1953; Interview with F. G. Repin, Moscow, 2004; Aleksandr Bovin, *XX vek kak zhizn'* (Moscow: Zakharov, 2003), 29.

[10] This injunction, from Stalin's 1946 speech before voters to the Soviets in Moscow, became a central mobilizing slogan in postwar higher learning. "Za dal'neishee razvitie sovetskoi nauki," *Stalinets*, 23 April 1953: 1.

[11] On the prestige of old institutes in the Soviet context, see George Z. F. Bereday, "Class Tensions in Soviet Education," in George Z. F. Bereday and Jaan Pennar (eds.), *The Politics of Soviet Education* (Westport, CT: Greenwood Press, 1976), 164–74.

[12] Interview with D. A. Berestov, Moscow, 2004.

[13] V. V. Voevodin (ed.), *Neuzheli iubilei? Ne veriu!* (Moscow: NIVTs MGU, 2004), 48.

[14] For the competitiveness of admissions to the universities, see data in Benjamin Tromly, "Reimagining the Soviet Intelligentsia: Student Politics and University Life, 1948–1964" (Ph.D. diss., Harvard University, 2007), 70.

[15] V. O. Shevchuk, *Na berezi chasu: Mii Kyiv. Vkhodyny: avtobiohrafichna opovid'-ese* (Kyiv: Vitae memoriae, 2002), 46–53.

others like him, university study was important for reasons that stemmed beyond pragmatic considerations; it represented a pathway to joining an intelligentsia of culture.

A student body fit for communism?

The reputation of universities as academic powerhouses shaped the student body that they trained. Unfortunately, the historian seeking to draw a social portrait of students in the late Stalin era encounters several obstacles. Historians of higher education always have trouble classifying student bodies according to social groups, in part because the language used to represent social divisions in the historical record is often ambiguous and inconsistent.[16] The task is particularly problematic in the Soviet context; perhaps appropriately, it is virtually impossible to identify the social makeup of the student body in the world's first socialist state. Ideological blinkers and definitional ambiguity complicated the definition of social groups, both within higher education and in Soviet society as a whole. When categorizing its subjects according to social class, the Soviet state employed a language of "social origin," one that focused on the social stations individuals inherited rather than the ones they occupied. Paradoxically, a Soviet citizen hailing from the working class could become a member of the Politburo or a professor yet retain worker status for life – and sometimes even pass it on to his or her progeny.[17] In the 1930s, Stalin deepened the quagmire by introducing the new doctrine that Soviet society, shorn of social contradictions, consisted of two "friendly" classes of workers and collective farmers along with a residual "intelligentsia" stratum. This tripartite division served as a remarkably vague guide to Soviet social realities. It was also an increasingly meaningless one in practical terms, at least in the realm of higher education. Given the exclusion of class considerations from admissions, higher education authorities simply stopped paying attention to the social origins of the student body in any sustained manner.

The uncertainty surrounding social groups in the Stalinist context obscured a clear trend in higher education: the over-representation of people hailing from the "intelligentsia," understood in Stalin's sense of an educational and occupational category, in the colleges. Table 2.1 shows that

---

[16] An insightful discussion of these problems is provided in Konrad Jarausch, "The Old 'New History of Education': A German Reconsideration," *History of Education Quarterly*, 26 (1986): 225–41.

[17] Sheila Fitzpatrick, "Ascribing Class: The Constitution of Social Identity in Soviet Russia," in Sheila Fitzpatrick (ed.), *Stalinism: New Directions* (London and New York: Routledge, 2000), 1–23.

Table 2.1 *Social composition of newly admitted students in selected Soviet higher education establishments (%)*

Institution	Workers	Collective farmers	Intelligentsia
Moscow University, 1953	12.5	5.5	82
Kyiv University, 1953	17.5	28.2	54.3
Saratov University Komsomol delegates, 1953	18	4	78
All colleges, 1955	24.4	13.0	62.6

Sources: TsMAM f. 1609, op. 2, d. 361, l. 13 (for MGU); TsDAHOU f. 1, op. 71, spr. 105, ark. 89 (KDU); GANISO f. 3234, op. 13, d. 30, l. 29 (SGU); Laurent Coumel, "The Scientist, the Pedagogue and the Party Official: Interest Groups, Public Opinion and Decision-making in the 1958 Education Reform," in Melanie Ilič and Jeremy Smith (eds.), *Soviet State and Society under Nikita Khrushchev* (London: Routledge, 2009), 68 (figures for the entire USSR). Lacking a corresponding figure for Saratov, I provide data on the social origins of the 589 delegates to the 1953 Komsomol conference. There is no obvious reason to assume that this group is unrepresentative in social terms.

the social selectivity of student bodies was particularly pronounced in the universities, institutions at the apex of the Soviet higher education system. Providing a rare glimpse of what the "intelligentsia" actually meant for at least the elite MGU, Table 2.2 shows that the premier university recruited heavily among the offspring of white-collar, educated professionals like scientists, engineers, doctors, bureaucrats, and teachers. In fact, all these official data surely exaggerate the representation of non-intelligentsia strata in universities' student bodies. Many "workers" and "peasants" derived this status through birth and had never labored in a factory or a collective farm. In 1956, a MGU official guessed that only 3–4 percent of the student body were composed of people who were "*themselves* workers and collective farmers."[18]

One should not stress the elite nature of the universities' student bodies too strongly. The state-defined educational and occupational category of intelligentsia was itself socially diverse, especially when juxtaposed with the middle classes that were crucial beneficiaries of higher learning in postwar West European societies. Stalin's "toiling intelligentsia" was a highly diverse and even inchoate social category. As Table 2.2 shows, a significant part of "intelligentsia" youth in the universities consisted of "state servants" or *sluzhashchie*, low-level mental laborers such as office workers, accounts

---

[18] TsAOPIM f. 478, op. 3, d. 38, l. 85. I have added emphasis.

Table 2.2 *Social composition of newly admitted students
in Moscow University, 1952 (%)*

Social origins of incoming students	Natural science departments (%)	Humanities departments (%)	Overall (%)
1. Intelligentsia including:	82.8	77.2	80.1
Party employees and military servicemen	18	23.4	19.7
Engineer-technical employees			
and scientific workers	24.6	16.3	21.5
Teachers and doctors	9.2	11.6	10
State employees (sluzhashchie)	31	25.9 .	28.9
2. Workers	13.7	16.7	14.6
3. Collective Farmers	3.5	6.1	4.5
Total	100	100	100

Sources: See the statistical report in TsMAM f. 1609, op. 2, d. 361, l. 13.

clerks, and train conductors who hardly fit the mold of intelligentsia in terms of academic, professional, or cultural accomplishments.[19] Also, the relative position of intelligentsia youth differed radically across different universities, as Table 2.1 shows. Social privilege was more pronounced in the Russian capitals than in the universities in the Russian provinces and especially in Ukraine (KDU's heavy recruitment from the Ukrainian countryside would later become important for ethnic identities, as Chapter 8 will explore). Nevertheless, the growing social inequality in university admissions was striking. By the early 1950s, universities had ceased to be motors of social mobility, instead helping educated people – broadly speaking, Stalin's "toiling intelligentsia" – to transmit this status to their progeny. Going further, central policies actively facilitated the elitist trend by relentlessly pushing merit as the sole criterion of admissions to college and even by introducing fees in secondary and higher education.[20]

The skewing of student bodies in favor of privileged social strata depended, of course, on a simple fact: youth from educated families tended to outperform their peers from the working class and the collective farmers in the system of competitive entrance exams. The tendency of higher educational systems to reproduce social stratification has thwarted

---

[19] For a useful discussion of the term *sluzhashchie* and its inconsistently drawn boundary with the intelligentsia, see Mervyn Matthews, *Class and Society in Soviet Russia* (New York: Walker, 1972), 148–49.
[20] Ibid., 291–92.

generations of reformers in the USSR and indeed around the world.[21] Without a doubt, the causes of the phenomenon in the postwar years were varied and deep-seated. Urban youth as a whole enjoyed many resources which were largely lacking in small towns and the countryside: high-quality schools, recruitment through university-sponsored academic competitions for school pupils ("Olympiads"), and academically focused extra-curricular clubs and organizations. As competition for placement rose in the mid-1950s, some solicitous parents from what one source calls the "well-paid intelligentsia" turned to hiring private tutors to help their children prepare for college entrance exams.[22] Just as important were the less tangible assets held by children of educated families, and especially by those from what were commonly called "intelligentsia families" (ones which could boast more than one generation of degreed members). No less important were the less tangible forms of cultural capital enjoyed by the offspring of educated families that were valuable assets in higher education such as an orientation toward academic success, good reading habits, proper speech, and a "cultured" bearing. As Pierre Bourdieu has argued in the context of modern France, universities often mask such accumulated social inequalities through what he calls an "ideology of gifts," the attribution of socially determined outcomes in educational success to natural talent alone.[23] Indeed, with its focus on academic merit and on oral examinations in admissions, the Soviet higher education system left wide scope for intelligentsia status to influence educational opportunities.

Dreaming of a (communist) ivory tower

Soviet university communities were not wholly comfortable with the emerging nature of their institutions as preserves of urban privilege and intelligentsia status. The Stalinist state remained deeply invested in forging a postwar intelligentsia that would be worthy of communist construction, and this meant that non-academic criteria found their way into the shaping of the student body. Central policies notwithstanding, communist class favoritism continued to influence admissions on the ground, as admissions committees

[21] For a classic account of the rise and fall of social engineering in early Soviet higher education, see James McClelland, "Proletarianizing the Student Body: The Soviet Experience during the New Economic Policy," *Past and Present*, 80 (1978): 122–46.

[22] TsAOPIM f. 4, op. 113, d. 41, l. 99.

[23] Pierre Bourdieu, *The State Nobility: Elite Schools in the Field of Power*, trans. Lauretta C. Clough (Stanford University Press, 1996), 251, 265–66.

in the universities tended to favor applicants from the working class or collective farmers on the assumption that they would be hard-working and politically reliable students.[24] A case in point was the admission to MGU in 1949 of Mikhail Gorbachev, a young member of the Communist Party whose exploits in a tractor brigade in his native Stavropol' Province earned him the designation of hero of socialist labor.[25] Offering admission to Gorbachev and others like him, university administrators showed they were ambivalent about peopling the universities on the basis of academic preparation alone – an attitude that suggested implicitly that knowledge had become a form of entitlement in Soviet society.

The party-state's involvement was far more extensive and methodical than such haphazard efforts by admissions committees to favor lower-class applicants. As recent literature has shown, the Stalinist state adopted an extensive system of categorizing its population into healthy and unhealthy parts. The war modified this system by providing new definitions of the system's domestic friends and potential enemies – notions that would envelop university life.[26] Benefitting from their war experiences were the veterans who entered higher education aided by preferential admission rules and, as discussed in Chapter 1, came to constitute a powerful if sometimes unruly group in the universities. At the other end of the spectrum was a massive new category of mistrusted citizens: those who had lived in territories occupied by Axis Powers, even if they had been forced laborers or prisoners of war at the time. Working in tandem with union-wide police and party bodies, the higher education system discriminated against wartime returnees of all kinds during the admissions process, often blocking their applications entirely.[27] As a result, a constant feature of postwar university politics was a cat-and-mouse game in which young people with allegedly questionable wartime biographies – and, indeed, any other blots on their records – hid information about their experiences and identities from hostile and suspicious state authorities.[28]

[24] Interview with D. A. Berestov, Moscow, 2004; "Vospitanie istoriko-arkhivnogo instituta-Kazakhstantsev," *Otechestvennye arkhivy*, no. 4 (2002): 64.
[25] Mikhail Sergeevich Gorbachev, *Memoirs* (New York: Doubleday, 1996), 41.
[26] For this broad trend, see Amir Weiner, *Making Sense of War: The Second World War and the Fate of the Bolshevik Revolution* (Princeton University Press, 2001).
[27] For an overview of the topic, see V. N. Zemskov, "Repatriatsiia sovetskikh grazhdan i ikh dal'neishaia sud'ba," *Sotsiologicheskie issledovaniia*, no. 5 (1995), at *Vtoraia mirovaia voina, Velikaia Otechestvennaia voina*, www.pseudology.org/Pobeda/Repatriacia1944_1956.htm (accessed 5 February 2012).
[28] The hiding and unmasking of identities as a characteristic of Stalinism is a theme in Sheila Fitzpatrick, *Everyday Stalinism. Ordinary Life in Extraordinary Times: Soviet Russia in the 1930s* (New York: Oxford University Press, 2000), 193–94, 216.

Tragically, dissimulation only raised the stakes; "If he hid this, it means he was afraid, and that means he committed sins," reasoned a KDU youth activist Gubenko on the case of a student Petrushevich who had studied in the Kyiv Medical Institute during the Nazi occupation.[29] To be sure, political controls over admission were not always airtight, and compromised people frequently found their way into the universities: non-Komsomol members, relatives of "enemies of the people," and individuals who had lived on occupied territory (even Gorbachev's Stavropol' had been under occupation for a short time).[30] Nevertheless, the constant search for compromising biographical details among applicants, students, and faculty alike – against the backdrop of a higher education system that functioned on meritocratic principles – underscored the coexistence of different models of constituting the future intelligentsia.

The operation of academic principles in peopling the student body came under challenge from another source: the influence of party elites. As recent work has shown, political corruption was particularly strong in the early postwar years, a result of sweeping power being consolidated in the hands of administrative elites and of the disruption of property relations during the war.[31] In this context, university study, increasingly prestigious and hard to obtain after the war, became a desired commodity for young people of elite backgrounds and their parents – and, therefore, a target for influence-peddling. Of course, corruption is inherently difficult to detect, let alone measure. However, the instances when behind-the-scenes practices gained public exposure leave no doubt that corruption in admissions – and, indeed, in the functioning of the higher learning system as a whole – was a constant reality in the postwar period. In 1952, the top Komsomol official in the Ukrainian Republic reported to the party that several Kyiv institutes had admitted children of powerful officials with poor entrance exam scores or none at all. In one case, the son of the deputy prime minister of the Ukrainian Council of Ministers had been allowed to repeat his first year of study at KDU

---

[29] DAKO f. 9912, op. 1, spr. 5, ark. 62. See also ibid., spr. 12, ark. 129–30.
[30] Examples of such cases emerged from my interviews. Interview with F. Z. Shapiro, Kyiv, 2005 (non-membership in Komsomol) and Interview with B. V. Simonov, Moscow, 2003 (a son of an "enemy of the people" who did not hide this information during admission).
[31] See Cynthia Hooper, "A Darker 'Big Deal': Concealing Party Corruption, 1945–1953," in Juliane Fürst (ed.), *Late Stalinist Russia: Society between Reconstruction and Reinvention* (London: Routledge, 2006), 142–64 and James Heinzen, "A 'Campaign Spasm': Graft and the Limits of the 'Campaign' against Bribery after the Great Patriotic War," ibid., 123–41.

after receiving failing grades; when the result was the same a year later, the Komsomol organization asked that he be expelled, but in vain.[32]

Corruption in the universities proved particularly controversial given their reputations as sanctuaries of academic excellence. Expressing a common opinion, one graduate asserted that MGU was an impartial "temple of science" that was only open to those with "capabilities, knowledge, and brains," people who supposedly forsook the help of "parents, ranks, and positions or commercial auctions."[33] Accordingly, the subverting of academic procedures by elites called into question the university communities' very self-image. How could universities claim an exalted position if "brains" were not the only way to gain entrance to them? And what kind of intelligentsia would emerge from their walls? No doubt responding to such concerns, university communities and especially students were vocal in questioning the efforts of powerful office-holders to intervene on behalf of relatives or friends. A 1953 meeting of MGU rector Petrovskii with Komsomol activists became heated when several participants raised the issue of classmates who had gained admission "by special notes and orders" rather than through the regular competitive examinations. A student Lapshin explained that such individuals, who clearly came from privileged backgrounds, proved hopelessly unprepared for their studies. He also mentioned widespread embarrassment over the academic performance of a niece of Iurii Zhdanov, the overseer of higher education and science in the central party TsK, and alleged that such apparatchik children "undermined the authority of distinguished leaders."[34] Rector Petrovskii's response – that "one should not speak about such things" – underscored the political sensitivity of the issue and, indirectly, the dilemma that elite privilege posed for the idea of the incorruptible Soviet university.

Administrators and faculty in the universities had a more complicated relationship to string-pulling in admissions than Petrovskii's defensive reaction suggested. Many faculty members proved solicitous for their institutions' academic reputations; while no doubt succumbing to the power of "special notes and orders" in some cases, they might also resist the application of pressure from influential persons. Such ambivalence

---

[32] This Komsomol investigation was initiated by the party secretary of the republic L. G. Mel'nikov. It spurred a Komsomol campaign across Ukrainian higher education in which primary organizations "uncovered" and disciplined various feckless and lazy students, among whom many were offspring of the party-state elite. There is no indication that such a harsh response to elite privilege occurred elsewhere in the period. TsDAHOU f. 7, op. 13, spr. 106, ark. 8–13.

[33] N. B. Bikkenin, "Stseny obshchestvennoi i chastnoi zhizni: 'moi universitety'," *Svobodnaia mysl'*, 3 (2001): 75.

[34] TsMAM f. 1609, op. 2, d. 349, ll. 51–52. See also TsAOPIM f. 478, op. 3, d. 24, ll. 90–91.

concerning the use of patronage in higher learning extended to the Ministry of Higher Education as well. In 1951, a senior party bureaucrat in Saratov appealed to the head of the Administration of Universities K. F. Zhigach to ask for help in admitting A. N. Lapatina, the niece of one of his subordinates, to SGU. Zhigach responded with the recommendation that Lapatina spend more time studying for the entrance examinations.[35] Whatever the motivation of the ministry official in this case, the abrupt injunction to study harder shows how entrenched the norm of academic achievement had become in the universities.

Conflicts over corrupt practices in the universities gained focus through their connection to a seemingly unrelated issue: state affirmative action for national minorities. In a holdover from early Soviet policies of "indigenization," leading institutes of higher learning in Moscow and Leningrad enrolled yearly quotas of students from specific non-Russian republics, both the Union Republics and non-Russian areas of the RSFSR.[36] Administrative organs in the periphery selected the individuals to be admitted, who then were exempted from the competitive examination system. Designed to create national intelligentsias for underdeveloped Soviet peoples, the policy also worked to create a multinational (if far from representative) student body at a few flagship institutions in the capitals. This contrasted heavily with the student bodies of many universities like KDU and SGU, where the East Slavs (Russians, Ukrainians, and Belarusians) dominated among the student body (see Table 2.3).[37] Whatever its perceived advantages, the program in its postwar incarnation was little more than a way for party-state leaders – including some ethnic Russians – to secure places for their children in top-tier educational institutions in the capitals.[38] The nepotism of the arrangement was one reason why the students accepted "outside of competition" often performed badly in their studies; close to one half of the Kirghiz students admitted to Moscow and Leningrad institutes by this arrangement in the beginning of the 1950s dropped out.[39]

---

[35] GANISO f. 594, op. 2, d. 1890, ll. 234–35.

[36] Peter A. Blitstein, "Stalin's Nations: Soviet Nationality Policy between Planning and Primordialism, 1936–1953" (Ph.D. diss., University of California, Berkeley, 1999): 207–8. On the prewar national affirmative action in higher education, see Terry Martin, *The Affirmative Action Empire: Nations and Nationalism in the Soviet Union, 1923–1939* (Ithaca, NY: Cornell University Press, 2001), 373–76.

[37] GANISO f. 3234, op. 13, d. 30, l. 29.

[38] See the results of an investigation of the system of "extra-competition" admissions conducted by the MVO in 1955 in RGANI f. 5, op. 17, d. 475, ll. 124–27.

[39] This is from a 27 July 1951 note to TsK secretary G. M. Malenkov justifying the TsK Science Division's decision to decline the Kirghiz TsK's petition for 160 enrollees in central institutes. RGASPI f. 17, op. 133, d. 195, l. 105.

Table 2.3 *National composition of admitted students (%)*

Nationality	MGU, incoming class of 1952	KDU, incoming class of 1953
Russians	84.5	17.9
Ukrainians	4.6	79.7
Jews	0.9	1.3
All other nationalities	10	1.1
Total	100	100

Sources: The MGU source mentions twenty-two other Soviet nationalities ranging from Belarusians to Tuvans and Chuvashians. The Ukrainian source mentions simply thirteen "other nationalities." The figures for Jews reflect the anti-Semitic campaigns underway at the time, which are discussed in Chapter 3. TsMAM f. 1609, op. 2, d. 361, l. 14 and TsDAHOU f. 1, op. 71, spr. 105, ark. 89, 185.

The program to admit youth from non-Russian areas by administrative fiat was remarkably unpopular among university communities, students, and professors alike. In 1955 the top MGU Komsomol secretary B. Spiridonov stated that "the comrades demand decisively" an end to accepting students outside of the normal competitive scheme on the grounds of their dismal academic performance.[40] Chauvinism and racism might have played a role in the opinion of "the comrades"; a MGU student from Georgia remembers being called a "national cadre women" (*natsmenka*), a derisive term dating from early Soviet affirmative action campaigns.[41] Yet student hostility to the arrangement also reflected the academic elitism bred by the universities. The enrollment of under-prepared students through bureaucratic procedures called into question the universities' meritocratic image and, by extension, the students' own claims to social distinction. It also encouraged students to think about the sensitive topic of party privileges; Komsomol activists complained that the delegated non-Russians were mostly "children of ministers" who should only be admitted after sitting examinations in Moscow along with everyone else.[42] Despite periodic doubts raised in the university administrations and outright hostility to

[40] See the comments at a 1955 Lenin district Komsomol Conference. TsAOPIM f. 4013, op. 2, d. 104, l. 114.
[41] The student had gained admission through the normal channels. Interview with G. S. Tolmacheva, Moscow, January 2004.
[42] See the minutes of a joint plenary session of the MGU Party and Komsomol Committees on the role of the Youth League in the 1962 admissions campaign. TsAOPIM f. 6083, op. 1, d. 44, ll. 162, 185.

the program from the Komsomol TsK, however, the extra-competition enrollment from non-Russian areas continued.[43] The program was important for its broader implications as well as its divisive impact on universities. The ongoing functioning of state programs which promoted desired elements through higher education on extra-academic grounds – regardless of whether the groups were defined by war experience, social group, or nationality – showed that Bolshevik social engineering had the potential to throw into flux the universities and the status-conscious middle-strata that were their main social constituency.

"I will go where I am sent"

The challenges posed by external meddling in admissions troubled the social position of the postwar universities, but they also confirmed it. The universities' distinctive academic functions and their reputations as centers of Soviet culture ensured that they would remain exposed to myriad pressures from state and society. Along with admissions, postgraduate employment emerged as a flashpoint for universities' relationships with the Soviet order surrounding them. In the final year of study, each student passed through a system of administrative job allocation known simply as "distribution." Appearing at the university's commission for distribution, a body tasked with assigning graduates to a list of jobs generated by Soviet planning organs, he or she would receive a job assignment – or, sometimes, a few options from which to choose.[44] Regardless of its salary and geographic location, not to mention the housing and living conditions that would come with it, students had to accept the distribution assignment they received. Until 1956, refusing to take up a distribution assignment or leaving it before serving out a mandatory three-year term constituted a criminal offence.[45] Soviet administrators were unapologetic about the strong-arm

---

[43] RGASPI-M f. 1, op. 46, d. 255, l. 6.

[44] The commission normally consisted of the rector and university administrators, representatives of the college's "public organizations" (normally party, Komsomol, and trade unions), and "personnel from the ministries or particular enterprises which are seeking graduates to fill their manpower needs." Joel Joseph Schwartz, "The Young Communist League (1954–1962): A Study of Group Cooperation and Conflict in Soviet Society" (Ph.D. diss., Indiana University, 1965), 86.

[45] L. I. Karpov and V. A. Severtsev (eds.), *Vysshaia shkola: osnovnye postanovleniia, prikazy i instruktsii* (Moscow: Sovetskaia nauka, 1957), 207. Central decrees put certain limits on the powers of the distribution commissions: married couples were to be kept in the same locale, and graduates who supported non-working family members were to be allowed to remain at their current one. But graduates had no way to ensure that the distribution commissions honored these provisions. Nicholas De Witt, *Education and Professional Employment in the USSR* (Washington, DC: National Science Foundation, 1961), 362–63.

tactics that distribution imposed on educated elites. The distribution system was a much-needed administrative mechanism for directing educated
specialists to parts of the planned economy where they were needed – and
where they might not otherwise have set foot. In any case, the practice
seemed fully justified to party-state leaders, as it embodied the statist
utilitarianism that underpinned the entire higher education system: that
learning's value rested in its usefulness to the state.[46]

The coercive core of distribution nevertheless guaranteed that it would
put the patriotism of every graduate to the test – as party-state leaders well
understood. Every spring, university newspapers carried headlines like "At
the call of the Fatherland" and "The Homeland is waiting for you!"[47]
Accepting one's position, it was endlessly repeated, was nothing more
than a patriotic repayment of the debt owed to the state for one's free
education. In practice, patriotic rhetoric did not trump practical considerations for many young people involved. Despite the administrative controls
involved, the distribution system remained sensitive to the rules of the labor
market in its functioning. When the supply of positions met demand for
them – that is, when graduates were interested in jobs the state had to offer –
the system usually functioned smoothly. However, some graduates were
always dissatisfied with their job postings. One common problem was
geography. An inordinate number of higher learning establishments were
located in major cities, yet employment opportunities in many cases were
not. Few graduates relished the prospect of leaving for a small town or
village where living standards were far lower and cultural amenities virtually
non-existent.[48] Making matters worse were the severe Soviet residence
registration laws that made it difficult to return to the city after fulfilling
one's job assignment. As former MGU philology student A. P. Aleksandrova
put it, "of course, no one wanted to leave Moscow because that meant losing
Moscow forever."[49] The phenomenon of recalcitrant urbanites was not
limited to the capitals; the desire of graduates in Saratov and other provincial
centers to remain in the city after graduation pointed to a more fundamental

---

[46] The importance of distribution as a way of controlling and ultimately shaping the educated class is
suggested by its survival until the last years of the Soviet experiment. Stephen Solnick, *Stealing the
State: Control and Collapse in Soviet Institutions* (Cambridge, MA: Harvard University Press, 1998),
125–74.

[47] G. Enik, "Po zovu otchizny," *Stalinets*, 15 April 1952; "Vas zhdet rodina!" *Stalinets*, 15 April 1954.

[48] On postwar poverty, see Donald A. Filtzer, *The Hazards of Urban Life in Late Stalinist Russia: Health,
Hygiene, and Living Standards, 1943–1953* (Cambridge University Press, 2010); Elena Zubkova,
Poslevoennoe sovetskoe obshchesto: politika i povsednevnost', 1945–1953 (Moscow: ROSSPEN, 1999),
55–101.

[49] Interview with A. P. Aleksandrova, Moscow, March 2004.

disconnect between the urban character of higher learning and the logic of the Soviet planned economy.[50]

The specific nature of the universities posed additional problems for job distribution. Given the universities' role in transmitting fundamental and specialized knowledge in academic disciplines, Soviet planners had a difficult time defining their graduates in occupational terms. In practice, the universities often earmarked graduates for positions in graduate study, research and development, and higher-level teaching. This posed few problems in university fields such as physics, chemistry, and mathematics, where graduates were eagerly recruited by research institutes and enterprises in fields like rocket technology, jet aviation, and electronics, and, later, space programs. Whether concentrated in the major cities or in the closed and secret science cities springing up across the country, these career opportunities were prestigious and lucrative.[51] But the situation was starkly different in the humanities, social sciences, and life sciences, where research positions could not keep up with the production of graduates once the war-torn ranks of the Soviet professional classes had been replenished. Adding to the problem, the positions earmarked for graduates in these fields were less clustered in the major urban centers. Seeking outlets for growing university student bodies, the party leadership at the end of the 1940s began to send increasing numbers of university graduates to teach in primary and secondary schools.[52] While logical from the planners' point of view, this move created a gap between state expectations and the career ambitions of university graduates. Geography complicated matters, as most university graduates received assignments in schools in rural areas and in distant parts of the country such as Central Asia, in part due to competition for more desirable positions in urban schools from graduates of the specialized pedagogical institutes. In this sense, distribution to the schools entailed a dual demotion from the academic summit of the USSR to a non-valued occupational group and from the cultural center to a supposedly uncivilized periphery.

The crisis surrounding the distribution system in the universities forced graduates to grapple with their identities as members of the Soviet intelligentsia, and particularly their commitments to state, society, and learning itself. The vast majority of students felt the party's call to patriotic service,

[50] RGANI f. 5, op. 17, d. 430, ll. 93–98.
[51] Careers for university science graduates are described in GARF f. 9396, op. 2, d. 1089, l. 11; TsMAM f. 1609, op. 2, d. 503, ll. 22, 23.
[52] See the 1955 discussion of the MVO in GARF f. 9396, op. 1, d. 700, l. 34.

internalizing the duty was to go "wherever I am sent," as A. Degtiarenko recalled of her move from Moscow to Penza.[53] Such a feeling of indebtedness was part and parcel of Soviet patriotic identities, but it took on particular resonance for young intellectuals starting their careers. The entire purpose of higher learning was to bring the store of culture one had accumulated in the university to the people; to refuse to leave the relatively wealthy cities for the periphery was not only unpatriotic but a move fit for selfish and uncultured "philistines," as an MGU economics student asserted.[54] But self-styled cultural missionaries might think twice when they saw life in the villages and small towns up close. An MGU geography student, Beliakova, who had recently returned from a curricular training expedition in an unnamed village "far from Moscow," expressed disgust at the prospect of working in such a "terrible hole in the wall." There were few young people and "the entire local intelligentsia [consisted] of one doctor and one teacher," she stressed.[55] Likewise, future Ukrainian dissident Leonid Pliushch left Odessa University halfway through his studies to work in a village school. After exposure to the conservatism, drunkenness, and cynicism of the schoolteachers he absconded to Kyiv to resume his studies.[56] True *intelligenty* were agents of enlightenment, but many students blinked when forced with pursuing the task in the trenches rather than in the familiar comfort of the cities.

Also complicating the distribution system was the fact that the cultural mission of the intelligentsia was open to different interpretations. Many graduates of the Russian and Ukrainian universities felt that their job prospects should match their academic training – which meant graduate training or work in research. At a 1957 MGU Party Committee meeting, the party secretary of the Biology and Soil Science Department complained that students were trained to think that the university was "an institution that trains scientists and that they will graduate as scientists."[57] If seeking to remain in Moscow or Kyiv after graduation could easily be construed as petty-bourgeois, it must have seemed harder to say the same about a graduate who sought to contribute to Soviet science, especially if this meant employing one's professional training to the fullest. In fact, such a position led some students to oppose the distribution system in the name of

---

[53] See the alumni publication of the 1959 graduating class of the MGU Mechanics and Mathematics Department. Voevodin (ed.), *Neuzheli iubilei*, 46.
[54] See the stenographic record of a 1957 Komsomol meeting in TsAOPIM f. 6083, op. 1, d. 5, l. 49.
[55] TsMAM f. 26, op. 26, op. 1, d. 14, l. 56.
[56] Leonid Plyushch, *History's Carnival: A Dissident's Autobiography*, ed. and trans. Marco Carynnyk (New York: Harcourt Brace Jovanovich, 1979), 20–25.
[57] TsAOPIM f. 478, op. 3, d. 67, ll. 23–24.

state utility. One interview subject recalled that a classmate at MGU rejected his assignment to teach in Central Asia, defending himself in court on the grounds that he had received a specialized education from the state and had a duty to make sure that his knowledge be utilized properly.[58] In a much milder form, this line of opposition to placement in teaching positions found quite public expression in the universities. The heavily censored SGU newspaper carried a story written by a student alleging that "the university gives people knowledge that can be employed in ways other than teaching."[59] The education system had generated intellectual elites whose abilities it could not harness; what constituted truly loyal action in this context was an open question. Clearly, students and professors articulated different ideas about how graduates should act in the distribution process. This reflected the open-endedness of the Soviet intelligentsia, a social construct which housed divergent commitments: to state service, to mass enlightenment, to pure science, and, not least, to the social aspirations of of the middle-strata professionals.

The depth of resentment toward distribution in the universities was no mystery in the halls of power; at a conference in Moscow, the minister of higher education conceded that university graduates found teaching work humiliating.[60] Moreover, the ministry was well aware of the quiet subversion that plagued the state's distribution plans, even during the late Stalin era when repercussions could be high. Efforts to outwit the distribution bureaucracy ranged from devious and semi-legal (using contacts to secure a job in advance of the distribution commission's meeting) to downright illegal (forging documents about one's bad health, not arriving for work assignments, or deserting before the mandatory three years had expired).[61] A particularly effective legal strategy was the marriage of convenience: as distribution commissions were instructed not to divide married couples, graduates anticipating undesired assignments could arrange to stay in the city through last-minute marriages to classmates or other individuals with the appropriate living papers. While the extent of the practice is impossible to measure, it is clear that strategic marriage choices were an endemic reality in the postwar universities. Sources mention only female graduates resorting to this strategy, and it is true that women made up a majority of the student

---

[58] Interview with A. F. Sergeev, Moscow, 2003. While I did not find archival corroboration of this episode, the very fact that it was recalled by a university alumnus reflected student perceptions of the distribution system during the period.

[59] E. Kocherba, "Poedem tuda, kuda poshliet rodina," *Stalinets*, 26 December 1952: 2.

[60] GARF-R f. 9396, f. 2, d. 1200, l. 121.

[61] See the excellent account in Schwartz, "The Young Communist League," ch. 3.

body in several university departments designated to train teachers, such as those of philology, biology and soil science, history, and geology.[62] But the fact that strategic marriages were associated primarily with women might also speak to Soviet gender norms. In official discourse, taking an assignment in distant lands was associated with male-coded traits of strength, bravery, and self-sacrifice – standards women might be forgiven for failing to live up to. The political machinations surrounding distribution sometimes invoked the trope of female frailty. A feuilleton in the central press depicted a Moscow official who intervened on behalf of his daughter at the Moscow Law Institute, complaining that the dean of her department was trying to "finish her off" by assigning her to work in the Gorno-Altai Autonomous Province.[63] Clearly, tensions in distribution made gender a space for contestation among state officials, students, and other interested parties, much as they did for the notion of an intelligentsia.

If the state's determination to assign university graduates to the schools drew mixed reactions from students, it also created new forms of solidarity within the universities. In particular, graduates and their professors sometimes discovered that they had common interests in confronting the inflexible and draconian distribution system. Faculty members in affected fields had reason to be unhappy with the job distribution crisis of the 1950s. As in all educational systems, the status of Soviet professors was invested in the fates of their graduates. The schools campaign impacted faculty further in 1955, when the post-Stalin collective leadership and education bureaucracy determined that universities should send the majority of graduates in *all* disciplines to the secondary schools. In conjunction with this measure, MVO cut enrollments in several humanities and social science disciplines that had posed problems for distribution and expanded pedagogical training in university curricula.[64] Both lowered enrollments and the proclaimed goal of the universities' "pedagogization" went against established practices in the universities, and most of all their academic purpose as centers of (relatively) pure science. When the SGU Philology Department sought to increase pedagogical training in the curriculum, it met with sharp faculty resistance at an Academic Council meeting. Privileging work in schools over specialized philological studies

---

[62] For an indication of this gendered disciplinal division, see data on the classes entering MGU in 1948–49 and 1959–60. TsMAM f. 1609, op. 2, d. 253a, l. 3 and ibid., d. 529, l. 13. For the same pattern across higher education enrollments, see De Witt, *Education and Professional Employment*, 347.

[63] S. Narinyani, "Pozhalei Marinu," *Pravda*, 6 May 1954: 2.

[64] See the Councils of Ministers decree "On Additional Measures to Regulate the Training of Specialists with Higher Education," in L. I. Karpov and V. A. Severtsev (eds.), *Higher School: Main Decrees, Orders, and Instructions*, vol. 2 (New York: U.S. Joint Publications Research Service, 1959), 24–27.

would work against the "broad humanitarian education" that was the mission of the university, Professor E. I. Pokusaev asserted.[65]

Faculty in the less affected physical sciences also saw the new mandate to devote greater resources to training schoolteachers as a violation of the university's identity as a center of science. At a 1955 conference of university rectors, A. D. Aleksandrov of Leningrad University criticized the MVO for viewing universities in a narrow economic framework and ignoring their role as generators of scientific knowledge. Commenting on the policy of curtailing training in disciplines that were difficult to account for in distribution, Aleksandrov suggested that the ministry was following a slogan of "bash the universities," an approach that would only harm Soviet science in the long run.[66] Aleksandrov's trenchant criticism of the ministry's policies seemed to evoke the attack on universities during Stalin's Great Break, a precedent that many of the rectors in the audience would have remembered with unease if not horror. For substantial parts of the university communities, then, efforts to shape higher learning to fit state manpower needs seemed a betrayal of the universities' very mission.

The students affected by the schools campaign, of course, felt they had even more to lose. In searching for ways to avoid the uncultured periphery, they discovered that they could take advantage of an irrational circumstance characteristic of the planned economy. Just at the time when the university communities were tasked with training them in growing numbers, the demand for secondary school teachers fell as smaller cohorts of youth born during the war entered the schools.[67] A remarkable situation arose: graduates of elite institutions traveled across the country to be refused jobs that were considered low-grade in the first place. In 1956, an unnamed MGU Philology Department graduate wrote an angry letter to a student friend, addressed as Vil' Matveevich, complaining about his experience of being denied work in a provincial school. He could not, the anonymous student wrote, "be reconciled with the rude, bureaucratic, empty talk that our graduates met at their distribution places." The student's letter also expressed disillusionment with MGU, which had done "nothing to ensure that its alumni can exist tolerably."[68] The note reached the higher education overseers in TsK, indicating the seriousness with which the party leadership viewed the problem of unemployed graduates. And with good reason: the humiliation of passing

[65] GASO f. R-332, op. 2, d. 126, ll. 7–12.   [66] See GARF, f. 9396, op. 2, d. 1200, ll. 52–55.

[67] The overall number of primary and secondary pupils in the USSR shrank from 33.4 million in 1950 to 1951 to 28.7 million in 1957 to 1958. See the 1958 order of the Russian Bureau of the TsK in RGANI f. 5, op. 15, d. 88, ll. 1–6.

[68] RGANI f. 5, op. 35, d. 15, l. 36.

from importance to uselessness is one that has gripped university graduates in many historical contexts, sometimes with disastrous consequences.

The tragic situation, however, carried a silver lining. Faced with the disastrous experiences of their graduates, university distribution commissions began to take advantage of a loophole in the distribution statutes by allowing graduates to find their own postgraduate employment, what was unofficially yet meaningfully called a "free diploma."[69] At the same time, students developed their own strategies for subverting the schools campaign, for instance by signing off on distribution assignments but either not taking them up or quickly leaving them. In 1954, 43 of the 114 MGU history graduates sent to secondary schools returned to Moscow with certificates stating they were not needed at their designated place of work; as the department's party secretary posited, "they went there [to the provinces] for the sole purpose of procuring those certificates."[70] Provincial graduates proved just as recalcitrant. In 1955, SGU could confirm that only 300 of 471 had taken up the jobs for which they had signed up.[71] It seemed as if the state had failed in its agenda of controlling the career paths of its servitors, a development that called into doubt the broader social construct of a docile and service-oriented Soviet intelligentsia.

Given the listless response from university administrators, it fell to the university party organizations to enforce the unpopular distribution system. University party members had a great deal at stake in the distribution crisis, as a disproportionate number of them taught in the humanities departments where the distribution crisis was most severe. Perhaps for this reason, the punitive regime for transgressions of the distribution system was mild during the late Stalinist period, at least considering the draconian laws involved and the patriotic propaganda surrounding the issue. The KDU party secretary I. P. Karnaukhov stated in 1950 that he had been in the university for five years but had "never heard" of a student who refused to take up a job assignment being "called to legal responsibility."[72] He went on to describe an episode in which three philosophy graduates – all party members – had refused to sign off on distribution assignments to provincial cultural enlightenment organizations. The department's party organization expelled the students but found their decision overruled by higher-ranking party

[69] Distribution commissions in higher learning could grant a student a "right to independent job placement" if they were unable to locate an appropriate distribution position for a graduate – meaning one that fit his or her curricular "specialization." Karpov and Severtsev (eds.), *Vysshaia shkola: osnovnye postanovleniia*, 206–10.

[70] TsAOPIM f. 478, op. 3, d. 13, l. 9.   [71] GANISO f. 594, op. 2, d. 3317, l. 199.

[72] DAKO f. 458, op. 3, spr. 96, ark. 98.

bureaucrats; eventually, the three students received highly coveted positions as graduate students at the Institute of Philosophy in Kyiv. It was no wonder they had refused their assignments, Karnaukhov explained, for it was "not entirely serious for one to graduate from the Philosophy Department and then become the instructor for monuments in Voroshilovohrad Province" – a comment that drew laughter from the assembled party members. Implicitly, Karnaukhov recognized that the university's mission of producing fundamental knowledge could take precedence over the demands of the distribution bureaucracy. In the following years, when the risk of expressing critical comments had fallen, party members teaching in the hard-hit humanities articulated their discontent at the distribution crisis for their students more clearly. At MGU, influential former rector I. S. Galkin complained at a rector's office meeting that recent cuts in enrollments to the humanities represented an "anti-state approach"; "after all, this is the capital's university," he intoned, a statement that again asserted the status of the postwar university against a bureaucracy that had allegedly violated it.[73]

Students protesting the perquisites of the party elite, professors undermining state-mandated employment plans, party activists invoking the pursuit of pure knowledge – such are some of the unlikely positions generated by admissions and job distribution policies in the first postwar decade. As this chapter has shown, these two points of contact between colleges and the broader community created dissatisfaction among university communities and sometimes even resistance to state orders. One reading of the conflicts discussed here might be to posit a fundamental gulf between the universities and the bureaucratic structures that controlled them. However, such a tidy scheme does not do justice to the ways the forging of a postwar intelligentsia divided university communities themselves. If some students decried the exercise of party power and the corrupt practices of elites in determining admissions, others benefitted from them. For every student bent on obtaining a cushy job in the capital, there were several others who followed state orders on the assumption that anything else would be a manifestation of self-interested and uncultured instincts.

Rather than expressing a strict dichotomy between university and regime, what stands out in the episodes discussed here are the ways they revealed differing conceptions of the universities and their function of producing highly qualified members of the Soviet intelligentsia. While celebrated and promoted after the war, the university communities had to juggle multiple

[73] TsMAM f. 1609, op. 2, d. 429, l. 18.

relationships with the surrounding society and the overbearing party-state that controlled it. Called on to admit the best and brightest, the university was also compelled to admit less academically prepared youth either favored by the state or pushed through by its avaricious servitors. Encouraged to make themselves into top-level centers for training researchers, the university was compelled to produce cadres for other branches of the economy according to the restrictive logic of state plans. At issue here were different notions of the place of higher learning in society and ultimately of the intelligentsia, an ambiguous social category that combined state service, cultural construction, and social elitism. Pulled in different directions, university communities struggled to interpret their position as elite educational institutions in a communist system – a balancing act that sometimes put university commun-ities at odds with agencies and constituencies of the system they served. In this sense, the universities provide an example of the lack of surety about "the rules of social life," a broader characteristic of Stalin-era society after the social, intellectual, and cultural transformations of the 1930s.[74]

University students were placed unwittingly at the center of the Soviet intelligentsia conundrum, and their responses to the conflicts described in this chapter reflected this fact. A fundamental social trend in postwar higher learning was the consolidation of intelligentsia as a social category defined by academic knowledge and the transcendent and universal culture that supposedly accompanied it. As institutions that furthered academic pursuits and gave them social value, universities were instrumental in constituting and widening this social construct in postwar society. Conflicts in admis-sions and distribution placements showed that the state's promotion of university learning had unpredictable consequences. Students and profes-sors who criticized or evaded state actions in these realms were inspired, at least in part, by the stature of the university and the cultural mission reflected by it. Questioning illicit dealings in admissions showed just how entrenched the image of the university as an incorruptible ivory tower had become. Likewise, students who resisted job distribution placements found motivation in their commitment to science and in the social entitlement made possible by their university studies. While adorning the universities with social status and the trappings of tradition, the party-state was never fully comfortable with the institutions it had created or with the young specialists who emerged from them.

---

[74] See Stephen Lovell, *Summerfolk: A History of the Dacha, 1710–2000* (Ithaca, NY: Cornell University Press, 2003), 159–62.

PART II

The emergence of Stalin's intelligentsia, 1948–1956

CHAPTER 3

Making intellectuals cosmopolitan
Stalinist patriotism, anti-Semitism, and the intelligentsia

Stalin was notoriously suspicious. It might seem anomalous, however, that he was particularly wary of the Soviet intelligentsia, the social group that his regime had constructed before the war. During the onset of the Cold War, the dictator expressed concern that the intelligentsia was not prepared for the challenges facing the country. In 1947, he told a hand-picked audience of party leaders and heads of the Union of Soviet Writers – precisely the kind of behind-closed-doors Kremlin meeting that dominated postwar party politics – that the "average intelligentsia" of professors and writers had "been insufficiently trained in the feeling of Soviet patriotism" and had an "unwarranted admiration for foreign culture."[1] Acting to forestall this trend, Stalin set in motion a series of initiatives to "raise the militant Soviet-patriotic spirit" among the intelligentsia, a process that began shortly after the war with widely publicized resolutions and party discussions on ideological matters which exposed the ideological mistakes of prominent cultural figures, scientists, and scholars.[2] Within a few years, patriotic reeducation took an anti-Semitic turn, as a highly publicized campaign against "rootless cosmopolitans" in the intelligentsia coincided with the imposition of widespread restrictions and political recriminations targeting Jews in Soviet professional life. The anti-Jewish phase of the broader patriotic drive was still gaining steam at the time of Stalin's death with the murky "Doctors' Plot," a wave of arrests directed at a concocted conspiracy of Kremlin doctors seeking to kill state leaders with Zionist and American support.[3]

---

[1] G. V. Kostyrchenko, *Stalin protiv "kosmopolitov": vlast' i evreiskaia intelligentsiia v SSSR* (Moscow: ROSSPEN, 2009), 122.
[2] The phrase is from Zhdanov's 1947 speech to the Cominform in D. G. Nadzhafov and Z. S. Belousova (eds.), *Stalin i kosmopolitizm: dokumenty agitpropa TsK KPSS, 1945–1953* (Moscow: Materik, 2005), 141.
[3] Ibid., 651–52. Stalin's agenda in initiating the Doctors' Plot is still unclear. David Brandenberger, "Stalin's Last Crime? Recent Scholarship on Postwar Soviet Antisemitism and the Doctor's Plot," *Kritika*, 6 (2005): 187–204.

Historians have often presented ethnic nationalism as the main context for postwar chauvinism and anti-Semitism. Continuing its wartime line, the party embraced Russian ethnocentrism as the centerpiece of its postwar ideology, thereby appealing to Russians basking in victory but frustrating Ukrainian national aspirations and leaving Soviet Jews, many of whom embraced proletarian internationalism, dispossessed.[4] While not casting doubt on the ethnic component of postwar Stalinism, this chapter shows that Russocentric pride was not the only issue shaping postwar patriotic campaigns in the universities. The social construct of the Soviet intelligentsia was an important factor in both the creation and popular reception of late Stalinist ideology. For academic elites, a crucial aspect of Stalin's anti-Western ideological agenda was its perceived anti-intellectualism, understood in this context as a stigmatization of intellectual endeavors and their practitioners as distant from a mythologized Soviet people. Given the status of higher learning and learned professions after the war, anti-intellectualism of this type proved highly divisive in the postwar universities. Public attacks on respected academic authorities on grounds of insufficient patriotism met with the active support or tacit approval from some elements in the universities. However, they also created the impression that the intelligentsia and its culture had been put on trial, which was something which many students and professors could not accept. The barely camouflaged anti-Semitic thrust of Stalin's patriotic initiatives only deepened the disruption of university life by entangling the official category of intelligentsia with the explosive issue of Jewish ethnicity. On the whole, postwar ideological initiatives intended to transform the intelligentsia instead focused attention on it as a social construct and a locus of identity.

Nation and class in the Zhdanovshchina

Stalin's postwar initiatives on the ideological front emerged in the context of the early Cold War. As relations with the recent Allies soured, Stalin set in

---

[4] Studies that stress the centrality of ethno-nationalism in the period include Geoffrey A. Hosking, *Rulers and Victims: The Russians in the Soviet Union* (Cambridge, MA: Harvard University Press, 2006), 225; Serhy Yekelchyk, "Celebrating the Soviet Present: The Zhdanovshchina Campaign in Ukrainian Literature and the Arts, 1946–1948," in Donald J. Raleigh (ed.), *Provincial Landscapes: Local Dimensions of Soviet Power, 1917–1953* (University of Pittsburgh Press, 2001), 262–3 and David Brandenberger, *National Bolshevism: Stalinist Mass Culture and the Formation of Modern Russian National Identity, 1931–1956* (Cambridge, MA: Harvard University Press, 2002).

motion campaigns to "discipline the intelligentsia" and to "drive it into an ideological war with the capitalist West."[5] At the same time, Stalin's varied efforts at patriotic reeducation of the intelligentsia reflected his concern that the educated stratum might prove disloyal to the regime – fears that, if certainly inflated, were not totally baseless. As recent research has shown, parts of Soviet educated society hoped for an evolution of Stalinism after the war: writers and musicians who had grown used to a wider scope of wartime creative license, scientists who hoped to expand international contacts, enlightened bureaucrats who sought to rationalize Soviet institutions, and isolated citizens who mulled over the need for liberalizing reforms and sometimes – with almost unbelievable naivety – wrote Stalin directly with their suggestions to hold free elections or to free political prisoners.[6] Some historians, mirroring Stalin's own assumptions, read all of this as budding intellectual resistance to Soviet communism.[7] It would be more accurate to posit the existence among educated Soviet citizens of a widespread yet inchoate sense of open possibilities, one that often reflected a patriotic belief in the transformative powers of a Soviet order now freed from murderous occupation and capitalist encirclement. Such nuances, it is true, meant little to Stalin, who saw postwar optimism as inimical to his domestic priorities, particularly in light of the expanding Cold War.

While the notion that Stalin aimed at ideological retrenchment is commonplace, the specific contours of the ideology promoted by the party have proved elusive. The conventional term used to describe the postwar efforts to discipline the intelligentsia is the Zhdanovshchina or "time of Zhdanov" after Stalin's lieutenant responsible for ideological affairs. The term is misleading, and not only because the decisive role in the campaigns was always Stalin's.[8] The Zhdanovshchina draws an artificial division between the initiatives of the era of Zhdanov's ascendancy – the high-profile resolutions on the arts – and the period after his death in 1948 when the goal of instilling patriotism in the intelligentsia continued in more virulent and sometimes violent form. Rather, a single form of party patriotic ideology

---

[5] Yoram Gorlizki and Oleg Khlevniuk, *Cold Peace: Stalin and the Soviet Ruling Circle, 1945–53* (New York: Oxford University Press, 2004), 32.

[6] N. L. Krementsov, *Stalinist Science* (Princeton University Press, 1997), 98–128; Julie Hessler, "A Postwar Perestroika? Toward a History of Private Enterprise in the USSR," *Slavic Review*, 57 (1998): 516–42; Elena Zubkova, *Poslevoennoe sovetskoe obshchesto: politika i povsednevnost', 1945–1953* (Moscow: ROSSPEN, 1999), 154–62. See also the documents in Elena Zubkova (ed.), *Sovetskaia zhizn', 1945–1953* (Moscow: ROSSPEN, 2003), 392–94, 417–22, 429–35.

[7] The most influential work in this vein is Elena Zubkova, *Poslevoennoe sovetskoe obshchesto*.

[8] Kees Boterbloem, *The Life and Times of Andrei Zhdanov, 1896–1948* (Montreal: McGill-Queen's University Press, 2004), 434.

characterized the late Stalin years, albeit one that took on an increasingly anti-Semitic nature before Stalin's death.

Recent literature has depicted postwar patriotism in strikingly different ways, as either a shoring up of Marxist-Leninist doctrine after the war or a celebration of Russian ethnic pride.[9] Both approaches are incomplete. Instead, the distinctive characteristic of postwar ideology was a close merger of communist and Russian national frameworks. The overall imperative of opposing the capitalist West dictated that the new superpower refurbish its Marxist credentials while extending the Russocentric fervor that marked the war years. In the ideological admixture that resulted, Marxism and Russian national interests would become mutually reinforcing constructs. Russia was virtuous because it was both a great nation and the center of international revolution; conversely, the West was evil because it was bourgeois and because it was historically and irrevocably anti-Russian.[10] Accordingly, the Soviet people needed to liberate themselves ideologically from two existential threats: the fetters of international capitalism and a national inferiority complex that had long plagued Russia. The notoriously obscurantist aspects of late Stalinist propaganda – the denial of the scientific and technological accomplishments of the Americans as a fraudulent myth or the ascribing of scientific discoveries of the past like the radio and the light bulb to Russian scientists – derived from the radical psychological break that the propaganda apparatus sought to affect.[11]

The dual thrust of late Stalinist patriotism as a Soviet and Russian phenomenon also accounts for its distinctive characteristics and mode of implementation. First, while the hyper-chauvinism of postwar rhetoric was a far cry from early Soviet ideology, the mass publicity through which it was conveyed was highly reminiscent of older Bolshevik propaganda practices. In a period of overwhelming censorship and secrecy, the party made sure to project the main initiatives of the patriotic drive to the public through a range of channels: specially convened "discussions" under party auspices, meetings in the primary party cells and other venues, and sometimes in the press. Second, the rhetoric of the campaign drew on class-based populism. Demagogic appeals to the masses were apparent from the first major salvo of

---

[9] Compare Brandenberger, *National Bolshevism*, 196 and Amir Weiner, "The Making of a Dominant Myth: The Second World War and the Construction of Political Identities within the Soviet Polity," *Russian Review*, 55 (1996): 638–60.

[10] Precedents for pursuing national agendas within Marxism are discussed in Roman Szporluk, *Communism and Nationalism: Karl Marx Versus Friedrich List* (New York: Oxford University Press, 1988), 48.

[11] See the 1947 document "Zakrytoe pis'mo TsK VKP(b) o dele professorov Kluevoi i Roskina," published in Nadzhafov and Belousova (eds.), *Stalin i kosmopolitizm*, 125.

the campaign, the 1946 party resolution calling two Leningrad literary journals to task for publishing works by major Russian writers Mikhail Zoshchenko and Anna Akhmatova. The resolution alleged that the two had committed a national heresy by expressing servile respect for the West. But it also identified the two wayward writers as class enemies in all but name by alleging that they had infiltrated the fortress of socialism with bourgeois culture.[12] This was especially true in the resolution's treatment of Akhmatova, who was criticized precisely for connections to reactionary cultural trends of the old regime: spirituality, sensuality, and pessimism.

The condemnation of select Soviet intellectuals as bourgeois raised the issue of the overall allegiances of the Soviet intelligentsia, a social group that contained many former class aliens. In fact, the treatment of the intelligentsia in conjunction with the patriotic campaigns was highly confused. The propaganda apparatus took pains to distinguish the healthy Soviet intelligentsia from the corrupted individuals whose patriotism it found lacking. Moreover, if Akhmatova's ties to the old regime came under scrutiny, the regime simultaneously valorized the old intelligentsia in party discourse and mass culture alike, part of a broader turn to the Russian past which reached its apex under late Stalinism. In this vein, a closed party letter from 1947 explained that "kowtowing to the West" was a tradition instilled by the "national defeatism" of pre-revolutionary exploiting classes, not the old intelligentsia; a novel of the period drew a similar picture by portraying a professor of pre-revolutionary vintage as a proud Russian and a Soviet patriot.[13] However, party rhetoric sometimes recalled the anti-intellectualism of early Bolshevism when the regime, bereft of its own red intelligentsia, had been forced to rely on specialists borrowed from the old regime even while viewing them as class enemies. As during the 1920s, "putrid intellectuals" were deemed guilty of unhealthy, formalistic, abstract, and elitist endeavors that did little to help the common people.[14] Certainly, many Soviet citizens saw the new patriotic rhetoric as a return to the anti-intellectualism of the early Soviet period – and not surprisingly, some members of the university communities were among them. In his diary, MGU linguist S. B. Bernshtein reacted to a party discussion of the 1946 resolution at the department by comparing it to the "leftist extremes" of

[12] Andrei Aleksandrovich Zhdanov, *Essays on Literature, Philosophy, and Music* (New York: International Publishers, 1950), 14–15.
[13] "Zakrytoe pis'mo TsK VKP(b)," 125; G. Ts. Svirskii, "Zdravstvui, universitet! Roman. Chast' pervaia," *Oktiabr'*, no. 1 (1952): 17–18.
[14] For the phrase, see Konstantin Azadovskii and Boris Egorov, "From Anti-Westernism to Anti-Semitism," *Journal of Cold War Studies*, 4 (2002): 74.

Stalin's Great Break fifteen years before.[15] In short, the socialist and populist trappings of postwar patriotism conjured up memories of anti-intellectualism, even as a contrary trend of lionizing the intelligentsia took hold in Soviet life.

From "kowtower to the West" to "rootless cosmopolitans"

Postwar patriotism deepened its impact on the universities when it merged with anti-Semitism. The emergence of anti-Semitism as a component of state discourse and policy in the postwar period seemed an outrageous anomaly to many citizens in the land of the Soviets – and with good reason. Jews were integral participants in the core social groups of the Soviet regime: party-state elites, new intelligentsia, and urban society more generally. In its first years, the Soviet state had offered many Jews both concrete opportunities for professional mobility and, just as importantly, a more general sense of belonging that had often been sorely lacking for previous generations.[16] Yet the tenuous position of Jews in the Soviet order became clear after Stalin's state reformulated its attitude to ethnicity in the 1930s. The Bolsheviks had first pursued an ambitious agenda of equalizing the Soviet nations en route to communism, a radical agenda which entailed promoting non-Russian languages and cultures at the expense of the previously dominant Russian equivalents. In the 1930s, Stalin turned this policy on its head. Not only did the party proclaim Russians and their culture the first among equals; it also embraced ethnic primordialism in its own right by celebrating the ancient pedigree and cultures of the Soviet nations (or, at least, of those possessing official status in the system of Soviet statehood).[17] By its very nature, this new view of Soviet nations complicated the status of the Jews, a diasporic people who fell short of the rather traditional Soviet markers of nationhood like a common territory and language, even as they held a prominent position in Russian society and culture.[18]

Stalin's Russocentrism threatened to disrupt conventional paths to Jewish belonging under Soviet socialism. In the interwar period, some

---

[15] See the diary entry in S. B. Bernshtein, *Zigzagi pamiati: vospominaniia, dnevnikovye zapisi* (Moscow: Institut slavianovedeniia RAN, 2002), 99–100.

[16] For these arguments, see Yuri Slezkine, *The Jewish Century* (Princeton University Press, 2004), 238–39.

[17] For this broader shift in nationalities policies, see Terry Martin, *The Affirmative Action Empire: Nations and Nationalism in the Soviet Union, 1923–1939* (Ithaca, NY: Cornell University Press, 2001), 394–431.

[18] Benjamin Pinkus, *The Soviet Government and the Jews, 1948–1967: A Documented Study* (Cambridge University Press, 2008), 11–16, 34.

Jews had abandoned not only religion but Jewish identity in its entirety, inspired by the promise of an egalitarian and universalist future. But the new rigidity of ethno-national belonging in the 1930s meant that Jews would occupy a position at the bottom of the Soviet hierarchy of nationalities, even as rapid assimilation of the Jews remained the stated goal of the Soviet state. The clearest indication of this reality was the encoding of Jewishness as a nationality under point five on internal passports – a fact that would come to inspire dark humor among Jews about being "invalids of the fifth group." And if complete assimilation was not possible, the alternative strategy of embracing a hybrid Jewish-Soviet identity became difficult as well, in part because the state curtailed the rich Yiddish-language cultural sphere that had thrived in the first years of the Soviet system.[19]

It was World War II that made the awkward status of the Jews in the USSR a reality and crystallized anti-Semitism as a component of postwar rule. Soviet Jews confronted a dual tragedy, as the mass murder of Jews in territories occupied by the Axis Powers as part of Hitler's final solution coincided with the growth of widespread anti-Semitic sentiments on the home front. The chauvinistic Russocentrism of the party-state, extreme social instability, and the echo of Nazi racial ideology – especially among populations in the Soviet West which had experienced it firsthand – fed anti-Semitism among everyday Soviet citizens. Stories about Jews spending the war on the "Tashkent front," that is, profiting comfortably in evacuation, gained widespread circulation in Soviet society. It was in this context that bureaucrats first undertook clearly anti-Semitic initiatives such as purges in the cultural sphere and more informal restrictions on hiring practices and college admissions, all of which was met with top-level approval or benign neglect.[20]

The increasingly bald official anti-Semitism after the war gave Stalin's patriotic campaigns an infusion of energy. The early patriotic reeducation campaign traditionally known as Zhdanovshchina had limited direct impact on intellectual elites as a whole, or at least far less than the harsh language contained in its resolutions on literature and music might have led one to expect. For instance, the party's creation of "Honor Courts" in Soviet

---

[19] See Anna Shternshis, *Soviet and Kosher: Jewish Popular Culture in the Soviet Union, 1923–1939* (Bloomington: Indiana University Press, 2006).

[20] For popular and official anti-Semitism during the war see Kostyrchenko, *Stalin protiv "kosmopolitov,"* 75–110; Mordechai Altshuler, "Antisemitism in Ukraine Toward the End of the Second World War," *Jews in Eastern Europe*, 3 (1993): 40–81. See also Zvi Y. Gitelman, *A Century of Ambivalence: The Jews of Russia and the Soviet Union, 1881 to the Present* (Bloomington: Indiana University Press, 2001), 121–31. It is important to distinguish this generalized anti-Semitism from anti-Zionism, which was widespread in state terror campaigns of the 1930s but is better understood in the context of the anti-religious initiatives of Soviet socialism.

ministries to hold up to public wrath administrators and intellectuals who
"kowtowed to the West" – a new patriotic campaign sparked by the case of
two Soviet scientists accused of passing advances in cancer research to the
United States – quickly ran up against bureaucratic inertia and self-defense
and petered out.[21] Faced with a seemingly recalcitrant intelligentsia and the
deepening Cold War, Stalin redoubled his efforts by recasting the patriotic
drive as a struggle against "rootless cosmopolitans" within the intelligentsia.
The term burst into official discourse in 1949 with an article in *Pravda*
condemning a number of mostly Jewish theater critics as carriers of a
"cosmopolitanism which is deeply repulsive to Soviet man," a signal from
the center which spawned frenetic searches for cosmopolitans in other
cultural and scientific fields.[22] Although similar in its anti-Western thrust,
anticosmopolitanism differed from Zhdanovshchina in two important
ways. A hostile element seeking to undermine the Soviet people from
within, the "rootless cosmopolitan" was a decidedly more threatening figure
than a perhaps naïve and misled "kowtower to the West." Most of all, the
campaign harnessed anti-Semitic passions for the purpose of firming up
political loyalty in the intelligentsia. The construct of cosmopolitanism was
a necessary fig-leaf for anti-Semitic policies which the party could never
openly embrace without weakening its Marxist credentials.[23]

The new campaign's internal enemy rhetoric and anti-Semitism ensured
that it would make deep inroads on the educated classes. As leading centers of
learning and institutions where Jews were well represented, universities
became a focal point for the struggle with cosmopolitanism. Responding to
the press campaign, college party organizations and administrators held
hastily organized meetings to discuss the "struggle against cosmopolitanism"
in their own midst. These were fearful and unpredictable encounters designed
to elicit mass denunciation, dubbed euphemistically "criticism and self-
criticism." Future literary critic Iu. M. Lotman captured the mood of one
such meeting at Leningrad University with a sketch of rabid dogs with foam
pouring from their mouths.[24] The party soon reeled in this highly public
hunt for cosmopolitans, but the campaign continued in a more bureaucratic

---

[21] On this episode, see Zubkova, *Poslevoennoe sovetskoe obshchesto*, 187–92.

[22] Pinkus, *The Soviet Government and the Jews*, 183–84.

[23] Kostyrchenko, *Stalin protiv "kosmopolitov*," 119. See also A. V. Fateev, *Obraz vraga v sovetskoi
propagande: 1945–1954 gg.* (Moscow: Rossiiskaia akademiia nauk, Institut rossiiskoi istorii, 1999),
102–4.

[24] P. S. Reifman, "Dela davno minuvshikh dnei," *Vyshgorod*, no. 3 (1998): 23. See also V. P. Smirnov,
"Anatolii Vasil'evich Ado: chelovek, prepodavatel', uchenyi (1928–1995)," *Novaia i noveishaia istoriia*,
no. 1 (1997): 189.

guise until Stalin's death.[25] Moreover, in higher education the anticosmopolitan campaign of 1949 was only one part of a broader set of restrictions placed
on Jews in the period, which included an informal yet thoroughly implemented system of restrictions on admissions to the universities and other elite
higher education institutions, episodic anti-Semitic harassment by party and
Komsomol organizations, and pervasive discrimination against Jewish graduates during the yearly job distribution process.[26]

The struggle against cosmopolitanism and the broader anti-Semitic
policies it accompanied were deeply disruptive of university life. In an
important recent rethinking of the campaign, Kirill Tomoff shows that
Soviet composers managed to blunt the impact of anticosmopolitanism by
exploiting its vague conceptual parameters and by utilizing their own
professional expertise.[27] As this approach would suggest, the campaign's
impact on higher education was not uniform or all-encompassing.
Cosmopolitanism was pursued more aggressively in Moscow and Kyiv,
where university politics were entangled with high-level political infighting,
than in the Russian and Ukrainian provinces. Moreover, the broader anti-
Semitic manifestations of the campaign were more pronounced in Ukraine
than in Russia; it was well known among Jews in Ukraine that gaining
entrance to higher education in Russia was easier than at home.[28] Although
the topic is quite understudied, it seems likely that the particular aggressive-
ness of measures toward Jews in Ukrainian higher learning reflected initiatives at the republic level as well as anti-Semitic attitudes on the ground.[29]
Finally, the campaign also affected specific fields and disciplines differently,
with the main brunt of the attack falling on the creative arts, the humanities,
and the social sciences – all ideology-saturated disciplines in which party
officials had extensive experience locating ideological infractions.[30]

---

[25] On this transition, see Kostyrchenko, *V plenu u krasnogo faraona*, 205–6.

[26] By the time of Stalin's death, roughly 1 percent of the incoming class to universities was Jewish, a
figure roughly proportionate to their share of the population but vastly reduced from previous years.
As a point of comparison, Jews made up 13 percent of higher education students in the Soviet Union
in 1935. Pinkus, *The Soviet Government and the Jews*, 29–30.

[27] Kirill Tomoff, *Creative Union: The Professional Organization of Soviet Composers, 1939–1953* (Ithaca,
NY: Cornell University Press, 2006), 152–88.

[28] Mordechai Altshuler et al. (eds.), *Sovetskie evrei pishut Il'e Erenburgu: 1943–1966* (Jerusalem: Yad
Vashem, 1993), 297–302; interview with D. F. Rozental', Moscow, 2004.

[29] For postwar Ukrainian anti-Semitism, see Amir Weiner, *Making Sense of War: The Second World War
and the Fate of the Bolshevik Revolution* (Princeton University Press), 229–30, 290–7. On the
formative role of Ukrainian party leaders during the Zhdanovshchina proper, see Yekelchyk,
"Celebrating the Soviet Present," 262–63.

[30] See the note on party meetings in MGU devoted to the "struggle with cosmopolitanism," reproduced
in G. V. Kostyrchenko (ed. and comp.), *Gosudarstvennyi antisemitizm v SSSR: ot nachala do kul'minatsii, 1938–1953* (Moscow: "Mezhdunarodnyi fond "Demokratiia," 2005), 322–24.

The impact of anticosmopolitanism and anti-Semitism more broadly on the universities was, however, extremely deep. In contrast to the situation among composers, the party pursued the campaign aggressively in higher education and left university communities little room for maneuver in off-setting it. And even if it led to firings and arrests in specific fields and areas and left others relatively untouched, anticosmopolitanism impacted university communities as a whole. In part, the accepted Stalinist norm of guilt by association put large sections of the university communities at risk; once a scholar was labeled a "rootless cosmopolitan," his or her close associates or graduate students also came under suspicion. More broadly, large parts of university communities felt themselves to be at risk regardless of their nation-ality or area of expertise. As Tomoff stresses, the very construct of the cosmopolitan carried a "diverse array of coexistent meanings," including anti-Semitism, fear of foreign influence, and pro-Russian bias.[31] Yet this lack of conceptual clarity only expanded the campaign's presumptive scope, as evidence of "kowtowing to the West" and "slandering Russian culture" could be found virtually everywhere in the universities. Long-accepted academic positions and conventions became ideologically suspect, with the new party line also being applied retroactively to scholarship published years before. Even the non-Jewish party secretary at MGU was forced to defend himself against accusations of cosmopolitanism when a junior instructor questioned his referencing of foreign scholarship in a book on soil science.[32] It seemed as if the party was attacking intellectuals as a group by deliberately provoking the "base passions of vulgar and philistine circles," as one professor recalled years later.[33] The fact that the new ideological line coincided with scientific workers' material position and status made the entire situation all the more disorienting.

The vague mandates of the campaign also deepened its impact by encouraging denunciation. The climate of insecurity in the universities depended on – and sometimes fed into – the willingness of members of university communities, both students and professors, to report signs of cosmopolitanism among their colleagues. Evaluating the motives that led citizens to send unsolicited signals to power is extremely difficult, as denunciations as documents are inherently skewed in the direction of what the regime wanted to hear (or what people thought it did).[34]

---

[31] Tomoff, *Creative Union*, 153.
[32] E. M. Sergeev, *Moskovskii universitet – vzgliad skvoz' gody* (Moscow: Izdatel'stvo Moskovskogo universiteta, 1992), 187–88.
[33] E. V. Gutnova, *Perezhitoe* (Moscow: ROSSPEN, 2001), 259.
[34] For discussion of denunciations as an historical source, see Sheila Fitzpatrick, "Signals from Below: Soviet Letters of Denunciation of the 1930s," *The Journal of Modern History*, 68 (1996): 831–66.

Contextual analysis suggests that the campaign was highly intertwined with factional disputes in the Soviet academic world. At the MGU Philosophy Department, a group of Soviet philosophers headed by G. F. Aleksandrov, former TsK official and current head of the Institute of Philosophy in the Academy of Sciences, accused their longstanding nemesis Z. Ia. Beletskii of cosmopolitanism; as chair of the Department of Dialectical and Historical Materialism, the latter had allegedly spread anti-party views with the help of "tendentiously selected cadres of mostly Jewish origins."[35] One can only assume that the anti-Semitic card was a convenient way to tarnish the divisive Beletskii, who had accused Aleksandrov of "Menshevik idealism" during the TsK Philosophy discussion a few years before. And despite the clear anti-Semitic nature of the dispute, there were Jewish scholars on both sides.[36] Making the meaning of cosmopolitanism even more elusive, Beletskii's many allies sought to appropriate the language of Stalinist demonology, alleging that their enemies were "the real cosmopolitans" who had hid their slanderous claims behind party slogans.[37] Clearly, cosmopolitanism was a flexible label that scholars could harness to pursue longstanding conflicts.[38]

Regardless of their motivations, professors' and students' willingness to denounce their colleagues confirmed the new party line. In some cases, everyday participation in late Stalinist politics helped to merge the anti-Semitic and anti-intellectual aspects of official ideology. This process was on display in a denunciation to the TsK alleging that several Jewish professors and students at the Moscow Polygraphic Institute had "sabotaged the struggle against cosmopolitanism." The document's author Ganiushkin, the head of the History and Philosophy Department, linked Jewish

---

[35] See the letter of the heads of the Institute of Philosophy to Malenkov in Nadzhafov and Belousova (eds.), *Stalin i kosmopolitizm: dokumenty*, 326–28.

[36] In later reminiscences, Professor T. I. Oizerman, a Jew and one of Beletskii's foes, did not mention the role of anticosmopolitanism and anti-Semitism in the conflicts of the time. "Iz besed s akademikom T. I. Oizermanom," in V. A. Lektorskii (ed.), *Kak eto bylo: vospominaniia i razmyshleniia* (Moscow: ROSSPEN, 2010), 143–54. For Beletskii's role in the 1946 philosophy discussion, see Ethan Pollock, *Stalin and the Soviet Science Wars* (Princeton University Press, 2006), 24–26 and Gennadii Batygin and Inna Deviatko, "The Case of Professor Z. Ia. Beletskii," *Russian Studies in Philosophy*, 33 (2010): 73–96.

[37] See the TsK information note on a February 1950 party meeting at the MGU Philosophy Department reproduced in Nadzhafov and Belousova (eds.), *Stalin i kosmopolitizm*, 558.

[38] The outcome of the political accusations of Beletskii also shows how the anticosmopolitanism campaign and its seemingly categorical language operated in different ways based on institutional settings. Probably with the help of Stalin, Beletskii managed to remain at MGU throughout the crisis, despite coming under vociferous attack by party officialdom for a year. See G. V. Kostyrchenko, *Tainaia politika Stalina: vlast' i antisemitizm* (Moscow: "Mezhdunarodnye otnosheniia," 2003), 566–71.

nationality with a near-caricature of intelligentsia. For instance, Ganiushkin alleged that many Jewish students had "their own apartments and parents" in the capital and refused to take up work on the periphery after gradu-ation.[39] This assertion contained a kernel of truth, as Jewish students across the country sought to avoid prejudicial job assignments by any means possible, sometimes taking the risky step of refusing to sign their appoint-ment papers.[40] But Jewish students were hardly the only ones seeking to remain in the city after graduation, as Chapter 2 showed. The author of the denunciation, consciously or not, depicted Jews as representative of a broader social elitism that parts of the university communities perceived after the war. A similar conflation of Jewishness and intellectualism under-scored Ganiushkin's criticism of a group of Jewish students, including several influential party members. He accused them of hounding an unpop-ular Russian literature professor called Krestova; allegedly, a student had brought to the teacher's apartment a Tsarist-era publication of Pushkin's poetry and read a provocative quotation to expose Krestova's reactionary political beliefs. In this instance, the students' Jewishness and their harmful freethinking emerge as different sides of the same coin. For at least some party members, then, Jewishness had become a symbol of the intelligentsia in the most seditious and elitist definition of the term – a kind of social scapegoating that had long marked anti-Semitic thought in Russia and elsewhere.

This denunciation's strident anti-Semitism was not the norm in the universities, where Jews had long held positions of authority. Yet even faculty members and students who stood aside from the campaign and remained unsympathetic to its chauvinistic principles found it difficult to avoid speaking the language of postwar Soviet patriotism. The hunt for cosmopolitans, much like Stalinist culture as a whole, depended on public performances in which actions and underlying beliefs were difficult to untangle.[41] A case in point was the MGU Russian historian S. S. Dmitriev, whose diaries chronicling the period have been published in recent years. The MGU History Department was torn apart by the anticosmopolitan campaign of 1949, with several leading figures forced to

[39] RGASPI f. 17, op. 133, d. 197, ll. 57–58.
[40] See examples in KDU Komsomol Committee protocols. DAKO f. 9912, op. 1, spr. 29, ark. 4, 67, 77 and ibid., spr. 13, ark. 9.
[41] The classic work on performance in Stalinist culture is Jeffrey Brooks, *Thank You, Comrade Stalin! Soviet Public Culture from Revolution to Cold War* (Princeton University Press, 1999). See also Jan Tomasz Gross, *Revolution from Abroad: The Soviet Conquest of Poland's Western Ukraine and Western Belorussia* (Princeton University Press, 2002), 71–124.

leave the institution in disgrace. Dmitriev's position became tenuous when his friend N. L. Rubinshtein was exposed as a cosmopolitan and Dmitriev's work came under criticism in party circles for an alleged over-reliance on foreign and bourgeois sources.[42] Dmitriev's diaries demonstrate that he viewed the hunt for anti-patriotic cosmopolitanism with revulsion, seeing it as fundamentally an assault on the intelligentsia. He characterized the campaign as "a chaotic shaking of thoughts and people" that was disorienting to "people of intellectual activities." He also clearly rejected the campaign's primitive and unscholarly logic; with biting sarcasm and a strong dose of gender stereotyping, he suggested that all women, "great cosmopolitans in matters of fashion," should be exposed as ideological enemies.[43]

Dmitriev's thoughts during the campaign were nevertheless ambivalent. During the height of the campaign, his diary employs the term "cosmopolitanism" in full seriousness as a way to interrogate his own motives. "Again and again" he came to the conclusion that he was not guilty of cosmopolitanism, as he had "always sought to instill Soviet patriotism" in his work. While this entry perhaps served as preparation for a public recanting that he would soon in fact offer, the diary also demonstrated a less benign utilization of the language of anticosmopolitanism. For instance, Dmitriev alleged that his opponents at the university, graduate students mostly of Jewish origins, were in fact the real "cosmopolitans trying to deflect the blow from themselves."[44] Dmitriev's inconsistent view of the campaign in a diary meant for private consumption reflects the ways that fear and social instability enabled the internalization of Stalin-era ideological categories. It also highlighted the complicated relationship of at least some non-party academics, particularly in the humanities and social sciences, to late Stalinist ideology. A specialist on the Slavophiles of the nineteenth century, Dmitriev benefitted from the revival of Russocentric history that culminated in the postwar patriotism campaigns.[45] Perhaps Dmitriev understood the new party line as a confirmation of the conservative turn in Soviet culture, the very trend that had made it possible for non-Marxist scholars like him to remain in the universities.[46] In any case, Dmitriev and probably

---

[42] See Kostyrchenko, *Tainaia politika Stalina*, 581–86.
[43] His term was *liudi intelligentnykh zaniatii*. S. S. Dmitriev, "Iz dnevnikov Sergeia Sergeevicha Dmitrieva," *Otechestvennaia istoriia*, no. 3 (1999): 146.
[44] Ibid., 148.
[45] John Keep, "Sergei Sergeevich Dmitriev and his Diary," *Kritika*, 4 (2003): 712–19, 733.
[46] For one case of scientists using the chauvinist turn in Soviet culture to their advantage – the opportunist rehabilitation of rocket scientist K. E. Tsiolkovskii – see Asif A. Siddiqi, *The Red Rockets' Glare: Spaceflight and the Soviet Imagination, 1857–1957* (Cambridge University Press, 2010), 296–301.

many others in the university saw the danger of anticosmopolitanism in its populist and anti-intellectual nature as much as in its chauvinistic language.

Victimhood and the intelligentsia

If Dmitriev's response to anticosmopolitanism was ambivalent, one would expect a more forthright embrace of the campaign from students. Lacking the pre-revolutionary mindset that Dmitriev and other professors of his generation to some extent maintained, students were inherently more receptive to the messages conveyed by Stalin's regime. Yet the public vilifying of cosmopolitans and the broader anti-Semitic policies that accompanied it met with volatile responses among students. Expressions of both forthright acceptance of the new patriotism and categorical rejection of it found expression in university life. Underscoring this disagreement was the question of how intellectualism and Sovietness were to be combined. As the patriotic campaignism shook and sometimes unraveled the universities' previously firm hierarchies of intellectual authority, students looked on with either enthusiasm or dread.

The campaign had a devastating impact on Jewish students, many of whom had rarely experienced anti-Semitism in the past. In a letter to writer Il'ia Ehrenburg in 1947, V. V. Aizenberg, a Jewish student at the Moscow Institute of Communication Engineers, recounted that wartime anti-Semitism had forced him to ponder his Jewish origins for the first time. Before he had only remembered that he was a Jew when filling out state questionnaires, but now, he fumed, he saw that he was a "Yid," responsible for "failures at the front and high prices in the rear." Perhaps he was even responsible for the war itself – in his account, many Russians felt that Hitler had only invaded the USSR in order to secure the destruction of the Jews.[47] The sense of being excluded from the Soviet community hung over all the Jews and led to different personal and social coping mechanisms. Many Jewish students strove to convince themselves that they belonged to the Soviet project as before, ignoring evidence of widening state discrimination. D. Ye. Gordon, a Komsomol activist of Jewish descent at SGU, recalled being disturbed by the repression of cosmopolitans, yet maintained the conviction that "Stalin doesn't know anything about it; it's just that these local authorities are behaving this way."[48] Of course, the Stalinist state

---

[47] Altshuler et al. (eds.), *Sovetskie evrei pishut Il'e Erenburgu*, 271–72.
[48] Interview with D. Ye. Gordon, Saratov, 2004.

encouraged this naïve belief in Stalin as a beacon of hope – and, sometimes, as an instance of last resort – through its relentless popularization of the leader cult and the practice of encouraging citizens to write appeals to national leaders.[49] Nevertheless, the refrain "if only Stalin knew" was evidence of students' often fierce determination to maintain faith in the righteousness of the party line. Many students of Jewish origins clung to such hopes, as the alternative was to accept that Jews had been ostracized from Soviet society. In an extreme articulation of this essentially defensive position, a MGU student, N. K. Shor, understood the anti-Semitic over-tones of the party purges but nevertheless hoped that the state would destroy its Jewish enemies "so that there would be no more reason for worry and suffering."[50]

Denial and obfuscation were difficult to maintain for Jewish students, in part because of the mobilizational scope of the campaigns mentioned above. The blatant anti-Semitism of postwar patriotism was hard to ignore: the search for cosmopolitan errors in the universities occurred in plain view of the students, while Komsomol organizations sometimes compelled their members to vote in favor of disciplinary sanctions. In this context, it is hardly surprising that Jewish students came under consistent criticism for demonstrating insufficient support of the campaign or even downright obstruction of it. Outspoken criticism of the campaign sometimes emerged, as in the case of Leizina of the Kyiv Polytechnic Institute, who was alleged to have told a Marxism-Leninism teacher that the nationalities question in the Soviet Union was resolved formally and that "in our country Jews are harassed like the Negroes in America," adding that she considered both the USSR and Israel her homelands.[51] Identification with Israel led three MGU students to discuss a plan to flee across the Soviet–Turkish border. One of them, the MGU law student M. D. Margulis, testified to the MGB that he was deeply affected by the "fomenting of national hatreds" in the anticosmopolitan campaign, and particularly by the convention in the press of revealing the original Jewish names of figures who had adopted pen names.[52] The two cases show the inherent slipperiness of the party's patriotic ideology: hostility to "the fomenting of national hatreds" and

---

[49] This point is made eloquently in Lewis Siegelbaum and Andrei Sokolov, *Stalinism as a Way of Life: A Narrative in Documents* (New Haven, CT: Yale University Press, 2000), 217–28, 231–33.

[50] DRZ f. 1, op. 1, d. R-472, l. 584.   [51] DAKO f. 9912, op. 1, spr. 29, ark. 63.

[52] GARF f. 8131, op. 31, d. 97889, ll. 6–13. As mentioned in Chapter 1, many political opposition groups in the Stalin era were products of the heated imagination and bureaucratic interests of the security services. While not confirmed by other sources, the veracity of the charges in this case is suggested by the fact that the three individuals were released after Stalin's death and then re-sentenced in 1955, when the post-Stalinist leadership was pursuing very different repressive policies.

commiseration with the "negroes in America" both belonged firmly to
official ideological discourse, suggesting that some Soviet students evaluated
the new campaign through long-established ideological prisms.

Student hostility to postwar patriotic campaigns also found more sustained expression in the postwar universities, sometimes relying on underhanded tactics that lowered the risk of political reprisals. According to
instructors for the Ukrainian party TsK, large numbers of students at the
Kyiv Polytechnic Institute voted for Jewish candidates in low-level
Komsomol elections, rejecting the officially vetted candidates; for instance,
117 students voted to reinstate one Jewish activist who had only recently
been fired from Komsomol work.[53] While the nationality of these
Komsomol voters is left unclear, it is not implausible to suggest that the
group contained some ethnic Russians and Ukrainians, among whom feelings of solidarity with Jews were far from rare. Biographical sources contain
only rare mention of anti-Semitic feelings among students in the universities. To take one example, then MGU student A. A.Verbovskaia's mother
was arrested in connection with the Doctors' Plot, and she herself was
driven into total isolation as the daughter of an enemy of the people. Yet she
claimed in a recent interview that she never detected traces of anti-Semitism
among her classmates.[54] Likewise, Shor at MGU was shocked to hear an
anti-Semitic remark directed at her in the cafeteria, as she had not encountered anything like that at her department, where "somehow no distinction
was made between Jews and non-Jews."[55]

Cases of pushback against anti-Semitic policies emerged against the
backdrop of a broader rethinking of Jewish identity in the student body.
In an echo of the late Tsarist Empire, discrimination led to new forms of
Jewish identity among assimilated Jews.[56] In articulating a positive image of
Jewish identity, Jewish students looked to the Soviet intelligentsia for
models of self-understanding. V. V. Aizenberg, whose bitter account of
discovering his Jewish origins after experiencing wartime anti-Semitism
has been mentioned, found a silver lining in the idea that the Jews'
"blood and ideas enriched the spiritual life of humanity" by bringing the
world the Bible, Christianity, and Marx (in that order).[57] Similar

---

[53] See the report sent by a group of party instructors to their superiors in TsDAHOU f. 1, op. 71, spr.
104, ark. 63–68, published in Mikhail Mitsel (ed. and comp.), *Evrei Ukrainy v 1943–1953 gg.: ocherki
dokumentirovannoi istorii* (Kyiv: Dukh i litera, 2004), 175–77.
[54] Interview with A. A. Verbovskaia, Moscow, 2004.   [55] DRZ f. 1, op. 1, d. R-472, l. 584.
[56] Cf. John Klier, *Russians, Jews, and the Pogroms of 1881–1882* (Cambridge University Press, 2011),
255–364.
[57] Altshuler et al. (eds.), *Sovetskie evrei pishut Il'e Erenburgu*, 271–72.

articulation of a Jewish intellectual and cultural mission found expression in a curious literary genre that emerged in the universities in the period: poems that Jewish students compiled, distributed to friends, and sometimes read at social occasions. Many of these poems built on an uncensored version of a 1945 poem by Margarita Aliger – unique for Soviet literature of the time in embracing Jewish identity and addressing the Holocaust – along with various responses to it.[58] These poems, which frequently fell into the hands of the secret police, provide a window onto the efforts of young Soviet Jews to come to terms with new experiences of marginalization. One such poem uncovered by party organs in KDU echoed Aizenberg's assertion of a Jewish civilizing mission:

> Did our small intimidated people
> Really spend so little energy
> To raise old Russia
> From the shadows and swamps?[59]

Here the Jews appeared as true Soviet *intelligenty* bringing consciousness to Russia, an identity that had obvious appeal to idealistic Soviet students destined to fill the ranks of the intelligentsia of the future.

Jewish students merged nation and intelligentsia in such sources for a host of pressing social and psychological reasons. Emphasizing one's intellectual credentials promised Jewish students something of an explanation for why they experienced hatred from their Soviet brothers and sisters. A student poem in MGU called "The Misfortune of Jews Is That They Are Intelligent" lamented that Jews were cursed for "striving for knowledge and living wisdom."[60] Reducing Soviet anti-Semitism to a symptom of a broader anti-intellectualism also allowed Jews to make common cause with the highly educated gentiles that surrounded them, at least in symbolic terms. In 1952, the regime discovered that several mostly Jewish Komsomol activists at the Potemkin Pedagogical Institute in Moscow had, at private meetings, criticized the department's party bureau for anti-Semitic policies like handing Jewish graduates undesirable distribution assignments. At a department-level Komsomol meeting, these students were made to confess to having held "nationalistic

---

[58] See the editor's comments in Kostyrchenko (ed. and comp.), *Gosudarstvennyi antisemitizm v SSSR*, 500.

[59] Published in Iurii Shapoval, *Ukraina XX stolittia: osobi ta podii v kontektsi vazhkoi istorii* (Kyiv: "Heneza," 2001), 242.

[60] See the informational note on the case of V.A. Edel'shtein in Kostyrchenko (ed. and comp.), *Gosudarstvennyi antisemitizm v SSSR*, 499–501.

conversations," but the student Kaminskaia held her ground, insisting not
only that "a wave of anti-Semitism swept the country after the war," but
also that "my close acquaintances from the intelligentsia, doctors, engineers, lawyers, students" shared her views.[61]

The idea that the intelligentsia, however defined, was solidly on the side
of the Jews was wishful thinking: as denunciations from the universities
demonstrated, education and intellectual accomplishments did not trans-
late tidily into rejection of postwar ideological priorities. As the party
secretary of the Kyiv Pedagogical Institute admitted in late March 1949 –
notably, when the campaign in the press was already dying down – he and
his comrades had received a flood of far-fetched denunciations against
suspected "rootless cosmopolitans," including some from students that
targeted hated professors.[62] Yet Kaminskaia's claim made sense against
the backdrop of postwar university politics. Given the well-integrated
position of Jews in educated society, sympathetic non-Jewish classmates
and colleagues were not an isolated group – particularly in light of the Jews'
efforts to depict themselves as *intelligenty* above all.

The stakes were no less high when professors rather than students fell
under suspicion in conjunction with the patriotic campaigns. While some
students used the campaign to lash out at university authorities, others,
disturbed by witnessing the spectacle of professors persecuted on demagogic
charges, actively defended them within the very limited means they possessed. The case of Iulian Grigorievich Oksman at SGU showed the complex politics touched off by the victimization of professors in the patriotic
campaigns. Oksman, a prominent Leningrad literary scholar who was
arrested on ideological grounds in the 1930s and only freed in 1946, found
himself in virtual exile at SGU in the postwar years. Oksman built up a cult
following among students who listened to him with "bated breath," as he
commented in a letter from the period; years later, his devoted students
depicted him as a true intellectual who stood out against the backdrop of
Stalinists and "provincial" time servers.[63] Whether or not this evaluation
contains a measure of retrospective justification, it is undeniable that a part
of the student body at the Philology Department embraced Oksman in

[61] See the report from Komsomol TsK secretary N.A. Mikhailov to TsK party secretary G.M.
Malenkov. Kaminskaia was expelled from the institute for nationalism. RGASPI-M f. 1, op. 46, d.
162, ll. 103–4, 108.
[62] DAKO f. 1, op. 9, d. 264, ll. 27–28.
[63] K.P. Bogachaevskaia (ed.), "Iu. G. Oksman v Saratove: pis'ma 1947–1957," *Voprosy literatury*, 5
(1993): 244, 237, 256; M.K. Azadovskii et al., *Perepiska: 1944–1954* (Moscow: Novoe literaturnoe
obozrenie, 1998), 138; Interview with D. Ye. Prokhvatilov, Saratov, 2004.

the face of high-level pressure. In October 1949, the central newspaper *Literaturnaia gazeta* (*Literary Gazette*) criticized Oksman's article in a SGU publication.[64] Following Stalinist custom, the Philology Department organized a public discussion of the article with members of the city's political elite in attendance. In a letter to a friend, Oksman recalled the meeting, which lasted from seven in the evening to three in the morning:

> The most unpleasant thing was the student demonstration in my honor, very energetic and unanimous. I am very afraid that the city authorities did not like this at all. It stands to reason that if I had known about the moods of the students, I would have talked to the *aktiv* and I would not have allowed either the ovations or the speeches against the *Literary Gazette*.[65]

In Oksman's account of the episode, students proved willing to hijack a politically charged scholarly event. Moreover, Oksman suggested that they had done so with at least the implicit permission of the *aktiv*, the institutionalized unit of political leaders in the student milieu. Surprisingly, they seemed to have done so without suffering political recriminations, perhaps because Oksman himself emerged from the episode relatively unscathed.[66]

A variety of motives must have inspired the students to defend Oksman in such a risky way. To some extent, Oksman's followers were merely showing their fealty to a respected professor, thereby affirming the deference that university administrators expected of them. However, Oksman's influence over the students was far from universal; one of Oksman's student followers recalled that the "originality" of his teaching drew rapturous responses from some students but hostile responses from others.[67] As this suggests, students seem to have seen Oksman as a model *intelligent*, a person of unusual academic integrity and moral stature. Moreover, criticism of Oksman in the central press did nothing to diminish his reputation and might have even enhanced it. The oppositional political implications of the students' defense of Oksman were clear in an episode recalled by one of Oksman's Saratov students. Soon before Stalin's death, Oksman lent an old and officially discredited book to a student of his seminar, one Andrianov, who promptly

---

[64] Oksman's article, "A. Kol'tsov and the secret 'Society of the Independents,'" as well as pieces by other scholars, was criticized for lacking "contemporary relevance." G. Permiakov, "A zhizn', znai sebe, idet i prokhodit ...' (Ob uchenykh zapiskakh saratovskogo universiteta, 1948, t. XX)," *Literaturnaia gazeta*, 5 October 1949: 7, cited in Azadovskii et al., *Perepiska*, 130, 132.
[65] See Bogachaevskaia (ed.), "Iu. G. Oksman v Saratove," 233.
[66] Azadovskii et al., *Perepiska*, 133–34. [67] Interview with P. R. Krastins, Saratov, 2004.

gave the book to the secret police.[68] At a meeting of the seminar, Oksman confronted Andrianov with the statement, "we don't need commissars in this seminar – we need hard workers." Oksman then asserted that as a professor of Russian literature he had "a right to read what [he] needed to." As his former student recalled, "We were silent when he talked about Andrianov but we were all outraged."[69] As Chapter 1 noted, it was not uncommon for postwar students to view their elderly professors with reverence, particularly in the specific social setting of the special seminars. In this case, however, Oksman represented a politicized vision of the old *intelligent*, a figure who defended knowledge from the inroads of political authorities.

The public support that a circle of Saratov students offered their embattled professor was not typical of the period, but neither was it an anomaly. Archival sources and memoir literature reveal several similar episodes of students siding with professors who were censured for ideological mistakes. In Gor'kii University in 1951, Professor A. G. Meier came under criticism for "past mistakes tied to kowtowing to the West" – including belittling the works of nineteenth-century mathematician N. I. Lobachevskii in lectures – at a meeting of the academic council of the Physics and Mathematics Department. Just a few hours later, Meier died of a stroke. His funeral became, in the party report's characterization, "a demonstration": "students carried his coffin by hand all the way to the cemetery, and the coffin was covered in wreaths." Later, a crowd of students went to the university's Party Committee and the rector's office "demanding the creation of a commission to investigate who brought down Meier."[70] Although the document does not indicate if students were punished for their actions, the party TsK saw the episode as troubling enough to warrant firing the university's rector for "allowing suspicious individuals to use the funeral for anti-Soviet announcements."[71] Subtler forms of showing support for professors also emerged, such as offering a victimized professor a bouquet of

---

[68] Although archival research in Saratov did not confirm this story, it did make clear that Oksman was in political danger during Stalin's last months. In 1952, an unidentified party official at SGU stated, "In the near future the question of Professor Oksman will be decided." GANISO f. 594, op. 2, d. 2302, l. 158.

[69] Interview with D. Ye. Prokhvatilov, Saratov, 2004. See also the account in Viktor Seleznev, *Kto vybiraet svobodu. Saratov: khronika inakomysliia, 1920–1980-e gody* (Borisoglebsk: "Poliarnaia zvezda," 2010), 59–60.

[70] RGASPI f. 17, op. 133, d. 192, ll. 210–14. See also I. V. Berel'kovskii, *Sovetskaia nauchno-pedagogicheskaia intelligentsiia i ideologiia totalitarizma v kontse 1920-k–nachale 1950-kh gg: bor'ba s inakomysliem: po materialam Nizhegorodskoi gubernii-Gor'kovskoi oblasti* (Moscow: MGGU, 2007), 181–82.

[71] According to S. S. Dmitriev's diary, a group of MGU students sought permission to hold a similarly symbolic funeral reception for a recent (Jewish) graduate who had committed suicide after defending the "cosmopolitan" Rubinshtein at her place of work in Ivanovo. Dmitriev, "Iz dnevnikov," 149.

flowers or a standing ovation after a lecture.[72] However rare such episodes were, public displays of solidarity with figures vilified by party authorities showed that the intelligentsia was open to varied interpretations. More specifically, the cultural mission of the intelligentsia – a myth that universities did so much to entrench – could become fused with the politically suspect values of academic freedom and the sanctity of the individual.

In February 1953 an anonymous letter reached party-state leaders that protested anti-Semitic policies organized "up on high." Coming just weeks after the public announcement of the Doctors' Plot, the letter's anonymous author – who called himself "a Russian *intelligent*, a Russian person, and a Soviet person" – rejected the anti-Semitic actions that had enveloped postwar Soviet state and society. Anti-Semitism contradicted Marxism-Leninism, the author asserted; unlike Jewish oppression of the past like the Beilis and Dreyfus cases, there could be no "historical and economic explanation" for anti-Semitism under socialism.[73] In his view, anti-Semitism was particularly morally repugnant to the Soviet intelligentsia. The "best part of the Russian intelligentsia," which the writer equated with "the advanced, honest and decent Soviet people," viewed the anti-Semitic "ravings" of the official press – especially its efforts to depict Jewish scholars and cultural figures as "rogues and cheats" – with disgust. The Russian intelligentsia, "in the best sense of the word," had always rejected Judeophobia.[74]

The letter's wholesale rejection of anti-Semitic policies demonstrated how views of the intelligentsia structured responses to late Stalinism. The pursuit of chauvinistic patriotism through means that harkened back to early Bolshevism – mass mobilization, populist rhetoric, and the encouragement of a climate of assault on established authorities – sent shockwaves through the otherwise flourishing postwar universities. Stalin envisioned postwar patriotic political campaigns as a way to reaffirm political loyalty among the educated classes. However, the party intrusions into academic communities that stemmed from them called attention to the intelligentsia, a category that fixed the place of intellectuals in society in unstable ways. In some cases, intelligentsia became conceptually distinct from the Soviet

---

[72] See the account of such events at a 1951 SGU party conference and the March 1949 report from KDU party secretary "on measures of the party organization of Kyiv State University in the struggle against manifestations of Cosmopolitanism in pedagogical and scientific work." GANISO f. 594, op. 2, d. 1890, ll. 12, 14; TsDAHOU f. 1, op. 70, spr. 1810, ark. 1–14, published in Shapoval, *Ukraina XX stolittia*, 234.

[73] Alfred Dreyfus was a French officer sentenced to life imprisonment for treason in the late nineteenth century; Menahem Mendel Beilis was a Ukrainian Jew tried by a Tsarist court for blood libel in 1913.

[74] Altshuler et al. (eds.), *Sovetskie evrei pishut Il'e Erenburgu*, 310–15.

power structures, providing individuals such as the letter writer with a framework within which to question the new party line.

The connection between late Stalinist ideological priorities and the category of intelligentsia was not, however, straightforward. The term itself was plagued by lingering confusion. Even the anonymous letter writer above had to concede, almost reluctantly, that there were "different senses of the word," or different ways of understanding the place of highly educated citizens in Soviet society. Those who viewed themselves as constituting the intelligentsia might be in disagreement about the category's meaning and implications. If the intelligentsia was defined as being a progressive force, affiliation with the Communist Party was, in theory, the hallmark of the *intelligent*. Moreover, the chauvinistic populism of late Stalinism rekindled older Bolshevik criticism of the intelligentsia as unprincipled, seditious, and distant from the people's cause. Indeed, an anti-intelligentsia patriotism, one which might be seen as particularly suited to the pervasive insecurity of the early Cold War, took hold among some members of the university communities. The willingness of some students and professors to denounce colleagues who published abroad or utilized foreign sources suggests the hold of anti-intelligentsia attitudes, even if one accepts that a dose of cynicism was also at work.

The intelligentsia proved a divisive factor in Stalin's efforts to instill an anti-Western and anti-Semitic model of Soviet patriotism. As mentioned above, scholars have stressed how Stalin's postwar patriotism shaped ethnic identities in the period. The unresolved issue of Soviet intellectualism intertwined with these different ethnic identities in unpredictable ways. For many educated Russians within the universities and without, the perception that the postwar patriotism was fundamentally anti-intellectual limited the edifying effects that its emphasis on Russian priorities past and present might otherwise have had. Indeed, in the long run many intellectuals would come to spurn Stalin's postwar patriotism and sometimes even Russian nationalism as such as backward and obscurantist, boiling it down to jokes in circulation during the period such as the now-famous quip about the Soviet Union as the "homeland of elephants."[75] As Chapter 8 will show, the rediscovery of the nation among postwar educated Ukrainians emerged through close association with notions of the intelligentsia. And without a doubt, the Soviet intelligentsia was most important to Soviet Jews, many of whom found in it a more appealing and, in Soviet conditions, safer form of

---

[75] Cf. Ludmila Alexeyeva and Paul Goldberg, *The Thaw Generation: Coming of Age in the Post-Stalin Era* (Boston: Little, Brown, 1990), 38–39.

self-identification than a clearly defined Jewish identity. As Yuri Slezkine has written, by the late Soviet years, the Soviet state "had trouble telling the Jews and the intelligentsia apart."[76] In all these ways, the perception that the late Stalinist state was distrustful of its intellectual elites shaped the articulation of ethnic identities in the postwar Soviet Union, at least among educated elites. Ironically, Stalin's efforts to fight intellectuals' perceived lack of patriotism proved a self-fulfilling prophecy.

[76] Slezkine, *The Jewish Century*, 340.

CHAPTER 4

Stalinist science and the fracturing of academic authority

In June 1950, N. S. Koshkina, a philology student at Leningrad University, wrote a letter to Stalin. A few weeks earlier, the Soviet leader had published a piece in *Pravda* entitled "Concerning Marxism in Linguistics." With this article and two others which followed later that year, the general secretary rejected N. A. Marr's Marxist research school, one that had long enjoyed dominance in Soviet linguistics. The party immediately hailed Stalin's contribution to linguistics as "a guiding beacon for creative development of different branches of Soviet science" and even "a new contribution to the treasure-chest of Marxism-Leninism."[1] However, Koshkina was not convinced and she wrote to Stalin for answers. At the outset, she stressed that a work by Stalin was correct by definition, as she had been educated on his books and articles and saw his "every word as a holy sacrament." She then proceeded to dissect Stalin's arguments in a highly critical manner. Stalin had rejected Marr's argument that language belonged to the Marxist superstructure together with politics and culture, and along with it the notion that languages developed in stages based on modes of economic production.[2] Here, Koshkina asserted, Stalin had approached language too narrowly by considering only vocabulary and grammatical structure; these aspects were only the form of language, while the content of language was thought itself. Following this reasoning, the language of socialist society was indeed different from that of capitalist Russia, as Marr had claimed. Koshkina conceded that her reasoning was surely flawed and asked Stalin to point out her mistakes to her. "I cannot live further with such doubts in my soul," she concluded.[3]

[1] "Znamonosets mira," *Stalinets*, 7 November 1950: 1.
[2] For an overview of Marrism and Stalinism in linguistics, see Ethan Pollock, *Stalin and the Soviet Science Wars* (Princeton University Press, 2006), 104–35.
[3] RGASPI f. 17, op. 132, d. 337, ll. 10–15, published in Elena Zubkova (ed.), *Sovetskaia zhizn', 1945–1953* (Moscow: ROSSPEN, 2003), 487–91.

Koshkina's letter points to the confusion surrounding the place of Marxism in scientific discourse in Stalin's final years. The aging dictator oversaw a series of scientific "discussions" in the postwar years which brought the TsK and ultimately Stalin himself into the matter of resolving scientific disputes. Koshkina's attempt to engage Stalin in scholarly discussion, while exceptionally naïve, was entirely logical given the propaganda trope of the leader as a principled scholar and theorist. Indeed, Stalin described his intervention in linguistics as a rejection of an "Arakcheev regime" prevailing in the discipline, by which he meant an authoritarian state of affairs that prevented a free flow of clashing opinions.[4]

Recent studies have cast doubt on the old notion that Stalin's foray into science was merely a sign of his deepening irrationality and megalomania. Rather, Stalin's objectives in science appear far more coherent: to reconcile Marxism with modern scientific developments in order to strengthen the communist order. Nevertheless, as Ethan Pollock has shown, the postwar party discussions led to confusion rather than clarity, paralysis rather than scientific advance, in part because party interventions – and especially those that came from Stalin's pen – were both inherently unquestionable and open to varying interpretations.[5] Enemies and supporters of Marr faced the same dilemma. The MGU linguist S. B. Bernshtein had long flouted Soviet orthodoxy by teaching a course in comparative Slavic linguistics, an approach that contradicted the universalist assumptions of the Marrist approach. When he first read Stalin's interjection in linguistics, Bernshtein was "filled with deep gratitude," even if he disagreed with parts of it. But he quickly became concerned with the canonization of Stalin's works, which limited the scope of research while also setting in motion a "powerful wave of vulgarization" (fueled, in his view, by Marrists who switched scientific camps with cynical ease).[6] Koshkina's epistemological confusion – her willingness to question Stalin even while comparing his work to scripture – was, then, an exaggerated illustration of a broader dilemma in the late Stalinist intellectual situation.

---

[4] Ethan Pollock, "Stalin as the Coryphaeus of Science: Ideology and Knowledge in the Post-War Years," in Sarah Davies and James R. Harris (eds.), *Stalin: A New History* (Cambridge University Press, 2005), 271–88. Count A. A. Arakcheev, a general under Aleksandr I, was a symbol of military rule and reaction in Soviet culture.

[5] Pollock, *Stalin and the Soviet Science Wars*, 13–15.

[6] See the diary entries from July to November 1950 in S. B. Bernshtein, *Zigzagi pamiati: vospominaniia, dnevnikovye zapisi* (Moscow: Institut slavianovedeniia RAN, 2002), 152–55.

The universities were at the epicenter of the "science wars" of late Stalinism. Yet late Stalinist higher learning has received little attention in the literature on the subject. When it has been studied, the picture of a tightly controlled and unquestioningly politicized university has predominated – in implicit contrast to the better-studied Academies of Sciences, where scientists wielded some degree of professional agency in shaping research agendas even at the peak of late Stalinism.[7] However, the realm of higher learning was more meaningful for late Stalinist science than this suggests. Reaching correct understandings of Marxism's place in different branches of knowledge was particularly important in higher education, where the groundwork for the future of Soviet science was prepared. And while it is true that higher education was subject to more bureaucratic control than the academy, the late Stalinist entanglements of party power and science shaped college life in myriad and sometimes unpredictable ways. Stalin's foray into linguistics, for instance, sent relevant departments in universities into convulsions as careers were made and broken, and curricula, teaching, and scholarship were reinvented virtually overnight. These disruptive shifts in academic discourse and practice produced an intellectual uncertainty among students that was a rarity in Soviet higher learning. Faced with conflicting intellectual authorities, students sometimes took sides in the scientific conflicts that had enveloped the universities and were playing out in front of their eyes. Following exploration of late Stalinist conflicts in biology and physics, the chapter examines debates about higher learning after 1953 to show how conflicts over learning and the societal roles of its practitioners continued to shape university life in the post-Stalin years.

The people's science and the people's intelligentsia

If debating Stalin was highly unusual, writing to him for answers to scientific problems made good sense in the Soviet context. In official discourse, the principle that Marxism-Leninism was scientific and therefore consistent with all realms of knowledge was beyond challenge. Yet the precise contours of this relationship were unclear, making the question of applying Marxism to any given field a complicated endeavor. Did science belong to the societal base or the ideological superstructure? Was Soviet science one branch of a universal scientific enterprise or was it somehow distinctly socialist? Clear answers were not forthcoming. On the one hand, Bolshevism's steadfast materialism dictated that science provide access to objective truth about the world, an

---

[7] N. L. Krementsov, *Stalinist Science* (Princeton University Press, 1997), 227–36.

approach that left little space for an exceptionalist notion of a Soviet science. On the other hand, it was hard for Soviet Marxists to accept the proposition that the generation of knowledge occurred outside ideological mandates, all the more so because science (*nauka*) was understood to include the humanities and social sciences, disciplines which Soviet leaders saw as straightforwardly ideological. What resulted from these contrasting impulses was a fluid ideological-scientific language which housed various philosophical and methodological approaches awkwardly. Soviet scientists might adopt any number of positions on the intersection of Marxism and science: a defense of the concept of a specifically proletarian science, a merging of Marxism and other scientific methodologies, or even the minimalist standpoint that Marxism could not determine science's substance but could only comment on its philosophical implications.[8]

During the early Cold War, the hardening of ideological positions and Stalin's patriotic drives on the home front seemed to create new space for a distinctly Soviet science. In 1948, Stalin gave official support to the teachings of agrobiologist T. D. Lysenko, who rejected modern genetics in favor of the inheritability of acquired characteristics.[9] While his opportunist promises of multiplying crop yields had established Lysenko in the wake of the disaster of collectivization, he had nonetheless been unable to dislodge his scientific opponents during decades of acrimonious conflict. Stalin's anti-Western patriotism allowed Lysenko to redefine the dispute in genetics as one between Soviet and Western priorities – an interpretation to which the reputations of his opponents in Western scientific communities lent credence.[10] With Stalin's approval, a 1948 session of the Lenin All-Union Academy of Agricultural Sciences (henceforth VASKhNIL) endorsed Lysenko's teachings that there were "two worlds, two ideologies" in biology: the materialist, Soviet, proletarian science based on the teaching of I. V. Michurin and formal genetics, which were idealist, Western, and bourgeois. The open support of a communist agenda saw a new phenomenon in Soviet science: the imposition of a virtually uncontrolled tyranny in a scientific discipline which was supported by the full repressive apparatus of the Soviet party-state.

The universities were a critical sphere for the Lysenkoist power grab. Geneticists had long held powerful positions in higher education

---

[8] See Loren R. Graham, *Science in Russia and the Soviet Union: A Short History* (Cambridge University Press, 1993), 99–120.

[9] For an overview of Lysenko's scientific beliefs and work, see Krementsov, *Stalinist Science*, 121–36.

[10] Conflict in biology emerged in close association with the early phases of patriotic mobilization discussed in Chapter 3. Ibid., 130–31.

establishments.[11] Under minister S. V. Kaftanov, the higher education bureaucracy pursued the Lysenkoist agenda aggressively, defining its goal in uncompromising terms as an "arming of students and scientists with progressive Michurinist teaching and a decisive uprooting of the reactionary idealist Weismannist (Mendelist-Morganist) trend" in biology.[12] The ministry's efforts included firing hundreds of professors who had opposed Lysenko, closing or restructuring university departments of genetics, overhauling curricula, and banning textbooks.[13] To prevent challenges from Lysenko's opponents down the road, the party restructured the central Supreme Attestation Commission, the body that approved all academic degrees and titles across the USSR, and even revoked some degrees retroactively.[14]

Lysenkoism's impact on higher learning extended far beyond the "organizational measures" that state and party authorities undertook. Just as important was the ideological framework that justified these measures. Lysenko presented university communities with a conception of scientific pursuit as a specifically Soviet and class-conscious endeavor. In his presentation, Soviet science belonged to the people doubly: it emerged from common-sense work in the fields and it brought practical benefits to the country. While the image of the "peasant biologist" is sometimes written off as evidence of Lysenko's fraudulence, it was taken quite seriously during the period. Even his opponents conceded that he was charismatic; as one geneticist commented, Lysenko made an unforgettable impression with "his hoarse voice, his passionate invective, his emaciated figure – that of a veritable Savonarola!"[15] The comparison was apt: like the Florentine friar, Lysenko combined prophecies of future greatness (abundant harvests) with attacks on the powers-that-be (established scientific elites who opposed him). It is true that Stalin himself prevented Lysenko from adopting the language of class war; while personally editing Lysenko's speech to the 1948

---

[11] Zhores A. Medvedev, *The Rise and Fall of T. D. Lysenko*, trans. I. Michael Lerner (New York: Columbia University Press, 1969), 105, 110, 128–29; A. S. Sonin, "'Delo' Zhebraka i Dubinina," *VIET*, 1 (2000): 34–37. On Kaftanov, see Krementsov, *Stalinist Science*, 147–48, 201, 233–35.

[12] See E. V. Il'chenko (ed. and comp.), *Akademik I. G. Petrovskii – rektor Moskovskogo universiteta* (Moscow: Izdatel'stvo Moskovskogo universiteta, 2001), 166–67, 120–21. The demonized figures were the historical founders of genetics and evolutionary biology Gregor Johann Mendel, Thomas Hunt Morgan, and August Weismann.

[13] Douglas R. Weiner, *A Little Corner of Freedom: Russian Nature Protection from Stalin to Gorbachev* (Berkeley: University of California Press, 1999), 213.

[14] Valerii Soifer, *Vlast' i nauka: razgrom kommunistami genetiki v SSSR* (Moscow: Izdatel'stvo "CheRo," 2002), 688–89.

[15] Eleanor D. Manevich, *Such Were the Times: A Personal View of the Lysenko Era in the USSR* (Northampton, MA: Pittenbruach Press, 1990), 27.

VASKhNIL session, the dictator methodically replaced the word "bourgeois" with "idealist" or "reactionary."[16] Nonetheless, Lysenko and his supporters employed Marxist doctrine in all but name, portraying their opponents as privileged gentlemen of pre-revolutionary origins who pursued obscure scientific work at the people's expense.

Lysenkoism's identity as people's science was at odds with postwar universities' focus on pure learning as well as its role as a source of social status. Against the backdrop of the intelligentsia's rising prominence and material compensation, the effort to destroy a branch of science in the name of communist orthodoxy appeared illogical and dangerous. This was one reason why the onslaught of Lysenkoism met with immediate resistance in higher education. When college administrators sought to evade orders – like the director of a Kyiv institute who allegedly dragged his feet in implementing orders to fire two compromised departmental heads – they met with swift party discipline.[17] As a result, faculty practiced more subtle forms of evasion, in some cases taking advantage of the fact that provincial institutions came under less central scrutiny during the campaign. At the height of Lysenko's power, an opponent of the Lysenkoist camp, S. S. Khokhlov, was appointed chair of the SGU Genetics and Darwinism Department and subsequently became vice-rector for research. In 1951, the university Party Committee and rector's office staged a three-day open discussion of Khokhlov's work on evolution in plants at which the scholar came under censure for standing on "the position of Weismannists." At the meeting, Khokhlov refused to recant and several of his colleagues defended his work; the graduate student V. A. Kumakov announced provocatively that young scientific workers would leave the discussion with their opinions unchanged.[18] Nevertheless, Khokhlov remained at the university by (temporarily) switching the research agenda of his department to the innocuous study of oak trees and grape cultivation – a strategy of marshaling institutional resources also pursued by prominent biologists in the Academy of Sciences in the period.[19]

[16] Pollock, *Stalin and the Soviet Science Wars*, 56–57.

[17] See the 21 January 1949 Odessa Provincial Party Committee resolution on reforming the Biology Department of the Kyiv Forestry Institute in TsDAHOU f. 1, op. 23, spr. 5925, ark. 28–31. See also an analogous case regarding the director of the Kharkiv Medical Institute R. I. Sharlai. Ibid., spr. 5067, ark. 56–57.

[18] See the account in L. Z. Zakharov, "O diskussii po knige S. S. Khokhlova 'Perspektivy evoliutsii vyshchykh rastenii," *Stalinets*, 15 May 1951: 2 and the Provincial Party Committee's criticism of the meeting in GANISO f. 594, op. 2, d. 1890, l. 148.

[19] Mark B. Adams, "Science, Ideology, and Structure: The Kol'tsov Institute, 1900–1970," in Linda L. Lubrano and Susan Gross Solomon (eds.), *The Social Context of Soviet Science* (Boulder, CO:

The situation differed in tightly controlled Moscow and Leningrad universities, where the VASKhNIL session set in motion a thorough purging of Lysenko's opponents. Yet even there some individual professors employed what Mark Adams has called "protective ideological mimicry," or simulated compliance with the new line. Upon discovering a recently hung portrait of Lysenko in a classroom, the Leningrad biology professor L. I. Kursanov grimaced and told his students: "this is academician Lysenko, Denis Trofimych, who made all sorts of discoveries ... They will tell you about this in other courses, but we are studying lower plant organisms."[20] More importantly, faculty members soon launched a challenge against Lysenkoism by attacking I. I. Prezent, Lysenko's close associate who led the purge in the universities through his positions as dean of the newly renamed Biology and Soil Science Department at MGU as well as chair of new Departments of Darwinism in both Russian capitals. At an early 1950 *aktiv* meeting, party members at MGU, including the secretary of the party organization in the Biology and Soil Science Department, charged Prezent – no doubt, as a surrogate for Lysenko – for trying to "run down, malign, and drive out honest working scholars"; they also gave their criticisms a denunciatory character by accusing Prezent of political sins like assigning works by "enemies of the people" in his courses.[21] After Prezent was removed from his positions and expelled from the party in late 1951 in connection with "dishonorable personal behavior," the hold of Lysenkoism weakened in higher learning. Perhaps hedging his bets on the party line in biology, the dean of the Leningrad Biology and Soil Science Department, the erstwhile ally of Lysenko N. V. Turbin, rehired a geneticist to the faculty and mandated intensive study of classical genetics in the framework of his course "Michurinist genetics" (on the pretext that "each biologist must know what he is struggling against").[22]

Westview Press, 1980), 173–201. For Khokhlov's research agenda, see N. A. Shishkinskaia, "K 100-letiiu Sergeia Spiridonovicha Khokhlova," *Vavilovskii zhurnal genetiki i selektsii*, 1 (2011): 199, www.bionet.nsc.ru/vogis/pict_pdf/2011/15_1/17.pdf (accessed 27 May 2012).

[20] N. N. Vorontsov, "Sobytiia kontsa 40-kh gg. v biologii: vzgliad iunnata," *Voprosy istorii estestvoznanii i tekhniki*, 1 (2001): 219. See Mark B. Adams, "Biology in the Soviet Academy of Sciences, 1953–1965: A Case Study in Soviet Science Policy," in John R. Thomas and Ursula M. Kruse-Vaucienne (eds.), *Soviet Science and Technology: Domestic and Foreign Perspectives: Based on a Workshop Held at Airlie House, Virginia, on November 18–21, 1976* (Washington, DC: Published for the National Science Foundation by the George Washington University, 1977), 163.

[21] D. G. Nadzhafov and Z. S. Belousova (eds.), *Stalin i kosmopolitizm: dokumenty agitpropa TsK KPSS, 1945–1953* (Moscow: Materik, 2005), 550–1; Sergeev, *Moskovskii universitet*, 188–89.

[22] Shortly before Stalin's death, Turbin shocked the faculty by openly criticizing Lysenko's ideas on species formation and intra-species competition at a university scientific meeting. T. A. Ginetsinskaia, "Biofak Leningradskogo universiteta posle sessii VASKhNIL," in M. G. Iaroshevskii (ed.), *Repressirovannaia nauka* (Leningrad: Nauka, Leningradskoe otdelenie, 1991), 117, 123.

The softening grip of Lysenko before 1953 was a product of the political calculus of Stalin – always eager to stoke divisions among strategic elites – much more than of actions undertaken by scholars to oppose the party line in biology. However, the various forms of faculty opposition to Lysenko were meaningful in the way they brought the intelligentsia into focus. Many professors were driven to oppose Lysenko out of scientific convictions or long-held personal animosities. But their reaction also constituted a rejection of Lysenkoism's mode of discourse, specifically its dogmatic claims and populist rhetoric. Parts of the professoriate saw the struggle with Lysenkoism as a conflict between real science and fraudulent science, intelligentsia and pseudo-intelligentsia, and ultimately good and evil. In 1947, MGU biology professor L. A. Zinkevich told a friend about his colleagues who have "defected shamelessly into the putrid camp" of Lysenkoists; evidently "belonging to the intelligentsia [*intelligentnost'*] is far too little to make one a decent person," he lamented.[23] Zinkevich's account reflected a habitual attitude among academic elites: that science and moral substance were intertwined – or, at least, would be if the *intelligenty* lived up to their true calling.

Students had a different vantage point on the sharp changes spearheaded by the triumph of Lysenko – that of the lecture hall rather than the murky world of academic infighting. While distanced from decision-making, students were no less involved in Lysenkoism than their professors. Unlike faculty members who were already aligned with one camp or another – or chose to switch between them – cohorts in several academic classes in biology and related disciplines faced the disorienting task of unlearning and relearning their core areas of study in short order. Not surprisingly, student responses to the contrasting truth claims of the opposing "Michurinist" and geneticist positions were intertangled with broader questions about the meaning of the intelligentsia and its knowledge. Without a doubt, Lysenko's persona as a revolutionary scientist appealed to many students who had an almost instinctual adherence to revolutionary causes. T. M. Panchenko grew up in a small Ukrainian town and enrolled in the MGU Biology and Soil Science Department in 1955 – notably, when Lysenko's position was already under attack within the universities and without. Decades later, he reflected on two lectures delivered by Lysenko himself that he had attended. The agrobiologist "spoke on general biological and philosophical questions simply, easily and even primitively," "puzzling

[23] S. B. Bernshtein, *Zigzagi pamiati: vospominaniia, dnevnikovye zapisi* (Moscow: Institut slavianovedeniia RAN, 2002), 93.

his audience with clever questions like, 'what comes first, the chicken or the egg?'" If there is irony here, it was evidently absent at the time: Panchenko had liked what Lysenko said and how he said it, even as he noted that the general mood of the audience was "tension-filled" and "unfriendly."[24] Postwar students were inundated with the notion that learning had a broader social mission, and that "Soviet science serves the people with its belief and truth."[25] As an embodiment of popular science, Lysenko must have seemed to some students as a prototype for what a truly Soviet intellectual should look like.

The intelligentsia ideal, however, could also be read in different ways. The student body also produced substantial opposition to the Lysenkoist campaign that drew on very different ideas about intelligentsia identity. When a young teaching assistant at Leningrad University criticized the ideas of Lysenko's associate O. B. Lepeshinskaia to a room of students, not only did no one denounce her to the authorities, but her reputation among the students instantly rose.[26] On one level, such skepticism about the new scientific orthodoxy showed that the habits of academic life – debate, skepticism, detachment – died hard. More fundamentally, student hostility to Lysenko stemmed from the social status that accompanied the intelligentsia's cultural mission. Accustomed to the valorization of intellectual pursuits, students were ill-prepared for the populist tone and *ad hominem* attacks that accompanied Lysenko's ascendancy. While a philology student in Leningrad, P. S. Reifman did not understand the scientific issues at stake in biology, but was shocked by how the Lysenkoists spoke with hatred about their opponents.[27] Although he might have lacked the language to express it at the time, Reifman clearly held the attitude that learning was entitled to a degree of internal integrity, if not autonomy – a commitment that might well have stemmed from the stature of university learning.

The forceful entrenching of Lysenkoism in the universities also politicized professorial authority. Mirroring contemporaneous events in the anticosmopolitan campaign discussed in Chapter 3, students responded particularly sharply to the criticism and denigration of respected professors.

[24] DRZ f. 1, op. 1, d. R-305, T. M. Panchenko.
[25] "Vooruzhat' studentov peredovoi naukoi," *Stalinets*, 25 December 1951: 1. For expressions of socialist idealism among biology majors in the period, see M. V. Guseev et al. (eds.), *Avtoportrety pokoleniia biologov MGU: vypuskniki biofaka MGU o biofake, ob uchiteliakh, o sebe, 1950–2000* (Moscow: Izdatel'stvo MGU, 2000), 488–89. See also Kathleen Smith, "'Acts Incompatible with the Title of Komsomol': Studying Genetics in the Age of Lysenko," a paper presented at the 2009 Association for Slavic, East European, and Eurasian Studies National Convention in Boston.
[26] Ginetsinskaia, "Biofak Leningradskogo universiteta," 120–21.
[27] P. S. Reifman, "Dela davno minuvshikh dnei," *Vyshgorod*, 3 (1998): 23.

In 1951, the newspaper of the Moscow Medical Institute alleged that Professor M. A. Baron, the chairman of the Sub-Department of Histology, had "reformed himself only formally according to the latest decisions of VASKhNIL." When the Biology Department's Academic Council held the expected "discussion" of the article, an estimated 350 agitated students showed up to show support for Baron. According to a report on the institute compiled by the Komsomol TsK, a "considerable part of the student body fell hostage to backwards moods, speaking out about the incorrectness of the article and its lack of objectivity." When the dean declared that the meeting was for faculty only, the students "loudly expressed their displeasure and protested this" while a crowd of 150 students "stood near the doors and tried to enter the hall using force."[28] Archival evidence does not make clear whether the Moscow Medical Institute students opposed Lysenkoism and its postulate about two sciences on principle, or rather felt that local authorities were acting unfairly in the specific case of Baron. In any event, this remarkable case of open mobilization against college authorities reflected a belief that the pro-Lysenko methods of scientific debate violated the respect that intellectuals deserved. In this and other episodes of student solidarity with professors accused of anti-Lysenkoism, the professor in question became the standard-bearer of truth and hence a moral authority.[29] In short, the Lysenko campaign spurred different readings of the Soviet intelligentsia, with some students seeing opponents of party-enshrined scientific truth as the true *intelligenty*.

As the Komsomol report on the scandal revealed, defending professors against officially endorsed criticism was to be read as a sign of "backward moods," an abandonment of the pursuit of proper consciousness befitting a Soviet intellectual. There can be no doubt that some students shared this position. But even the most aggressive and ideologically militant students might feel the pull of intelligentsia culture and feel uneasy about the use of force to decide scientific debates. In a recent interview, D. D. Berezkin, a Komsomol leader and party member studying at SGU in the late 1940s, recalled of the Lysenko and anticosmopolitan campaigns that "in those days we were very politicized, especially us at the history faculty. And these so-called groups supported it, thought that we were doing the right thing." He

---

[28] See the Komsomol TsK inspection of the institute organization dated 1 October 1951. RGASPI-M f. 1, op. 46, d. 162, ll. 198–200.

[29] See episodes recounted in Medvedev, *The Rise and Fall*, 129; Raissa L. Berg, *Acquired Traits: Memoirs of a Geneticist from the Soviet Union*, trans. David Lowe (New York: Viking, 1988), 273; TsDAVO f. 4621, op. 1, spr. 60, ark. 14.

then recalled S. S. Khokhlov, the maligned botanist described above, as "a large, beautiful man, very much a refined intellectual (*intelligentnyi*)."[30] This description might be the product of later rethinking of his Stalin-era experiences rather than an indication of Berezkin's mindset at the time. Nevertheless, Berezkin's account was, at the least, a reflection of the respect for the old intelligentsia that was a resilient and widespread feature of the university milieu.

Lysenkoism remained a source of division for university communities long after Stalinism. The political upheaval that followed Stalin's death in 1953 fueled hopes for a reversal of the party's position in the life sciences and genetics in particular. With the political course of the party's collective leadership in question, scientists challenged Lysenko's theories openly while, in the universities, the resurgent opponents of Lysenko sought – sometimes with the help of deans, rectors, and scholars in other fields – to reintroduce classical genetics into the curriculum.[31] Across the USSR, small groups of students voiced their approval of such a turn by attacking Lysenko in the colleges' heavily policed wall newspapers or even, in one case, by participating in an underground biology seminar.[32] Lysenkoism, however, remained the official doctrine in Soviet biology, in large part because its demagogic promises of transformative discoveries proved well suited to the agricultural experiments and impulsive style of N. S. Khrushchev.[33] Though weakened in the following years, the Lysenkoist niches in the universities would survive until the arrival of a more pragmatic post-Khrushchev leadership. While central prerogatives were decisive, Lysenkoism's resilience in the universities underscored the difficulties it posed for Soviet higher learning. The Lysenko episode is often treated as a cautionary tale about the dangers of political intervention in science, but this reading suggests that politics and science were clear entities to participants in the drama. Instead, it should be stressed that Lysenkoism divided educated society from within, raising unresolved questions about how the Soviet intelligentsia was to be understood.

---

[30] Interview with D. D. Berezkin, Saratov, 2004.

[31] On the role of MGU rector Petrovskii in a boisterous conflict at the Biology and Social Science Department, see the comments of party secretary V. V. Dobrovol'skii in TsAOPIM f. 478, op. 3, d. 67, ll. 28–30.

[32] For student support of a report on formal genetics by professor D. P. Protsenko in KDU, see DAKO f. 158, op. 5, spr. 221, ark. 7. See also V. Gruzdev, "Stennoi pechatiu nuzhno rukovodit'," *Moskovskii universitet*, 17 January 1957: 2 and Ekaterina Pavlova, "Delo sestr Liapunovykh," *Znanie-sila*, 8 (1998), www.znanie-sila.ru/online/issue_177.html (accessed 12 January 2010).

[33] David Joravsky, *The Lysenko Affair* (Cambridge, MA: Harvard University Press, 1970), 161–62.

A beautiful new world: physics and the "atomic shield"

The party diktat involved in the Lysenko episode was not the only possible outcome of the ideological-scientific debates of the 1940s. During Lysenko's ascendancy, a struggle over the place of Marxist ideology in physics came to a very different conclusion. At the root of this conflict was the scientific and ideological clash between two loosely defined collectivities. One side consisted of the elite of Soviet theoretical physics at the Academy of Sciences; their opponents were physicists and philosophers centered at MGU, unified by the conviction that the new physics of relativity and quantum mechanics were "idealist" and therefore at odds with dialectical materialism. This standoff cannot be reduced to a simple dichotomy between ideology and science, as scholars in both camps had to speak a hybrid language that incorporated elements of Marxism. Nevertheless, the dispute took on decidedly non-academic ideological and personal overtones in the context of late Stalinism. Physicists at the Academy of Sciences gained ascendance through their role in the top-priority atomic program and tried to extend their influence into the universities. In contrast, the university physicists and philosophers sought to frame the disagreement in terms of postwar patriotic rhetoric, depicting the academy physicists as aping the ideas of physicists in the bourgeois West at the expense of Russian scholarship.[34]

Several factors would seem to have pointed to the imminent success of the university physicists: official support of Lysenko's two sciences rhetoric, the chauvinism of official patriotism and their opponents' close ties to international science and (in some cases) Jewish origins. Nevertheless, the attempt to construct a distinctly Soviet physics failed resoundingly. Historians of science concur that the importance of academy physicists for the atomic program – what amounted to an "atomic shield" – protected Soviet scientists from a party discussion in 1949 on idealism in physics that might have thrown the field into flux.[35] However, the conflict in physics continued unabated, and university politics at MGU remained at its center. The Physics Department, dominated by the university physicists, came under challenge in 1951 with the appointment of mathematician

---

[34] See Paul R. Josephson, "Stalinism and Science: Physics and Philosophical Disputes in the USSR, 1930–1955," in Michael David-Fox and György Péteri (eds.), *Academia in Upheaval: Origins, Transfers, and Transformations of the Communist Academic Regime in Russia and East Central Europe* (Westport, CT: Bergin & Garvey, 2000), 105–40 and A. V. Andreev, *Fiziki ne shutiat: stranitsy sotsial'noi istorii nauchno-issledovatel'skogo instituta fiziki pri MGU (1922–1954 gg.)* (Moscow: Progress-Traditsiia, 2000), 115–22, 132–35.

[35] Here I rely on the detailed discussion of the planning of the conference in Pollock, *Stalin and the Soviet Science Wars*, 83–93.

I. G. Petrovskii as rector. Following government instructions, Petrovskii sought to raise the scientific profile of the university by recruiting prominent scholars from the Academy of Sciences to teach at the university.[36] In a 1952 letter to the head of the country's atomic program, L. P. Beria, Petrovskii asserted that the poor training of specialists at the MGU Physics Department required the removal of its current dean and the recruitment of academy physicists affiliated with the atomic program (some of whom had been driven away from the university in recent years).[37] The university physicists, along with some party-minded social scientists, relied on their strengths in the party organization to challenge Petrovskii. Besides casting aspersions on Petrovskii's political reliability (as shown by his lack of party membership and suspect social origins), party members in the Physics Department and their allies in other departments took the rector to task for "orienting himself only toward scholars with great names" and ignoring the input of the party organization in making personnel decisions.[38] This line of attack appealed to parts of the faculty for several reasons: it defended the sometimes shaky political clout of the party organization, it played on a feeling of resentment toward the influential Academy of Sciences some harbored, and it seemed to follow the imperative of forging a specifically Soviet science.

Opposition to Petrovskii met with little sympathy at the apex of the party-state, where the indispensability of leading physicists to the atomic program trumped other considerations. Nevertheless, the department remained in the hands of the university physicists in October 1953, when the department's yearly Komsomol conference, normally a routine event, met. Led by a group of fifth-year students, the conference became a forum for lodging wide-ranging criticisms of the department's faculty and its leadership. Resolving to send a letter to the Central Committee with their complaints, the students alleged that instruction at the department lagged behind contemporary scientific developments, especially in theoretical physics. They also alleged that the departmental leadership had driven "first-class scientists" from the institution and favored under-qualified

[36] See the 1950 Council of Ministers resolution "on Measures for Aiding MGU." RGASPI f. 17, op. 133, d. 191, ll. 184–90.

[37] For Petrovskii's role in the conflict, see G. I. Kiselev, "Moscow State University Physics Alumni and the Soviet Atomic Project," *Physics – Uspekhi*, 48 (2005): 1254–56 and TsMAM f. 1609, op. 2, d. 335, ll. 1–2, 3–4, 16–17.

[38] See a report on a June 1953 meeting of the university party *aktiv* as well as a letter criticizing Petrovskii from the deputy dean of the MGU Physics Department F. A. Korolev in RGANI f. 5, op. 17, d. 434, ll. 66–68, 70–73, 76–77. Petrovskii's biography is outlined somewhat hagiographically in Il'chenko (ed. and comp.), *Akademik I. G. Petrovskii*, 1–83.

scholars in their place.[39] With thinly veiled aggression, the Komsomol activist Vladimir Neudachin proclaimed to the faculty, "It seems to me that no one will underestimate your merits, but instead we will get to the bottom of this and everyone will get what he deserves" – a statement that generated "prolonged applause" in the hall.[40]

The students' revolt against their teachers had its origins in the specific institutional and social setting of the MGU Physics Department. Physics students in the capital had witnessed the postwar infighting in physics up close, and many had come to view the university physicists as backward pseudo-scientists who were holding back Soviet scientific advances. Sometime in the early 1950s, senior student Gerzen Kopylov wrote "Evgenii Stromynkin," a satirical poem about the MGU Physics Department set to Pushkin's classic, *Evgenii Onegin* (Stromynka was the region in Moscow where the main dormitories for MGU students were then located). In this poem, Kopylov satirized a meeting of the stronghold of the university physicists, the MGU seminar on the philosophy of physics, whose participants were depicted asserting "that Einstein is stupid | that Bohr is a swine | that a physicist is not a macro-instrument (*makropribor*) | but a social phenomenon."[41] On at least one occasion, the students' rejection of university physics found public expression. In 1948, the philosophy seminar that Kopylov had satirized discussed a paper by academy scientist M. A. Markov which set out to prove that Bohr's quantum mechanics were compatible with dialectical materialism. A. A. Maksimov, a philosopher who had published an attack on Markov for defending Western idealist physics, took the podium. What a party report called "groups of students in close ranks" applauded Markov and "yelled sharply" during Maksimov's comments, a scene that led the MGU Party Committee to bar the admission of students to the seminar's meetings in the future.[42]

[39] A useful description by eyewitnesses is Iu. V. Gaponov et al., "Studencheskie vystupleniia 1953 goda na fizfake MGU kak sotsial'noe ekho atomnogo proekta," in V. P. Vizgin (ed.), *Istoriia sovetskogo atomnogo proekta: dokumenty, vospominaniia, issledovaniia* (Moscow: Ianus-K, 1998), www.russcience. euro.ru/papers/gkkozap.htm (accessed 2 October 2013).

[40] In Russian, *vozdadut kazhdomu po zaslugam*. A printed transcript of the second meeting of the conference on 23 October 1953 provides information on the students' qualms. "Stenogramma komsomol'skoi konferentsii fizicheskogo fakul'teta, zasedanie 23 oktiabria 1953 g.," 3–4, 45 (on the academy physicists), 8–9, 12–13, 14, 17, 29, 34 (on incompetent teachers), and 17, 61, 65, 73 (on creative learning). The minutes of this meeting, which are absent from the archives, are in the personal archive of S. F. Litvinenko.

[41] See Andreev, *Fiziki ne shutiat*, 138–40; Svetlana Kovaleva, *Ty pomnish, fizfak?* (Moscow: Pomatur, 2003), 16. The entire text of the poem has been published: G. I. Kopylov, "Evgenii Stromynkin," in *Voprosy istorii estestvoznanii i tekhniki*, 2 (1998), 96–122. See also A. V. Kessenykh, "Poema o zhizni molodogo Sovetskogo fizika 40-kh–50-kh godov (Kommentarii k poeme G. I. Kopylova 'Evgenii Stromynkin')," ibid., 123.

[42] The Russian is *splochennye gruppy studentov*. Andreev, *Fiziki ne shutiat*, 137.

This episode resembled other responses to late Stalinist ideological innovations in that it involved a moralistic embrace of a specific scholar as a
purveyor of progressive science. In 1953, however, the physics students went
further by challenging the entire mode of instruction and structure of authority at the department. In doing so, the physics students demonstrated their
unique sense of empowerment within the university and in the Soviet project
more generally. Several of the ringleaders of the Komsomol meeting were
themselves specializing in nuclear physics, and had contact with academy
scientists tied to the atomic program.[43] Physics was critical for Soviet military
and economic might in the future; moreover, given what Paul Josephson has
called the "domestication" of the atom in Soviet public culture – the belief
that atomic science could serve as a "panacea for economic and social
problems" – physics students could see themselves as heroic innovators as
well as strategic assets to the state.[44] This was in stark contrast to the biology
conflict, in which geneticists were hampered by their inability to match
Lysenko's promises of tangible and immediate scientific gains to the regime.

An important circumstance in the students' challenging of departmental
authorities was the recent move of the Physics Department from the cramped
university buildings in downtown Moscow to the new state-of-the-art campus in the Lenin Hills. The Soviet press presented the new campus as a gift of
the benevolent Soviet state to the people, one which was to be repaid by them
through devoted labor.[45] This patriotic rhetoric inspired the physics students'
criticism of the department. Writing decades later, a participant in the
student conference explained that the new MGU campus signified a "fantas-
tic breakthrough from the difficult everyday life of the postwar years to a new
beautiful world – the world of science that was calling us to new exploits, to
selfless study." The obstructionist line of the departmental leadership, which
steadfastly refused to consider student concerns, hindered the students from
"living in a new way."[46] Paradoxically, furthering Soviet science required an
overturning of power relations in the department. It was the physicists'
disciplinary assuredness, their self-confidence as crucial figures in the Soviet
future, which encouraged them to redefine the terms on which they would
serve the party-state.

---

[43] Kovaleva, *Ty pomnish*, 17–18.
[44] Paul R. Josephson, "Atomic-Powered Communism: Nuclear Culture in the Postwar USSR," *Slavic Review*, 55 (1996): 298.
[45] Cf. "Velikaia zabota o Sovetskoi nauke," *Moskovskii universitet*, 29 August 1953: 1.
[46] See Gaponov et al., "Studencheskie vystupleniia, 1953 goda" and Iu. V. Gaponov, "Otryvki iz nenapisannogo: 'iznachalie'," *VIET*, 1 (2001): 215–16. See also the words of Zakharov in "Stenogramma," 47
and TsAOPIM f. 6083, op. 1, d. 3, l. 154.

Departmental authorities were hardly mollified by the students' desire to harness progressive science for the Soviet project. The dean's office and party organization attempted to discredit the students' initiative as political subversion. At a university-wide party meeting held soon after the Komsomol meeting, deputy dean of the Physics Department F. A. Korolev accused one student of giving a speech "of a Trotskyist character" and alleged that the Komsomols had acted on the schemes of academy physicists; for good measure, Professor V. F. Nozdrev alleged that a Komsomol leader of the conference was the son of a persecuted Bukharinist.[47] The students gained immunity from these accusations from a seemingly unlikely source: the party apparatus. E. A. Furtseva, secretary of the Moscow organization of the CPSU, offered a spirited defense of the students at an MGU party conference held shortly after the Komsomol conference. In her presentation, the students' desire to write to the TsK was a product of their "patriotic feeling"; if the students' "placing of questions" took "not completely correct forms," this was the fault of the party leaders of the Physics Department, who had long ignored serious problems in the training of cadres.[48]

The students emerged unscathed from the episode. More remarkable still, they soon witnessed the thorough shakeup of the Physics Department that they sought, as the academy physicists captured the last bastion of their longstanding opponents. Participants in the Komsomol meeting have since claimed that they played a major role in the outcome of the battle over Soviet physics in the 1950s. The student protest at the department could not have strengthened the position of the university physicists, particularly as they had frequently stressed that their scientific positions were a guarantee of student ideological purity. However, the student action was less important in shaping events at the university than were political developments at the apex of party power. A December 1953 joint letter from the Minister of Culture P. K. Ponomarenko, the Minister of Medium Machine-Building V. A. Malyshev, and the President of the Academy of Sciences M. V. Keldysh to G. M. Malenkov and Khrushchev that set in motion the reorganization of the department made no mention of the Komsomol conference.[49] In any case, the position of the university physicists in the halls of power in Moscow had already been drastically weakened by the time of Stalin's death. Regardless of its impact on the politics of science in the USSR as a whole, the episode at the Physics Department was crucial for university politics in the period. It showed that university academic life

---

[47] TsAOPIM f. 478, op. 3, d. 1, ll. 107–10, 115–20, 232.   [48] Ibid., ll. 236–8.
[49] See Andreev, *Fiziki ne shutiat*, 145.

could move in the direction of greater disciplinal integrity and academic autonomy, forming a contrast to the situation in biology.

The MGU physics episode also suggested that students could make a convincing claim to represent a distinctive model of intelligentsia, one in which autonomous action and service of the party-state could be mutually constitutive. In the coming decade, physics students at MGU and across the country would seek to act on this notion of an independent-minded yet loyal intelligentsia. A case in point was the Komsomol organization of the MGU Physics Department, which combined extreme enthusiasm for affairs in the Youth League with close and often cantankerous engagement in curricular matters in the department. The students' patriotic assertiveness remained closely tied to their pride in the discipline of physics, and reflected what Douglas Weiner has called the "corporativist" and "castelike" quality of Soviet "scientific public opinion."[50] Physics students' disciplinary mega-lomania found expression in cliquish traditions such as elaborately staged "physics operas" and yearly Archimedes rallies featuring students dressed up as great scientists of the past.[51] Though it was largely limited to a specific discipline, the physicists' insular yet patriotic version of intelligentsia identity illustrated the broader variability of the concept in Soviet conditions.

De-Stalinizing the Soviet classroom?

The overhaul at the MGU Physics Department stemmed from Stalin-era higher learning, but its dénouement fell in the period of flux and re-evaluation that followed Stalin's death. Already during the dictator's last years, Stalin's retinue seems to have formed something of an informal consensus about the need for measured liberalization in economic, political, and foreign policies pursued after the war.[52] After Stalin's death, a collective leadership in the Politburo promptly set about alternatively softening or dismantling what they perceived as the excesses of Stalin's final years: concocted terror plots, the virtually unrestrained role of the political police, the labor camp system, and excessive state obligations in the countryside. These reforms – all occurring against the backdrop of Khrushchev's attempts to find common ground with the West – reached a climax in 1956, when the first secretary gave a scathing report to a party congress

---

[50] Weiner, *A Little Corner of Freedom*, 8.

[51] A book that reads like a compendium of the Khrushchev-era folklore of the physics students is Kovaleva, *Ty pomnish, fizfak?*

[52] Yoram Gorlizki and Oleg Khlevniuk, *Cold Peace: Stalin and the Soviet Ruling Circle, 1945–53* (New York: Oxford University Press, 2004), 123–42.

attacking the "cult of personality" of Stalin and acknowledging some of its bloodier manifestations.[53] In the year of popular upheaval and public discussion that followed, Stalin-era higher learning underwent far-reaching scrutiny. This post-Stalin discussion in higher education differed principally from the party discussions under Stalin; rather than centrally guided exercises to find scientific truth in specific disciplines, the discussions of 1956 focused on the overall organization of higher learning, including curricula, methods of instruction and evaluation (what was called the "learning process" or *uchebnyi protsess*). And while following central mandates, the post-Stalin discussions drew explicitly on public discourse in the press as well as in the loosening public spaces of the colleges themselves. However, as under Stalinism, public discussions engaged fundamental questions about the role of university governance, student politics, and the nature of the intelligentsia.

György Lukács characterized socialist universities as "huge high schools," and the comparison gives a sense of the narrow and rigid kind of learning that predominated during the Stalin era and indeed beyond.[54] Curricula were absurdly detailed and voluminous. To take but one example, in 1952 second-year philology students at KDU were asked to read 16,000 pages of literature and "familiarize themselves" with 220 writers in a single semester.[55] Instruction was equally laborious, with students being subjected to mandatory yet frequently repetitive or academically irrelevant lectures that often totaled more than forty hours a week.[56] In order to ensure compliance among students, Stalinist higher learning relied on extensive petty discipline. Academic group "elders" (*starosty*) enforced attendance among their peers, while Komsomol cells were tasked with pressuring their members to maintain passing grades and, more broadly, with pursuing their studies with rigor. The inevitable outcome of this educational overkill was rote-learning, as students regurgitated material from lectures at oral examinations while rarely consulting books.

The origins of Soviet methods in higher learning lay in Stalin's Great Break, when the regime defined the core priority in higher learning as the hasty production of specialists capable of working in the planned economy. This utilitarian objective – to provide narrow professional training which

[53] A useful overview of the politics of the early post-Stalin years is William Taubman, *Khrushchev: The Man and His Era* (New York: Norton, 2003), 236–69.
[54] This is drawn from Ivan T. Berend's review of John Connelly's *Captive University* in *Slavic Review*, 61 (2002): 132–33.
[55] TsDAHOU f. 7, op. 13, spr. 106, ark. 216.
[56] See a March 1952 meeting of the SGU Komsomol *aktiv* in GANISO f. 3234, op. 13, d. 17, l. 44.

would equip students to perform specific occupational tasks – remained a defining characteristic of Soviet higher learning, even in the universities where it seemed least applicable.[57] The notorious political orthodoxy of Soviet curricula also increased the stiffness of the Soviet academic regime. Students in all disciplines spent a large part of their time in dry and doctrinaire "social science" courses in Political Economy, Dialectical and Historical Materialism, and History of the Communist Party.[58] In its narrowness, doctrinarism, and statist inflexibility, Soviet higher learning aimed to produce a Soviet intelligentsia as politically docile as it was technically competent.

The Stalinist pedagogical regime proved unpopular among students for many reasons. According to one faculty member, some MGU students suffered from "nervous exhaustion" from having to sit in class for so many hours taking notes (often on an empty stomach).[59] The Kyiv student Iamshanov expressed the idea in colorful, or rather black-and-white, terms: during a Marxism lecture he passed around a picture of a skeleton with the caption, "Image of the student in the USSR."[60] Beyond its drudgery and strain, the Stalinist academic process appeared fundamentally flawed in what would today be called its educational outcomes. The system held out note-taking and memorization as the apex of academic achievement and devalued critical thinking. It also made rule-breaking a standard and perhaps necessary part of student life. Predictably, skipping class, sometimes with the connivance of one's student "elder," was widespread, especially as one could always borrow lecture notes from a classmate.[61] If a struggling student was still not prepared for exams, he or she could resort to tried-and-true methods of cheating. Academic dishonesty was so rampant in higher learning that Komsomol committees looked leniently on students caught red-handed. At the height of late Stalinism, a student using a common ploy – she had stolen a ticket in order to prepare for an oral examination in advance – received a minimal Komsomol punishment, one

[57] Nicholas De Witt, *Education and Professional Employment in the USSR* (Washington, DC: National Science Foundation, 1961), 225.

[58] These subjects, mandatory for all higher education students, were focused in special sub-departments (*kafedry*) that were not subordinated to specific departments. See a 1954 order on the structure of this curriculum in GARF f. 9396, op. 1, d. 643, ll. 262–64.

[59] See the 1953 comments of MGU Philology Department dean M. N. Zozulia in TsAOPIM f. 478, op. 3, d. 1, l. 113.

[60] DAKO f. 158, op. 3, spr. 11, ark. 165.

[61] For cases of negligent elders, see TsAOPIM f. 478, op. 3, d. 24, l. 96; GANISO f. 3234, op. 13, d. 66, l. 48. For similar strategies in interwar Soviet student life, see Peter Konecny, "Library Hooligans and Others: Law, Order, and Student Culture in Leningrad, 1924–1938," *Journal of Social History*, 30 (1996): 97–128.

that did not even figure in her personal records come graduation time.[62] Often, getting by as a student meant resorting to unseemly or downright dishonest behavior that sat uncomfortably with the ubiquitous talk of academic excellence and veneration for learning in the universities.

Policymakers were far from oblivious to the systemic distortions of the academic enterprise in Soviet universities. The journal of the MVO carried articles bemoaning the uncreative and incompetent work of many professors (albeit rarely by name), noting that some had turned their lectures into verbatim dictations.[63] Moreover, students sometimes voiced their frustrations with their studies, most often by lodging complaints through Komsomol but also sometimes through spontaneous protests like that of the SGU students who stormed out of the classroom to protest a mediocre professor, leaving the hapless Komsomol organizer alone in the classroom.[64] However, the rigidities and flawed organization of the Stalinist classroom withstood challenge from within. The overseers of higher education – much like administrators throughout the Soviet state – were constrained by the exigencies of the planned educational regime, just as the students were. Officials in the MVO evaluated the performance of their bailiwick in terms of aggregate data on student grades and attendance submitted from below. This method of measuring academic performance provided an easy way to send reassuring signals up the chain of command and created an overall illusion of progress, even if the officials involved must have understood that the numbers underwent massive falsification on the ground.[65] The perverse incentives that plagued the entire planned economy helped to maintain the Stalinist pedagogical regime.

The historical caesura of Stalin's death and the softening of the political line that followed it seemed to present an opportunity to push for fundamental changes in Soviet higher education. The Soviet higher education bureaucracy encouraged this perception by drawing attention to flaws in higher learning, for instance by calling on faculty to remove unnecessary material from study plans and emphasizing that "the state widely supports all initiatives to improve the training of specialists."[66] In mid 1956, several scholars responded to such calls by initiating a discussion in the press about

---

[62] DAKO f. 9912, op. 1, spr. 13, ark. 9–10.
[63] "Protiv proiavlenii shkoliarstva v vysshchei shkole," *VVSh*, no. 7 (1952): 1–2.
[64] This episode was discussed at a 1953 Komsomol meeting. GANISO f. 3234, op. 13, d. 30, l. 54.
[65] For one example of the top-down evaluation of higher education establishments based on attendance figures, see GANISO f. 3234, op. 13, d. 31, l. 63.
[66] "Vsemerno povyshat' kachestvoh uchebnoi raboty," *VVSh*, no. 2 (1954): 2; E. B. Khlebutin, "Aktivnyi organizator vospitaniia molodezi," *VVSh*, no. 5 (1953): 35–37.

the need for "free attendance" in higher education establishments, by which they meant an end to the mandatory attendance of classes by students. Art historian B. I. Brodskii claimed that the existing system's "spirit of the primary school (*shkoliarstvo*)" and "petty unrelenting guardianship" robbed "a person of all independence and initiative." Doing away with attendance rules would allow students to work "consciously and independently" by focusing on specific problems and questions according to academic need instead of being overwhelmed with unneeded information.[67] It would also force teachers to improve their craft, "sweeping away as with a broom" the most incompetent teachers, who "read their course year after year in a monotone from the same piece of paper."[68] In any case, they pointed out, many students were skipping class already; at least giving them the right to determine their schedules would raise their sense of responsibility.[69]

Faculty would seem to have a vested interest in avoiding the "sweep" Brodskii foretold. But a part of faculty embraced his logic that loosening the draconian rules hampering higher learning would invigorate it. In fact, the call for a less regimented classroom coincided with aspirations among university professors for a less bureaucratic and more associational model of governance. A. D. Aleksandrov, the rector of Leningrad University, endorsed free attendance but also made a call for greater university self-government; academic councils should be freely elected rather than appointed (as they currently were), and they should have greater powers at the expense of the powerful directors and rectors. Lowering oversight over both faculty and students would make universities into "schools of creative thought" rather than the sterile and narrow centers for training specialists, Aleksandrov felt.[70] Clearly, parts of the Soviet university communities gravitated toward what Talcott Parsons called "collegial associationalism," a looser form of administration suited to the modern university's specialization and inherent "intellectual venturesomeness."[71] Aleksandrov stopped far short of espousing academic freedom in the Western sense, let alone demanding institutional guarantees of it. He did, however, call for the state to recognize the principle that higher learning, by its very nature, required a lesser degree of top-down control than it had experienced during the Stalin years.

---

[67] B. I. Brodskii, "Vysshaia shkola i ego pitomtsy," *Literaturnaia gazeta*, 2 August 1956: 2.
[68] See a note by Professor A. Burganov of Tadzhik University in *Literaturnaia gazeta*, 15 September 1956: 2.
[69] TsAOPIM f. 478, op. 3, d. 210, l. 62.
[70] A. Aleksandrov, "Shkola tvorcheskoi mysli," *Literaturnaia gazeta*, 4 September 1956: 2.
[71] Talcott Parsons, "The Strange Case of Academic Organization," *The Journal of Higher Education*, 42 (1971): 486–89.

Shirkers or socialist citizens?

Conflict surrounding curricular matters within faculty generated heated engagement among students, just as it did during the biology and physics disputes a few years before. In 1956, the question of "free attendance" and proposals for a loosening of the academic regime dominated the public sphere of the universities, which was itself rapidly developing as a place for freer debate in the wake of de-Stalinization. The call for ending grueling oversight in higher education appealed to wide parts of the student body, and not simply because it promised students an easier existence. Echoing the physics students at MGU, many students supported free attendance as part of a patriotic agenda of improving the quality of learning. Allowing students to determine the use of their time and work independently would make them better specialists, SGU Komsomol activist Lobova asserted.[72] In this viewpoint, eschewing harmful and backward controls would help revitalize Soviet higher learning and, by extension, socialism itself. The independent student groups proliferating during the period – the focus of Chapter 5 – also embraced free attendance, in large part because they identified with the reformers' ideal of a creative and informal higher learning which would replace the stifling pedagogical status quo. For these critically minded students, ending attendance controls fit a broader agenda of freeing the country from Stalinism through intellectual engagement. An unsanctioned journal created by philology students at the Urals University called "Searching" (*V poiskakh*) presented student "self-education" as a way of restoring the "humanitarian life of the country" that had been destroyed during the Stalin years.[73]

Opponents of innovation often ignored the argument that a looser pedagogical regime would revitalize higher learning. Instead, they focused on the official mission of Soviet higher learning, that of "training highly qualified specialists according to the economic plans of the country."[74] For instance, a professor of technical sciences, K. Zhadin, warned that tampering with the current system would harm state interests. Free attendance would encourage truants and other malicious "violators of labor discipline," the dropout rate would soar, and the "eternal students" of imperial Russia would reappear, costing the state massive and unnecessary expenditure.[75]

---

[72] See Lobova's speech at a 1956 Komsomol meeting in GANISO f. 3234, op. 13, d. 92, l. 5.

[73] RGANI f. 5, op. 37, d. 2, ll. 144–47, in Iu. G. Burtin (ed. and comp.), "Studencheskoe brozhenie v SSSR (konets 1956 g.)," *Voprosy istorii*, 1 (1997): 21.

[74] See the note by higher education teacher M. Mal'chenko from Kharkiv oblast in *Literaturnaia gazeta*, 15 September 1956: 2.

[75] K. Zhadin, "Nashi za i protiv," *Literaturnaia gazeta*, 15 September 1956: 2.

At the heart of the debate was a "question of trust," as the MGU physics Komsomol leader Iurii Gaponov put it.[76] Could students be allowed to have input into their own development as future members of the Soviet intelligentsia? Replying in the affirmative, reform-minded students sought to persuade the professors of their good intentions. As a KDU journalism student assured the skeptics, "if a lecturer reads a lecture well, no one will leave it."[77] But to some professors and students, this formulation seemed woefully inadequate, as it placed responsibility for learning on the professors alone – a reversal of the top-down nature of Soviet pedagogical practices. Party officials rejected out of hand the notion that feckless and pampered students were up to the challenge of policing their own attendance, let alone of offering meaningful insight into curricular matters. The KDU party secretary I. P. Karnaukhov told a meeting of Komsomol activists that free attendance could only be discussed in a hypothetical future when the state would need fewer specialists. In any case, he added for good measure, Komsomols would not be part of the discussion.[78]

As this suggests, defenders of the pedagogical old regime based their arguments on a decidedly pessimistic view of the younger generation. The current student body, Zhadin warned, was not "isolated from backwards people, carriers of the holdovers of the past."[79] Such comments make it tempting to see this debate as a clash of generations, with the Stalinist elders calling for continued close control of higher education and postwar youth embracing intellectual freedom. The struggle did not, however, fall neatly along generational lines. The original supporters of pedagogical innovation were professors who sought a less regimented form of higher learning, an aspiration Aleksandrov attributed to a substantial part of the university faculty. Conversely, some students agreed with the disciplinarian status quo: at MGU, a student party member named Konovalov drew on the Stalin-era trope of "double dealers" by asserting at a Komsomol meeting that "shirkers (*progul'schiki*) [were] hiding behind discussions about the overburdening of students."[80]

Rather than representing a clash of generations, debates about free attendance highlighted divided notions about the place of an intelligentsia in Soviet society. The opponents of free attendance rejected the very premise of the reform – that students were capable and indeed uniquely positioned to contribute to the instruction they received.[81] Instead, they

---

[76] Gaponov, "Otryvki iz nenapisannogo," 217.   [77] DAKO f. 9912, op. 1, spr. 41, ark. 65.
[78] Ibid.   [79] Zhadin, "Nashi za i protiv."   [80] TsAOPIM f. 478, op. 3, d. 210, l. 72.
[81] F. Drobyshev, "Ne nado stroit' illiuzii," *Literaturnaia gazeta*, 15 September 1956: 2.

stressed that the state was sole arbiter of higher learning, whose interests therefore surpassed those of the professors and students. In contrast, the supporters of free attendance viewed the holders of learning far more optimistically, stressing not only the ability but the necessity of colleges to conduct their affairs without excessive state intervention. For at least some of the reformers, this vision was rooted in a more democratic vision of Soviet socialism. For instance, Brodskii called the higher education establishment a "breeding ground of national culture," a "school of citizenship," and a "nursery of the democratic habits of the future."[82] A seemingly mundane debate about lecture attendance raised fundamental questions about the place of intellectuals in society, showing that the intelligentsia would remain an unsettled category after Stalin's death.

Divisions over the Stalinist academic regime only sharpened when they passed from discussion to practice. Responding to the discussion in the press, the MVO issued "instructive letter #I-100" in September 1956, which tasked individual higher education establishments with facilitating the "independent work" of students. Although it fell far short of endorsing free attendance in the way it was usually envisioned, the letter provided some scope for loosening controls in higher learning by suggesting that colleges excise material that students could access outside the curriculum and, more controversially, by clearing the way for colleges to grant particularly successful students the right to study according to "individual plans," meaning in essence that not all parts of the curriculum would apply to them.[83] If the letter's provisions were vague and non-binding, at least they left room for institutions to generate their own initiatives.

The moment of seemingly incipient change in higher learning succumbed to the crisis that embroiled the country in late 1956, when the party-state suppressed a revolution in Hungary and struggled to put an end to signs of ideological dissent in the USSR. By the end of 1956, it was clear that the party-state would not follow the MVO instructional letter with more radical reforms of the attendance regime – or, for that matter, of other components of Soviet higher education.[84] Regardless of the impact of broader political developments, however, the chances of restructuring Stalinist higher education along the lines reformers sought were hardly auspicious. "Instructive letter #I-100" did not lead to substantial experimentation in curricula or pedagogy. For reasons of both professional pride

---

[82] Brodskii, "Vysshaia shkola."
[83] See the description of the letter in GANISO f. 3234, op. 13, d. 92, l. 38.
[84] TsAOPIM f. 6083, op. 1, d. 5, l. 87.

and self-interest, professors proved reluctant to cut teaching in their own disciplines and classes, even as they realized the overall curriculum was severely bloated. For instance, the KDU Department of Ukrainian Literature easily found cases of repeated material: recent TsK resolutions on ideology were being discussed at length in virtually all its classes, such as History of Ukrainian Literature, Literary Theory, and even Ukrainian Folklore. But the Department was unwilling to go far in lightening students' coursework on the grounds that giving too much leeway for independent work would only harm their "systematic knowledge."[85] As a way to compensate for their inaction, many faculty members suggested cutting study hours in disciplines that they saw as less academically important, which generally meant the dogmatic and highly repetitive social sciences curriculum as well as military training classes. However, the MVO expressly forbid rectors to tamper with these parts of the curriculum, tying the hands of faculty administrators in the universities.[86]

Colleges which did undertake experiments in softening academic discipline were also rarely pleased with the results. Early in 1957, the vice-rector of KDU claimed that students were using the day per week which had been left free from classes for leisure activities rather than poring over books in the library or working in the laboratory.[87] MGU philosophy professor T. I. Oizerman went so far to suggest that any day freed from classes could only be productive if it was "organized and controlled like any day of classes," with students actually signing in and out at the department office – a suggestion that seemed at odds with the spirit of the envisioned reforms.[88] Meanwhile, some faculty members had deep misgivings about the letter's mechanism for providing the best students with individualized curricula. As one SGU professor wondered, would specially gifted students granted free attendance not walk around "with raised noses" and "break away from the collective"?[89] An effort to reinvigorate the Stalinist academic practices had foundered on many obstacles: the resistance of Moscow authorities to downsize ideological indoctrination in higher learning, the reluctance of faculty to cut their own lecture hours, and, most of all, a pervasive skepticism about relying on student initiative in higher learning.

[85] DAK f. 1246, op. 21, spr. 775, ark. 16–17.
[86] GASO f. 332, op. 2, d. 82, ll. 46–47. See a similar account of the situation at the MGU History Department in E. V. Gutnova, *Perezhitoe* (Moscow: ROSSPEN, 2001), 286–88.
[87] See the comments of KDU historian P. P. Udovychenko at an early 1957 Komsomol meeting in DAKO f. 9912, op. 1, d. 43, l. 46.
[88] Iu. A. Saltanov, "Mnenie uchenykh Moskovskogo universiteta," *VVSh*, no. 7 (1957): 62.
[89] See comments made at a session of the all-university academic council in 1958. GASO f. 332, op. 2, d. 82, ll. 76, 80.

While institutions continued to discuss the instructional letter until the end of the decade, the tweaking of curricula it produced was far from the original vision of a university driven by student independence and research.[90]

Remembering the postwar years, former faculty and students often depict universities as centers of intellectual integrity and moral substance subjected to irrational intrusions by an oppressive state. As a geologist put it colorfully, MGU had an "inner pride" that reflected its long history of struggle for autonomy; this made it inherently oppositional to the Soviet regime and ensured that faculty and students did not become the "total bastards" that the communist regime would otherwise have made of them.[91] However biased and totalizing, the picture of a university wedded to academic freedom contains a kernel of truth. As the chapter has shown, some faculty and students sought, sometimes at considerable personal risk, to maintain space where intellectual exchange could proceed with a greater degree of agency than the party-state would allow. Moreover, the persistent if scattered efforts at the grassroots level to diminish perceived excesses of ideological and bureaucratic control can be understood as a product of the universities and specifically the values of academic rigor and pure learning and the social status that held a tenacious place in them.

The story of late Stalinism in higher learning and its early aftermath, however, cannot be reduced to the simple dichotomies of knowledge and power or university and regime. Rather, late Stalinist intervention in higher learning spurred divisions within the universities themselves. Postwar disputes about physics, biology, and pedagogical practices showed not only a lack of consensus about scientific truths but also contestation over the core principles that underlay Soviet higher learning. First, the issue of whether learning should be somehow specifically Soviet or proletarian was an intractable one for the Soviet universities during the late Stalin period. Responses to Lysenkoism showed that the notion of a "people's science" held significant appeal. In the case of physics, the crude application of party principles to science carried less weight among the students. Yet even here, the patriotic thrust of the students' Komsomol initiative showed that the students understood science to have a Soviet character, in its objectives if not in its form. Second, the disputes explored in this chapter shed light on the problem of autonomy and control in higher learning and Soviet intellectual life as a whole. Did the distinguished "temples of science"

[90] P. D. Baliasov, "Nuzhna bol'shaia tvorcheskaia rabota kollektiva," *VVSh*, no. 9 (1957): 49–55.
[91] Interview with Iu. D. Ivanov, Moscow, 2003.

require a special form of leeway in order to serve the Soviet system? The actions of the physics students seemed to constitute an affirmative answer to this question, and post-Stalin reformers made the case openly. Yet opponents of calls for a less regimented university were never in short supply within the universities, among both professors and students. In their view, the universities were indistinguishable from the Soviet order they served, and therefore had to remain immersed in its norms.

Universities are perhaps fractious institutions by their very nature. As György Péteri has argued, the one eternal feature of universities is the "never-ceasing contestation about what 'the idea of the university' should be."[92] In the Soviet context, this existential problem of university life was entangled with the conceptual web of the intelligentsia. Most could agree – and had to agree – that higher learning belonged to the people who were building socialism. The party was committed to the principle that the intelligentsia was a subservient stratum that served the people's state through learning and mass enlightenment. The scientific and pedagogical disputes of the period saw the articulation of the idea that intellectuals, as carriers of culture, should help define the terms on which service was rendered. In academic affairs as in other realms, intellectuals remained ambivalent figures, servants of Soviet society who had a tendency to see themselves as its leaders.

---

[92] György Péteri, "The Communist Idea of the University: An Essay Inspired by the Hungarian Experience," in John Connelly and Michael Grüttner (eds.), *Universities under Dictatorship* (University Park: Pennsylvania State University Press, 2005), 141.

CHAPTER 5

De-Stalinization and intellectual salvationism

In early November 1956, students at the Kazan' Finance and Economics Institute created a "society for the study of questions of economy and culture." The leaders of the initiative, the Komsomol activists Gadzhiev and Kataev, announced the creation of a "circle of independent study" at a Youth League meeting and invited anyone interested to take part. At the meeting, Gadzhiev delivered reports to fifteen students on unusual and controversial topics: "Is man the driving force of society?" and "is the cult of personality a product of socialist society?" Despite its seemingly benign origins, the undertaking soon sparked the interest of the highest political officials of the country; the short-lived society ended with the expulsion of several of the participants from the institute.[1]

This episode of student protest belonged to the period of ideological ferment that accompanied de-Stalinization. In February 1956, Khrushchev denounced Stalin's "cult of personality" at the Twentieth Party Congress of the Communist Party. The so-called "secret speech" was a bombshell for Soviet society, as millions of citizens who had recently viewed the leader with devotion struggled to make sense of Khrushchev's revelations of mass terror and misrule. While the speech produced a range of responses, young people were especially active in articulating one approach to the recent past that caused concern among party leaders: an over-eager embrace of Khrushchev's criticism of Stalin and his era. The "circle of independent study" in Kazan' suggests two seemingly discordant aspects of student mobilization around an anti-Stalinist platform. The "circle of independent study" in Kazan' is striking for its political naivety. Demonstrating a seeming ignorance about the limits of accepted discourse, the students – including ranking Komsomol activists – advertised their endeavor at the highly public setting of a Youth League meeting. The immediate historical context of November 1956 would hardly seem one fitting for open political

---

[1] RGASPI-M f. 1, op. 46, d. 192, ll. 153–54.

action. While the students debated history and communist theory, Soviet armed forces were suppressing revolution in Hungary and the KGB, party and Komsomol organizations were undertaking targeted repression against critics at home and in higher education in particular.[2]

Another seeming anomaly was the way the students presented their agenda in academic terms. By calling their initiative a "circle," the students seemed to liken it to the student scientific societies and cultural clubs that were an everyday reality in the postwar universities; perhaps inadvertently, however, the description also conjured up a core institution in intelligentsia history, the *kruzhok* of like-minded and critically thinking intellectuals.[3] Nevertheless, the Kazan' students clearly understood the purpose of their endeavor as an intellectual exercise, one that approached the problem of transition to post-Stalinism through the prism of ostensibly disinterested and objective discourse. The institute's top Komsomol official also seemed to treat it as a valid intellectual endeavor when he attended the society's inaugural meeting and, while criticizing Gadzhiev for referencing Voice of America and BBC broadcasts, did not inform higher authorities of the meeting.[4]

The naïve and academic nature of the Kazan' case suggests the complexity of university politics during de-Stalinization. Recent scholarship has presented students as an essentially oppositional group, determined to press Khrushchev's tentative criticisms of Stalin to their logical conclusions.[5] This literature exaggerates the anti-Soviet motives of student rebels and treats an oppositional fringe as representative of the student body as a whole.[6] In part, these oversights reflect the use of newly available archival documents,

---

[2] See Polly Jones, "From the Secret Speech to the Burial of Stalin: Real and Ideal Responses to De-Stalinization," in Polly Jones (ed.), *The Dilemmas of De-Stalinization: Negotiating Cultural and Social Change in the Khrushchev Era* (London: Routledge, 2006), 41–51. Throughout I use the term de-Stalinization in the narrow sense to convey the dismantling of the cult of Stalin rather than as a shorthand for broader liberalizing trends in the period.

[3] To be sure, the *kruzhok* involved a thorough rejection of surrounding realities in a way that was far different from the social networks constructed by students in this period. For the role of the *kruzhok* and its extension into the Soviet period, see Barbara Walker, *Maximilian Voloshin and the Russian Literary Circle: Culture and Survival in Revolutionary Times* (Bloomington: Indiana University Press, 2005).

[4] The role of foreign radio broadcasts in student politics is considered in Chapter 7.

[5] Elena Zubkova, *Obshchestvo i reformy* (Moscow: Rossiia molodaia, 1993); Vladislav Zubok, *Zhivago's Children: The Last Russian Intelligentsia* (Cambridge, MA: Belknap Press, 2009), 60–87; Kathleen E. Smith, "A New Generation of Political Prisoners: 'Anti-Soviet' Students, 1956–1957," *The Soviet and Post-Soviet Review*, 32 (2005): 191–208; A. V. Pyzhikov, "Sources of Dissidence: Soviet Youth after the Twentieth Party Congress," *Russian Social Science Review*, 45 (2004): 66–79; L. V. Silina, *Nastroeniia sovetskogo studenchestva, 1945–1964* (Moscow: Russkii mir, 2004); Karl E. Loewenstein, "Re-Emergence of Public Opinion in the Soviet Union: Khrushchev and Responses to the Secret Speech," *Europe-Asia Studies*, 58 (2006): 1331–33.

[6] My argument is limited to Russia and the parts of Ukraine that had been Soviet before 1939. Reactions to the secret speech differed sharply among youth in the Western periphery of the USSR, territories

which provide ample room for a distorted view of the students by focusing exclusively and in black-and-white terms on "ideological deviations" in the universities. This literature also suffers from adopting uncritically the viewpoint of many historical actors during de-Stalinization – specifically, their belief that intellectuals were purifying a Soviet society insufficiently "Thawed" from the Stalin period.

This chapter views unrest in the universities as the product of a broader interaction among learning, identity, and the crisis of post-Stalinism. Recreating the thinking of specific student rebels, it argues that university life and the ideas about the intelligentsia that it nourished formed the critical context for student reactions to de-Stalinization. Faced with Khrushchev's rewriting of Soviet history and the ideological and personal dilemmas it posed, many students redoubled their efforts to become cultured *intelligenty*, elaborating on modes of intellectual self-fashioning that had been present in the late Stalinist universities. Embrace of the intelligentsia cultural mission was a logical response to a time of upheaval, but it also brought dissension into the universities by interconnecting de-Stalinization with debates about the intelligentsia.

Stalin's death, Khrushchev's riddle, and university culture

The conventional starting point for de-Stalinization – and, more broadly, the liberalizing trends of the period which scholars have traditionally called the "Thaw" in Soviet life – is Stalin's death. This is hardly surprising given Stalin's role as the driving force of the Soviet system, even in his final months. Along with much else, higher education underwent several crucial changes soon after Stalin's death. In line with what one historian has called the "exceptional liberalism" of the repressive apparatus immediately after 1953, the routine functions of the secret police on campus – recruiting informers to conduct surveillance, acting on "signals" concerning political dangers received from citizens – narrowed in scope.[7] At the same time, Komsomol underwent a process of reform that undid some of the

integrated into the country through war and where older anti-Soviet moods remained strong. See William Jay Risch, *The Ukrainian West: Culture and the Fate of Empire in Soviet Lviv* (Cambridge, MA: Harvard University Press, 2011), 179–219, and Amir Weiner, "The Empires Pay a Visit: Gulag Returnees, East European Rebellions, and Soviet Frontier Politics," *The Journal of Modern History*, 78 (2006): 333–76.

[7] Elena Papovian, "Primenenie stat'i 58–10 UK RSFSR v 1957–1958 gg.: po materialam verkhovnego suda i prokuratury SSSR v GARF," in L. S. Ereminaia and E. B. Zhemkova (eds.), *Korni travy: sbornik stat'ei molodykh istorikov* (Moscow, "Zvenia," 1996), 73.

bureaucratic immobility that had plagued the organization for years. A centrally organized campaign against "bureaucracy" in the ranks sparked a turnover in ranking cadres and a shrinking of the apparat and spurred activists to criticize the "petty guardianship and regimentation" of higher Komsomol bodies.[8] In the long run, this campaign weakened oversight in the organization while providing a language of socialist democracy and anti-bureaucratism – embodied in slogans like "being closer to the masses" and "banishing formalism in work with youth" – which would soon prove formidable weapons in the hands of young communist reformers.[9]

But too great an emphasis on Stalin's death as the pivotal moment in Soviet history, at least with regard to the politics of educated society, risks obscuring other trends in the period. While the loss of Stalin was a defining moment for every Soviet citizen, its implications were hardly clear at the time. It is unconvincing to posit a direct link between Stalin's passing and a "Thawing" of public opinion. The vast majority of students saw the event as a tragedy. In one recollection of a typical scene, students at the SGU History Department, devoted to Stalin "to the last drop of their blood," had a meeting on the event at which everyone cried.[10] Rather than feeling liberated, students and other educated citizens responded to Stalin's death with despair and even a sense of paralysis, and this applied to many of the people who had long harbored doubts about the leader as well as the much larger group of those committed to him.[11] As one Moscow student asked, "How will we live, who will lead us?"[12] The shock produced by Stalin's death illustrated a fundamental fact about the politics of educated society during de-Stalinization. Rather than being an elemental reaction to the end of an inhumane era, anti-Stalin politics emerged in close dialogue with the unsettled and ambivalent post-Stalin leadership.

Focusing on Stalin's death as the start of a Thaw in Soviet society also obscures continuities across the 1953 divide. Recent writing has pointed to the late Stalin period as a generator of different aspects of the Thaw, from

---

[8] RGASPI-M f. 1, op. 3, d. 889, ll. 340–50, 356–57. On liberalizing shifts in elections within Komsomol in the period, see Gleb Tsipursky, "Integration, Celebration, and Challenge: Soviet Youth and Elections, 1953–1968," in Ralph Jessen et al. (eds.), *Voting for Hitler and Stalin Elections under 20th Century Dictatorships* (Frankfurt: Campus Verlag, 2011), 81–102.

[9] Nikolai Solokhin, "Podsnezhniki 'ottepeli,'" in V. Dolinin and B. Ivanov (eds.), *Samizdat: po materialam konferentsii "30 let nezavisimoi pechati. 1950–80 gody" Sankt-Peterburg, 25–27 aprelia 1992 g.* (St. Petersburg: Nauchno-informatsionnyi tsentr "Memorial," 1993), 25.

[10] Interview with G. R. Davydov, Saratov, 2005.

[11] Vladimir Bukovsky, *To Build a Castle: My Life as a Dissenter* (New York: Viking Press, 1979), 99–100; Iu. G. Burtin, *Ispoved' shestidesiatnika* (Moscow: Progress-Traditsiia, 2003), 16–18.

[12] Interview with D. F. Rozental', Moscow, 2004. Aleksandr M. Nekrich, *Forsake Fear: Memoirs of an Historian* (Boston: Unwin Hyman, 1991), 73–74.

the liveliness of youthful cultural consumption to the humanist themes of post-1953 literature: the sincere depiction of life, a focus on individual fulfillment, and criticism of bureaucracy.[13] In the same pattern, student activism of the de-Stalinization period emerged from the social and intellectual milieu of higher learning under late Stalinism. As Chapter 1 showed, the universities were social environments where youth interacted most closely with "culture," understood in the specific contemporaneous sense of a socialist civilizing mission. Far from being inherently oppositional, the idealistic pursuit of culture was a core component of postwar student life, one which the higher education bureaucracy cultivated.

The moderating reforms that followed Stalin's death transformed the scale of student cultural life, as a less fearful environment made it possible to bring independent intellectual exploration into public settings in ways that were impossible just a few years before. Growing numbers of students participated in university literary associations sponsored by writers' unions and publishing houses which aimed to help aspiring writers and critics hone their craft.[14] Sometimes with minimal party oversight, intellectually minded students used these organizations to share ideas, form social networks, and ultimately to claim roles as independent interlocutors of Soviet culture.[15] In Leningrad, poetry readings at the Polytechnic Institute under the auspices of a literary club reportedly drew audiences upward of 1,000 young people from across the city.[16] Provincial universities also saw the emergence of officially recognized yet intellectually boisterous cultural spaces. At SGU, a "literary-creative section" provided a university-wide forum for intellectual discourse among cultural savants, including several former participants of the now disbanded wall newspaper BOKS discussed in Chapter 1. When one E. Kaganov presented a mediocre poem entitled "The Lion and the Person" that he had entered in a university poetry contest, the BOKS veteran Viktor Seleznev proclaimed ironically that the poem was a monumental work on the contradictions of the slave-holding system.[17] If this was the distinctive public culture of the Thaw – erudite, deviant, and

---

[13] Katerina Clark, *The Soviet Novel: History as Ritual* (Bloomington: Indiana University Press, 2000), 189–250. A wide-ranging treatment of the theme with regard to youth is Juliane Fürst, *Stalin's Last Generation: Soviet Post-War Youth and the Emergence of Mature Socialism* (Oxford University Press, 2010).

[14] See Emily Lygo, "The Need for New Voices: Writers' Union Policy towards Young Writers, 1953–64," in Jones (ed.), *The Dilemmas of De-Stalinization*, 193–208.

[15] Vladimir Kuznetsov, *Istoriia odnoi kompanii* (Moscow: Izdanie avtora, 1995), 17–18.

[16] See Vladimir Britashinskii, "Studencheskoe poeticheskoe dvizhenie v Leningrade v nachale ottepeli," *Novoe literaturnoe obozrenie*, no. 14 (1995): 167–68 and Solokhin, "Podsnezhniki 'ottepeli,'" 23–24.

[17] "Protiv oposhleniia kritiki," *Stalinets*, 8 May 1954: 1; Interview with V. Seleznev, Saratov, 2004.

clever – it was also an extension of a longer tradition of student highbrow creativity.

The special link of universities to Soviet culture provided a critical context for the events of 1956, when Khrushchev denounced Stalin at the Twentieth Party Congress. Scholarly accounts often stress the speech's incomplete account of the Stalin period, particularly its failure to acknowledge the tragedy of collectivization and the fate of non-communist victims of the regime. This critique is true but misses the point. In the context of the time, Khrushchev's lurid recounting of Stalin's misdeeds – including persecution of honest communists, strategic mistakes during World War II, ruination of (postwar) Soviet agriculture, and propagation of his own cult – was explosive.[18] The boldness of the speech reflected Khrushchev's confidence that history was on the side of Soviet communism; expunging the ghost of Stalin and resurrecting Leninism would redouble citizens' dedication to the party.[19] This was not as unrealistic an idea as commentators have sometimes argued, at least with regard to youth. Among Russian and Ukrainian students, the speech triggered widespread patriotism and enthusiasm about the communist project. As the Ukrainian literary critic Ivan Svitlychnyi recalled wistfully in a later speech, it had seemed immediately after the Twentieth Party Congress that "all national problems would resolve themselves at one blow, and that nothing was left except to march ceremoniously with upraised fists on the path to communism."[20]

The problem with Khrushchev's criticism of the cult of personality was less its stridency – or lack thereof – as its inconsistency. Khrushchev wanted to spur enthusiasm for a de-Stalinized communist project while leaving the institutions and elites of the Stalin period in place. This contradictory objective was at the root of the report's tortured account of the Stalin period. According to Khrushchev, Stalin was a bloody dictator but also a great Marxist who had tragically gone astray; the Communist Party had never deviated from the historically correct path of socialist construction, even as its leaders had been held in terror and ignorance by Stalin.[21] The speech provided just as confusing a blueprint for the future as it did an analysis of the past. Because the speech blamed the terror and misrule of past years

---

[18] "O kul'te lichnosti i ego posledstviiakh: doklad N. S. Khrushcheva XX s'ezdu Kommunisticheskoi partii sovetskogo soiuza 25 fevralia 1956 g.," in L. A. Kirshner and S. A. Prokhvatilova (eds.), *Svet i teni "velikogo desiatiletiia": N. S. Khrushchev i ego vremia* (Leningrad: Lenizdat, 1989), 46–105.

[19] William Taubman, *Khrushchev: The Man and His Era* (New York: Norton, 2003), 276–81.

[20] "Speech Delivered by Ivan Svitlychnyi in Memory of Vasyl Symonenko (Kyiv Medical Institute, 1963)," *Ukrainian Herald: Underground Magazine from Ukraine, Issue IV* (Munich: ABN Press Bureau, 1972), 109.

[21] "O kul'te lichnosti i ego posledstviiakh," 101–3.

on Stalin and a narrow circle of his minions alone, the process of "overcoming the cult of personality and its consequences" might be limited to a clear rejection of the recently departed leader. But the Khrushchev leadership also suggested that "the cult of personality," in some form, had outlasted the dictator. The congress's resolution called on the party to "fully restore the Leninist principles of Soviet socialist democracy" as expressed in the constitution and to "struggle against the arbitrary power of people who are abusing their authority."[22] Dissemination of the report deepened the sense that Soviet leaders were unsure of their objectives. Even as the report was read aloud at party, Komsomol, and even general enterprise meetings across the country, it retained the official designation "not for distribution" and copies of it were carefully controlled through party channels.[23]

The leadership's mixed signals on the Stalin question disoriented the ruling party. What would represent a loyal response to de-Stalinization and how should deviations from it be handled? These questions remained unanswered in the course of 1956. Soon after the congress, the country's leadership became convinced that excessive *support* of de-Stalinization – rather than opposition to it – was the most dangerous ideological tendency in Soviet society. Following this conviction, the party TsK issued three letters to party members in the course of the year that sought to place boundaries on interpretation of the secret speech at the feverish discussions that had absorbed Soviet society, instructing party organizations to intervene in cases when "freedom of discussion" and healthy "criticism" had crossed "the line of party mindedness" and turned into "slander."[24] The very language of this interjection suggests the bind into which Khrushchev had put the party: Soviet citizens had responded to the party's call to condemn Stalin's cult of personality, yet their efforts often exceeded admissible limits. The situation was deeply disorienting to the party's apparatus and middle ranks, which wilted when confronted with public discussions that were moving in unpredictable directions – of course, the exact opposite of what Khrushchev had intended when he opened the Stalin question.[25]

The uncertainty created by de-Stalinization was especially pronounced in the universities. Students who had come of age at the height of the Stalin

---

[22] Ibid., 103–5.
[23] On the speech's distribution, see K. Aimermakher et al. (eds.), *Doklad N. S. Khrushcheva o kul'te lichnosti Stalina na XX s'ezde KPSS: dokumenty* (Moscow: ROSSPEN, 2002), 253, 278.
[24] Ibid., 288–90, 352–68, 378–85, 393–401.
[25] Party documentation shows that terms like "violations of inner-party discipline" were debated even within the TsK itself. RGANI f. 5, op. 30, d. 186, ll. 158–64.

era usually expressed shock at Khrushchev's revelations about the recent past and immediately sensed that the explanations of the speech were incomplete, or at least demanded further discussion. A lecturer sent from the Moscow City Party Committee to the MGU dormitories met with "a rumble of dissatisfaction" from the students when he called Stalin a "rank-and-file communist" – certainly a clumsy effort to convey Khrushchev's wavering attitude toward the departed leader.[26] Of course, the party had elaborate mechanisms for communicating its message in higher education, including the ideological social science curriculum that was mandatory for all students and propaganda work conducted in a variety of settings. Yet these instruments posed their own problems in the context of ideological upheaval. The social science teachers, guardians of ideological purity in higher learning, were in as much disarray as the students; indeed, the entire social sciences curriculum remained up in the air while the ministry set about commissioning a textbook that would replace the previously defini-tive *Short Course of the History of the Communist Party*.[27] Lacking in clear instructions and sometimes themselves confused about the situation in the country, most professors had to grapple with Stalin's scientific authority in haphazard ways, for instance by expunging his works from syllabi or quoting Stalin's texts in their lectures without attributing their source.[28] No wonder that ideological social science seminars – classes that were usually dry expositions of party doctrines – became unpredictable and confrontational events as discussions from the hallways and dormitories found their way into the classroom. In short, the usual channels of convey-ing party priorities to students, never fully effective even in the more clear-cut conditions of Stalinism, seemed especially unequal to the task in 1956.

The disarray of university party authorities in the wake of the Twentieth Party Congress had drastic consequences, as students themselves had to fill the ideological void left by the discrediting of Stalinist orthodoxy. In the wake of the secret speech, an open-ended campus debate swept through the universities in which every aspect of Soviet life and its history came under scrutiny. In the process, the lower rungs of Komsomol and the other mass organizations came to resemble debating societies which often flaunted control from above. Significantly, the clear majority of the "incorrect and anti-Soviet statements" for which students were punished through party

[26] RGANI f. 5, op. 35, d. 179, l. 28.
[27] Cf. "Novoe v prepodavanii obshchestvennykh nauk," *VVSh*, no. 7 (1956): 1–5. See the insightful treatment of clashes in party history at MGU in Polly Jones, "Revisions, Revisionism, or Dissent? Stalinist History and 'Stalinist' Historians in the Thaw," unpublished manuscript.
[28] TsDAHOU f. 1, op. 24, spr. 4255, ark. 167.

channels in 1956 and 1957 occurred at Komsomol meetings.[29] The student body was doubly confused. As mentioned in the case of the students in Kazan', the party's ultimate intentions were unclear and therefore the parameters of discourse seemed unsettled, despite its increasingly conservative line on de-Stalinization. More fundamentally, students were unsure of their own positions. For the vast majority of Soviet students who had been loyal to the leader, Khrushchev's revelations threw much in doubt: the identity of a figure previously held sacred, the entire course of Soviet history, and one's own past identity as a Soviet citizen of the Stalin era. Not surprisingly, classmates and comrades discovered that they held widely divergent thoughts about the Stalin question and everything that came with it. Ivan and Timur, roommates and close friends at MGU, argued heatedly into the night so loudly that the "disturbed students in adjoining rooms beat against the wall." Ivan's "genes spoke, even howled in favor of exposing Stalin's 'deeds,'" whereas Timur remained a "fervent Stalinist."[30] Many others were beset with uncertainty: a student at Irkutsk University lamented at a Komsomol conference that unbelief had "firmly occupied [his] whole life," "suffocating" him.[31]

Such all-consuming doubt finds scarce mention in work that presents 1956 as a year of liberation in the universities, with the frequent suggestion that students were essentially or perhaps monolithically in favor of deepening de-Stalinization.[32] In reality, disunity and confusion dominated the universities. As elsewhere in Soviet society, opposition to de-Stalinization remained widespread along with support of it. Unabashed pro-Stalinists reproduced the longstanding trope of the leader's infallibility: "the evil Beria, Molotov, and Kaganovich deceived him" and were responsible for the terror, the argument went.[33] Moreover, citizens who accepted Khrushchev's revelations in factual

---

[29] This critical point is made in Gennadii Kuzovkin, "Partiino-komsomol'skie presledovaniia po politicheskim motivam v period rannei 'ottepeli'," in Ereminaia and Zhemkova (eds.), *Korni travy*, 95–96.

[30] N. T. Bakaev, *Na mekhmat kto popal ... Ivan, ne pomniashii rodstvo i potomok Ghingis Khana* (Moscow: Knizhnyi dom "Moskovskii universitet," 2000), 12–13. Despite its artful title, Bakaev's book is a memoir.

[31] L. I. Borodin, *Bez vybora: avtobiograficheskoe povestvovanie* (Moscow: Molodaia gvardiia, 2003), 62.

[32] See the literature in note 5 of this chapter. Zubok provides a more nuanced account by stressing widespread debate, the presence of "naïve Stalinists" in the universities, and the ongoing importance of "socialist romanticism," but follows this literature in suggesting that protest was near-universal in higher education. "The ability to think independently and hold unauthorized public discussions about Stalinism led by logical progression to public protest," he posits. Zubok, *Zhivago's Children*, 62–67.

[33] Here I quote a former student who sought to characterize the discussions about the Stalin cult among his acquaintances. Interview with G. P. Dudkin and E. R. Dudkina, Moscow, 2004. See also Aleksandr Gidoni, *Solntse idet s zapada: kniga vospominanii* (Toronto: Sovremennik, 1980), 26.

terms did not necessarily support the leadership's move against the deceased leader. Despite his faults, as many pointed out, Stalin had led the country to victory in war. In any case, the inconsistencies of the speech and its dissemination proved troubling to patriotic Soviet citizens, regardless of their views of Stalin. At a KDU Party meeting on the Twentieth Party Congress, an unidentified party member asked whether it had been correct to publish the report at all, even as a closed letter to a party congress.[34] An implicit attack on Khrushchev from the perspective of party interests, this approach demonstrates how some students and faculty members in 1956 longed for the mood of unity that dominated Stalin-era public culture but now seemed lost for good.

Culture-building after Stalin

Depicting students en masse as proto-dissidents also oversimplifies the anti-Stalinist moods that did emerge in the sphere of higher learning in 1956. Particularly poorly explored is the fundamental issue of the relationship between "culture" and politics in educated society during the Khrushchev era. Scholarly work has often depicted the high culture associated with the Thaw as a surrogate civic sphere in which anti-Stalinist political impulses found expression.[35] This perspective is invaluable for understanding a period when poems, novels, and films were indeed at the forefront of political debate.

Seeing the culture of the Thaw as a vehicle for political impulses alone is nonetheless conceptually incomplete. Thaw-era activists saw their activities as a struggle against the Stalinist past, but they also maintained the mindset of the Soviet intelligentsia as a whole. Accordingly, they saw culture as the wellspring of civilized values and also as a much-coveted source of social status. The high purpose and broad contours of the concept of culture during the Thaw found reflection in the diligence with which many students sought to immerse themselves in cultural activities. Writing decades later, a Muscovite recalled her student years in the 1950s as an all-consuming pursuit of true culture: sitting in on lectures delivered by noted scholars at different institutes across the capital, taking part in student poetry readings, working on the wall newspaper, reading the thick journal

---

[34] TsDAHOU f. 1, op. 71, spr. 4255, ark. 14.
[35] For this approach, see Michael Urban, "Regime and Politics in the Pre-Political Period," in Michael Urban et al. (eds.), *The Rebirth of Politics in Russia* (Cambridge University Press, 1997), 36–39.

Novyi mir avidly, and attending every notable cultural event – a concert by Sviatoslav Richter, a new French film – even if it meant spending a night in line for a ticket.[36] On one level, such devoted pursuit of culture – which seemed an odd accompaniment to the lightness and informality of many expressions of the Thaw – reproduced longstanding intelligentsia and Soviet practices of "working on oneself" or mastering one's impulses in the name of a higher state of consciousness.[37] It also represented the value that learning, in both its formal and less tangible forms, had long held for the middle strata in the USSR: that of acquiring cultural capital and cementing one's place in an intelligentsia.

The Thaw, then, represented the splicing together of a political agenda of de-Stalinization and longstanding modes of Soviet culture-building. A widespread view among educated critics of Stalin was that "the cult of personality and its consequences" – its cruelty, dishonesty, and bureaucratic indifference – were a symptom of moral backwardness. Accordingly, the "period of the cult" could be overcome with the civilizing zeal of an intelligentsia carrying culture to the masses. An independent student pub- lication that appeared at the Leningrad Polytechnic Institute, entitled simply *Kul'tura*, captured this agenda of cultural and political revival. The paper bemoaned the "stagnation, clichés, and falsehood" of official cultural expression and called on students to "speak the truth of life," even if it meant coming into conflict with intolerant "high-ranking people."[38] Evident here was a central concern of the individuals associating themselves with the Thaw: the search for new and genuine forms of cultural expression that, it was hoped, would create a harmonious, humane, and integrated society. This was an optimistic and idealistic reading of the country's post- Stalin predicament, one that subsumed the thorny questions of historical evaluation and responsibility into a broader narrative of cultural renewal. Thinking about Stalin in this way was a logical response to the ideological chaos of 1956; culture was a clearly progressive part of the Soviet project which one could embrace unhesitatingly. Also, students might imagine that

---

[36] "Pozdravliaem s iubileem zamechatel'nogo cheloveka, talantlivogo kollegu, nashu sokursnitsu!" *Pervogo sentabria*, no. 4 (2007), www.rus.1september.ru/article.php?ID=200700401 (accessed 5 May 2011); Iryna Zhylenko, "Homo feriens," *Suchasnist'*, no. 10 (1997): 19.

[37] On Soviet practices of selfhood, see Jochen Hellbeck, *Revolution on my Mind: Writing a Diary under Stalin* (Cambridge, MA: Harvard University Press, 2006), 115–64, and Oleg Kharkhordin, *The Collective and the Individual in Russia: A Study of Practices* (Berkeley: University of California Press, 1999), 231–78.

[38] The KGB unearthed documents on "Culture" in 1965 when they arrested Boris Zeligson, an important figure in the episode and also under investigation at the time for participation in the "Bell" or (*Kolokol*) oppositional group. Arkhiv UFSB SPb, Arkh no: P-51433, tom 14, 195.

they were well placed to spearhead such a post-Stalin cultural offensive: if enlightenment was what the Soviet project needed, who better to provide it than the intellectual elites of the future?

The problem was that culture could only purify the country of the cult if it was itself liberated from Stalin-era restrictions. This made achieving cultural freedom the central aim of the Thaw. By challenging "high-ranking people" in the Soviet system, the young cultural activists believed that they could confront the moral failings of society at their point of origin. For this reason, major cultural controversies covered in the Soviet press, particularly those surrounding specific literary works, constituted defining events of the Thaw, in the capitals and provinces alike. The first such episode occurred when the press attacked literary critics who railed against the "sugar-coating" (*lakirovka*) of unpleasant realities in fictional works, an implicit critique of censorship and writers' self-censorship. A larger *cause célèbre* came in 1956 with Vladimir Dudintsev's *Not by Bread Alone*, a novel depicting the struggle of the amateur inventor Lopatkin to gain acceptance of his superior pipe-casting machine in the face of cruel and corrupt bureaucrats.[39] The novel's plot, and particularly the way it presented the virtuous thinker as a mover of progress, held immediate appeal for students who had struck upon an intelligentsia-centered narrative of the recent Soviet past. The appeal of the book only grew when the Soviet press lambasted Dudintsev for depicting Soviet society in too negative a light. In a phenomenon widespread in Thaw culture, a literary work merged with real-life drama as the novel's story of *intelligent* versus bureaucrat was reenacted in the struggle between Dudintsev and his critics.[40] The party played into this interpretation through its heavy-handed arguments – for instance, that Dudintsev's book represented "freedom of creativity in a bourgeois-anarchic and individualist spirit" – which seemed almost calculated to insult idealistic and socialist Soviet students.[41]

The Dudintsev melodrama brought to the fore the construct of a culture-bearing intelligentsia. Students mobilized in defense of Dudintsev at hastily convened discussions of *Not by Bread Alone* at colleges across the country.

[39] Vladimir Dudintsev, *Not by Bread Alone*, trans. Edith Bone (New York: Dutton, 1957). For an outstanding account of the literary politics of 1956, see M. R. Zezina, *Sovetskaia khudozhestvennaia intelligentsiia i vlast' v 1950-e–60-e gody* (Moscow: Dialog MGU, 1999), 181–203.

[40] On the interconnection between fiction and reality in the affair, see Susanne Schattenberg, "'Democracy' or 'Despotism'? How the Secret Speech was Translated into Everyday Life," in Polly Jones (ed.), *The Dilemmas of De-Stalinization: Negotiating Cultural and Social Change in the Khrushchev Era* (London: Routledge, 2006), 64–79.

[41] This quotation is drawn from materials generated by the Komsomol TsK in preparation for a discussion of ideological problems in higher learning. RGASPI-M f. 1, op. 46, d. 192, l. 103.

Readers' conferences were a commonplace means for what higher education authorities called students' "aesthetic and moral education," but the Dudintsev discussions strayed far from the didactic purpose intended for them. As Denis Kozlov has observed, agitation surrounding the book reproduced a language of vilification that bore some resemblance to the discourse of the Stalin period.[42] Indeed, some students felt that the book was a litmus test for post-Stalin citizenship; referring to the arch villain of *Not by Bread Alone*, a graduate student at Leningrad University argued that "those who do not agree that the novel is truth" were "themselves Drozdovs, referring to the novel's villain." At the same time, the plot of *Not by Bread Alone* and the plight of its author provided students and other sympathetic readers with a parable for the role of Soviet intellectuals in society. At the Leningrad discussion mentioned above, the student Orlovskii gave a speech asserting that Lopatkin and Drozdov were in competition for the allegiance of "the people." The Drozdovs had brought the masses onto their side by demagogically convincing them that the Lopatkins lived "at the expense of others, but Drozdov works selflessly"; in fact, as *Not by Bread Alone* had shown, the reality was exactly the opposite.[43] Whether he wanted to or not, Dudintsev had provided his readers with a powerful allegory for understanding the intelligentsia as the guiding force of Soviet society, one which could compete with the party for the right to represent the people's interests.

Taking the side of Dudintsev rhetorically was also a way to make a statement about oneself. Students who saw the culture-bearing intelligentsia as an answer to the Soviet system's ills were simultaneously imagining themselves as members of this collectivity. This personal aspect of the Thaw found expression in a distinctive literary genre of 1956: the self-produced and independent student cultural publications that arose at Soviet colleges across the country carrying names like "The Literary Front of the Literature Department," "Scandal," "Heresy," and the already mentioned "Culture."[44] The *Literary Bulletin*, a wall newspaper that first appeared in the foyer of the MGU Mechanics and Mathematics Department in early 1956, demonstrated the place of self-fashioning in Thaw cultural activism. The paper reported widely on current events and cultural novelties: an interview with the first cohort of French exchange students in MGU, the

---

[42] Denis Kozlov, "Naming the Social Evil: The Readers of *Novyi mir* and Vladimir Dudintsev's *Not by Bread Alone*, 1956–59 and Beyond," in Jones (ed.), *The Dilemmas of De-Stalinization*, 80–98.

[43] See the student-composed minutes of this November meeting in R. I. Pimenov, *Vospominaniia* (Moscow: informatsionno-ekspertnaia gruppa "Panorama," 1996), 41–45.

[44] This phenomenon has been brought to light by an excellent primary-source volume that traces the origins of samizdat in Leningrad. Dolinin and Ivanov (eds.), *Samizdat*.

work of van Gogh.[45] Despite its seemingly innocuous character, however, the paper immediately led to a test of wills between the students and the department-level party authorities, who tore down each successive issue of the bulletin only to see a new copy the following day bearing the words "if you tear it down it will reappear!"

This tense standoff reflected more than just the party's jealous hold on public space in the university. Although the *Literary Bulletin* never published calls to revolution, it espoused an ideological program that proved unacceptable to departmental authorities, including many faculty members. Above all, the participants in the *Literary Bulletin* were eager – and to party officials, over-eager – supporters of "overcoming the cult of personality." In retrospect, their view of de-Stalinization hardly appears extreme. Like many other young rebels in 1956, the mathematics students saw their cultural initiatives as part of a process by which Soviet socialism would overcome its Stalin-era distortions. Decades later, Mikhail Beletskii recalled that he and his friends saw the paper as support for the "new power" that would "take everything into account" and "construct a fair socialism."[46] The party's increasingly conservative course after the Twentieth Party Congress did not extinguish their faith in the regeneration of socialism from within; when Vadim Iankov, a radical classmate at the department, asserted that the country was "ruled by a gang," his friends engaged in the *Literary Bulletin* responded with shock and dismay.[47] Nevertheless, students' enthusiastic support of the Twentieth Party Congress struck a raw nerve in some faculty members who feared the questions about responsibility for the past which were arising in various formal and informal settings.[48] I. I. Dmitriev, then a young faculty member at the MGU Geography Department, remembers students' questions of him in 1956: "What were you doing [during the Stalin years]? You are a communist and you entered the party at the front, so just who are you (*kto ty takoi*)?" "I am your teacher, I am your educator," Dmitriev answered rhetorically in an interview over forty years later, clearly disturbed by the memory of these encounters.[49]

The *Literary Bulletin*, like many other autonomous student initiatives in 1956, saw culture as the means of pursuing the purification of Soviet

[45] See the comments by Liubarskii in Iu. G. Burtin (ed. and comp.), "Studencheskoe brozhenie v SSSR (konets 1956 g.)," *Voprosy istorii*, 1 (1997): 5.
[46] Interview with Mikhail Beletskii, Kyiv, 2005.   [47] Interview with F. G. Repin, Moscow, 2004.
[48] For discussion of the politics of historical responsibility in the different context of the Gnesin Music Academy in Moscow during de-Stalinization, see Stephen Bittner, *The Many Lives of Khrushchev's Thaw: Experience and Memory in Moscow's Arbat* (Ithaca, NY: Cornell University Press, 2008), 44–47.
[49] Interview with I. I. Dmitriev, Moscow, 2003.

socialism. A cultural reading of de-Stalinization was evident in Mikhail Beletskii's article in the *Literary Bulletin* on Mark Shcheglov, a young literary critic who graduated from MGU in 1953 and died of tuberculosis of the bones three years later. Shcheglov's articles in the literary journal *Novyi mir* became a sensation among young readers because of what his classmate at MGU Vladimir Lakshin called their "genuinely live words, open mockery of routine and clichés, and youthful passion and irony."[50] To Beletskii, Shcheglov represented the martyrdom under Stalin of true intellectuals, those who defended "the right of a person to courageous thoughts, words, and actions."[51] However, Beletskii's article ended on a decidedly optimistic note when it seemed to prophesy a liberated future society – characteristically, one described in essentially cultural terms as a place where the literary criticism sections of Soviet journals would be "imbued with living thought, thought that ignites people, prevents them from sleeping at night, and that forces blood to flow more swiftly in their veins."[52] Clearly, this was an intelligentsia-centered historical narrative, one in which intellectuals struggling for creative freedom would spark a moral revival of Soviet society as a whole.

The veneration of Shcheglov hints at the crucial place the notion of personality occupied in student activism during the period. As Elena Zubkova has argued, a distinctive feature of campus politics after the Twentieth Party Congress was the emergence of new student leaders, "bright personalities" who gained influence through their "character" rather than political connections.[53] This statement does not situate "character" in its proper social framework. While many student activists in the period lacked Komsomol positions as Zubkova suggests, they often had well-established "personalities" nonetheless – ones that rested on claims to cultural and intellectual distinction.[54] The principal figures in the *Literary Bulletin* and similar groups were well connected in the universities through academic and cultural activities, and they often hailed from "intelligentsia

---

[50] Lakshin appeared in Chapter 1 as a performer of a *kapustnik*. Vladimir Lakshin, "Mark Shcheglov – 'vechnyi iunosha,'" in *Golosa i litsa* (Moscow: Geleos, 2004), 21.

[51] This depiction seems to be a mythologizing one: Shcheglov's posthumously published student diaries suggest that he saw himself as a contented Soviet *intelligent* rather than as a martyr. Mark Shcheglov et al., *Studencheskie tetradi* (Moscow Izdatel'stvo "Sovetskaia Rossiia," 1973), 11–13.

[52] Mikhail Beletskii kindly provided me with a retyped copy of his piece "Mark Shcheglov."

[53] See Zubkova cited in Ia. N. Zasurskii (ed.), *Polveka na Mokhovoi (1947–1997)* (Moscow: Moskovskii gos. universitet im. M. V. Lomonosova, Fakul'tet zhurnalistiki, 1997), 100.

[54] Indeed, the Russian word *lichnost'* (translated as either "personality" or "individual") refers to the individual as a carrier of universal values. Kharkhordin, *The Collective and the Individual in Russia*, 184–90.

backgrounds." Kronid Liubarskii, a founder of the *Literary Bulletin*, could trace his roots to the Russian nobility through his mother; while a student, he circulated copies of poems by Lev Gumilev, Federico García Lorca, and Walt Whitman among his friends.[55] During the post-Stalinist confusion, such cultural aficionados proved well-positioned to become leaders of the nascent movement for cultural revival, in the process showing classmates the path to becoming what one participant in the affair called a "creative person" who could "intervene in what is happening in life."[56]

The students' intelligentsia self-fashioning had clear origins in the state-sanctioned cultural project that was so widely expressed in the postwar universities. After all, if the Soviet intelligentsia was to bring civilized values to the people, its individual members had a duty to become embodiments of truthfulness and moral transparency. However, the students' publication expressed this motif, in itself innocuous, in a way which some faculty members perceived as an implicit challenge. At a party meeting, mathematics professor K. A. Kulikov related with horror a conversation he had with the participants of the *Literary Bulletin*: "What a high opinion of themselves they have! They look at us as backward people!"[57] Indeed, many professors at MGU and at other institutions viewed student cultural activism with a dismissive attitude, as if to assert their own mastery over the cultural sphere. For instance, the Leningrad University philology professor V. Ia. Propp told his students that he did not plan to attend the dispute on *Not by Bread Alone* (mentioned above) on the grounds that the book had little aesthetic value.[58]

Although it created divisions among faculty and students in MGU, the *Literary Bulletin* was ultimately uprooted by forces far beyond the universities. In the course of the year, the students managed to continue releasing the paper as university Komsomol activists equivocated, seeking to reason with them and resisting pressure from above to act more resolutely – an uneasy situation that highlighted how the repressive policy of the regime remained in flux. The situation changed radically in November in the context of unrest in the Eastern bloc and especially the Hungarian Revolution. In December, the TsK instructed local party organizations to stop the "sallies of anti-Soviet hostile elements," putting into motion a campaign of political repression across the country that was wider in scope

---

[55] Kronid Liubarskii, *"Kronid": izbrannye stat'i K. Liubarskogo* (Moscow: Rossiiskii gos. gumanitarnyi universitet, 2001), 29.
[56] TsMAM f. 1609, op. 2, d. 416, l. 56.   [57] TsAOPIM f. 478, op. 3, d. 38, l. 67.
[58] See the recollections of Liudmila Iezuitova in L. Ia. Lur'e and Irina Maliarova (eds.), *1956 god: seredina veka* (St. Petersburg: Neva, 2007), 408.

than anything that would follow in Soviet history.[59] The Presidium explicitly identified youth as a target of the repressive campaign, which was pursued through both the KGB and the party and its subordinate institutions. Contrary to customary assumptions, neither students nor educated citizens formed the main group of victims of this campaign.[60] While the numbers are unclear, perhaps fewer than 100 students were arrested by the KGB and a similar number probably applies to students expelled from party and Komsomol organizations (although many more students were surely given various warnings and signals through both these different repressive channels).[61] Despite its selective character, however, the repressive campaign at the end of 1956 transformed the political situation in the universities, as previously common ideological infractions came to carry far graver penalties.

The tipping point for the *Literary Bulletin* was its fourth issue that materialized on 9 November, just five days after the Soviets' second invasion of Budapest. Marking the thirty-ninth anniversary of the October Revolution, the paper contained a symbol that gave the party officials pause: "a chained worker stands against the background of a red ray and reaches towards a bell."[62] Fanning the flames, the contributor Eduard Stotskii published a synopsis of John Reed's *Ten Days that Shook the World* sprinkled with quotations from it praising Trotskii, Zinoviev, and Kamenev as leaders of the revolution (all were still designated as enemies of the people by the Soviet state).[63] Stotskii was no Trotskyite. In all likelihood, he flirted with ideological heresy to test the limits of the party's commitment to de-Stalinization and to make a claim to intellectual freedom. The authorities took the bait: the Mechanics and Mathematics Department Party Bureau accused the bulletin of "propagandizing the enemies of the working class Trotskii and Zinoviev."[64]

---

[59] See A. A. Fursenko et al. (eds.), *Prezidium TsK KPSS 1954–1964, Tom 1: Chernovye protokol'nye zapisi zasedanii. Stenogrammy* (Moscow: ROSSPEN, 2004), 202, 979–80.

[60] For the now disproven view that intelligentsia and students were the primary victims of state repression in the period, see Zubok, *Zhivago's Children*, 81.

[61] The best reconstruction of the campaign shows that in 1957, the main year of repression, some 2,121 people were convicted of counter-revolutionary crimes as defined by article 58 of the RSFSR Criminal Code. Of these, only 4.6 percent (almost 100 people) were "students" (*uchashchiesia*), a category that included pupils of secondary schools and factory schools as well as students of higher education institutions. See Papovian, "Primenenie stat'i 58–10," in Ereminaia and Zhemkova (eds.), *Korni travy*, 85. For a sense of the scope of Komsomol repressions, see RGASPI-M f. 1, op. 46, d. 327, ll. 172–73. On the division between KGB and party-Komsomol in the repression in higher education, see Kuzovkin, "Partiino-komsomol'skie presledovaniia."

[62] TsAOPIM f. 4, op. 113, d. 41, l. 11.

[63] Notably, Stotskii had read Reed in the "special storage division" (*spetskhran*) library stacks at MGU, access to which became easier during de-Stalinization. Ibid., f. 478, op. 3, d. 38, l. 7.

[64] Ibid., l. 8.

Perhaps caving in to party pressure, the dean of the department, prominent mathematician A. N. Kolmogorov, issued an order for the expulsion of three of the *Literary Bulletin*'s ringleaders (Beletskii, Stotskii, and Mikhail Vainshtein). This set the stage for an emotionally charged Komsomol meeting – speeches were constantly punctured with jeers and foot stomping – which broke all precedents by voting against the expulsion of the three students.[65] Despite its outcome, however, the meeting also demonstrated the divisiveness of the *Literary Bulletin* and other student groups like it for students and faculty in 1956. Kolmogorov, who looked "simply unwell" at the meeting according to one member of the audience, did not embrace the party's charges of subversion but did criticize the students' overall attitude in a way that might well have resonated among some parts of the department.[66] By referencing Trotskii, Kolmogorov asserted, Stotskii was guilty of the egotistical attitude that "now everything is allowed, I want to show off."[67] The students' self-importance was also criticized by Iulii Poliusuk, a member of the bulletin's editorial board. Evidently seeking to calm the agitated assembly, Poliusuk gave a telling characterization of the mood of one part of the Komsomol gathering: they viewed the three students as "martyrs," which he characterized as "some sort of intelligentsia nonsense."[68] The comment demonstrated an important dynamic of student politics in 1956: just as during the campaigns under late Stalinism discussed in Chapters 3 and 4, party-state repression in the universities often burnished the reputation of the victims by giving them moral stature. At the same time, by labeling (however honestly) the furor over the *Literary Bulletin* as "intelligentsia nonsense," Poliusuk cast light on the large part of the student body, which had little sympathy for the students in question. The agenda of spearheading de-Stalinization through culture inspired some students but smacked of cultural elitism to others.

Marxist revisionism reborn

The *Literary Bulletin* and other student cultural endeavors like it steered clear of programmatic demands, instead seeing in self-directed cultural activities a way to humanize the Soviet order. The prevalence of morally charged culture-building, however, does not mean that the ideas of

[65] TsAOPIM f. 478, op. 3, d. 38, l. 8; RGANI f. 4, op. 16, d. 1098, ll. 44–47, published in Burtin (ed. and comp.), "Studencheskoe brozhenie," 10.
[66] Il'ia Ioslovich, "Universitet i iashchik," *Den' i noch'*, no. 3 (2010), "Megalit: Evraziiskii zhurnal'nyi portal," www.promegalit.ru/publics.php?id=1638 (accessed 23 September 2012).
[67] TsMAM f. 1609, op. 2, d. 416, l. 8.   [68] In Russian, *intelligentnaia erunda*. Ibid., l. 13.

Marxism-Leninism played a marginal role in campus unrest. A wide range of young thinkers, usually dubbed "revisionists," sought to articulate a Marxist vision of democratic socialism.[69] Although a pejorative term, revisionism nonetheless helps to delineate a strain of doctrinaire Marxist dissent that played an important role during de-Stalinization in the universities and beyond. Revisionist thinkers held as sacrosanct the revolutionary goals of the October Revolution, yet interpreted them in ways that challenged the Stalin and post-Stalin order fundamentally. A fitting case study for capturing revisionism's origins and implications is Mikhail Molostvov, a Leningrad University philosophy student who formed an underground circle that would eventually succumb to the party-state's campaign against perceived anti-Soviet activities.

Molostvov wrote a tract called *Status Quo* that captured revisionism's blend of revolutionary romanticism and sweeping political critique. It attacked Stalinism but also the post-Stalin leadership in categorical terms. Khrushchev had provided an inadequate view of Stalin's rule, Molostvov argued. Whereas the secret speech explained the brutality of Stalin's dictatorship as a result of the cult of personality, Molostvov reversed the relationship. In fact, worship of the leader was merely one symptom of an entrenched system of political exploitation, an "artificial division of society into rulers and ruled without a class base," that could be preserved only through violence.[70] Against this backdrop, the post-Stalin leadership's reforms to date represented only "playing at democracy," offering society limited concessions that the deleterious economic effects of Stalinism had made necessary in any case. As power still belonged to a monopolistic bureaucracy that ruled in its own interests, Molostvov asserted, Stalinism and post-Stalinism were essentially the same.[71]

Molostvov's pessimistic view of Soviet history sat uncomfortably with an idealized vision of Leninism as both as a golden age and a roadmap to the correct revolutionary path. If many student activists of the period looked to cultural figures like Dudinstev or Shcheglov as model *intelligenty*, revisionists revered Lenin as revolutionary theorist, clearly an intellectual of a

---

[69] Here culture-building and revisionism should be seen as ideal types, insofar as many students straddled both kinds of thinking. An overview of revisionisms during the Cold War is Karl Reyman and Herman Singer, "The Origins and Significance of East European Revisionism," in Leopold Labedz (ed.), *Revisionism: Essays on the History of Marxist Ideas* (Plainview, NY: Books for Libraries Press, 1974), 215–22.

[70] Molostvov and his companions N. D. Solokhin, L. Ia. Garanin, and E. A. Kozlov were convicted in October 1958 on charges of counter-revolutionary agitation and propaganda. Arkhiv UFSB SPb, arkh no: P-66655, tom 4, 75–76.

[71] Ibid., tom 4, 73, 5.

different ilk. Like many other revisionists, Molostvov drew many of his ideas from Lenin's *State and Revolution*, particularly the work's description of a communist order in which workers would elect and recall officials and take an active role in administration while bureaucrats would be paid no more than qualified workers.[72] Similarly, *Status Quo* called for a return of proletarian democracy (though notably *not* "illusory" bourgeois democracy), which meant a freeing of the ossified Soviets and the party itself from hierarchical control and "a countrywide repentance by the accomplices of Stalin and a countrywide rehabilitation of the victims of Stalinist terror" – something, perhaps, like a Soviet truth and reconciliation commission. Molostvov's plans for societal and economic organization were vaguer but no less sweeping: a sharp curtailment of all social privileges accruing to the ruling party and workers' control over production on the model of Yugoslavian and Polish workers' Soviets.[73] In a sense, then, Molostvov's revisionism paralleled cultural activism in providing an optimistic prognosis for the Soviet project after Stalin: history would return to its proper Leninist course, a conclusion that could be confirmed scientifically by applying Marxist analysis to current conditions.

Molostvov's idealization of Leninist communism did not detract from his trenchant criticism of Soviet political realities. Yet his attack on current Soviet rulers in the name of Leninism posed a paradox faced by all communist oppositionists of the period. If Lenin's rule had represented the true course of the Revolution, why had history gone so far off course with Stalin? Explaining such a major historical wrong turn without abandoning Marxism's historical logic was a tall order, but the credibility of any project endorsing the Soviet revolutionary narrative depended on it. Molostvov's treatment of revolutionary history responded to this predicament with considerable sophistication, at least given the historical context in which it was written. After the October Revolution, he argued, the continued existence of class interests within the country as well as capitalist hostility from without required the young revolutionary state to develop a strong administrative apparatus and to enforce party unity. This goal, however, could be achieved in two ways: either through top-down control and iron discipline or through a genuinely "Leninist path" of control from below and reliance on the working class. After Lenin's death, the party leaders drifted spontaneously toward the first path because it seemed the easier one, thereby concentrating political power and setting the stage for Stalin's seizure of power.[74] Molostvov's account of Bolshevism might seem unsatisfactory to current-day historians.

[72] Ibid., tom 1, 84–85ob.   [73] Ibid., tom 4, 84, 69.   [74] Ibid., 63–64.

Nevertheless, its attempt at rigorous and dispassionate Marxist historical analysis – common, in varying degrees, to other revisionist groups in the period – distinguished it from the mainstream of student anti-Stalinists who tended to view history in morally and emotionally charged terms.

This kind of thinking appealed to a specific subset of the student body. Molostvov's own biography shows how revisionist thinking emerged from distinct personal and collegiate experiences. Like the *Literary Bulletin* leaders, he hailed from an old intellectual family – his parents were actors and his father descended from the Russian nobility – and he grew up with this social group's reverent attitude toward books. As Molostvov claimed at his trial, classic works in the Russian revolutionary tradition had "formed [his] self" and "seemed to be written from his soul."[75] Study at the Leningrad University Philosophy Department leavened this bookish revolutionary engagement with academic rigor. Like Molostvov, many revisionists majored in social sciences such as history and philosophy, disciplines that were dominated by Marxist methodology.[76] Study in these institutions seemed to empower students within the universities and the Soviet project as a whole, in some sense echoing the physics students discussed in Chapter 4. The party had entrusted philosophers and historians to study subjects of the highest political sensitivity, and their institutions positioned them to pursue party careers should they choose to do so. Not surprisingly, many of the revisionists also had extensive experience in party-political life: two members of the group were members of the departmental Komsomol Bureau, while Molostvov himself headed the department's student scientific society.[77] As with cultural leaders in the student body, student revisionists were well placed to apply their intellectual abilities and interests to political issues.

The universities also enabled the critical thrust of Molostvov's party intellectualism. University history and philosophy departments constituted an intellectual environment that was surprisingly rich given their function of training ideological workers.[78] Some of their professors approached

---

[75] He mentioned Nikolai Chernyshevskii's *What is to be Done?*, Anton Makarenko's *Flags on the Towers*, and Aleksandr Herzen's *Life and Thoughts*. Ibid., 100–103.

[76] In 1956, these included the "Molostvov Group" (centered on the LGU Philosophy Department), the "Trofimov Group" (whose leader, Viktor Trofimov studied at the Herzen Leningrad Pedagogical Institute History Department), and the "Krasnopevtsev Group" (centered on the MGU History Department). On all of these groups, see S. D. Rozhdestvenskii, "Materialy istorii samodeiatel'nykh ob'edinenii v SSSR posle 1945 goda," *Pamiat': istoricheskii sbornik*, 5 (1981): 226–86.

[77] Arkhiv UFSB SPb, arkh no: P-66655, tom 1, 216.

[78] This argument does not apply to the social science sub-departments, which taught a separate part of the curriculum in all colleges and were often staffed by former party activists with poor academic credentials. RGASPI-M f. 1, op. 46, d. 192, ll. 47–48.

Marxism as a body of thought subject to critical evaluation rather than as state-sanctified dogma. In philosophy departments, moreover, approved textbooks were lacking, meaning that students learned from lecturers and their own reading of primary sources.[79] Regardless of its causes, the degree of academic integrity in the ideological fields was surprising: Molostvov wrote a senior research paper on Hegel's *Phenomenology of Spirit* with references to György Lukács' *The Young Hegel*, for which he received a top grade (although his university character reference would include the phrase "disposed toward revisionism").[80] In this environment, some students came to believe that they were interpreters of the regime's ideology rather than merely its future purveyors, an intellectual framework they quickly applied to make sense of the haphazard rejection of Stalin-era policies by the post-Stalin leadership. In this sense, the revisionists, like the cultural activists, found in the intellectual process itself an answer to the ideological dislocation of the period.

Going to the brink: the Hungarian Revolution

Molostvov's self-fashioning as a party theorist informed his political actions during de-Stalinization. Nikolai Solokhin, a friend and discussion partner of Molostvov, wrote a piece in his diary that he called "the Manifesto of the Working Class." It contained a telling political slogan: "not against the party, but for it, after making it our own."[81] This was more than a rhetorical flourish. Molostvov and his companions saw themselves as ideological insiders with a privileged vantage point on Soviet socialism. In this spirit, *Status Quo* takes the form of a polemic against "party philistines," uneducated apparatchiks whose knowledge of Marx, Engels, and Lenin was limited to isolated quotations in Stalin's *Short Course*. The students' stance of internal Bolshevik critique accounted for some surprising and contradictory ideas. Molostvov accepted the progressive character of Stalinist industrialization and collectivization, despite acknowledging their vast and largely unnecessary social and economic costs. And while calling for democratization, Molostvov thought it had to serve the interests of the party rather than having value in its own right: "freedom of speech and print and

---

[79] See Aleksandr Piatigorskii and Vadim Sadovskii, "Kak my izuchali filosofiu: Moskovskii universitet, 50-e gody," *Svobodnaia mysl'*, 2 (1993): 42–54.

[80] M. M. Molostvov, "Na starosti ia snova zhivu," *Kuranty*, no. 174, 23 November 1995: 1 and "Revizionizm – 58 (iz vospominanii)," in N. G. Okhotin et al. (eds.), *Zven'ia: istoricheskii al'manakh*, vol. 1 (Moscow: Progress, 1991), 579–81.

[81] Arkhiv UFSB SPb, arkh no: P-66655, tom 1, 174.

the right to vote are necessary instruments of the dictatorship of the proletariat, no less important than the militia and the corrective labor camp," he opined.[82] In addition to being a fervent Marxist, Molostvov was a Soviet patriot who placed the interests of the Communist Party – at least how he saw them – front and center.

Molostvov's attachment to the Soviet system helps to explain why he and his companions were slow to turn from underground discussion to oppositional activity. The critical turning point for Molostvov and nascent student protests more generally was unrest elsewhere in the Eastern bloc in the fall of 1956, namely the peaceful transfer of power in Poland and the bloody suppression of mass revolution in Hungary. Frustrated with the uneven course of the Soviet party leadership in the course of the year, some student radicals came to look to Eastern Europe as a model for de-Stalinization in the USSR. On the whole, the Soviet suppression of revolution in Hungary put a damper on such cross-bloc influences, as students and educated citizens more generally rallied to the flag under the impression of press stories accusing the rebels of fascist ties and terrorist methods. A tiny fraction of the Soviet student body, however, viewed rebellions in Eastern Europe favorably, and they generally held revisionist views. For Molostvov and some others, contact with exchange students from the people's democracies might have helped account for their favorable views of the Hungarian Revolution.[83] More important in drawing revisionists to protest in the Soviet near abroad was their deep attachment to revolution. As Molostvov explained years later, he had been deeply impressed that "young people with moods like ours appeared in the streets and talked about freedom."[84] In any case, it was against the backdrop of rising tensions in Eastern Europe in October that Molostvov took to public political protest for the first time. At a heavily attended university Komsomol Conference in October, Molostvov gave a speech calling for the Soviet press to tell the truth about events in Poland and Hungary and pronouncing that "achieving full

---

[82] These comments are from *Status Quo*. Ibid., tom 4, 70 ("party philistines," labor camps), 76 (industrialization).

[83] See the account of his friendship with a Hungarian student in the interrogation of E. A. Dmitriev, ibid., tom 2, 120. For discussion of students from the people's democracies in Soviet higher learning as well as Soviet student politics in 1956, see Patryk Babiracki, "Imperial Heresies: Polish Students in the Soviet Union, 1948–1957," *Ab Imperio*, 4 (2007), 199–236; Benjamin Tromly, "Brother or Other? East European Students in Soviet Higher Education Establishments, 1948–1956," forthcoming in *European History Quarterly*.

[84] "Borot'sa i stradat: eto ne odno i to zhe (interviu s narodnym deputatom RSFSR Mikhailom Molostvovym")," text of unidentified radio interview dated 23 October 1990, M. M. Molostvov Papers, NITs "Memorial" SPb: 3.

openness (*glasnost'*) in all matters" was necessary in the struggle against the cult of personality.[85]

Molostvov's political agenda, however, was more tentative than this speech would suggest. He curtailed his provocative speech-making after receiving threats from university party officials (he would graduate on schedule but received a job posting to an agricultural institute in Omsk instead of gaining entry to graduate school as he had hoped).[86] More than fear alone, though, Molostvov's reluctance to engage in full-fledged dissent reflected his paradoxical position as a loyal opponent of the regime. In fact, despite his harsh critique of the current party leadership, Molostvov harbored a hope that it would start to listen to its sympathetic critics – that is, to revisionists like him. This naïve hope was more logical than it seems. Molostvov believed that the party's problems should be addressed from within and, insofar as the revolution demanded it, ultimately would be. And as a good Marxist-Leninist, he also believed in the possibility of understanding history scientifically, and no doubt saw his own writings in this way. In other words, the regime would eventually turn to building true Leninism, and Molostvov would find a role in the process. This helps to explain Molostvov's political calculations: apart from open agitation in Komsomol, the only strategy for dissent that he seemed to entertain was to send a manifesto to the party TsK outlining his ideas, which might "become known to a large circle of people," as he explained to KGB interrogators.[87] Molostvov expressed his hopes for a political career more provocatively while parting with his friends in 1957 to take up work in Omsk: "We will meet either in jail or in the government."[88]

Unsurprisingly, the former occurred. When Molostvov and his companions arrived in Leningrad to renew their philosophical discussions – an endeavor they semi-facetiously called a "congress of the Philosophizing Brotherhood" – they were promptly arrested by the well-informed KGB. The Molostvov group exemplified the dilemmas that plagued other student groups which supported de-Stalinization on the basis of Marxist-Leninist doctrine. To be sure, not all the revisionists were as reluctant to act in opposition as Molostvov and his comrades; other young intellectuals with revisionist ideas formed underground parties with programs and distributed leaflets, efforts no less bold for being quickly uncovered by the KGB.

---

[85] Molostvov, "Revizionizm – 58," 584.   [86] Arkhiv UFSB SPb, arkh no: P-66655, tom 1, 73–75.
[87] Ibid., 97.
[88] An interview with Molostvov in A. Koreniuk, "Dissident, perezhivshii dve perestroiki," unidentified article, n.d., M. M. Molostvov Papers, NIITs "Memorial" SPb.

Nevertheless, Molostvov was representative of revisionism's irresoluteness, its almost instinctive hope that the current political regime would make strides toward restoring their idealized picture of the Leninist heritage.[89] Another factor that hobbled the revisionist circles was their propensity toward internal division. While often forming around a single figure who had penned a theoretical tract like *Status Quo*, revisionist circles tended to produce principled disagreement about almost everything save the applicability of Marxism to history. In part, this was because the kind of people interested in revisionism – professional Marxism specialists, Youth League activists – were rarely willing to subordinate themselves to a leader. For instance, Molostvov's friends immediately rejected *Status Quo* for interpreting Stalin's rule too subjectively and for demanding democratization instead of focusing on immediate improvement in Soviet living standards.[90] A personal-doctrinal dispute with Solokhin became so heated that the two friends broke off all communication for a few weeks.[91]

Molostvov's group was also typical in its marginal influence on university opinion as a whole. Well connected in Komsomol circles, Molostvov and his friends enjoyed the benevolent tolerance of their classmates; when a classmate attacked Molostvov and his friends for revisionist sins in the department's wall newspaper, the Komsomol organization rose to his defense. Yet the revisionist circles remained a fringe phenomenon in the universities. The vast majority of students would have rejected the radical implications of *Status Quo*. Moreover, revisionists tended to limit their discussions to small social circles on purpose, as they looked askance at peers who were unable or unwilling to engage in serious Marxist analysis. During a KGB interrogation Molostvov explained that he had sought to prevent his group's discussions from reaching a broader public; he "did not want to become like those philistines who get together and say all sorts of rumors about the political system in the USSR, about members of the Soviet government."[92] This political-intellectual elitism found reinforcement in the male ethos that the revisionists often adopted. The "Krasnopevtsev Group" at MGU, for instance, decided not to open discussions with a female classmate because she was "too feminine."[93] Ambivalent about the regime they were opposing, internally divided and largely isolated

[89] Pimenov, "Odin politicheskii protsess," 65–69; Rozhdestvenskii, "Materialy istorii."
[90] Arkhiv UFSB SPb, arkh no: P-66655, tom 1, 99ob–100. On divisions in other revisionist groups, see V. V. Iofe, *Granitsy smysla: stat'i, vystupleniia, esse* (St. Petersburg: Memorial, 2002), 176–86; Vladimir Men'shikov, "Mysli po povodu . . ." *Karta*, no. 17–18 (1997): 74.
[91] Arkhiv UFSB SPb, arkh no: P-66655, tom 1, 103ob–104.   [92] Ibid., 65.
[93] Interview with G. S. Tolmacheva, Moscow, 2004.

from their peers, the revisionists were nevertheless viewed as a serious political threat by the Communist Party. The reason was clear enough: for a post-Stalin leadership seeking to revive the party idealism, a challenge from a Leninist perspective – especially one coming from specialists in ideological matters being carefully groomed by the state – appeared especially dangerous.

The "unifying concern" of the cultural Thaw, Nancy Condee writes, was "studied deviance, a self-conscious and stylized set of codes that were ostensibly concerned with norm and deviance but were equally eloquent in their anxiety about the containment of conflict."[94] Often lionized for its uncompromising character, student protest in 1956 conforms to this picture of oppositionists concerned about the implications of their critical thoughts and ideas. As Condee argues, this was because intellectuals associating themselves with the Thaw had considerable sympathy toward the reformist Khrushchev regime. In a broader sense, however, participants in the Thaw employed "a self-conscious and stylized set of codes" because they were seeking to create a specific kind of "imagined community," that of an intelligentsia that would remedy Soviet society through its ideas and the moral vision that was assumed to come with them. Some reform-minded students were more concerned with narrowly cultural activities, while others embraced the revisionist project of finding a Marxist answer to the post-Stalin situation. In both cases, being a part of the student Thaw meant accepting a set of assumptions: that knowledge was progressive, that ignorance had been at the root of the calamities of the Stalin era, and that those who wielded advanced knowledge had a special duty to improve society by correcting this deficiency.

As explosive as these ideas proved in the universities, they need to be understood in the context of longstanding patterns of Soviet intellectual life and discourse more broadly. As Jochen Hellbeck has argued on the basis of diaries from the 1930s, Soviet rule "prodded individuals to consciously identify with the revolution" and thereby to "comprehend themselves as active participants in the drama of history," a mode of revolutionary selfhood that demanded constant efforts at self-improvement.[95] The students examined in this chapter provide an interesting contrast to Hellbeck's diary writers. Students active in the independent politics of 1956, in their vast

[94] Nancy Condee, "Cultural Codes of the Thaw," in William Taubman et al. (eds.), *Nikita Khrushchev* (New Haven, CT: Yale University Press, 2000), 168.

[95] Hellbeck, *Revolution on my Mind*, 6; Igal Halfin, *From Darkness to Light: Class, Consciousness, and Salvation in Revolutionary Russia* (University of Pittsburgh Press, 2000).

majority, shared the view that they were agents in the building of communism, even if some thought in Marxist-Leninist categories more systematically than others. However, their relationships to "ideology" differed sharply from the eschatological vision which Hellbeck and others have described for the interwar period in three important respects. First, elaborating on Khrushchev's narrative, students of the 1950s understood revolutionary history as a circuitous route, one that passed from a Leninist golden age to a Stalinist perversion and then back again. Second, they saw revolutionary history as a process in which an intelligentsia played a decisive role. Learning and culture – whether Beletskii's embrace of cultural expression or Molostvov's revising of Soviet ideology – provided the key to moving history forward past the "cult of personality." In other words, the students understood themselves in terms of historical development and "self-transformation," but the content of these terms had shifted.

A third difference from the interwar period was the importance of immediate social context for revolutionary thinking. In establishing intelligentsia as a collective entity on which to hang their hopes – and with which to form their own identities – students were working with material close at hand. Student rebels thought of themselves in universal terms as carriers of culture or articulators of a cleansed Marxism-Leninism; in both scenarios, they were building on ideas and notions of the intellectual that they encountered in everyday life in the universities. Indeed, student activism emerged from activities common to postwar students as a whole. Molostvov's *Status Quo* originated in curricular study and belonged in style and tone to the oeuvre of a professional Soviet philosopher.[96] Cultural experimentation, even when pursued by mathematicians in the *Literary Bulletin*, also reflected everyday collegiate life in its reworking of the cultural activities whose value had always lain in their connection to the Soviet civilizing process.

The attempt to constitute a de-Stalinizing intelligentsia, and the "studied deviance" it entailed, also produced widespread discord in the universities. The brandishing of intelligentsia "codes" struck many students and professors as unconvincing and even presumptuous; by presenting the struggle against Stalinism as the true mark of the intelligentsia, the Thaw activists were implicitly challenging the claims of more apolitical people to belong to it. Just as importantly, even student supporters of the Thaw found themselves confused about the means necessary to pursue it. In confronting post-Stalinism, student rebels had embraced two modes of self-understanding

[96] On this point, see V. Ioffe's introductory remarks in Molostvov, "Revizionizm – 58," 578.

that seemed to be ideological *terra firma*: Soviet culture-building and the study of Marxism-Leninism. However, their efforts were ideologically ambivalent, as they involved grafting familiar modes of intelligentsia behavior and belonging onto an oppositional political agenda. And while languages of cultural and socialist revival predominated among student supporters of de-Stalinization, strains of future cacophony could already be heard in the rare student protestor who rejected Marxism altogether for the sake of alternative commitments such as Russian populism or an idealized vision of the United States.[97] Perhaps the most serious challenge to the students' Thaw, however, was the fact that their vision of the Soviet future was limited to an insular university milieu and remained marginalized in the wider Soviet order. Meanwhile, the Khrushchev leadership was itself striving to revive communist idealism and had every intention of dictating what form it should take.

---

[97] An example of the first commitment was the Leningrad mathematician Revol't Pimenov. See Benjamin Tromly, "Intelligentsia Self-Fashioning in the Postwar Soviet Union: Revol't Pimenov's Political Struggle, 1949–1957," *Kritika*, 13 (2012): 151–76. For student pro-Americanism, see GARF f. 8131, op. 31, d. 78607, ll. 2–9.

PART III

Revolutionary dreaming and intelligentsia divisions, 1957–1964

CHAPTER 6

Back to the future
Populist social engineering under Khrushchev

Nikita Khrushchev attended the graduation ceremony of the MGU Physics Department in 1959. The prestige of physics could not be higher; the first artificial Earth satellite had been launched into orbit a little over a year before, an accomplishment the Soviet regime hailed as a sign of its superiority in science. But if the graduates hoped to bask in the praise of the first secretary they were in for a surprise. Launching into one of his customary tirades, Khrushchev warned the graduates of the dangers of social elitism. Recalling a speaker before him who predicted that the graduates would take part in interplanetary flights, Khrushchev criticized what he saw as his implicit assumption: that physicists' creative work made them "distinct from earthly and mortal people." Rather than seeking individual distinction, the graduates should remember than any labor useful to society was "worthy of praise and respect"; in the end, not only scientists but even street cleaners were to be thanked for producing "our famous rockets," he added. Humility and respect for simple toilers was necessary if university graduates wished to become worthy members of "our great collective, our Soviet people."[1]

Khrushchev's call for modesty among MGU graduates belonged to a broader shift in party policies towards students and educated society as a whole in the late 1950s. When the dust had settled after the crisis of 1956, the Khrushchev leadership curtailed the campaign to combat anti-Soviet moods in Soviet society and secured his hold on power by out-maneuvering hard-liners in the Presidium (dubbed an "anti-party group") in May 1957. Freed from internal constraints and buoyed by the country's brisk economic

[1] "'Chelovek, okonchivshii universitet s otlichiem, v zhizni mozhet etogo otlichiia ne poluchit': Vystuplenie N. S. Khrushcheva na vypuske fizicheskogo fakul'teta Moskovskogo gosudarstvennogo universiteta imeni M. V. Lomonosova 20 ianvaria 1959 g.," *Istochnik*, 6 (2003): 97–101. A few edited lines of the speech were made known to the broader university community in "Rabotaite goriacho, s entusiazmom!" *Moskovskii universitet*, 22 January 1959: 1.

expansion, Khrushchev initiated a period of widespread reforms of Soviet institutions, all pursued under the quixotic objective of building communism in quick order. A central part of Khrushchev's ideological agenda was addressing what he saw as a malignancy in Soviet society: the Stalin-era intelligentsia had become self-serving and distant from society as a whole, and it used its stranglehold on the education system for this purpose. Moreover, a new party consensus linked the dominance of the privileged offspring of the intelligentsia in the colleges to social and political ills such as a widespread disrespect for labor in Soviet society and the "anti-Soviet moods" of educated citizens in 1956.

Khrushchev's rebuke to the ambitious physics graduates summarized the narrative: the students had undertaken flights of (cosmic) egoism and would have to be reformed by re-immersion in the people and its values. The path to rehabilitation was physical labor, which ensured "the harmonious development of the individual," the synchronization of the interests of the individual and the collective, and therefore the health of society as a whole.[2] Khrushchev unleashed two major campaigns in higher learning that sought to create a more socially rooted and service-minded intelligentsia. An overhaul of admissions aimed to fill the colleges with people with direct labor experience who, it was assumed, would be more willing to serve the party-state unquestioningly. Also, in the same years, the party undertook a campaign to direct students to Komsomol-sponsored labor projects designed to close the gap between the life of the mind and the world of work, the prestige of science and the character-building of simple toil.

All this was in the spirit of the times: "reforging" and "reeducation" were watchwords in a period when the party-state sought to mold minds, habits, and everyday life in preparation for communism.[3] At the same time, the new campaign flew in the face of the practices and norms of postwar higher learning and the universities in particular. As discussed in Chapter 2, universities had come to occupy a firm place in postwar Soviet life as strategic training centers, cherished national symbols, and a basis for social prestige among the educated middle strata in the Soviet population. Indeed, Khrushchev was showing the scope of his utopianism by asking Soviet physics graduates not to be proud of their knowledge and future occupations.

---

[2] See Khrushchev's comments to the 1963 TsK plenum on ideological questions in RGANI f. 2, op. 1, d. 335, ll. 8–25.
[3] See Miriam Dobson, *Khrushchev's Cold Summer: Gulag Returnees, Crime, and the Fate of Reform after Stalin* (Ithaca, NY: Cornell University Press, 2009) and Susan Reid, "Cold War in the Kitchen: Gender and De-Stalinization of Consumer Taste in the Soviet Union under Khrushchev," *Slavic Review*, 61 (2002): 215–17.

Accordingly, the offensive in the universities, like Khrushchev's initiatives in other areas, raised difficult questions about higher education, intelligentsia, and society for a number of different social or institutional constituencies: students (and their parents), professors, and, in a different way, Soviet political leaders themselves. Could practices and values from other parts of Soviet life be grafted onto higher education? Would demands to perform physical labor energize university communities or disrupt them? These questions were only complicated by their historical resonances. As Khrushchev understood it, the path to the future lay in reviving past ideas and practices; the attempt to repeople the intelligentsia with toilers drew directly on the playbook of Stalin's Great Break (1928–1932). How would early revolutionary practices function in the conditions of the postwar USSR? In the end, Khrushchev's attempt to transform the universities would misfire, as party policies collided with entrenched university communities, yielding unpredictable results.

The intelligentsia disowned

Khrushchev's very decision to speak to the MGU physics students reflected the important place of higher learning in his plans for transforming the Soviet project. Two overlapping issues explain the Khrushchev leadership's preoccupation with education, and particularly the elite higher learning constituted by the universities: an intelligentsia problem and a youth problem. First, as noted above, Khrushchev viewed Soviet intellectuals as a self-serving social group which had lost its will to work for the rest of society.[4] Khrushchev saw this as a consequence of Stalin's cult of personality, one which was every bit as pernicious as the terror against communists: the dictator, he alleged, had stopped relying on "the working class and the people," instead creating an elitist "social stratum around himself," a process he likened to "bribing the intelligentsia."[5] Reclaiming the intelligentsia for the people meant confronting higher learning, as it was here that the intelligentsia had managed to establish itself as a self-reproducing caste. Khrushchev's analysis contained some truth, even if his allegations of intelligentsia betrayal belonged firmly to Bolshevik discourse in its Khrushchevian variant. As discussed in Chapter 2, higher learning and universities in particular became increasingly dominated by the offspring of educated society during the Stalin period. The trend

---

[4] N. S. Khrushchev, "Rech' na XIII-om s'ezde VLKSM," *Komsomol'skaia zhizn'*, no. 1 (1958): 11.
[5] See Khrushchev's comments at a 1963 party plenum on ideological questions in RGANI f. 2, op. 1, d. 638, ll. 26–27.

toward elitism only gained momentum in the mid-1950s, when large cohorts of school graduates who had been too young to serve in the war flooded higher education. Authorities looked with concern at increasing instances of string-pulling in admissions, particularly in the medal system for school graduates with top grades.[6]

Odious to Khrushchev in its own right, the rise of intelligentsia privilege in the universities also appeared to explain major problems confronting the Soviet state. The leader thought that the determination of young people to gain higher education degrees drained the blue-collar workforce of recruits – a serious concern given the demographic effects of the war.[7] At issue were deep-seated cultural assumptions, as Khrushchev realized: too many Soviet intellectuals ingrained in their children the belief that "it is obligatory for one to complete a higher education establishment, and best of all Moscow University."[8] Soviet leaders were also convinced that the elitism of the student body had helped to bring about the ideological upheavals in the universities following de-Stalinization. A Komsomol TsK analysis stressed that the recent wave of student political opposition had been the product of "white-handed" students who led an "idle lifestyle"; it was only "one step" from idleness to "nihilism and pessimism, haughtiness and immodesty," the youth leaders stressed.[9] This reading of the situation also had some support in the universities' party organizations. N. S. Stroganov, the party secretary at the MGU Biology and Soil Science Department, complained in 1955 that youth "from intelligentsia families (*iz sem'ei intelligentov*)" had a tendency to "criticize everything" in university life without any sense of personal responsibility.[10] Such a class-based line of thinking was highly simplistic, but it was nonetheless an understandable one for communists who witnessed the overall trend toward social elitism in the universities and the growing importance of intelligentsia culture for students in the context of de-Stalinization, as discussed in Chapter 5.

The party bolstered its analysis of youth deviation with simple conservative rhetoric reminiscent of what works on youth culture have called "bourgeois moral panics."[11] Just like the perception of class snobbery, the

---

[6] TsDAVO f. 4621, op. 1, spr. 95, ark. 61–65; GARF f. 9396, op. 2, d. 1203, ll. 58–66.
[7] See Khrushchev, "Rech' na XIII-om s'ezde": 11 and Laurent Coumel, "L'appareil du parti et la réforme scolaire de 1958: Un cas d'opposition à Hruščev," *Cahiers du Monde Russe et Soviétique*, 47 (2007): 177–78.
[8] "'Chelovek, okonchivshii universitet'," 98.   [9] RGANI f. 5, op. 30, d. 179, l. 100.
[10] See the minutes of a 1955 party conference at TsAOPIM f. 478, op. 3, d. 24, l. 83.
[11] Concern with the moral traits of educated youth fed on a broader "moral panic" about youth delinquency in the late Stalin years. Juliane Fürst, *Stalin's Last Generation: Soviet Post-War Youth and the Emergence of Mature Socialism* (Oxford University Press, 2010), 167–99.

view that students were frivolous and disrespectful gripped defenders of
party orthodoxy in the universities. At university party cell meetings, faculty
and staff expressed exasperation with what they saw as students expressing
"excessive pride" (*chvanlivost'*) and "putting on airs" (*zaznaistvo*), recounting episodes of students refusing to greet a professor in the hallway, holding
drunken parties in the dormitories, and (horror of horrors) wearing their
overcoats during lectures.[12] The students' lack of respect was the result of
their over-solicitous "mamashas and papashas," Khrushchev believed. It was
also a broader generational phenomenon: youth coming of age in the 1950s
had not experienced the Soviet regime's foundational events, namely the
Revolution, Civil War, and Great Patriotic War (allegedly, their childhood
experiences of the last were already too far in the past and not particularly
conducive to patriotic behavior in any case).[13] According to the Komsomol
TsK, youth's ignorance about "the huge difficulties that the Soviet people
had to overcome before it could reach today's heights" accounted for its
complacency and "frivolous relationship to life."[14] Indeed, for all his talk of
revolution, Khrushchev's vision of social change was rooted firmly in the
past; his was to be a "second cultural revolution" with all the reflexivity this
implies.[15] Indeed, some college party leaders joined the first secretary in
waxing nostalgic about their own student experiences in the workers'
faculties (*rabfaky*), the accelerated courses for communist workers during
the First Five Year Plan. F. N. Zauzolkov, a Communist Party history
teacher at MGU, received "warm applause" from his fellow party members
when he contrasted the current generation of students who behaved like
"young masters" with the *rabfak* students, for whom there had been "no
question" of unworthy behavior.[16]

The regime's perceptions of interlocked intelligentsia and youth problems called for recreating the student body and through it the intelligentsia
as a whole. Beginning in 1955, admission rules to higher education establishments – which had long operated almost exclusively on performance in

---

[12] See for instance the minutes of an *aktiv* meeting of the Saratov University Komsomol on "ideological character-formation work in the dormitories," dated 5 March 1953. GANISO f. 3234, op. 13, d. 17, ll. 69–83.
[13] Anxiety about the disruptive nature of youth's war experiences was longstanding. See Ann Livschiz, "Children's Lives after Zoia's Death: Order, Emotions, and Heroism in Children's Lives and Literature in the Post-War Soviet Union," in Juliane Fürst (ed.), *Late Stalinist Russia: Society between Reconstruction and Reinvention* (London and New York: Routledge, 2006), 192–208.
[14] See the 1956 document entitled "Materialy TsK VLKSM ob ideologicheskoi rabote sredi molodezhi." RGANI f. 5, op. 30, d. 179, ll. 101–2.
[15] Victor Buchli, *An Archaeology of Socialism* (Oxford: Berg, 1999), 137.
[16] TsAOPIM f. 478, op. 3, d. 38, l. 53.

competitive examinations and accomplishment in school (particularly the granting of "medals" to top pupils) – began to take account of applicants' labor experiences. The key transformation came in 1958 with the legislation, "On Strengthening Ties between School and Life," which called for 80 percent of admission slots to higher education establishments to be reserved for individuals with "two or more years of gainful employment" (who were called "production candidates") as well as demobilized servicemen of the armed forces; only the remaining 20 percent would remain open to competition from graduates of the secondary schools.[17] The introduction of a labor-based quota system of admissions would serve multiple purposes. If school graduates began their working careers before applying to college, they would lose what Khrushchev called a "lordly contempt for physical labor," and some much-needed young bodies would remain in the labor force permanently.[18] The admissions quotas would also result in a thoroughly transformed student body. Whether they hailed from the toiling masses or had spent a few years among them, the production candidates and ex-servicemen would enter the universities with a hard-working and humble attitude. The result would be a student body with "less demagoguery and fewer words," as a Komsomol activist at MGU put it bluntly.[19] The new student body would also be a better return on investment for the Soviet state. Understanding that "any useful labor is considered honorable in Soviet society," students would study diligently and then work according to their state-designated job assignments – a critical consideration given the near-breakdown of the "distribution" system discussed in Chapter 2.

No doubt realizing how radical these aims were, the party-state leaders bolstered the turn to promoting toilers with a set of reforms in other areas of higher education. First, new curricula increased the exposure of students to practical work as part of their studies. It was envisioned that students would spend entire semesters working full-time at institutions affiliated with the college or in the economy at large while attending classes in the evening – a

[17] For extensive discussion of the changes as well as translations of the different republic laws passed in 1958, see Nicholas De Witt, *Education and Professional Employment in the USSR* (Washington, DC: National Science Foundation, 1961), 248–49, 558–74. In Russian, the production candidates were often referred to as *stazhniki* (those who had served a required work term) or *proizvodstvenniki* (producers).

[18] Ibid., 241.

[19] See the comments made in 1957 by Khmeletskii at the MGU Mechanics and Mathematics Department. TsAOPIM f. 6083, op. 1, d. 5, l. 17. The specifically political logic of the reform found reflection in the requirement that all college applicants furnish a "character reference" from a party, Komsomol, or trade union cell. Such a direct role for the "public organizations" in admissions to higher education had not existed since Stalin's Great Break. De Witt, *Education and Professional Employment*, 248–49.

provision that would help to reshape the minority of future students who would enter higher education without work experience. Second, the MVO expanded the evening and correspondence divisions of higher education establishments at the expense of their "stationary," meaning full-time, divisions.[20] Finally, the leadership pursued a policy of curtailing higher education enrollments in major cities of European Russia in favor of expanding higher learning in Siberia, the Far East, and Central Asia. Prying higher learning away from the core to the peripheries would help to recruit a more service-minded intelligentsia while lessening the persistent problem of urban graduates refusing to take up job positions in distant corners of the country.[21] Taken together, these innovations constituted a radical attempt to redefine Soviet studenthood as a part-time status pursued by working citizens, something that would reduce the distinctness and allure of the *studenchestvo* in Soviet society. It may have been too late for Khrushchev to salvage the MGU physics graduates, but future student cohorts would learn that they were "earthly and mortal" Soviet citizens.

Remaking the *studenchestvo*

The new vision of a toiling student body proved immediately controversial in university communities and educated society more generally. Academicians and professors in the sciences in particular feared that requiring young people to perform labor before undertaking higher study would set them back academically. As Laurent Coumel has shown, this opposition influenced the reforms' ultimate shape, as Khrushchev backed away from some of his more radical plans – for instance, replacing traditional secondary schools with work-production arrangements and requiring all students to have production experience before admission – after scholars and educators voiced their concerns to party officials.[22] When the party submitted the resulting "Thesis" on the reforms to public discussion, moreover, influential scientists like A. N. Kolmogorov, A. D. Sakharov, and even the president of the Academy of Sciences A. N. Nesmeianov spoke out publicly about the harmful impact of breaking up the traditional academic path to higher

---

[20] De Witt, *Education and Professional Employment*, 265–69.
[21] The connection between the reforms in higher learning, distribution, and expansion of higher education in the peripheries is spelled out in M. A. Prokofiev, "Puti uluchsheniia raboty vuzov," *VVSh*, no. 8 (1957): 3–10.
[22] Laurent Coumel, "The Scientist, the Pedagogue and the Party Official: Interest Groups, Public Opinion and Decision-making in the 1958 Education Reform," in Melanie Ilič and Jeremy Smith (eds.), *Soviet State and Society under Nikita Khrushchev* (London: Routledge, 2009), 71–76.

education. Despite this mobilization of scientists to influence party policy, however, significant parts of the university faculty shared Khrushchev's vision of a student body redeemed through toil. Indeed, even some professors who were concerned with the impact of the proposed reforms had grown concerned that admissions to universities had developed a "caste nature."[23] From the start, then, university communities balanced affinity for the reforms' goals with deep concerns about their academic costs.

Current students and recent graduates of intelligentsia origins had a much more immediate interest in the campaign. The shift in admissions seemed to be targeted against them. The Leningrad mathematician Revol't Pimenov, soon to be arrested for cobbling together an anti-Soviet group, took a position that many others shared: admitting only youth working at production to the universities would be "a blow against science."[24] Yet the position that science should be the preserve of people from educated society was a decidedly awkward one for students given the hold of socialist principles among them. Some students thought they would lead a revolution, but none of them anticipated becoming a target of one. Igor' Dedkov, a student of "revisionist" views who spearheaded a grassroots takeover of the MGU Journalism Department Komsomol organization in 1956, exemplified the difficulty of balancing intelligentsia identity and communist ideology. In his diary, Dedkov expressed mixed reactions to a *Komsomol'skaia Pravda* article announcing the promotion of producers to higher learning: "On the one hand it is fair and on the other hand it is sad." Acknowledging that he might be "too ill with denial to see the truth," Dedkov was nonetheless repelled by the article's "insinuating contrast of producer-youth to school pupils," which seemed a "newly woven platitude."[25] Clearly, Dedkov could hardly reject Khrushchev's campaign on ideological grounds, but he recoiled at the idea that intellectuals might be viewed as a suspect social class. Perhaps expressing the same idea, several students at SGU, when asked to record their social origins in a "list of delegates" at a 1956 Komsomol conference, offered facetious answers like "female student" and "bachelor."[26]

[23] As early as 1954, the Ukrainian party TsK received suggestions for some sort of a pre-admission production requirement from college administrators and party committees across the republic. TsDAHOU f. 1, op. 24, spr. 3792, ark. 204, 209–10; Coumel, "The Scientist," 74.
[24] UFSB SPb, arkh no: P-81390, t. 5 (konvert).
[25] Igor' Dedkov, *Dnevnik 1953–1994* (Moscow: Progress-Pleiada, 2005), 18. On Dedkov's activities in 1956, see Elena Zubkova, *Obshchestvo i reformy* (Moscow: Rossiia molodaia, 1993), 135–43.
[26] GANISO f. 3234, op. 13, d. 92, l. 6.

At stake for many students was the meaning of the intelligentsia and their place in it. Khrushchev justified his new social promotion policies using a populist and class-inflected political lexicon. In a controversial speech to Komsomol activists in November 1956, Khrushchev recounted an episode told to him by "Romanian comrades" about a visit by a group of workers to an educational institution. Khrushchev quoted the workers' message to students with approval: "for the time being you are living on what we are creating, so you should study well. If you do not like our ways, which we have established with blood and toil, go and work and others will come and study in your place."[27] Students saw their exclusion from the "we" in this speech as a threat, and not an empty one in the context of the wave of repressions that had enveloped higher learning following the Hungarian Revolution. Implicit in Khrushchev's words was a modified definition of intelligentsia: rather than social elites, the students or future intelligentsia were a class of service that was dependent on the good will of the masses. This was clearly a challenge to core social identities held by many students. At an MGU Komsomol meeting in December 1956, a philology student challenged the speech's depiction of Soviet society, asserting that Khrushchev was wrong to "divide the workers and students," asking: "Who were students if not children of the workers?" And was it not "a fact that [the students] make criticisms that are a matter of importance for the whole people?"[28] Indirectly, this comment underscores how the construct of intelligentsia was developing in the period among students. During de-Stalinization, many students became convinced that the intelligentsia was both consummately Soviet (the "children of workers") but also the cultural and moral leaders of society which improved the Soviet order by "making criticisms" of it. Khrushchev denied both assumptions. Far from being society's leaders who might speak for the "whole people," they were its servants who relied on its benevolence.

Students and academicians critical of the reform might have felt vindicated when the universities set about implementing the admissions changes. It quickly emerged that the new procedures would prove disruptive in the colleges. Applicants to higher learning who fit the criteria of production candidates or demobilized servicemen had often been out of school for years and proved unprepared for sitting the entrance exams for the universities. In 1958, over 60 percent of applicants from the two privileged

---

[27] "Meeting of Moscow Youth Devoted to Awarding of Order of Lenin to Y.C.L.," *Pravda*, 10 November 1956: 1–2; reproduced in *CDSP*, 8, no. 45 (1956): 12–13.
[28] TsAOPIM f. 4, op. 113, d. 41, l. 90.

admissions groups who sat the entrance examinations received failing scores.[29] The high-powered universities faced particular difficulty in following the new admissions guidelines. Few producers and ex-servicemen applied to the universities, as they were usually discouraged by the universities' carefully cultivated reputation of academic excellence. A frustrated Moscow Physics Department administrator, I. Alekseev, discovered that there was a "widespread opinion" that "only wunderkinds get admitted to MGU," and the situation for provincial universities was different only in degree.[30] The result was that the universities, so used to sitting at the top of the higher education system, now lagged behind in fulfilling state mandates: if over 60 percent of students admitted to all institutes in the USSR in 1958 were production candidates and ex-servicemen, the corresponding figure was forty-two in MGU.[31] Most higher education establishments had to resort to unanticipated measures like running multiple entrance examinations and lowering standards of evaluation in order to enroll the required numbers of toilers and ex-servicemen.

The campaign placed the universities in a difficult situation. Under pressure from above to fulfill the new quotas, universities struggled to find applicants who both qualified for the privileged admissions and were capable of passing entrance exams. To this end, the universities mobilized professors to travel the country to drum up interest in the provinces, and also to run evening courses to prepare people with production experience for admission (Komsomol joined the act by creating its own classes using young volunteers).[32] At the same time, the Ministries of Higher Education in Moscow and the Union Republics allowed the universities to break the rules.[33] The new admissions quotas were not forced upon university departments of mathematics, physics, and chemistry, meaning that the vast bulk of the student body in these disciplines remained recent school graduates as before – a development that would remain a point of contention between universities and their ministry overseers for years.[34] Supporters of the reform

[29] See the report on higher education enrollments in 1958 from the Komsomol TsK division of work with student youth to the league's TsK secretariat. RGASPI-M f. 1, op. 46, d. 223, l. 44.
[30] I. Alekseev, "Priemnye eksameny pokazhut," *Moskovskii universitet*, 13 June 1959, 1. See also a July 1960 Komsomol TsK report on preparations for the upcoming academic year in Saratov Province. RGASPI-M f. 1, op. 46, d. 261, l. 186.
[31] Ibid., d. 223, l. 43. See also the figures in De Witt, *Education and Professional Employment*, 265.
[32] GARF-R 605, op. 1, d. 812, l. 24.
[33] MVO was split into a reduced all-Union agency and separate republic bodies in 1959.
[34] On the social composition of these departments in SGU, see GANISO f. 652, op. 1, d. 6, 85. For ongoing contestation between the Russian Republic MVO and the universities, see GARF-R f. 605, op. 1, d. 10, l. 16.

claimed that these challenges were worth the trouble; in the long run, the recruits from outside the intelligentsia would become more serious specialists and, as noted above, shore up the job distribution system. Yet the experiences of the universities, more so than in less prestigious branches of higher learning, showed that the campaign had failed to balance ideological imperatives and academic standards.

Regardless of the difficulties the universities experienced in fulfilling the new admissions requirements, the education reforms erected considerable hurdles for young people from educated backgrounds trying to find their way into the colleges. Many of these young people were deeply troubled by the notion that their path to higher education would be blocked entirely. As Boris Vail', a student in Leningrad at the time, put it, "an orientation toward higher education was inculcated" in Soviet youths from childhood, and the alternatives to higher learning – serving in the army or industrial labor – were far from attractive.[35] Here an unexpected circumstance helped to shape the experiences of millions of young people: the ambiguity of the admissions reforms themselves. The reforms were clearly meant as an attack on privilege. For instance, new rules made students' state stipends dependent on their parents' income level (an innovation that infuriated children from elite families who were now forced to rely exclusively on family support during their studies).[36] However, the different reforms carefully avoided the category of class in favor of that of labor experience, meaning that the favored admission groups would remain accessible, in theory, to intelligentsia children. While avoiding class discrimination might have made sense given the focus on correction rather than exclusion in Khrushchev-era policies, another aspect of the reform was more puzzling.[37] A young person could fulfill the two-year labor requirement not only in industry or agriculture but also "in other branches of the economy and culture" – meaning, in essence, any kind of gainful employment.[38] The party's failure to define "production experience" threatened to strip from labor the ideological and social qualities the party-state had assigned to it. This moderation might have reflected Khrushchev's own ambivalence

---

[35] Boris Vail', *Osobo opasnyi* (London: Overseas Publications Interchange, 1980), 149. The appeal of academic education also posed problems for reforms of secondary education in the period. See Loretta Dawn Fleurs, "Education Reform in Moscow Secondary Schools, 1958–1964" (Ph.D. diss., Princeton University, 1999).

[36] RGASPI-M f. 1, op. 46, d. 233, ll. 1–3.

[37] On the discourse and policies of correction during the Khrushchev era, see Dobson, *Khrushchev's Cold Summer*.

[38] *Pravila priema i programmy priemnykh ekzamenov dlia postupaiushchikh v vysschie uchebnye zavedeniia SSSR* (Moscow: "Sovetskaia nauka," 1957), 9.

about the campaign; the first secretary's love–hate relationship with intellectuals is well known.[39] More importantly, it underscored how reluctant the political leadership was to push ideological correctness at the cost of future scientific development.

Educated society proved eager to take advantage of the reform's critical loopholes. Countless young people of intelligentsia social origins gained production candidate status by working for two years after secondary school in decidedly "mental labor" settings such as factory administrations or even scientific research institutes. In many cases, racking up production experience involved a degree of string-pulling as well; witness the Odessa University applicant who gained production candidate status by working once a week in the crèche managed by her mother, who diligently falsified the number of hours in her daughter's work papers.[40] Another creative way that intelligentsia youth made their way to higher education involved no toil at all: they enrolled in the less prestigious but rapidly expanding correspondence and extension divisions of the universities, in direct violation of the requirement that students in these institutions be employed full-time, and then transferred to the full-time divisions.[41] In short, the reforms left plenty of channels for urban professionals and hereditary "Soviet intelligentsia" to infiltrate the envisioned stratum of toiling students.

However forgiving its mandates were in practice, the education reforms remained quite unpopular among many students. In fact, the very ease with which students violated the spirit if not the letter of the new laws went far in discrediting them. At a joint plenary session of the MGU Party Committee and Komsomol Committee in 1962, the Philology Department activist M. Remneva complained that young people completed the pre-college work requirement formally, "for the sake of a check mark." She then posed a provocative question: "Does a philologist really need work experience in the first place? This is not an entirely rational decision."[42] Lacking justification in terms of its original goal of proletarian character-building – and in most cases not offering anything in terms of academic growth – the production requirement seemed to be nothing more than an unwanted break in one's studies. And if some students had positive experiences working for two years or more

---

[39] William Taubman, *Khrushchev: The Man and his Era* (New York: Norton, 2003), 127–32, 382–88.

[40] TsDAHOU f. 1, op. 71, spr. 239, ark. 72; "Itogi novogo priema v universitet," *Moskovskii universitet*, 6 August 1958: 1.

[41] A 1964 Komsomol TsK report, "Questions on the Further Development of Correspondence and Evening Education," describes the applicant pool to these divisions in detail. RGASPI-M f. 1, op. 46, d. 364, ll. 1–8.

[42] TsAOPIM f. 6083, op. 1, d. 44, l. 181.

before enrolling in higher learning, they articulated the value of the work in terms of material interests rather than ideological or academic advancement. According to a Western tourist who talked to many students, the opinion was widespread that it was "a good idea to earn some money for a while" so as to enter the impoverished student existence with some savings.[43] Ironically, a reform that harkened back to Bolshevik values of labor and social unity was feeding careerism and materialism.

The education reforms' other components also did little to meet their goal of deepening students' connection to the toiling masses. Curricular internships that the reform introduced appeared just as unnecessary and disruptive to students as the production requirement. Students often found that they were treated dismissively as untrained labor in institutions beyond the universities' walls. It is not surprising that merging the activities of educational institutions and the productive economy, entities with very different mandates, proved difficult. But this disconnect was particularly damaging to student morale given the broader ideological pretensions of the education reforms. In 1960, MGU student Nikolaeva complained at a Party History seminar that at the printing shop where she was an intern, "comradely, proletarian relations between workers" were non-existent and students were being exploited.[44] Likewise, the Komsomol rank-and-file was decidedly unenthusiastic about participating in activities tied to the education reforms, such as tutoring production candidates for the entrance exams without pay.[45] Khrushchev had intended the reforms to build a sense of student solidarity with the wider society, but social distance seemed as large as ever – in part because students found themselves acting in ways that contradicted the image of the virtuous toiler presented to them.

Intelligenty with a firm step

The ultimate political impact of the higher education measures rested on the new recruits themselves. In official thinking, the lack of "people of labor" in the universities meant that "the worldview of the largest part of the students emerged spontaneously, under the influence of bookish institute life"; the production candidates would purify the students' consciousness

[43] "Interview with a Western Traveler who Visited the USSR in 1958, 1959, and 1960," BR # 5–61, 19 April 1961, RFE/RL, HIA, 530/2, 9.
[44] RGASPI-M f. 1, op. 46, d. 271, l. 46; DAKO f. 158, op. 6, spr. 26, ark. 2.
[45] The problems of preparatory courses are outlined in a 1958 report note of the Ukrainian Ministry of Higher Education to the Moscow TsK. TsDAVO f. 4621, op. 1, spr. 95, ark. 122.

by bringing them "knowledge filtered by conscious laboring life."[46] The production candidates and ex-servicemen were indeed different from their classmates who entered university right after secondary school. They more often claimed worker or collective farmer social origins and, not surprisingly, they were older on average.[47] Perhaps most importantly, they had higher levels of party membership, which offered the university party organizations a larger direct foothold in the student body than it had possessed since the influx of veterans right after the war.[48]

University authorities hoped that the new recruits would strengthen a student *aktiv* which had been badly demoralized by the ideological crisis of de-Stalinization. An article in the MGU newspaper claimed that one could immediately recognize a demobilized soldier by his "good carriage, cleanliness, bearing, and firm military step"; it noted that these new recruits "tried to bring all these healthy military traditions into student life."[49] There can be no doubt that many students carried habits which had been acquired in more regimented social settings, military or otherwise. In KDU, one student activist explained, the production candidates and soldiers prepared thoroughly for social science seminars, the bland ideological discussion classes that many students had come to view with scarcely hidden boredom and irritation.[50] And at least some of the students who came from secondary schools were influenced by the new worker- and soldier-students: one interview subject thought that she and her peers might have become "hooligans" if not for the influence of the older production candidates.[51]

The influx of students that fit the party's biographical criteria did not, however, give party and Komsomol organizations in higher education the shot in the arm authorities hoped it would. The central problem was the endemic academic troubles of many of the production candidates and ex-servicemen, who had difficulty adapting to the rhythms and expectations of student life. At a meeting of first-course production candidates at the MGU Journalism Department, the overriding sentiment was that it was "hard to

[46] RGASPI-M f. 1, op. 46, d. 379, l. 25.
[47] To take one example, two-thirds of the production candidates to KDU in 1958 were workers and collective farmers, a significantly higher percentage than for the entering class as a whole. DAKO f. 158, op. 5, spr. 263, ark. 22. On changing age patterns, see RGASPI-M f. 1, op. 46, d. 318, l. 1.
[48] In the early 1960s, roughly 15 percent of the entering classes to MGU and KDU were party members or candidates, which was roughly five times as large as the same figure a decade before in the case of MGU. TsDAHOU f. 1, op. 71, spr. 239, ark. 66; TsAOPIM f. 478, op. 4. d. 1040, ll. 142–3; TsMAM f.1609, op. 2, d. 388, l. 14.
[49] M. T. Smirnov, "Sovety i pozhelaniia," *Moskovskii universitet*, 30 August 1958: 1.
[50] See the December 1959 Komsomol Committee discussion of studying Marxism-Leninism at the KDU Biology and Soil Science Department. DAKO f. 9912, op. 1, spr. 54, ark. 197.
[51] Interview with L. N. Dmitrievna, Moscow, 2003.

study, hard to organize one's time, hard to do everything that the teachers demand of us" – difficulties that were only deepened by the troubling situation of older production candidates who had to support families on paltry student stipends.[52] Many production candidates found themselves on the brink of academic failure, a situation that was hardly conducive to Komsomol activism.[53] In fact, the new recruits might have proven as much a problem for party and Komsomol as an asset for them, as a "battle for the preservation of the new recruits" came to absorb a large part of their time and energy.[54]

The new beneficiaries of Soviet social mobility were also, in many cases, far from confident in their mandate to remake the student body. They might have brought distinct habits with them, but once in the universities they confronted an entrenched university environment with its hierarchies of academic achievement and culturedness that they could hardly ignore. In an interview, a former production candidate remembered not only studying ardently to catch up with classmates from "intelligentsia" origins but also going to museums and the theater to "raise her intellectual level" – a comment which suggests that some of the new recruits held cultural inferiority complexes, as had indeed many university students from non-intelligentsia (and non-urban) backgrounds in the preceding years.[55] The ambivalent feelings some of the new recruits must have felt towards the universities found reflection in a Komsomol speech of Loginov, a first-year MGU philology student and worker. He complained that in university seminars, the professors "oriented themselves toward the students from the ten-year school," who had an easier time mastering course material. Yet Loginov also demonstrated that he had himself internalized some of the university's cultural hierarchy: taking the podium, he apologized that he still had not "learned to speak beautifully" and proceeded to read his speech from a notebook.[56] In simultaneously expressing bitterness toward university hierarchies and seeking their approval, Loginov exemplified the limited effect of the admissions reforms on the university milieu. Changing the composition of the student body and transforming its ethos proved very different things.

The Soviet government eventually curtailed the social mobility campaign it had championed. If their initial responses had been varied, university

---

[52] V. Klimov, "O moem druge," *Moskovskii universitet*, 22 October 1959: 2.
[53] TsAOPIM f. 478, op. 3, d. 84, 93, 101; DAKO f. 9912, op. 1, d. 54, l. 190.
[54] Cf. 1957 MGU Komsomol Committee discussions of the reforms. TsAOPIM f. 6083, op. 1, d. 5, l. 129.
[55] Interview with A. P. Aleksandrova, Moscow, March 2004.   [56] TsAOPIM f. 6083, op. 1, d. 5, l. 94.

professors increasingly came to believe that "it was better to return to admitting school graduates, as it is too hard for producers to study."[57] Other parts of the reform also lost the support of faculty, such as the expanding system of "production training" that cut into classroom time and forced the universities to seek often unstable partnerships with institutions across the country.[58] The reform began losing momentum by the early 1960s. With official sanction, several universities created special secondary schools devoted to preparing applicants for university programs in the physical sciences.[59] At the same time, MGU and other leading institutes undermined the reform in unsanctioned ways as well. In a spontaneous move toward academic tracking, the capital's university along with other institutions also began placing school graduates and production candidates into separate academic groups.[60] The higher education bureaucracy cracked down on this quiet undoing of the reform in Moscow, but the broader message was clear: the faculty at universities and other elite higher education establishments had lost the conviction that poorly prepared entrants could perform at the level of school graduates. A Moscow student thought that colleges in the capital "tried to avoid" admitting unprepared production candidates whenever possible, and the fact that the pre-reform social profile of MGU barely changed in the early 1960s (as shown in Table 6.1) seems to confirm this perception.[61]

Ironically, the political leadership in Moscow came to similar conclusions once Khrushchev, the author of the reform, had been removed from the scene. The decisive unwinding of the campaign came in 1965 when new admissions rules allowed the colleges to set the quota for production candidates according to their share of the applicant pool.[62] The revision allowed the universities and other institutions with a predominantly

[57] See a February 1962 Komsomol report on Komsomol work in MGU. RGASPI-M f. 1, op. 46, d. 318, l. 16.

[58] Iu. Iu. Baturina, "Organizatsionnye izmeneniia v uchebnom protsesse vysshikh uchebnykh zavedenii v 1956–1965 godakh (na primere nizhnego povolzh'ia)," *Vestnik Cheliabinskogo gosudarstvennogo universiteta*, 179, no. 41, ser. "Istoriia," 100–101, www.lib.csu.ru/vch/179/017.pdf (accessed 9 July 2012).

[59] On the special schools, see Henry Chauncey, "Interviews with Soviet Educators on Recent Developments and the Current Status of Education in the U.S.S.R.: Report of Visit to the Soviet Union Sponsored by the United States Office of Education under the Auspices of the US–USSR Cultural Exchange Agreement for 1964–65" (May 1965), 210–11.

[60] See GARF-R f. 605, op. 1, d. 12, l. 50 and "The Mood of Soviet Students as Reflected in Some Comments by a Tourist to the West," BR # 22–65, 26 April 1965, RFE/RL, HIA, 1–2.

[61] Changes in the social composition of the student body were much more pronounced at KDU, where the intelligentsia category for admissions in 1956 was 56.3 percent and declined to 44.5 by 1960. DAKO f. 158, op. 6, spr. 20, ark. 8.

[62] Mervyn Matthews, *Education in the Soviet Union: Policies and Institutions since Stalin* (London and Boston: Allen & Unwin, 1982), 157.

Table 6.1 *Social origins of incoming classes to Moscow State University (%)*

Year	"Employees and intelligentsia"	Workers	Collective farmers
1956	70	20.2	9.8
1957	63.3	30.8	5.9
1958	66	30	4
1959	58	37	5
1960	68.8	25.4	5.8
1961	69.2	25.8	5

Sources: The figure for 1956 is for the total MGU student body, while the other figures refer to incoming students only. These figures were culled from several different sources. TsAOPIM f. 478, op. 3, d. 38, l. 85; ibid., f. 6083, op. 1, d. 5, l. 128; ibid., f. 478, op. 3, d. 80, l. 19; RGASPI-M f. 1, op. 46, d. 223, l. 44; ibid., d. 318, l. 36.

school-graduate and "intelligentsia" applicant pool to curtail the acceptance of laboring youth and ex-servicemen sharply. Soviet higher learning, and the universities especially, quickly returned to the status quo of training young people straight from secondary school – if 57.1 percent of all Soviet students in 1960 were producers and ex-servicemen, the corresponding figure was 27.3 in 1965 and just 13.1 a year later.[63] The Komsomol apparat leader M. I. Zhuravleva recalled the Council of Ministers meeting where the matter was discussed: the Youth League had been a "fierce proponent" of keeping the admissions reform in place but lost the argument with higher education bureaucrats when confronted with "objective information": dropout rates had soared so high (up to 30 percent at some institutions) that the admissions quotas had become "a luxury that could not be maintained."[64]

The intelligentsia had defeated Khrushchev's crude effort to intrude in their affairs. Such, at least, was the narrative on the education reforms that would come to dominate academic communities in the following decades,

[63] S. V. Volkov, *Intellektual'nyi sloi v sovetskom obshchestve* (St. Petersburg: Fond "Razvitie," Institut nauchnoi informatsii po obshchestvennym naukam RAN, 1999), 39. See also the reports on sharp changes in admissions to several elite higher education establishments in 1965 in RGASPI-M f. 1, op. 46, d. 378, ll. 30–34, 40–42, 58 and M. N. Rutkevich and F. R. Filippov, "Social Sources of Recruitment of the Intelligentsia," in Murray Yanowitch and Wesley A. Fisher (eds.), *Social Stratification and Mobility in the USSR* (White Plains, NY: International Arts and Sciences Press, 1973), 248.
[64] RGASPI-M f. 1, op. 5, d. 1096, ll. 143–44.

when the universities' elite reputations met few challenges from pragmatic party elites careful not to repeat their predecessor's radicalism. Viewing the universities' experience of the education reforms as an irrational and irrelevant episode, however, ignores the impact of the reforms on Soviet higher learning and indeed the intelligentsia generally. Reinjecting Bolshevik social conflict into higher learning – if only in a lukewarm Khrushchevian form – had a demoralizing impact on university communities. By calling into question their access to higher learning, the regime had forced Soviet intellectuals young and old to act on narrow material interests in ways that were not easily reconcilable with the image of the intelligentsia as the conscience of society. Ironically, Khrushchev's endeavor to weaken the elitist nature of the intelligentsia had only made it more visible.

To far-away lands

Attempts to transform the students were not confined to the universities themselves. In 1954, Khrushchev announced the settlement of large tracts of uncultivated land in Kazakhstan and Siberia in an effort to rectify the chronic underperformance of Stalin-era agriculture once and for all.[65] The Virgin Lands settlement was central to Khrushchev's vision of a revitalized post-Stalin communism; characteristically, in its rapid movement of people to great construction tasks and its call to production heroics, it harkened back to Stalin's Great Break. Little wonder, then, that the regime connected this campaign to its ambitious plans to reconstruct the Soviet intelligentsia. In the late 1950s, Komsomol mobilized large numbers of young students and workers from across the country to work as seasonal laborers in the Virgin Lands. In 1958 over 220,000 students spent their summer vacations toiling in the fields or helping with construction, sometimes thousands of miles from home.[66] For the party-state, mobilized youth constituted a useful addition to the labor pool of new settlers struggling to work land recently put under the plow. The seasonal laborer campaign also dovetailed with the educational reforms' aim of bringing intellectuals into contact with the toilers and their values. As a Komsomol TsK leader put it, by "tempering" students through hard labor and showing them "the huge

[65] Overall accounts include Michaela Pohl, "The Virgin Lands between Memory and Forgetting: People and Transformation in the Soviet Union, 1954–1960" (Ph.D. diss., Indiana University, 1999) and Martin McCauley, *Khrushchev and the Development of Soviet Agriculture: The Virgin Land Programme 1953–1964* (London: Macmillan, in association with the School of Slavonic and East European Studies, University of London, 1976).
[66] See materials on the work of college Komsomol organizations in RGASPI-M f. 1, op. 46, d. 239, l. 49.

opportunities of socialist agriculture," the Virgin Lands would be a "force against idlers and demagogues."[67]

The Virgin Lands episode was the centerpiece of a broader mania with labor projects that gripped Soviet higher learning in the late 1950s. Komsomol organizations had long pursued "public work" (*obshchestvennaia rabota*) among students, but the Khrushchev period redefined the nature and purpose of these efforts. Apart from week-long trips to the collective farms in the fall and various weekend labor call-ups, public work in the late Stalin era rarely involved much physical labor. Instead, students brought enlightenment to the masses by conducting talks with workers at nearby enterprises and construction sites on pre-approved topics (such as foreign affairs or scientific advancements), leading circles of secondary school students interested in science or technology, and "agitating" Soviet citizens to get them to vote in elections.[68] All of this could be dreary and demoralizing, but at least it corresponded to students' self-understanding as future carriers of culture. In sharp contrast, Komsomol in the Khrushchev era sponsored hard labor projects, often involving work in the fields of collective farms or at local construction sites, which took up the lion's share of students' summer vacations.[69] Such extended trips pursued a clear purpose which fit into Khrushchev's overall agenda for educated society: while bringing culture to the masses, students would also be learning from them. As the MGU Komsomol secretary A. N. Zelenin stated in 1957, "only in labor and continual communication with workers can one produce a correct view of life."[70]

Komsomol leaders saw labor projects as a panacea for the organization, which would finally inspire its members by providing them with "great deeds."[71] There was a degree of truth here. In 1956, the Komsomol TsK sent an appeal to all students to spend their summer in the Virgin Lands, emphasizing that the people's welfare depended on it: "never before in the Eastern regions of the country has bread been harvested from such a large area."[72] By all accounts, the call to duty found a willing audience. Crowds stormed the Komsomol offices to volunteer for the Virgin Lands

---

[67] RGASPI-M f. 1, op. 46, d. 202, ll. 37, 42.
[68] See the outline of activities conducted at KDU in the protocols of the Komsomol Committee meetings. DAKO f. 9912, op. 1, spr. 8, ark. 70. For interwar precedents, see Peter Konecny, *Builders and Deserters: Students, State, and Community in Leningrad, 1917–1941* (Montreal and Ithaca: McGill-Queen's University Press, 1999), 185–91.
[69] See a January 1957 report of the Student Division of the Komsomol TsK to the Party TsK. RGASPI-M f. 1, op. 46, d. 213, l. 6.
[70] TsAOPIM f. 478, op. 3, d. 67, l. 6.   [71] RGASPI-M f. 1, op. 46, d. 182, l. 20.
[72] Ibid., op. 3, d. 906, l. 122.

campaign; some were turned away but went anyway by stowing themselves in the trains.[73] To be sure, the recruiting process was not wholly voluntary. Komsomol gave each institution a target for recruitment and activists put pressure on their classmates to fulfill it. One former MGU history student recalled that Komsomol punished her for visiting her mother in the Caucasus instead of going to the Virgin Lands, seeing this as a manifestation of "aristocratism and hostility to the Komsomol system."[74] Some students at the Leningrad Electro-Technical Institute agreed to take part for fear of losing their stipends or of generating a compromising Komsomol record that might affect future career chances.[75] Yet pressure was not decisive in spurring many students to participate: as one former student recalled, "you didn't have to show any kind of certificate in order not to go. On the contrary, you had to ask them, to prove that you were useful [in order to be taken]."[76]

The mass mobilization for the Virgin Lands fits poorly with the usual story of 1956 as a year of student protest. In fact, the Virgin Lands campaign was well suited to the moods of students during the ideological fallout of de-Stalinization. Students eager to participate in molding the post-Stalin age now had visions, however murky, of valiant deeds: taming nature, bringing civilization to the periphery, and solving the deficient food supply of the country as a whole. At the same time, the campaign's sheer novelty was a welcome respite from the general sense of regimentation in Soviet college life, which had come to seem particularly galling after the secret speech. Authorities appealed to this desire for adventure in pitching the campaign to students: "if your heels are itching to move . . . if you aren't satisfied with looking at life through the windows of the lecture hall, then you cannot but go to the Virgin Lands!"[77] Underlying the patriotic and romantic appeal of the Virgin Lands was a sense that postwar youth finally had a chance to match the exploits of Soviet generations past. Fifty years after the campaign, MGU graduate E. A. Popova recalled her motivation for spending two summers at the Virgin Lands: "I went [there] on a Komsomol pass, from a feeling of duty; I lived with the thought that, after all, my contemporaries three or four years older than

[73] RGASPI-M f. 1, op. 46, d. 190, l. 75. For similar examples from Kyiv, see DAKO f. 9912, op. 2, spr. 6, ark. 33.
[74] Interview with G. S. Tolmacheva, Moscow, January 2004.
[75] RGASPI-M f. 1, op. 46, d. 213, l. 51.
[76] Interview with N. A. Yushchenko, Moscow, April 2004.
[77] "Slovo molodogo entuziasta Iu. Zhukova," *Moskovskii universitet*, 10 July 1958: 1.

me worked at military factories and slept at their machines."[78] Of course, many students avoided the campaign. But the usual motives of those who steered clear of participating – reluctance to leave the comfortable cities and fear of the unknown, often encouraged by fearful parents or even professors – could be written off as banal and petty-bourgeois during what seemed like a great historical moment.[79]

Student experiences at the Virgin Lands defy simple characterization. For some, the exciting commencement of the trip – starting with triumphal send-offs with marching bands and followed by exotic travels across the country – ended in disappointment. Khrushchev thought that "life itself" would mold the students into better citizens, but realities on the ground rarely matched his prediction. The "idiocy of rural life" was especially pronounced at the Virgin Lands, where living conditions in the recently formed state farms were haphazard and the chaotic intermixing of farmers, deported victims of Stalinist terror, and short-term laborers produced episodes of mass violence.[80] Students, poor but on a track to relative privilege, were hardly prepared for the hardships they faced: laboring in sixteen hour shifts, sleeping in the village school on an earthen floor infested with mice, relying on erratic food supplies, and suffering strange ailments from the foreign climate.[81] Labor experiences at the Virgin Lands did not live up to basic standards, let alone the romantic image the campaign seemed to promise. In an echo of Stalinist industrialization, the state farms' poor planning and the encouragement of maximal speed in production ("storming tactics") made accidents common. Students were run over by agricultural machines in the fields, flung to their death out of pick-up trucks, and buried alive in grain elevators.[82] Especially infuriating were the state-farm managers who frequently underpaid the students or left them without sufficient work. Such behavior not only produced numerous conflicts at the Virgin Lands but, in a broader sense, seemed to confirm the wider discourse about the evils of bureaucracy that had enveloped educated youth following the Twentieth Party Congress.[83] As if this were not enough,

---

[78] A. L. Nalepin (ed.), *Filologicheskii fakul'tet MGU, 1950–1955: zhizn' iubileinogo vypuska: vospomina-niia, dokumenty, materialy* (Moscow: Rossiiskii fond kul'tury "Rossiiskii arkhiv," 2003), 72.

[79] "Pishut nashi tovarishchi," *Moskovskii universitet,* 21 August 1956: 2.

[80] V. A. Kozlov, *Mass Uprisings in the USSR: Protest and Rebellion in the Post-Stalin Years,* trans. Elaine McClarnand MacKinnon (Armonk, NY: M. E. Sharpe, 2002), 72–86.

[81] TsAOPIM f. 478, op. 3, d. 67, l. 174; L. V. Silina, *Nastroeniia sovetskogo studenchestva, 1945–1964* (Moscow: Russkii mir, 2004), 67.

[82] "Doloi neschastnye sluchai!" *Moskovskii universitet na tseline,* 26 September 1958: 1 and, for Ukraine, TsDAHOU f. 1, op. 24, spr. 4299, ark. 262–63.

[83] Conflict over payment is mentioned in Anna Savchuk, "Skazka pro belogo bychka," *Moskovskii universitet,* 5 September 1958: 3 and Sergei Kara-Murza, *'Sovok' vspominaet* (Moscow: Algoritm, 2002), 201–3.

the students found themselves socially isolated from the settlers they were sent to help. The locals viewed the urban visitors with suspicion, as skeptical of the female students' make-up and dances as they were offended by the male students' habit of growing beards, which seemed a subtle mockery of peasant backwardness.[84]

While common enough, disaster and dismay did not dominate the experience of the Virgin Lands for many students. Precisely because of the hardships it entailed, the campaign generated a student subculture, a way of life that was distinct from that of the universities and the norms of Soviet youth more broadly. On the distant steppe, students experienced a form of independent group existence that was hardly possible in the regimented universities. Social solidarity grew around novel adventures and experiences: traveling across the country by train, drinking peasant home-brew, initiating romantic escapades, singing at the campfire, or even hunting wild hamsters on the steppe.[85] Laboring in a common cause had the same effect. Quickly, students at the Virgin Lands developed their own ethical code of hard work and discipline, captured in the oft-repeated phrase "he who works poorly does not respect his comrades."[86] These norms reflected a surprising fact: many students took extreme pleasure in the work they were performing, however dangerous and poorly paid. A Muscovite remarked that spending a summer laboring at the Virgin Lands was one of the most meaningful parts of his experience as a physics student. In the university "we were lofty," he recalled, but living and working on the Kazakh steppe "we had been thrown into the earth and shown what life was really like. This period only enriched us."[87] While not expressed directly, one sees here the students' enthusiasm for Khrushchev's model of an intelligentsia tied both to the heights of culture and the virtue of the masses. The Virgin Lands enthusiasts were articulating a notion of serving the people through simple labor, one which could not have differed more from the agenda of cultural salvation that motivated university oppositionists in 1956, as Chapter 5 discussed.

---

[84] See Pohl, "The Virgin Lands Between Memory and Forgetting," 313–14 and TsAOPIM f. 478, op. 3, d. 67, l. 172–73.

[85] Valentina Maslova, *Paralleli i meridiany: povest' o shestidesiatykh*, vol. 2 (Saratov: "Sokol," 2002), 20; Vladimir Pozner, *Parting with Illusions: The Extraordinary Life and Controversial Views of the Soviet Union's Leading Commentator* (New York: Atlantic Monthly Press, 1990), 91–94.

[86] V. Dorokhov, "Nash pervyi voskresnik," *Moskovskii universitet*, 9 October 1958: 3. For the same phenomenon in other student work projects of the time, see Valerii Ronkin, *Na smenu dekabriam prikhodiat ianvari: vospominaniia byvshego brigadmil'tsa i podpol'shchika, a pozzhe-politzakliuchennogo i dissidenta* (Moscow: "Zvenia," 2003), 77.

[87] Interview with B. V. Simonov, Moscow, January 2004.

If the student Virgin Landers (*tselinniki*) constituted a subculture in the universities, it was one that closely modeled Bolshevik ideals of labor and collectivism. In fact, the students created a more vibrant Komsomol life than that which they temporarily left in the universities, as a series of contrasts will help to drive home. Collegiate Komsomol organizations carried out often meaningless tasks passed down from a distant bureaucracy, but Komsomols at the Virgin Lands decided matters of great urgency such as finding food, organizing labor projects, and forcing lazy students to do their share of work – all, it was felt, for the people's cause. Activists on campus were trained to follow orders and otherwise impress their superiors, while those at the Virgin Lands had to earn the authority of their peers above all (their direct superiors in the party and Komsomol were far away).[88] In university Komsomol cells, power flowed from above rather than below; at the Virgin Lands, unswerving discipline often enjoyed the support of the rank-and-file. Student leaders in Kazakhstan expelled from the brigade a student who had traveled to Almaty for a few days without the permission of the group; the MGU newspaper commented that such a violation would hardly have been treated so harshly at the university.[89] Paradoxically, the regime's ideological goals for youth seemed most attainable when pursued at a distance from university power structures.

The student planet

So popular were the student Virgin Lands that they outlasted the campaign that gave rise to them. In 1958 the use of students as seasonal laborers ran into serious difficulties. Faced with poor weather conditions, a contingent of 220,000 student volunteers was idle through the summer months and had to remain well into the school year to take in the harvest.[90] University faculty, who had never been too excited about the Virgin Lands campaign, expressed open frustration with the disruption of studies and the academic troubles that some *tselinniki* experienced.[91] Faced with the dubious economic benefits of the campaign and growing discontent in the universities, the party shelved the experiment of using students as seasonal farm workers. While some students rejoiced, a group of Komsomol activists at the MGU

---

[88] V. Kondakov, "Tak rodilsia brigadier," *Moskovskii universitet na tseline*, 15 August 1958: 3.

[89] "Glavnaia tsel'," *Moskovskii universitet*, 19 July 1957: 1.

[90] Svetlana Kovaleva, *Ty pomnish, fizfak?* (Moscow: Pomatur, 2003), 34.

[91] See for instance the complaints of professors about the toll of the campaign on academic performance at a 1957 plenary meeting of the MGU Party Committee. TsAOPIM f. 478, op. 3, d. 58, ll. 113, 130, 134–35, 157.

Physics Department decided to renew the campaign in a new guise by organizing a "student construction detachment" (*studencheskii stroitel'nyi otriad*) to work at the Virgin Lands the next summer. The creators of the detachment sought to make the Virgin Lands experiment economically viable by replacing the ineffective army of mobilized laborers with small, well-trained, and self-governing groups of students focusing on construction, a bottleneck sector of the local economy.[92] While the first brigade of 330 students in 1959 was a success, the movement nevertheless operated for a few years without explicit patronage from major political bodies. The MVO opposed the initiative, while the central Komsomol authorities, sympathetic but chastened by the experience of the first incarnation of the student Virgin Lands, took a position of benevolent non-interference.[93] Despite these inauspicious beginnings, the construction detachments grew each year, drawing in participants from different departments at MGU and then from other institutions across the country. After Khrushchev himself blessed the movement in 1962, student construction detachments entered the Komsomol hierarchy, establishing a central headquarters under the Youth League's TsK.[94]

The construction brigades built on the student subculture of the first Virgin Lands campaign to create a full-fledged and student-led movement. From the start, the movement embraced party and Komsomol institutional models and practices. Responding to the chaos of the previous years' campaigns, the detachments instituted strict internal subordination, which they explicitly referred to using the Stalin-era term *edinonachalie* ("one-man management" or "undivided authority").[95] In an arrangement which reproduced the distinctively Soviet interpenetration of party and state, the detachments had "commissars" responsible for "internal-detachment life and ideological-political work among students and the local population."[96] Top-down control extended far into the private sphere of its members through a strictly enforced ban on drinking in the detachments – as a leader of the movement recalled, "with the dry law I was inflexible like that Marat or

---

[92] V. Pis'mennyi, "K tseline nado gotovit'sia zaranee," *Moskovskii universitet*, 13 November 1958: 3.

[93] Interview with G. P. Dudkin and E. R. Dudkina, Moscow, 2004. Such assertions of the movement's leaders are confirmed by the archival record. RGASPI-M f. 1, op. 46, d. 240, l. 112.

[94] On the expansion of the movement, see a 1963 report from the secretary of the Bulaevskii District Party Committee to TsK Komsomol on the first construction detachments in RGASPI-M f. 1, op. 46, d. 230, l. 67.

[95] T. Simonova, "Problemy minuvshei nedeli," *Molodoi tselinnik na studencheskoi stroike*, 19 June 1963: 4.

[96] Kovaleva, *Ty pomnish fizfak*, 43.

Danton ... I was a real swine" – while students who refused to work or merely "whined" about conditions faced harsh discipline.[97]

Combining ideological orthodoxy, hard work, and collectivism, youth at the Virgin Lands seemed to be the very embodiment of Khrushchev's intelligentsia. The irony was that the construction brigades' viability as a movement depended on maintaining a measured distance from political bureaucracies and adult authority structures more broadly. Although the detachments' leaders were selected by university administrations and Komsomol organizations, they exercised considerable self-governance on the steppe when their putative superiors were far away. They pointedly refused to allow university hierarchies to hold within their movement; one leader claimed that the activists spurned professors who came with them one year for clinging to signs of their superior social status such as eating separately from the students.[98] More importantly, the construction detachments never fulfilled the role party leaders at the universities envisioned for them, that of a "school of Komsomol cadres."[99] The freewheeling and self-reliant ethos of the Virgin Landers lacked a fitting outlet in the bureaucratic Komsomol cells in higher education.[100] As an activist at the MGU Physics Department exclaimed at a 1962 meeting, detachment members often experienced boredom upon returning to the Komsomol life of the university.[101] The students liked to call their movement the "Virgin Lands planet," a description that not only likened their efforts to the vaunted space program but also emphasized how it constituted a separate and inward-looking enterprise.

The construction brigades became a massive and institutionalized movement in the last decades of the USSR. In the process, they lost much of their early verve. While collectivism still prevailed, many students participated in the brigades because they offered substantial summer earnings, something especially important for "out-of-town" students who could not rely on regular support from home.[102] Explicitly communist agendas such as that of

[97] Interview with G. P. Dudkin, Moscow, 2004. On enforcement of the dry law, see "K tselinnomu meridianu," *Molodoi tselinnik na studencheskoi stroike*, 10 July 1963: 1. On "whiners," see a 1960 protocol of the Moscow City Committee of Komsomol at TsAOPIM f. 635, op. 14, d. 320, l. 15.

[98] "Tam mozhno bylo po-chestnomu rabotat'," *MSOshnik* [newspaper of the "Educational-Methodological Center of Youth-Student Brigades," Moscow] (2003): 7.

[99] TsAOPIM f. 6083, op. 1, d. 44, l. 194.

[100] See the results of a 1962 inspection of MGU conducted by the Komsomol TsK. RGASPI-M f. 1, op. 46, d. 318, l. 2.

[101] TsAOPIM f. 6083, op. 1, d. 46, l. 201.

[102] Petr Vail' and Aleksandr Genis, *60-e: mir sovetskogo cheloveka* (Moscow: "Novoe literaturnoe obozrenie," 1996), 130.

establishing redistributive "communes" in the Virgin Lands never took hold. By the end of the Khrushchev period, the central Komsomol officials' faith in productive labor as a cure for "youth problems" was passing; in 1965, a Komsomol leader regretted that the organization had become caught up in economic questions at the expense of pursuing the broader imperative of "character formation."[103] More broadly, the student Virgin Lands had always been more of a youthful subculture rather than a serious effort at transforming the intelligentsia from within. Privileged students' embrace of rugged toil – encapsulated in their motto, "graduate from the physics department as a foreman!" – always contained a degree of playfulness and artifice. The students were members of the educated class moonlighting as virtuous toilers. Significantly, when Khrushchev called for university graduates to move to the Virgin Lands permanently, virtually no one took up his call.[104] If intellectual self-fashioning was central to student politics in the period, the construction of a "toiling intellectual" at the Virgin Lands was its most quixotic product.

Khrushchev's appeal to physics graduates to merge with the Soviet people and shed their social distinction as scientific elites was not empty rhetoric. In the first post-Stalin decade universities were sites of social engineering in ways they had not been since Stalin's Great Break, as admissions reforms, curricular changes, and extra-curricular work projects all exposed students used to an insular university environment to non-academic labor. By the end of the period, however, much of the flurry of activity to transform students seemed to have missed the mark, at least in the elite universities. Here the students' social identities – not to mention their social makeup – had changed far less than hoped, while experiments in merging education and "life" had become unpopular among faculty and students alike. In contrast, the palpable excitement of large-scale Komsomol projects, and of the Virgin Lands campaign most of all, had struck deep roots in parts of the student body. Despite its ideological conformism, the movement of student construction brigades under Komsomol represented a successful grassroots initiative with few parallels in the period.[105] And yet campus engrossment in labor had also fallen short of expectations, as the impulse to merge students

---

[103] RGASPI-M f. 1, op. 5, d. 1097, ll. 76–77.
[104] See a February 1962 report on Komsomol work at MGU. RGASPI-M f. 1, op. 46, d. 318, l. 10.
[105] Points of comparison in the postwar years include student environmental movements and spontaneous student mobilization around political rituals such as May Day celebrations, political theatre, and political song festivals. See Douglas R. Weiner, *A Little Corner of Freedom: Russian Nature Protection from Stalin to Gorbachev* (Berkeley: University of California Press, 1999), 312–39 and A. G. Borzenkov, *Molodezh' i politika: vozmozhnosti i predely studencheskoi samodeiatel'nosti na vostoke Rossii, 1961–1991 gg.*, vol. 1 (Novosibirsk: Novosibirskii gos. universitet, 2002).

with society produced a vibrant student subculture rather than furthering the chimerical goal of humbling intellectual elites.

Khrushchev's endeavors to transform the Soviet *studenchestvo* provide an interesting perspective from which to consider the broader phenomenon of post-Stalin reformism. Western and Russian commentators have stressed the extent to which the Khrushchev-era reforms – and particularly the era's more utopian policy initiatives – were irrational, ill-planned, and unpopular. As an influential account has it, the period's reforms were "shocks that Khrushchev so mercilessly heaped on a bewildered people."[106] As this suggests, the inadequacy of the reforms stemmed from their author, a communist dreamer out of touch with current realities.[107] This narrative has much to recommend itself: many of the policies pursued under the aegis of accelerated communist construction proved disruptive to state and society, including those explored in this chapter. For this reason, Khrushchev's successors were eager to cast off some of his policy innovations, which they dismissed as his "hare-brained schemes."

The case of reformist policies directed at students also suggests the shortcomings of telling the usual narrative on Khrushchev's reformism as a string of irrational ideas. The first secretary's agenda for a "Second Cultural Revolution" generated significant backlash in the university communities. Yet the notion that a greater tie between "education and life" was needed had significant popularity in them, in part among faculty who had become convinced that students were becoming increasingly elitist and uncommitted to the Soviet order. Likewise, Komsomol labor mania quickly caught the imagination of Soviet students. The modifications and indeed reversals that both higher education reforms and Komsomol labor projects underwent in the period were hardly preordained, or at least did not seem so at the time. The party-state gave up on large-scale social promotion through higher education only after eight years of almost Sisyphean efforts to transform the student body; the mass employment of students as shock-laborers around the country was likewise of impressive scope. Finally, all the initiatives discussed in this chapter lived on in modified form after the political career of the Soviet leader who inspired them.

---

[106] Roy A. Medvedev and Zhores A. Medvedev, *Khrushchev: The Years in Power* (New York: Columbia University Press, 1976), 1. Valuable recent accounts that stress irrational goals as the hallmark of the Khrushchev leadership are A. V. Pyzhikov, *Khrushchevskaia ottepel', 1953–1964* (Moscow: OLMA-PRESS, 2002), 267, 274, 320–23 and Yoram Gorlizki, "Policing Post-Stalin Society: The Militsiia and Public Order under Khrushchev," *Cahiers du Monde Russe*, 44 (2003): 465–80. For an exception to this approach, see discussion of a "moment of optimism in Soviet criminal justice policy" in Dobson, *Khrushchev's Cold Summer*, 133–55.

[107] A useful volume that provides different perspectives on Khrushchev's goals is William Taubman et al. (eds.), *Nikita Khrushchev* (New Haven, CT: Yale University Press, 2000).

Khrushchevian principles of favoring the admission to higher education of people with work experience remained in a softened and perhaps more effective form until the collapse of the USSR, while student construction brigades became such an established part of late Soviet life that efforts to revive them have emerged in the Putin era.[108]

The revolutionary impulses of the late 1950s had a wider basis than the quixotic mind of Khrushchev, yet in practice they discredited themselves in the eyes of many members of educated society. In addressing this unanticipated outcome, it is worth stressing the challenges the reformist leadership faced. In articulating policies toward higher education and youth as in other areas, Khrushchev worked from the notion of a second, de-Stalinizing Cultural Revolution. During the Stalin period, higher education was a central part of cultural construction, but it had also become an engine of social stratification by serving the interests and feeding the social identities of Soviet educated society. Efforts to recreate a revolutionary model of higher learning and to merge educated elites into a mythologized vision of the toilers flew in the face of Stalin-era social interests and values. In this context, it is hardly surprising that the politics of Cultural Revolution, even if pursued in a surprisingly tentative form, produced confrontation with parts of university communities and indeed with educated society as a whole. The Soviet intelligentsia was a creation of the Stalin era, and its tenacity in the face of post-Stalin reformism should be seen as part of the checkered process of grappling with the legacy of the past that was so central to the Khrushchev era.

---

[108] A. V. Pyzhikov, "Reformirovanie sistemy obrazovaniia v SSSR v period 'ottepeli' (1953–1964 gg.)," *Voprosy Istorii*, no. 9 (2000): 102.

CHAPTER 7

Uncertain terrain
The intelligentsia and the Thaw

In 1959 Les' Taniuk, a first-year student at the Kyiv Theater Institute, reflected on the Soviet leader in his diary. Taniuk "truthfully like[d] Khrushchev and the principal things that he is doing," but also had grave reservations about the first secretary. He was troubled by Khrushchev's personality, "his talkativeness, the universalism of his advice and all-knowingness, his lack of *great* culture." The first secretary was only concerned with material ends, "means of production," and "bases," rather than "deep values of the spirit" and "conscience." All of this had degraded the Soviet people, which had freed itself from the fear of the Stalin era only to "become petty-bourgeois [*mishchanity*]." Evidently distasteful in its own terms, the neglect of culture under the first secretary's rule threatened to lead back to the "restoration" of Stalinism. Taniuk pinned his hopes for the future on "culture itself," for only in it could "moral criteria be preserved."[1]

Taniuk's comments anticipate a longstanding scholarly consensus on the place of "great culture" for the Khrushchev period. Literature and the arts became a national obsession in the period as writers and artists pushed for freer expression and young poets subverted Soviet aesthetic traditions, appearing in front of electric crowds that filled soccer stadiums. For its part, the Khrushchev leadership looked on nervously, alternatively supporting and attacking these new voices in the creative sphere. Scholarly accounts often present the culture of the Thaw as "proto-politics," in which intellectuals and their supporters sought to "create a new language of civic culture," a "framework of social and moral responsibility, truth and sincerity."[2]

---

[1] Les' Taniuk, *Tvory v 60-i tomakh. Tom IV: Schodennyky 1959–1960 rr.* (Kyiv: Al'terpres, 2004), 60.

[2] Vladislav Zubok, *Zhivago's Children: The Last Russian Intelligentsia* (Cambridge, MA: Belknap Press, 2009), 162 and Stephen Bittner, *The Many Lives of Khrushchev's Thaw: Experience and Memory in Moscow's Arbat* (Ithaca, NY: Cornell University Press, 2008), 174–210.

In such a reading, creative intellectuals and their audiences embraced a new model of citizenship as an effort to overcome the heritage of Stalinism and prevent its reoccurrence, an agenda that inevitably drew them into conflict with Soviet officials within and outside the cultural world who derived their authority and livelihoods from the Stalinist order.[3] Adding to this break with the regime, in most accounts, were the widening intellectual horizons that Soviet thinkers experienced through contact with the outside world, and especially with the USSR's essential constitutive Other, the capitalist West. In recent years, a burgeoning literature has complicated these assumptions about Thaw culture, for instance by stressing the rifts within the Soviet creative professions and the complicated reactions of Soviet audiences to the cultural innovations of the period.[4] And yet the fundamental interpretation still holds that the politics of educated society were about "de-Stalinization," the passage from one epoch to another. From this fundamental temporal divide flow several binary oppositions: old and new, false and authentic, stale and fresh, and evil and good.

Taniuk also points to a different aspect of the Thaw that is less often explored by scholarship – the longstanding *mission civilisatrice* that dominated Soviet intellectual life. During the Thaw as before, Soviet culture was geared toward civilizing the "petty-bourgeois" Soviet masses. For Taniuk as for the student rebels discussed in Chapter 5, intelligentsia culture seemed all the more urgent in the disorienting post-Stalin era as only it could overcome Stalinism, which was a moral failing predicated on a lack of enlightenment. Taniuk's invocation of the intelligentsia's cultural mission was not easily reducible to the binary oppositions implicit in the "proto-political" view outlined above. Indeed, the political implications of Taniuk's musings were anything but clear. If intellectuals were the carriers of culture and all that was thought to come with it, what attitude should they take to political leaders who seemed to have little respect for such matters? Khrushchev, a reformer but also widely seen at the time as hostile to intellectuals, posed a particular conundrum in this regard. Taniuk highlighted this by depicting the first secretary as a threat to post-Stalin development while expressing support for "the principal things he is doing."

---

[3] Particularly influential accounts in this idiom are Stephen Cohen, "The Stalin Question since Stalin," in Stephen Cohen (ed.), *An End to Silence: Uncensored Opinion in the Soviet Union: From Roy Medvedev's Underground Magazine 'Political Diary'* (New York: Norton, 1982), 22–50; Priscilla Johnson McMillan, *Khrushchev and the Arts: The Politics of Soviet Culture, 1962–1964* (Cambridge, MA: MIT Press, 1965).

[4] Historians who have forced reconsideration of the Thaw include Stephen Bittner, Susan E. Reid, Miriam Dobson, Polly Jones, Kristin Roth-Ey, Eleanory Gilburd and Denis Kozlov; their works are cited throughout this chapter and the book.

This chapter focuses on the place of the intelligentsia in the Thaw by examining student experiences of two important historical developments: the cultural debates of the period and the opening of the country to the capitalist West. Following a theme of Chapter 5, it presents the Thaw as a development which was intricately connected to social identities.[5] For students, the overarching concern of the Thaw was a moral revival of post-Stalin Soviet society, but they viewed this task through the prism of the culture-carrying Soviet intelligentsia. The conflation of the political task of overcoming Stalinism and the social identities that had along accompanied belonging to the intelligentsia – among them a commitment to learning and "culturedness" along with a consciousness of the prestige that was attached to these pursuits – shaped much of student politics in the 1960s. This connection was at the core of the Thaw and provided it with its distinctive mindset and intellectual framework. Nevertheless, the social questions raised by identification with the intelligentsia also created problems for students embracing the Thaw agenda of renewing Soviet society.

In just twenty years

The Thaw emerged during a period of historical optimism. The dawn of the 1960s saw a kind of revolutionary dreaming that had not held central stage for decades. Khrushchev announced that the "period of extensive construction of communism" had begun and that members of the younger generation would live to see communism in their lifetimes. A new party program elucidated the path to the future: Soviet society had finally surpassed the stage of the dictatorship of the proletariat, during which a conventional state was needed to repress remnants of the hostile classes. Rapidly freeing itself of social contradictions, the Soviet order was becoming a "state of all the people" in which the population could begin to administer themselves en route to the withering away of the state: "Each Soviet person must become an active participant in the administration of societal affairs!" Khrushchev proclaimed.[6] Rather than being a propaganda slogan alone, this vision

---

[5] The need to bring social groups into discussions of "de-Stalinization" is noted in Miriam Dobson, "The Post-Stalin Era: De-Stalinization, Daily Life, and Dissent," *Kritika*, 12 (2011): 912.

[6] N. S. Khrushchev, *An Account to the Party and the People: Report of the C.C. C.P.S.U. to the 22nd Party Congress of the Party, October 17, 1961* (Moscow: Foreign Languages Publishing House, 1961), 97–103. See also Alexander Titov, "The 1961 Party Programme and the Fate of Khrushchev's Reforms," in Melanie Ilič and Jeremy Smith (eds.), *Soviet State and Society under Nikita Khrushchev* (London: Routledge, 2009), 8–25.

found concrete application in reforms aiming to invest power in societal organizations (including the ossified Soviets and trade unions) at the expense of state bureaucracies and to shift work in such disparate spheres as policing, legal procedure, and party administration to (generally unpaid) volunteers.[7]

The leap to the future came via a detour to the troubled past. After five years of deafening silence, the party returned to the topic of the cult of personality at the proceedings of the Twenty-Second Party Congress. In contrast to the secret speech, the congress and limited discussions of it were conveyed in Soviet media; moreover, Stalin's name and image were excised from Soviet life and his remains removed from the mausoleum on Red Square. For all its decisiveness, however, the new wave of de-Stalinization produced far less upheaval in the universities than it had five years before. Critical discussions about the past and historical responsibility did occur in the dormitories and hallways, but with scattered exceptions, they did not overwhelm the university's public spaces as they had five years before.[8] In part, the more subdued response to the second round of de-Stalinization reflected the party's clearer articulation of its objectives. Gone were the secret speech's confusing presentation of Stalin and its vague definition of the limits of permitted criticism; this time, the congress made clear that de-Stalinization as a process was complete and Leninist norms of party life fully restored.[9] This shift was crucial in the universities: as discussed in Chapter 5, many young dissenters in the universities during the first wave of de-Stalinization had seen their actions as support for reformism within the Soviet leadership rather than as outright opposition to it. This brand of loyal – and sometimes naïve – extrapolation of party pronouncements was much harder to articulate in the firmer political situation of 1961.

The less heated responses of students to the second round of de-Stalinization also reflected changes in the student body. In 1956, students had reached adulthood during the Stalin period; they had a fresh memory of his rule; and, in many cases, they still maintained faith in the leader when Khrushchev attacked him. None of these conditions applied to the cohorts enrolled in the early 1960s.[10] This does not mean that this later generation

---

[7] A. V. Pyzhikov, *Khrushchevskaia ottepel', 1953–1964* (Moscow: OLMA-PRESS, 2002), 136, 246–51.

[8] For specific cases of student dissent related to the congress, see RGASPI-M f. 1, op. 46, d. 331, ll. 85, 120–25.

[9] N. S. Shevtsova (ed.), *XXII s'ezd Kommunisticheskoi partii sovetskogo soiuza – s'ezd stroitelei kommunizma; lektsii dlia studentov gosudarstvennykh universitetov* (Izdatel'stvo Moskovskogo universiteta, 1963), 20.

[10] Igor' Volgin, "Na ploshchadi Maiakovskogo materializovalos' vremia," in L. V. Polikovskaia (ed.), *My predchuvstvie – predtecha – : ploshchad' Maiakovskogo, 1958–1965* (Moscow: "Zvenia," 1997), 37.

was uninterested in the Stalinist past or that it tended to accept the party's account of it uncritically. On the contrary, anti-Stalinism was now *de rigueur* in many student circles as it had not been five years before, as clearly illustrated by the appearance of anti-Stalin themes in the repertoire of popular student songs in the early 1960s.[11] However, the explosiveness of the Stalin question had shrunk while confidence in the future had grown. A 1961 sociological study that aimed at discovering Soviet youth's view of itself – one of the first of its kind in the USSR – discovered a "highly positive emotional-psychological tone" among the vast majority of young people surveyed, students included.[12] The "cult of personality" appeared a thing of the past or, at least, would soon become one.[13] A French graduate student returned from a trip to the USSR with the impression that students believed that the "progress and advances" after 1953 were there for good and that the Stalin era was now a "closed book."[14]

Paradoxically, the students' overarching optimism about post-Stalin advances coincided with emerging disdain for the very figure that had done most to bring about them about. Many students agreed with Taniuk in supporting the general line of Khrushchev's policies while holding the leader in disregard. As Chapter 6 demonstrated, the party-state's embrace of social affirmative action through education, and the populist rhetoric that accompanied it, was deeply unpopular among university communities. More broadly, the first secretary himself, an impulsive, earthy, and poorly educated worker, came across as an embodiment of the party's disrespect for intelligentsia status.[15] A French student who spent a year studying at MGU was shocked by "the scornful gibes and the 'aesthetic' disgust that the very name of Khrushchev evoked in young people"; he was "a 'third rater,' a 'swindler,' the incarnation of rudeness and

---

[11] See for instance V. F. Lur'e (ed.), *Fol'klor i kul'turnaia sreda GULAGA* (St. Petersburg: Sovmestnoe izdanie Fonda "Za razvitie i vyzhivanie chelovechestva" i Izdatel'stva "Kraia Moskvy," 1994), 63–68.

[12] B. A. Grushin, *Chetyre zhizni Rossii v zerkale obshchestvennogo mneniia: ocherki massovogo soznaniia Rossii vo vremena Khrushcheva, Brezhneva, Gorbacheva, i El'tsina*, vol. 1 (Moscow: Progress-Traditsiia, 2001), 189–95; Pyzhikov, *Khrushchevskaia ottepel'*, 291.

[13] A telling indication of this change was the stress on the recovery and reintegration of victims of terror in literary works of the period. See Polly Jones, "Memories of Terror or Terrorizing Memories? Terror, Trauma and Survival in Soviet Culture of the Thaw," *Slavonic and East European Review*, 86 (2008): 346–71.

[14] "Interview with a French History Graduate Student back from Moscow," BR # 1–60, 4 January 1960, RFE/RL, HIA, 529/7, 5.

[15] Attitudes toward Khrushchev among intelligentsia warmed after his removal, which helped to obscure the gulf between them during his rule. William Taubman, *Khrushchev: The Man and His Era* (New York: Norton, 2003), 629–33.

disgrace."[16] Capturing this impression was one episode at MGU in 1961; students watching Khrushchev's televised speech following talks with Kennedy in Vienna broke into laughter when the first secretary spoke about the German Bundesrat, pronouncing it *Bunde-srat'* ("Shit Office").[17] In the larger scheme of things, Khrushchev's personality was no laughing matter, and not only because of its potential ramifications for the Berlin Crisis. If the path to a humanized Soviet Union depended on civilized behavior, the leader's lack of it was a serious matter indeed.

This loss of respect for Khrushchev – and the intelligentsia attitudes that underpinned it – tainted students' attitudes toward the lofty plan to build communism in twenty years. Despite the widespread appeal of a reformed socialism in the late 1950s, students' responses to the new line on communist construction were quite restrained, both in the capitals and in the provinces. At SGU, the mandatory social science classes and lectures on the new congress were decidedly humdrum events, particularly in the less ideologically driven exact science departments; one student allegedly opined that it was "pointless to read lectures about the XXII Congress to mathematicians, read them to the historians."[18] Questions posed to propagandists sent to explain the party's vision for the future suggest that many young people saw it as fantastical and unscientific: one asked, "Where will the funds come from to construct communism given the constant struggle between two systems?"[19] Just as damaging to student morale as the confusing picture of the communist future was the regime's failure to provide students with concrete outlets to help bring it about. Policies meant to presage the "state of all the people" in the universities were largely uninspiring. An example was the "self-service" (*samoobsluzhivanie*) campaign, which transferred everyday tasks in the universities from paid employees to the students themselves. Ostensibly an experiment in revolutionary practice, self-service was also a barely disguised strategy to humble cocky students, a goal wholly in line with the concurrent experiments with labor projects at the Virgin Lands and elsewhere (see Chapter 6).[20] Cleaning the

---

[16] "Report by a Frenchman Recently Returned from Moscow," BR # 22–50, 30 September 1958, RFE/RL, HIA, 529/3, 4.

[17] "Some Observations on Life in Moscow," BR # 24–61, 29 August 1961, RFE/RL, HIA, 530/2, 2.

[18] GANISO f. 652, op. 1, d. 4, l. 14. For a meeting on the Party Program at MGU, see David Robert, "Moscow State University," *Survey*, no. 51 (1964): 30.

[19] RGASPI-M f. 1, op. 5, d. 824, ll. 6–7.

[20] For further discussion of *samoobsluzhivanie* and citizen policing, another manifestation of the "state of all the people" in a collegiate context, see Benjamin Tromly, "The Rise and Decline of Soviet Patriotism: University Students in Khrushchev-Era Russia and Ukraine," *Nationalities Papers*, 37 (2009): 299–326.

hallways and operating the cloakrooms did not drum up much enthusiasm for communist construction, perhaps because it served as a reminder that the intelligentsia as a social group was meant to disappear as communism approached.

Khrushchev's culture wars

For growing parts of the student body, then, communist ideology had become unexciting, despite – and perhaps sometimes because of – the fact that it seemed an immutable reality. Culture filled the void. In some ways, Thaw culture constituted a substitute for old-style Komsomol collectivism, to which it indeed bore a family resemblance. For young people engaged in the Thaw, the project of bringing about a moral regeneration of society through culture recreated something like the pathos of creating a new world. The differences between the Thaw and Komsomol activism were overwhelming, however, and one of them deserves particular attention: the reliance of the former on the social construct of intelligentsia. However universal its objectives were, the Thaw was a creation of educated society and deeply connected to its social and cultural attitudes. And if the intelligentsia animated the Thaw, the central questions become how people made claims to belong to this group – and, indeed, how such claims found validation. Two such mechanisms stand out for the student milieu and require discussion: social networks and cultural consumption. As my discussion will make clear, these ways of marking oneself an *intelligent* made the Thaw possible yet also presented their own complications for the project.

The friendship networks of the Thaw were a product of postwar university life. Already during the late Stalin years, students with intellectual proclivities formed friendship groups whose loose and informal nature had contrasted with the official youth collectives, a development exemplified by the BOKS publication discussed in Chapter 1. In the Khrushchev years, these "companies" (*kompaniia*) became important centers of Thaw thinking, particularly in provincial settings far from the concentrated intellectual elites of the capitals.[21] For instance, a group of SGU students which met to read poetry and reflect on paintings gave itself the name VChIN (an acronym

---

[21] An account of the companies that does not focus on questions of intellectual identities is Juliane Fürst, "Friends in Private, Friends in Public: The Phenomenon of the Kompania among Soviet Youth in the 1950s and 1960s," in Lewis H. Siegelbaum (ed.), *Borders of Socialism: Private Spheres of Soviet Russia* (New York: Palgrave Macmillan, 2006), 229–50.

for "all that is interesting"). Highlighting their own intellectual distinction, they wrote a song in which they boasted that they "did not borrow the lightning of their thoughts | from the bookshelves."[22] In the capitals of Moscow and Kyiv, more elaborate companies emerged which brought students into contact with intellectually minded people outside the student milieu. The following description of a company in Moscow conveys a sense of the combination of intellectual concerns, political debate, and socializing in these social groupings: "Old *politzeki* [political prisoners] would be shouting something at young philologists, middle-aged physicists would be locked in hot debates with young poets, and some people I had never met would be doing unrecognizable dance steps to someone's scratched Glenn Miller record."[23] Regardless of their differences, companies were a place for adherents of the Thaw to imagine and even construct in microcosm the future society they desired – one dominated by erudition, truthful talk, and solidarity.

While companies represented distinct social worlds with their own values and habits, it is nonetheless true that university life provided students engaged in the Thaw with significant social space within which to function. As discussed in Chapter 1, the universities provided students with a rich array of cultural activities that had the explicit function of making them *Kulturträger* in the Soviet mold. Culture-building activities took on new urgency with the anticipated approach of communism in the Khrushchev years and the concomitant need to produce "fully and harmoniously developed, spiritually rich, morally clean, and physically strong" individuals.[24] Communist morality, ethics, and aesthetics became ersatz academic disciplines, while Komsomol undertook what one activist called a "crusade for culture," which saw students reading lectures to workers in volunteer "universities of culture" and traveling to distant villages to perform theatrical sketches.[25]

More importantly for the Thaw, the official focus on cultural construction widened the scope for less regimented forms of cultural activity, such as

[22] Vitalii Azef, "'Taina' 42-ei komnaty: odnazhdy v Khrushchevskuiu 'ottepel'," *Sovety: fakty, sobytiia*, 28 April 1991: 3.
[23] Ludmila Alexeyeva and Paul Goldberg, *The Thaw Generation: Coming of Age in the Post-Stalin Era* (Boston: Little, Brown, 1990), 84.
[24] These are the words of a participant in an October 1962 Komsomol seminar. RGASPI-M f. 1, op. 5, d. 824, l. 69. See Catriona Kelly, *Refining Russia: Advice Literature, Polite Culture, and Gender from Catherine to Yeltsin* (Oxford and New York: Oxford University Press, 2001), 313–20 and Deborah A. Field, *Private Life and Communist Morality in Khrushchev's Russia* (New York: Peter Lang Publishing, 2007).
[25] RGASPI-M f. 1, op. 5, d. 1096, l. 119. See also L. G. Dobrovol'skii, "Kurs marksistko-leniskoi etiki i nravstvennoe vospitanie molodezhi," *VVSh*, no. 3 (1962): 67–70.

an array of new youth clubs ("youth initiative groups") with varying focuses
and youth cafes where students could spend their evenings listening to
poetry and music and take part in more or less organized discussions.[26]
These institutions quickly took on a life of their own. In 1963, students
at MGU were holding "spontaneously organized disputes" without
Komsomol approval; at one of them, a student Glebov was heard criticizing
Lenin for "not understanding the revolutionary nature of new forms and
methods in art" – and not a single member of the Departmental Komsomol
Bureau took him to task, the university's top Komsomol secretary later
noted with disgust.[27] For their part, the new student cafes came to develop
the reputation among Komsomol leaders as "places for meetings of rogues
and for collective drinking binges and debauchery."[28] In short,
Khrushchev's goal of Cultural Revolution had the unintended consequence
of providing outlets for the cultural initiatives of the Thaw, including those
that would run afoul of party authorities.

The consumption of cultural artifacts was another critical building block
for the Thaw intelligentsia in the university environment. Shaping what art
and literature people should consume and how this was to be done was critical
to the Thaw project. This was certainly true of professional producers of
culture in the period; for instance, Susan E. Reid has argued that Khrushchev-
era Soviet designers and artists championed a "contemporary," moderately
modern and internationalist aestheticism, one that they saw as constitutive of
their intelligentsia cultural mission.[29] But it is also true that consumers of
Thaw culture defined their own rules of evaluating cultural artifacts. Given
the importance of written texts, student literary judgment presents itself as a
useful case for exploring how cultural consumption reflected intelligentsia
identities. Rather than being a simple reflection of personal proclivities,
reading was a socially constitutive act through which a future member of
the professional strata could make a claim to belong to the intelligentsia. At
the same time, the emergence of a Thaw literary canon gave shape to social

[26] A recent account on youth initiative clubs does not focus on the specific intellectual and cultural
context of higher education. Gleb Tsipursky, *Having Fun in the Thaw Youth Initiative Clubs in the
Post-Stalin Years* (University of Pittsburgh Press, 2012), 25–27, 33–36. See praise of the cafes in Saratov
and Kharkiv universities in RGASPI-M f. 1, op. 5, d. 802, l. 117.
[27] TsAOPIM f. 6083, op. 1, d. 54, ll. 19–21.
[28] See the minutes of a 1964 Komsomol TsK conference on the struggle against bourgeois ideology
among youth. RGASPI-M f. 1, op. 31, d. 975, ll. 79–80.
[29] Susan E. Reid, "Destalinization and Taste, 1953–1963," *Journal of Design History*, 10 (1997): 177–201.
The pioneering work on aesthetic taste as a matter of demarking social positions is Pierre Bourdieu,
Distinction: A Social Critique of the Judgement of Taste (Cambridge, MA: Harvard University Press,
1984).

networks which held in common the Thaw agenda of regenerating Soviet society. In this regard, the Thaw paralleled other student movements of the 1960s around the world in which lists of "required reading" helped to solidify campus opinion and to identify insiders and outsiders.[30] At the risk of oversimplification, two traits of student literary reception deserve special emphasis. First, in determining what to read and what sense to make of it, students valued innovations in artistic forms of all kinds. To an extent, at work here was a visceral reaction to the "monochrome" character of Soviet culture inherited from the Stalin period; as the young poet Tatiana Zhirmunskaia commented to a foreign visitor in 1965, if ten completely unknown poets put up a sign advertising an evening of poetry, they would be sure to fill a theater.[31] Rather than representing interest in novelty for its own sake, however, finding new forms of expression was critical to the overriding Thaw agenda of correcting the moral deformities of the Stalin period through culture. Only by talking about human problems in a sincere and ethical way, it was believed, could the constrictiveness, emptiness, and cynicism of the existing society be undone.[32] While specifically aimed at the Stalin question, some students saw the new sincere talk in a wider frame as a modern and progressive response to universal human problems. "It is impossible in the century of electronics and the atom bomb to retain previous positions," an MGU student argued; rather, one should "speak about the individual personality and the life that surrounds him with an entirely different language."[33] This statement makes clear the Thaw's connection to a distinctly Soviet understanding of culture – namely, that it constituted an all-embracing pursuit of civilization and progress.

A second pillar of Thaw taste was the paramount attention given to the moral authority of the writer. Stalinism had encouraged an intensely personal relationship between readers and writers, whom Stalin dubbed "engineers of the human soul."[34] Yet Khrushchev-era students diverged from the model

---

[30] Cf. Jeremi Suri, *Power and Protest: Global Revolution and the Rise of Détente* (Cambridge, MA: Harvard University Press, 2003), 88–130.

[31] See the account of a meeting with Tatiana Zhirmunskaia in Mihajlo Mihajlov, *Moscow Summer, 1964: A Traveler's Notebook* (New York: Farrar, Straus and Giroux, 1965), 48. On "monochrome" culture and its sources, see Stephen Lovell, *The Russian Reading Revolution: Print Culture in the Soviet and Post-Soviet Eras* (New York: St. Martin's Press, 2000), 21.

[32] The importance of language to the Thaw is a major theme in Slava Gerovitch, *From Newspeak to Cyberspeak: A History of Soviet Cybernetics* (Cambridge, MA: MIT Press, 2002).

[33] RGASPI-M f. 1, op. 31, d. 19, l. 46.

[34] See E. A. Dobrenko, *The Making of the State Reader: Social and Aesthetic Contexts of the Reception of Soviet Literature*, trans. Jesse M. Savage (Stanford University Press, 1997), 282–306 and Juliane Fürst, *Stalin's Last Generation: Soviet Post-War Youth and the Emergence of Mature Socialism* (Oxford University Press, 2010), 128–34.

Soviet reader in seeing the mark of the true writer not only in truthfulness
and moral purpose but also in freethinking and a refusal to compromise
one's principles. Indeed, student readers tended to divide contemporary
Soviet writers into conformists to be spurned and critical and progressive
writers to be applauded, categories that stabilized or shifted with the political
situation at any moment. A mass survey of youth reading habits in Leningrad
demonstrated that the popularity among students of writers like Vasilii
Aksenov, Robert Rozhdestvenskii, and others reached its apex in 1963 when
they came under harsh criticism in the central press; students were "taking
[them] under protection," the authors of the study posited.[35] And when
writers were perceived to fail at truth-telling, criticism could be harsh. One
exchange student referred to "top-flight" intellectuals at MGU spurning a
leader of the Thaw, Evgenii Evtushenko, for following up "Bab'i Yar," his
controversial poem about anti-Semitism and the Holocaust, with a series of
"sell out" poems.[36] The paramount role of writers' moral stature in influenc-
ing student readers also goes some way in explaining the popularity of writers
past and present whose works had been deleted from the Soviet canon and
were only beginning to be published in the 1960s. The "password" for
entering certain youthful social circles in Moscow during the period was
"knowledge of Gumilev, Pasternak, and Mandel'shtam" – all victims of
Soviet power.[37] Of course, reading is always a social act, but this was especially
crucial for the Thaw in the student milieu. Reading the right works and
poems – and having the right kinds of insight about them – showed that one
was an insider who carried the progressive culture on which the project of the
Thaw was built.

Grabbing hold of the philistines: the radicalization of the student Thaw

Establishing norms of aesthetic appreciation – just like the formation of
companies and other social networks described above – was a way for
students to embrace the Thaw mission of transforming Soviet society
through culture. However, the specific social mechanisms of the Thaw
life and the cultural elitism they reflected proved highly divisive when

---

[35] See a summary of the unpublished study by the staff at the Krupskaia Leningrad State Institute of
Culture dated 1 August 1964. RGASPI-M f. 1, op. 46, d. 352, ll. 20–21.
[36] "Moscow Revisited: A Russian-Speaking British Exchange Student's Observations on Soviet
Attitudes," BR # 27–63, n. d., RFE/RL, HIA, 530/5, 10.
[37] Bukovskii, "Gaid-park po-sovetski," in Polikovskaia (ed.), *My predchuvstvie – predtecha*, 10. Nikolai
Gumilev and Osip Mandel'shtam perished in the Stalinist terror. See below on Boris Pasternak.

students confronted the society over which they sought to establish cultural patronage. The polarizing character of the Thaw's intellectual vanguardism shaped the most famous episode of student protest during the Khrushchev period: the independent poetry readings at Maiakovskii Square in Moscow. The amateur readings began with official blessing in 1958 following a ceremony marking the erection of a statue to the avant-garde communist poet on the square. The free-wheeling events, at which anyone could take the rostrum regardless of professional qualifications, let alone official vetting, quickly became a magnet for young supporters of the Thaw throughout the capital, including some students who had come into conflict with Komsomol in the colleges. Not surprisingly, party authorities put an end to the reading of ideologically suspicious and provocative published and unpublished poems in downtown Moscow. But they reappeared in September 1960 through the initiative of a smaller group of young people from around the capital (according to one recollection, the audience for this second phase of the readings made up fewer than 100 people).[38] For about a year, a remarkable situation prevailed in which young poets read while Komsomol citizen policing forces tried to disrupt the proceedings. This contest for public space was clearly a much more radical endeavor than the usual university politics, even in their most boisterous 1956 form.[39]

In part because of their very public nature, the Maiakovskii Square readings have come to be remembered as a chapter in Soviet dissent – an interpretation with some merit given that several of its participants would come to participate in the human rights movement that emerged roughly five years later. But the poetry readings were in fact more ambivalent in their opposition to Soviet authorities than they are sometimes imagined, especially in their first semi-authorized phase. A variety of motives drew young people to the poetry readings: mere curiosity, a purely aesthetic interest in fin-de-siècle ("Silver Age") poetry, or even naïve hope that a reformist leadership would view the readings as support for the agenda of purging the system of lies and cynicism – a misreading of Khrushchev's intentions that the latter fed with his talk of socialist democracy and attaining communism.[40] To be sure, the activists who spearheaded the second,

[38] Alisa Gadasina, "'Maiakovka' dala nam vnutrennuiu svobodu," in Polikovskaia (ed.), *My predchuvst-vie – predtecha*, 103.

[39] V. N. Osipov, "Ploshchad' Maiakovskogo, stat'ia 70-ia," *Grani*, no. 80 (1971): 116. See also Evgenii Shterenfel'd, "Ya vypolnial funktsii okhrannika," in Polikovskaia (ed.), *My predchuvstvie – predtecha*, 121–23.

[40] Leonid Prikhozhan, "Postupilo takoe ukazanie . . .," ibid., 144; Volgin, "Na ploshchadi Maiakovskogo," 41. Liudmila Alexeyeva, *Soviet Dissent: Contemporary Movements for National, Religious, and Human Rights* (Middletown, CT: Wesleyan University Press, 1985), 270.

unsanctioned phase of the readings were a more radical lot. Boisterous political discussion emerged at the square. Its most important product was an underground oppositional group that was eventually uncovered by the KGB, bringing about an end to the readings in 1961. The group composed an ideological program founded on internal Marxist critique of Soviet communism discussed as "revisionism" (discussed in Chapter 5). More exceptional for the period was the plan a few participants discussed to assassinate Khrushchev, which a few of them saw as the only way to avert war during the Berlin Crisis.[41] Although this group was small, it is also true that the poetry the young people read at the square, including original works penned for the purpose, was often provocative, to say the least. Yurii Galanksov's "The Human Manifesto," the most notorious original poem performed at the square and which was widely distributed in the *samizdat* networks that grew up around it, called on its listeners:

> Do not believe the ministers, leaders and newspapers!
> Those who are lying face down, rise up!
> You see, there are globules of atomic death
> In the graveyards of the world's eye-sockets.

The determined young people who gathered every week to defend poets such as Galanskov from Komsomol toughs nonetheless presented a more uncertain agenda than the action at the square might suggest. For most of their participants, the goal of the readings was not revolution – indeed, even Galanskov's "Human Manifesto" could appear as a critique of capitalism rather than a call to arms – but the core Thaw project of bringing conscious-ness to the people. According to one participant's later recollections, the readers at the square "tried somehow to grab hold of the philistines walking past who stopped with their jaws dropping open"; their goal was "to interpret something for them, to convince them of something, to excite them, maybe even to insult them – anything to keep them from being indifferent."[42] Here the project of spurring cultural renewal through finding new means of expression was taken to its extreme, becoming a kind of collective rebuke to society for its lack of enlightenment. This paradoxical attitude underscored a broader dilemma of the student Thaw in the 1960s. The square's activists built on intelligentsia ideals in claiming moral guard-ianship over the people. At the same time, the Maiakovskii Square activists'

---

[41] See Anatolii Ivanov, "Gavrilo Printsip naoborot," in Polikovskaia (ed.), *My predchuvstvie – predtecha*, 237–38. These discussions never came close to being acted upon. See Eduard Kuznetsov, "Ya rodilsia na zemle ...," ibid., 222–23.

[42] Gadasina, "'Maiakovka' dala nam vnutrenniui svobodu," 102.

bleak reading of Soviet society and its potential for overcoming the Stalinist past led them to a rhetorical radicalism, one that could only isolate its participants from the Soviet order. Indeed, some of the readings' regular participants dropped out of college and adopted a bohemian lifestyle, devoting their time to the square and to late night poetry readings at friends' apartments, often accompanied by heavy drinking and drugs.[43] However the young people's self-imposed isolation should be understood, it certainly aided the regime in its efforts to "expose and ridicule young people who aspire to the role of 'poet-enlighteners' but in reality are ignoramuses and loafers," as Komsomol TsK assigned newspapers to do in the wake of the readings.[44]

With their clashes for public space, the Maiakovskii Square readings were a particularly radical manifestation of Thaw culture among youth. However, the more commonplace forms of student cultural consumption in the universities also became more politically charged in the early 1960s. A watershed in this regard was the Manezh Affair in late 1962, when Khrushchev lashed out at modernist and abstract painters at an exhibition of the Moscow Artists' Union, notoriously questioning their sexuality and threatening them with arrest or expulsion from the country.[45] The party-state leader's actions and the more restrictive party line in creative affairs that followed had several causes: behind-the-scenes agitation by conservative forces in the party, his humiliation of the Cuban Crisis which occurred just before, and a deepening perception that artistic circles were coming under Western influence.[46] For educated society, however, the episode inevitably encapsulated Khrushchev's hostility to intellectuals and his demagogic political style.

Khrushchev's intervention in the arts drew heated responses in the universities. For the most part, students who supported the Thaw had adopted a highly optimistic prognosis for cultural affairs in the USSR. During the period, the creative professions were enveloped in conflicts between loosely formed reformist and conservative factions, with the first secretary presiding inconsistently over the fray. Before 1962, however, students committed to the Thaw often chose to read this uncertain situation as a

---

[43] Vadim Pomeshchikov, "Appolon i Iura," ibid., 118; RGASPI-M f. 1, op. 32, d. 1026, ll. 39–40, reproduced ibid., 158.

[44] This is a quotation from the Komsomol TsK protocol from November 1961. RGASPI-M f. 1, op. 3, d. 1062, printed ibid., 254.

[45] An overview of the event and its ramifications is in Taubman, *Khrushchev*, 588–92.

[46] See this argument in Zubok, *Zhivago's Children*, 207–13. For the conflation of Western-ness and Thaw culture in the press, see A. Sukontsev and I. Shatunovskii, "Frenk Soldatkin – mestnyi chuzhezemets (fel'eton)," *Komsomol'skaia pravda*, 25 August 1960: 2.

bump on the road to ultimate cultural renewal, hailing the publication of each work that broke official taboos as proof that censorship and publication bans would soon become a thing of the past.[47] The Manezh Affair destabilized this interpretation: the already unpopular first secretary had now tied himself unambiguously to conservative priorities in the arts. A more strident tone in student thinking was clear at a meeting of the MGU "Club of Lovers of Art" attended by 300 students. According to a Komsomol report, speakers who praised Khrushchev's management of the arts were drowned out by whistling and screaming. The crux of many of the student speeches was that "one person or even collective cannot interfere in the matter of aesthetic conscious-ness and force his own opinion and that the press does not have the right to speak in the name of the people."[48] Under the impression of Khrushchev's demarche, some students adopted the view that the communist leadership and perhaps the party as a whole was a fundamental obstacle to the project of renewing the Soviet project through culture.

As at the Maiakovskii Square readings, students' investment in the Manezh Affair exposed the extent to which the student Thaw had become an insular social milieu. The exhibition of the Moscow Artists' Union which had sparked Khrushchev's intervention also brought to the surface social tensions in the Thaw. Susan E. Reid's sensitive reading of visitors' books for the exhibition suggests the ways that some students' support of controver-sial artists distanced them from the broader society. One Moscow student, whom Reid characterized as "confident in his cultural capital," talked about the need to elevate the aesthetic tastes of the masses; but another criticized "self-satisfied philistines" who condemned works of art they did not under-stand.[49] Juxtaposing these comments is useful. The first student was invok-ing the core Thaw task of de-Stalinization through intelligentsia enlightenment. In contrast, the second, by disdaining people for retaining Stalin-era tastes, exposed frustration with the unwillingness of many citizens to follow the intelligentsia's agenda. Clearly, some participants in the student Thaw were adopting a more combative stance toward both the party and the people who were supposed to embrace the intelligentsia's enlightening influence. A noncommittal bystander captured this shift in his

---

[47] An American graduate student who spent a year at MGU reported that such thinking was widespread among his Soviet classmates. "Interview with an American Student who Spent an Academic Year at the University of Moscow," BR # 2–63, 16 January 1963, RFE/RL, HIA, 530/5, 2 and Volgin, "Na ploshchadi Maiakovskogo," 44.

[48] RGASPI-M f. 1, op. 31, d. 19, ll. 46–48.

[49] Susan E. Reid, "In the Name of the People: The Manège Affair Revisited," *Kritika*, 6 (2005): 711, 714, 704, 709. As Reid notes, it is unclear whether the comments in the visitors' books were entered before or after Khrushchev's denunciation of the exhibition.

description of a "typical scene" at the 1962 exhibition. A "not very highly educated" member of the older generation would approach an abstract painting and ask in a Khrushchevian vein "what sort of smear is that?" A crowd of nearby young bystanders would then pounce on him and argue for hours on end.[50] In the student milieu, the Thaw proved to be a difficult endeavor: by tying the intelligentsia's cultural mission to an ambitious attempt to de-Stalinize the Soviet project, it worked to divide students from the very masses they ultimately sought to lead.

Confronting the wider world

In the summer of 1957, Moscow felt like the center of the world. The VI World Festival of Students and Youth brought thousands of young people from all corners of the world to the streets of Moscow and, to a lesser extent, other locations in the country. Coming in the wake of the Hungarian crisis, the event's purpose was to brighten the Soviet state's tarnished international reputation; more broadly, the regime sought to convince young people around the world that the country was advanced and dynamic. The result was an event that stressed friendship, universal values, and culture above ideology, an approach that differed sharply from the usual celebratory events organized by Moscow-dominated international youth organizations. Class enemies as well as friends were invited to the Moscow event in large numbers, and control over their movements was uncommonly loose.[51] More remarkable still, informal interaction between everyday Soviet citizens and the strange visitors was not only allowed but encouraged.[52] Crowds of young people mingled freely in the streets and visited Muscovites' apartments, creating a truly exuberant and even wild atmosphere; young people mobbed every single foreigner as if he were "somebody from another planet."[53]

---

[50] "A Conversation with a Young Soviet Engineer in London," BR # 12–63, 3 May 1963, RFE/RL, HIA, 530/5, 2.

[51] Of 34,000 youths who took part in the festival, some 21,000 came from "capitalist and post-colonial countries." Moreover, less than 40 percent of all the non-Soviet participants were "members of communist organizations." See the report of TsK VLKSM to TsK KPSS on 30 August 1957. RGANI f. 5, op. 30, d. 233, l. 156.

[52] See discussion of the festival's origins and organization in Eleonory Gilburd, "To See Paris and Die: Western Culture in the Soviet Union, 1950's and 1960's" (Ph.D. diss., University of California, Berkeley, 2010), 49–100 and Pia Koivunen, "The 1957 Moscow Youth Festival: Propagating a New, Peaceful Image of the Soviet Union," in Ilič and Smith (eds.), *Soviet State and Society*, 46–65.

[53] This is from a Soviet student who recorded his impressions of the event on tape, evidently for Radio Liberation. "Radio Liberation and the Moscow Youth Festival," BR # 14–58, 30 August 1957, RFE/RL, HIA, 529/2, 2. The complex politics of sexuality enabled by this proximity is the theme of

The festival was a defining event in a broader opening of the Soviet Union to the outside world, including the enemy states of the capitalist West. Khrushchev sought to transform the Cold War from an incipient military conflict to a competition of civilizations, a strategy of "peaceful coexistence" that required a dramatic (if, in practice, incomplete) rejection of the closed borders and xenophobia of the Stalin period. In analyzing the growing exposure of Soviet citizens to the outside world, commentators – and particularly people who were themselves involved in waging the cultural Cold War – have presented contact with the West as inherently corrosive of Soviet values and institutions. In this view, exposing Soviet intellectuals and students to "relentless standards" of "truth and comparison" – or, what is seen as the same thing, "Westernizing" them – meant that loyalty to Soviet institutions and ideas inevitably fell by the wayside.[54] However, the Youth Festival in fact provides evidence for a more complex account of how young Soviet citizens viewed the outside world, and especially how important "culture" was for them. If young people embraced things foreign with unqualified enthusiasm during the festival, this was in part because Komsomol itself espoused an internationalist vision among them, for instance by encouraging young people to befriend visitors and even organizing the study of foreign songs and dances.[55] At the same time, many young people participating in the festival took quite seriously the fact that they were representatives of Soviet culture for the outside world. In preparation for the festival, the colleges put cultural activities into high gear by staging "Festivals of Soviet Youth" that featured street festivities, holidays of song, youth balls, carnivals, and concerts.[56] Indeed, the consensus in Komsomol circles was that the festival had helped to strengthen Soviet culture, even if there was concern that foreigners had used the event to infiltrate Soviet society.

Recent treatments of the topic have offered a critical corrective on the simplistic "Westernization" perspective by emphasizing how Soviet contexts and ideas informed contacts with the West. Eleonory Gilburd has stressed that for many Khrushchev-era Soviet citizens – including cultural administrators, intellectuals, and youth – broadening ties with the West was about

Kristin Roth-Ey, "'Loose Girls' on the Loose: Sex, Propaganda, and the 1957 Youth Festival," in Susan E. Reid and Melanie Ilič (eds.), *Women in the Khrushchev Era* (Houndmills, Basingstoke and New York: Palgrave Macmillan, 2004), 75–95.

[54] Allen H. Kassof, "Scholarly Exchanges and the Collapse of Communism," *The Soviet and Post-Soviet Review*, 22 (1995): 263. See also Richmond, *Cultural Exchange and the Cold War: Raising the Iron Curtain* (University Park: Pennsylvania State University Press, 2003) and Walter L. Hixson, *Parting the Curtain: Propaganda, Culture, and the Cold War, 1945–1961* (New York: St. Martin's Press, 1997), 115–17.

[55] RGASPI-M f. 1, op. 46, d. 182, l. 74. See also Gilburd, "To See Paris and Die," 121–28.

[56] See RGASPI-M f. 1, op. 3, d. 889, l. 62 and TsAOPIM f. 478, op. 3, d. 52, ll. 5–6.

more than the narrowly political agenda of fighting the Cold War through the clash of civilizations. Rather, the "idea of a great humanistic culture shared by all" gained a foothold in official discourse, propelled by the tenets of socialist internationalism as well as the universalizing parameters of Soviet notions of civilization.[57] The anthropologist Alexei Yurchak highlights Soviet ways of thinking in his discussion of late Soviet youth's fascination with an "Imaginary West." In his account, Soviet socialism offered young people a confused framework for responding to foreign culture. Socialist internationalism undercut the simple binary oppositions of Cold War rhetoric; for instance, a Soviet citizen could find ideological justification for embracing capitalist culture in the writings of Lenin, which presented the dictum that any national culture contained competing progressive and reactionary elements. Responding to such confused ideological messages, young people appropriated and adapted Western cultural artifacts to their own environment without abandoning Soviet values as they understood them.[58]

This discussion builds on this literature by presenting intelligentsia as another crucial Soviet idea that colored perceptions of the Cold War enemy among students. In this perspective, students' belief in their cultural mission and the special status it brought helped to make the West appear both attractive and fundamentally foreign. A fitting focus for exploring this theme is student exchanges. Cultural exchange agreements with several Western countries, including the Lacy–Zarubin agreement with the United States in 1958, brought students from the capitalist world to study in the premier Soviet universities – and hence into contact with the Soviet intellectual elites of the future.[59] The Cold War enemy, however feared, had often appeared as a distant and even somewhat abstract entity for Soviet students and other citizens; now he or she lived and breathed in one's midst.[60] While the student exchanges made universities in Moscow, Leningrad, and (to a lesser extent) Kyiv central battlefields of the cultural Cold War, provincial institutes were much less affected, not to speak of those in closed cities like Saratov which remained off limits to foreigners entirely.

[57] See Gilburd, "To See Paris and Die," 22–30 and Ted Hopf, *Social Construction of International Politics: Identities and Foreign Policies, Moscow, 1955 and 1999* (Ithaca, NY: Cornell University Press, 2002), 92–98.
[58] Alexei Yurchak, *Everything was Forever, until it was No More: The Last Soviet Generation* (Princeton University Press, 2006), 158–205, at 164–65. Although focusing on the Brezhnev period and beyond, Yurchak suggests that this specific dynamic began in the late Stalin period.
[59] Yale Richmond, *Cultural Exchange and the Cold War*, 14–20.
[60] For Cold War hostilities in the context of previous Stalinist enemy politics, see Serhy Yekelchyk, "The Civic Duty to Hate: Stalinist Citizenship as Political Practice and Civic Emotion (Kiev, 1943–53)," *Kritika*, 7 (2006): 552.

Whatever the limits on direct contact with the West, the party saw it as a threat to the ideological makeup of Soviet society. Indeed, in Khrushchev's last years party and Komsomol discourse presented the "inroads of bourgeois ideology" as an almost existential threat to the Soviet order. Training students and graduate students from the capitalist West in the USSR was an exceptionally politicized affair. To be sure, Soviet higher education had already experienced extreme difficulty in training foreign students, both the longstanding cohorts of students from the people's democracies and the more recent ones from post-colonial or developing countries. Stalinist xenophobia, great power chauvinism, and – in the case of the students from the second group – racism all rendered Soviet internationalism hollow.[61] Nevertheless, the small groups of students from the West posed distinct problems for university authorities and students alike: if there was hope that fellow socialists and post-colonials would follow the Soviet historical path, there was none vis-à-vis the capitalist students who were treated as hostile elements to be contained from the outset.[62] KGB tracked the capitalist students from their arrival by sending covert agents to befriend them and plainclothesmen to follow them through the streets.[63] Soviet students quickly learned the dangers of associating with the capitalist students, and those who did so anyway sometimes implored the Westerners not to write about their experiences once back home for fear of retribution from university authorities.[64]

Such distrust was surely counter-productive. Some of the capitalist exchange students, and the Americans most of all, came to the USSR with the goal of fighting the cultural Cold War, but the suspicion and bureaucratic barriers they encountered at every turn only firmed

---

[61] See Julie Hessler, "Death of an African Student in Moscow: Race, Politics, and the Cold War," *Cahiers du Monde Russe et Soviétique*, 47 (2006): 33–64. The troubling consequences of Stalinist xenophobia for intra-bloc exchanges are the topic of Benjamin Tromly, "Brother or Other? East European Students in Soviet Higher Education Establishments, 1948–1956," forthcoming in *European History Quarterly*.

[62] In 1965, there were 21,236 foreign students and graduate students enrolled in higher education establishments, with 11,802 from people's democracies, 9,183 from post-colonial countries, and only 251 from "developed" capitalist countries. RGANI f. 5, op. 55, d. 136, l. 105.

[63] "Attitude and Mood of Some Young Soviet Citizens," BR # 20–57, 12 September 1957, RFE/RL, HIA, 529/7, 2. These practices had not changed a decade later, as shown by William Taubman, *The View from Lenin Hills: Soviet Youth in Ferment* (New York: Coward-McCann, 1967), 96–99. Westerners, especially graduate students trying to conduct research, also confronted endless bureaucratic hurdles from suspicious administrators in the universities and libraries. See the accounts gathered in Samuel H. Baron and Cathy A. Frierson (eds.), *Adventures in Russian Historical Research: Reminiscences of American Scholars from the Cold War to the Present* (Armonk, NY: M. E. Sharpe, 2003).

[64] "Attitude and Mood," 7.

their views.[65] Students from the West wasted no time in creating waves in the universities by entering into heated arguments with their Soviet over-seers and classmates – treated, in turn, by university administrative, party, and Komsomol authorities as hostile attacks to be repulsed by all means possible, short of those which would cause major diplomatic setbacks.[66] Despite this degree of political tension – and in part because of it – the capitalist students provide a useful context for examining the place of the West in the mindsets of Soviet students. Foreign students living in the midst of the Soviet students for months or even years had countless interactions with their Soviet peers which were not controlled by political authorities. Sometimes they were "amazed" at being "able to discuss politics freely and straightforwardly" with their Soviet classmates, as an American graduate student who studied from 1962 to 1963 at the MGU Economics Department – typically thought of as a pillar of party conservatism – reported.[67] Moreover, the foreigners were eager observers of Soviet student life, providing a sense of the immediate social contexts for student cultural and political discussions that Soviet sources sometimes leave obscure.[68]

The experiences of exchange students from capitalist countries leave no doubt about the extreme interest of Soviet students in the West. A case in point was students' all-consuming passion for foreign literature. The study of mass reading habits cited above revealed that virtually all students polled read foreign authors, with Erich Maria Remarque, Ernest Hemingway, Jack London, and Theodore Dreiser (in that order) being most popular.[69] Although the reading of Western literature was widespread among Soviet youth of all social stations, the depth and seriousness of engagement with it distinguished the students. Educated youth spent countless hours combing second-hand bookstores for books published abroad, waiting in line in libraries for dog-eared works in

---

[65] One of the early American exchange students recalled that he knew not one peer "whose views weren't hardened against the Soviet Union" while studying there. David C. Engerman, *Know Your Enemy: The Rise and Fall of America's Soviet Experts* (Oxford University Press, 2009), 88.

[66] For strategies of containing exchange students, which included mobilizing the Komsomol *aktiv* and settling supposedly ideological Soviet students in the dormitories close to them, see TsAOPIM f. 478, op. 3, d. 84, ll. 91–92.

[67] "Interview with an American Graduate who Spent Five Months at Moscow State University in the Economics Faculty," BR # 32–63, 12 August 1963, RFE/RL, HIA, 530/6, 1.

[68] In part, the foreigners' reports of the university scene provide a useful contrast to letters to authority, a type of primary source used widely in recent histories of the period which are composed by a self-selecting range of authors by definition. For thoughtful use of the letter to authority genre to study the Thaw, see Miriam Dobson, *Khrushchev's Cold Summer: Gulag Returnees, Crime, and the Fate of Reform after Stalin* (Ithaca, NY: Cornell University Press, 2009), esp. 10–12 and Denis Kozlov, *The Readers of Novyi Mir: Coming to Terms with the Stalinist Past* (Cambridge, MA: Harvard University Press, 2013).

[69] RGASPI-M f. 1, op. 46, d. 352, ll. 20–22.

translation, and even wading through literary texts in German, English, or French with dictionary in hand.[70] "Personality cults" arose around some Western writers, as evinced by Soviet youth who imitated Hemingway by talking in curt phrases, wearing turtlenecks, and growing beards.[71]

Reading such passionate interest in foreign writers as the symptom of a fundamental "Westernization" of Soviet youth would be a mistake. Rather, several aspects of the Soviet students' worldview during the Khrushchev period made foreign cultural artifacts meaningful, and prominent among them was the Thaw. Foreign writers, perhaps even more than the young poets of the Thaw, seemed to provide a genuine mode of expression – the antipode of the stale and conservative Soviet literature of the present – which might feed the cultural and societal renewal that Thaw activists eagerly anticipated. But even young intellectuals who did not embrace the Thaw developed a strong interest in foreign literature. This should hardly surprise given the internationalism of Soviet ideology in the Khrushchev period. If high culture was to be seen as a universally held value, then foreign literature – or, rather, those works which the Soviet state saw as sufficiently "progressive" to publish in translation – was part of the cultural baggage that the Soviet intellectual was duty-bound to amass.

Foreign literature also became a status symbol for young members of the educated strata. A Soviet defector from Kherson in Ukraine explained to Radio Liberty that consumption of foreign art served to distinguish between social groups among young people: "among youngsters of better education and higher social station it is considered gauche to read Soviet writers," he commented, with the only exception being the celebrated writers of the Thaw like Evtushenko and Rozhdestvenskii.[72] Status distinctions also held with regard to different foreign writers. A West German journalist who socialized extensively with intellectuals and students while living in Moscow explained that easier-to-read works by Heinrich Böll, Erich Maria Remarque, or Arthur Miller could "only move the reader in the provinces and the intellectual 'petty bourgeois'," even in their original editions; however, it was "almost a sin against the spirit" to be uninterested in finding the books of Uwe Johnson, Tennessee Williams, or Eugène Ionesco.[73] Although this respondent's sarcastic tone might give pause, there is no reason to doubt his claim that the

[70] "The Role of Western Literature in Soviet Intellectual Circles," BR # 22–63, 20 June 1963, RFE/RL, HIA, 530/5, 5–6.
[71] Alexeyeva and Goldberg, *The Thaw Generation*, 97.
[72] "Soviet Youth, as Seen by a Young Defector," BR # 14–63, 9 May 1963, RFE/RL, HIA, 530/5, 2.
[73] "The Role of Western Literature," 2.

appeal of foreign books depended on how hard they were to access as well as on their content – indeed, this should surprise given the role that considerations of scarcity played in shaping the habits and values of Soviet readers in general.[74] In short, on display in students' appreciation of foreign writers was the tight intertwining of the goals of the Thaw and the broader traits of educated society associated with the intelligentsia.

If high-brow literature from abroad was wholly compatible with Soviet intelligentsia identity, the situation was more complicated in the case of Western mass culture, and particularly popular music. The tremendous popularity of the latter in the universities is beyond question: Western exchange students discovered that their Soviet counterparts flocked to American concerts and listened religiously to jazz broadcasts on Voice of America (VOA).[75] Such forms of cultural consumption were deemed decidedly "low" by Soviet leaders – "men of the ancient régime when it came to culture," as a recent study characterizes them – and this was no doubt one reason why many Soviet adults saw listening and especially dancing to foreign music as a threat to the morality and political obligations of Soviet youth.[76] Nevertheless, interest in jazz and, later, rock and roll was primarily about the taste of forbidden fruit and bore no clear connection to oppositional "moods." Going further, Yurchak is surely correct in asserting that Soviet "authoritative discourse" was elastic enough to provide space for attachments to Western culture. An American scholar who had long discussions with students in Kyiv reported that, in the opinion of his informants, "interest in Western dress and Western jazz cannot be taken as a symbol of protest," as "many jazz fans are ardent members of Komsomol."[77] Indeed, Komsomol activists sometimes used the Youth League to lobby for jazz performances at college events.[78]

Despite its apolitical thrust, however, Western mass culture proved challenging for people preparing to enter the ranks of the intelligentsia.

---

[74] See Lovell, *The Russian Reading Revolution.*

[75] "Some Attitudes of Soviet Students in Moscow and Leningrad," BR # 76–65, 17 December 1965, RFE/RL, HIA, 531/2, 3.

[76] Kristin Roth-Ey, *Moscow Prime Time: How the Soviet Union Built the Media Empire that Lost the Cultural Cold War* (Ithaca, NY: Cornell University Press, 2011), 9. For the shifting relationships of the Soviet state to jazz, see Frederick Starr, *Red and Hot: The Fate of Jazz in the Soviet Union 1917–1991* (New York: Limelight editions, 1994).

[77] "Note from a Trip to the Soviet Union in the Spring of 1961," BR # 11–61, 17 May 1961, RFE/RL, HIA, 530/2, 12. A recent study argues that interest in Western culture among late Soviet youth was "countercultural" in nature, but in fact presents much evidence to the contrary. Sergei I. Zhuk, *Rock and Roll in the Rocket City: The West, Identity, and Ideology in Soviet Dniepropetrovsk, 1960–1985* (Washington, DC: Woodrow Wilson Center Press, 2010), 13, 67–68.

[78] TsAOPIM f. 5463, op. 1, d. 4, l. 117.

For students who took their cultural mission seriously – including many activists of the Thaw who held the ethical implications of learning sacred – real culture was high culture, not empty entertainment produced by and for markets. The predisposition of some students to serious culture informed their negative responses to the subculture of American-aping stylish youth called *stiliagi*, a phenomenon which arose in the Stalin period and continued throughout the Khrushchev years.[79] Despite the large interest they have generated among later scholars, *stiliagi* had a small presence in universities in the capitals and provinces (although their visibility on the dance floors at institute events was much larger). A part of the student body condemned the lifestyle of stylish youth, both for their deliberate rejection of collective life and for their reputation for drinking and sexual depravity – a stance that no doubt bore the imprint of press campaigns vilifying *stiliagi*.[80] In all likelihood, a more common attitude among adherents of the Thaw was to view *stiliagi* with scorn rather than with hatred or fear. In this view, while hardly subversive, wide ties, narrow pants, and boogie-woogie were decisively "petty-bourgeois" and uncultured.[81] The Kyiv students who met with the American academic noted above thought that students "most imitative of the West" were not "the most responsible elements" and certainly "not the ones among whom dissent on grounds of cultural freedom would spring."[82] The subtext of the formulation is clear: while there was nothing wrong with consuming Western mass culture, it should not come at the expense of the serious business of freeing Soviet society through enlightenment. Of course, such a ranking of cultural priorities reflected broader social realities, as it was largely students' special connection to culture which defined them as a social group.

Western mass culture might pose problems other than distracting students from serious culture. By its very nature, popular culture could not provide intellectual elites with the same kind of social status as the serious learning of an intelligentsia did. While students and intellectuals were at the forefront in embracing jazz and then rock and roll in the 1960s, tastes soon became democratized and lost their exclusive social function (as fashions always do).[83] Moreover, the pursuit of exotic foreign cultural

---

[79] The best account of the emergence of this phenomenon is Mark Edele, "Strange Young Men in Stalin's Moscow: The Birth and Life of the Stiliagi, 1945–1953," *Jahrbücher für Geschichte Osteuropas*, 50 (2002): 37–61.

[80] RGANI f. 5, op. 17, d. 529, ll. 104–5, 110–12. See also L. V. Silina, *Nastroeniia sovetskogo studenchestva, 1945–1964* (Moscow: Russkii mir, 2004), 131.

[81] Edele, "Strange Young Men," 42–43. [82] "Note from a Trip to the Soviet Union," 12.

[83] See the account of the social diffusion of these musical styles in Zhuk, *Rock and Roll in the Rocket City*, 65–81.

products – and, it is true, this applied to rare books as well as jazz albums or blue jeans – brought one into a shadowy world of illicit money-making. Students who supplemented their meager stipends by trading Western books on the black market provided a strange spectacle of high culture and its antithesis, one which must have proven uncomfortable for future *intelligenty*.[84] In short, students' association with the intelligentsia and their penchant for Western consumer culture coexisted awkwardly. This fact complicates Yurchak's presentation of Soviet youth drawing freely and comfortably on foreign culture to suit their cultural environment.[85] Soviet students might have imagined the West, but the ways they did so reflected their own contested social identities and interests.

Enemies in our midst?

It is also true that the West could not, in the end, be pried apart from questions of political ideology. Apart from being the mythic home of Hemingway and Glenn Miller, the West was the Cold War enemy – something that could hardly be forgotten given the widespread fear of catastrophic war in the period.[86] It is indeed striking that an idealized image of the West as a political and ideological entity – rather than a cultural one – took hold of some student minds in the period. This phenomenon emerged even in the closed city of Saratov, where direct contact with foreigners was totally lacking.[87] In 1961, the SGU Komsomol Committee heard the case of the student Churkin, who spoke openly about the advantages of life in foreign countries, including "freedom of speech in America" and multi-party democracy. When a member of the Komsomol Bureau stated that Churkin was indebted to the state for his education and much else besides, the latter responded that he owed it nothing: on the contrary, the "bureaucratic machine" was repressing him and seeking to prevent him from graduating. He declared that he could emigrate and finish

---

[84] "The Role of Western Literature," 4–5. For exploration of a similar tension in the context of Soviet tourism to the West, see Anne E. Gorsuch, *All This Is Your World: Soviet Tourism at Home and Abroad after Stalin* (Oxford University Press, 2011), 130–67.

[85] Yurchak only hints at this tension between Soviet culture and market-based culture for Soviet youth. *Everything was Forever*, 172–73.

[86] For a different context in which the "Imaginary West" took on very concrete implications, see Andrei Kozovoi, "Eye to Eye with the 'Main Enemy': Soviet Youth Travel to the United States," *Ab Imperio*, 2 (2011): 221–37.

[87] For an earlier and non-elite version of Soviet pro-Americanism, see Rosa Magnusdottir, "The Myth of 'Amerika' and Soviet Socialism: Perceptions and Realities in the Postwar Soviet Union," *The Soviet and Post-Soviet Review*, 31 (2004): 291–307.

university abroad "if it was necessary."[88] Although the outcome of this
conflict is unclear, Churkin was far from alone in pondering the possibility
of exit: in 1963, the KGB recorded almost 500 cases of people twenty years of
age or younger attempting to flee the country. This number, it was claimed,
was higher than in previous years.[89]

Ironically, the ideological possibilities of the West grew with Khrushchev's
ideological pronouncements, and particularly the promise that economic
production in the USSR would soon surpass that of the United States,
whose "sun was setting."[90] As at least one member of the leader's inner circle
feared, the ratcheting-up of expectations in the Cold War proved a dangerous
move for the government.[91] An economic downturn in 1962 forced the
government to take the dangerous and humiliating steps of raising prices
on staple foods and buying grain abroad, while instances of mass unrest more
severe than anything the country had seen for decades further discredited the
party-state's promises of plenty.[92] Disappointment with the failure of
Khrushchevism was clearly at work in the case of Churkin, who told his
Komsomol interrogators that he and many Soviet citizens "agreed with the
Molotovs" – that is, Khrushchev's conservative opponents whom he had
removed from power in 1957 – that "communism can't be built in twenty
years" and that the program's claim to this end was "all talk."

Although frustration with the course of Khrushchev's rule was widespread among students, Churkin's idealization of the West was hardly a
widely held position. Rather, student thinking about the West was multi-
dimensional and uncertain, as the experiences of the student exchanges
make immediately clear. Even though they read Hemingway and Salinger
with bated breath, Soviet students bombarded the American graduate
students with hostile questions about racism and unemployment; they
might eagerly befriend American classmates while discrediting everything
the latter said on the assumption that their companions surely belonged to
the exploiting class.[93] At the root of such ambivalence was a simple fact:

[88] GANISO f. 652, op. 1, d. 6, ll. 134–35.   [89] RGANI f. 2, op. 1, d. 626, ll. 101–10.
[90] N. S. Khrushchev, "On the Program of the Communist Party of the Soviet Union: Report by
   Comrade N. S. Khrushchev at the 22nd Congress of the Communist Party of the Soviet Union Oct.
   18, 1961," *Pravda*, 19 October 1961, in *CDSP*, 13, no. 44 (1961): 5–6.
[91] See O. V. Kuusinen's comments on the draft of the Party Program in Pyzhikov, *Khrushchevskaia
   ottepel'*, 341–45.
[92] Erik Kulavig, *Dissent in the Years of Khrushchev: Ten Stories about Disobedient Russians* (New York:
   Palgrave, 2002), 125–53.
[93] For a sense of such diverse responses, see "Interview with an American Student Who Spent an
   Academic Year at the University of Kiev," BR# 8–63, 25 March 1963, RFE/RL, HIA, 530/5, 2 and
   Loren R. Graham, *Moscow Stories* (Bloomington: Indiana University Press, 2006), 32–40.

students perceived the West according to their own values and ideas, and these frequently proved conflicted. And one important issue in this context was the social identity of the intelligentsia, a factor that influenced Soviet perceptions of the exchange students in disparate ways.

Intelligentsia thinking was crucial with regard to an issue central to the cultural Cold War: wealth and living standards. A member of the first cohort of American graduate students in Moscow reported that he handed out Sears Roebuck catalogues to his Soviet classmates, and recalled that they were "particularly effective" propaganda tools.[94] While surely awe-inspiring to Soviet students, images of plenty and the wide scope for unflattering comparisons they generated rarely produced principled pro-Westernism like that expressed by Churkin above. The obvious response – that material deprivations would evaporate en route to communism – is only part of the story. The Sears catalogue approach might fall flat for another reason: the values of the intelligentsia. One of the first French students to spend an academic year at MGU recalled that his Soviet peers "were aware that Americans live better than they do but qualified this by the fact that Americans were interested in the material but not in the spiritual aspects of life" – that is, the very sphere the intellectuals claimed as their own.[95] Indeed, intelligentsia identity provided a clear vantage point from which to decry the West, and America especially. An American graduate student felt that Soviet students – including those he called "anti-regime people" – looked at the luxuries of American life "with contempt and consider[ed] it a waste of time," citing as an example the contemporaneous American student fad of telephone booth cramming that had been lampooned in the Soviet press.[96] The poet Evtushenko took the idea to its natural conclusion in his autobiography (published in the West) by arguing that the rich nations showed a "grosser spirit and a weaker hold on moral principles" than Russia, which had been ennobled by suffering.[97] As these sentiments show, the intelligentsia's idealism and distaste for all things "petty-bourgeois" both contributed to – and, no doubt, fed off – the geopolitical divide of the Cold War.

---

[94] "Aspects of Soviet Life as Seen by American Exchange Student," BR # 39–59, 21 August 1959, RFE/RL, HIA, 529/3, 7.
[95] "Attitude and Mood of some Young Soviet Citizens," 6.
[96] "American History Student Who Spent an Academic Year at Moscow University," BR # 35–55, 23 July 1959, RFE/RL, HIA, 529/3, 3. See also the discussion of the trope of America as an uncultured parvenu in Susan E. Reid, "Who Will Beat Whom? Soviet Popular Reception of the American National Exhibition in Moscow, 1959," *Kritika*, 9 (2008): 896–900.
[97] Yevgeny Yevtushenko, *A Precocious Autobiography*, trans. Andrew R. MacAndrew (London: Collins and Harvill, 1963), 40–41.

The perception of superior Western wealth also played into a defensive stance toward the West among Soviet students. Whether many students held what a French student called "black envy and deep distrust" directed toward the West is unclear.[98] However, there can be no doubt that Western wealth and self-confidence threatened the claim to culturedness that was so central to the identities of Soviet students. Indeed, the capitalist exchange students served as a lightning rod for this more pervasive sense of insecurity in student identities. In 1957, three Soviet students wrote a piece in *Moskovskii universitet* attacking French exchange students who had allegedly conveyed a sense of their "superiority over uncultured Russians." The authors turned the tables on the French by alleging that the latter were the ones lacking in culture; Georges Niva, they alleged, did not clean his room and even swore at members of the sanitary commission who asked him to rectify the situation.[99] Though the publication was highly censored and the material was tendentious – many Soviet students were no more polite to the invasive sanitary commissions that Niva was, nor more "cultured" in their behavior in the dormitories generally – the article reflected the threat that the West posed for the students' core commitment of *kul'turnost'*.

There were, however, points of elective affinity between the West and intelligentsia ideals, particularly in the politicized way that Thaw activists viewed them. Western exchange students struck a raw nerve among Soviet citizens by emphasizing their enjoyment of many freedoms the latter lacked. An American graduate student thought he had impressed his Soviet contacts with his "assurances" that closed divisions did not exist in American libraries and that Soviet newspapers and magazines were available for purchase at newsstands.[100] More specifically, the "bourgeois freedoms" of information, conscience, and travel held obvious appeal for young adherents of the Thaw. Connecting the ideological clash of the Cold War to Thaw culture explicitly was the party's attack on Boris Pasternak, who was awarded a Nobel Prize for Literature after publishing *Doctor Zhivago* abroad in 1957. Very few Soviet students actually read the novel, which was not published in the USSR; exchange students who arrived with suitcases full of copies of the novel were reluctant to distribute them for fear of spurring political reprisals against their Soviet classmates. Nonetheless, Pasternak's real-life drama could hardly fail to appeal to students used to seeing writers

---

[98] "Report by a Frenchman," 3.
[99] Z. V. Kormanov, "Uvazhaemye gosti, davaite ne budem!" *Moskovskii universitet*, 6 April 1957: 3. On the defensive side of *kul'turnost'*, see also Eleonory Gilburd, "Picasso in Thaw Culture," *Cahiers du Monde Russe et Soviétique*, 47 (2006): 80–82.
[100] "Programming Suggestions," 3.

as moral authorities. In discussions on the subject with foreigners, some students expressed respect for Pasternak as someone who "dared to speak his mind right to the very end" – even if many others "took the Pravda line" by condemning *Doctor Zhivago* as slander against the revolution.[101] As this shows, identification with the intelligentsia produced mixed reactions to the West, complicating the usual emphasis in the literature on the unquestioned attractiveness of the latter in either its imaginary and real manifestations.

A complex pattern of attraction and rejection was also evident in the most widespread form of direct contact with the West for Soviet society: foreign radio broadcasts. It is clear that tuning in to what were popularly called "the voices" – mainly Voice of America and BBC – became widespread in the period and played a major role in popularizing American music. Yet the ideological ramifications of foreign broadcasting for students, as for other social groups, are more open to interpretation.[102] It is indisputable that "the voices" figured prominently in a series of KGB prosecutions of educated youth for anti-Soviet propaganda and agitation in the period; moreover, some of the defendants in these cases spoke the Western language of the Cold War in condemning Soviet "totalitarianism." (On the other hand, it also seems possible that the KGB had a vested interest in exaggerating the ideological dangers of Western radio for Soviet society.)[103] Obstacles to foreign broadcasting's ideological influence, however, were substantial. Most of all, it seems doubtful that the political material conveyed by Western radio reached student ears in the first place. While Soviet jamming of foreign radio broadcasters softened in the Khrushchev years, programs in Russian and other Soviet languages that dealt with domestic political affairs were usually blocked in the major cities; meanwhile, language skills muted the impact of English-language news on VOA

---

[101] "Interview with Frenchman Recently Returned from USSR," BR # 21–58, 12 September 1958, RFE/ RL, HIA, 529/3, 6. See the extensive discussion of letters supporting Pasternak in Denis Kozlov, "'I Have Not Read, But I Will Say': Soviet Literary Audiences and Changing Ideas of Social Membership, 1958–66," *Kritika*, 7 (2006): 564–74. See also "Some Observations by a French Graduate on his Return from a Year's Study in the USSR," BR # 15–59, 13 May 1959, RFE/RL, HIA, 529/3, 1.

[102] For differing evaluations for the period in question, compare Vladimir Tolz with Julie Corwin, "Soviet Reactions to Foreign Broadcasting in the 1950s," in A. Ross Johnson and R. Eugene Parta (eds.), *Cold War Broadcasting: Impact on the Soviet Union and Eastern Europe: A Collection of Studies and Documents* (Budapest: Central European University Press, 2010), 293–96 and V. A. Kozlov et al. (eds.), *Kramola: Inakomyslie v SSSR pri Khrushcheve i Brezhneve, 1953–1982 gg.: rassekrechennye dokumenty Verkhovnogo suda i Prokuratury SSSR* (Moscow: "Materik," 2005), 130.

[103] GARF f. 8131, op. 31, d. 96675, l. 16 and Robert Hornsby, "Voicing Discontent: Political Dissent from the Secret Speech to Khrushchev's Ouster," in Ilič and Smith (eds.), *Soviet State and Society*, 175. For the argument about the KGB's inflation of risk, see Roth-Ey, *Moscow Prime Time*, 141–44.

and BBC.[104] Even when more ideologically driven programming did find its target, it is far from clear that most Soviet students were open to what they heard. According to an American graduate student, the majority of student listeners "were inclined to discount much of the VOA news, regarding it as American propaganda."[105]

In a broader sense, however, foreign radio did have an impact on student minds, and the ways it did reflected the concerns of the student Thaw. Limited access to foreign radio crystallized the issue of freedom of expression and presented a tangible symbol of the limits of the Thaw. Indeed, even students who mistrusted the Western broadcasts often disagreed with censorship of them.[106] A group of students at the Belarus Polytechnic Institute arrested in 1963 had constructed a plan to blow up a nearby radio tower that was used for jamming foreign broadcasting. S. N. Khanzanov explained that the tower was a "direct violation of the individual personality"; his co-conspirator V. I. Khrapovitskii called it a "minimizing of human dignity."[107] In an indirect way, foreign radio had provided support for the Thaw and its ideals of virtuous freethinking and the liberated personality.

The idea of a Thaw offered Soviet citizens a powerful narrative on the Soviet project. Soviet history was poised between the Stalinist past and a more hopeful future, as forces for renewal confronted Stalinist stalwarts. Presiding over the drama was the Khrushchev leadership, which seemed to embody the transitional and basically unsatisfactory present with its espousal of novel policies rooted in archaic Bolshevik conceptions. The means to move history forward seemed simple: in order to dispel the ghosts of the cult of personality, one had to value the truth and act decently.

Inevitably, this blueprint for transforming society through free thought and expression proved difficult to implement in practice. The Thaw project seemed destined to create divisions, one cause of which this chapter has identified as student social identities. Ostensibly universal, the ideas of the Thaw in fact were bound up with the interests of a relatively narrow part of society: intellectual elites who had long been confident in their mission to civilize society and felt particularly duty-bound to assign themselves this

---

[104] The jamming policies of the Soviet leadership fluctuated with the major developments of the Cold War. See Michael Nelson, *War of the Black Heavens: The Battles of Western Broadcasting in the Cold War* (Syracuse University Press, 1997), 91–106.

[105] "Aspects of Soviet Life," 6.

[106] For articulations of student opposition to jamming of foreign radio, see RGANI f. 2, op. 1, d. 626, ll. 120–21.

[107] See the judicial conclusion (*zakliuchenie*) on the case sent by head of oversight over KGB in the Belarusian Procurator's Office. GARF f. 8131, op. 31, d. 95626, ll. 14, 19.

role in the wake of the Stalin period. Accordingly, the Thaw represented the transposing of idealized characteristics of intellectuals – intellectual integrity, willingness to debate, and autonomy – onto the rest of society and even onto history itself. An MGU student who wrote to Khrushchev to condemn his curbing of young writers in 1963 conveyed this link between intellectual identities and the march to communism. "We are trying to awaken creativity in every person – think, create and only then will communism be built," he stated; accordingly, the current "campaign against creativity" in the arts stunted history itself.[108] The notion that creative thought would bring communism – and, conversely, that ignorance was the root of reactionary tendencies – provided a neat illustration of the Thaw's inherent connection to educated society.

The problem was that not everyone accepted this conflation of intellectuality and historical progress. In fact, the limiting social content of the Thaw lifted its head at inopportune moments, complicating the students' seemingly straightforward agenda for Soviet society. While supporting the reformist moment in the Soviet leadership, young intellectuals despised its architect, a reaction that was understandable given his populist rhetoric but also conveyed a strain of cultural snobbishness. When struggling to produce a new and more genuine Soviet culture, they discovered that the masses might not share their tastes or even approve of their right to have them. And as they came into contact with real and imagined manifestations of the West, students made sense of them in ways that reflected the cultural assumptions and status concerns of Soviet intellectuals as much as the ideological underpinnings of Soviet discourse. The presentation of the Thaw as a struggle between new and old, good and bad, post-Stalin and Stalin – binary oppositions that scholars have too often reproduced in an unreflecting way – papers over thorny questions about the particular identities and interests of Soviet intellectuals. In the coming years, young educated citizens would begin to sense the social limits of the Thaw, and some would search for new ways to embrace the intelligentsia's cultural mission.

---

[108] "'My sobralis' dlia togo, chtoby iskrenne vyskazat' svoi mysli' (K istorii vstrech N. S. Khrushcheva s tvorcheskoi intelligentsiei v 1962 i 1963 gg.)," *Izvestiia TsK KPSS*, no. 11 (1990): 214–15.

CHAPTER 8

Higher learning and the nationalization
of the Thaw

In 1961, a Radio Liberty official interviewed N. I. Sereda, a 24-year-old Ukrainian electrical engineer and recent graduate of the Kyiv Polytechnic Institute. Given the circumstances – Sereda had defected to the West during a tourist trip to Vienna just months before – Radio Liberty expected to meet a staunch anti-communist.[1] Instead, they discovered someone who accepted "as gospel truth many of the tenets of Soviet propaganda" and was cynical about the freedom of the "free world." To be sure, the young Kyivan railed against the party, alleging that it consisted "primarily of opportunists and people who are using it for the advancement of their own personal interests." However, he espoused a "democratic socialism" in which the second concept seemed to predominate: in the future, only socialist parties would exist, he asserted, and the only difference between them would be "the methods and techniques which they would use to implement socialism." Despite having recently fled the country, Sereda was optimistic that this future society would be built, since "the overwhelming majority of the population" and especially youth believed staunchly in socialism and, being "sophisticated politically," would transform the system from within.

If these views caught Radio Liberty off-guard – in fact, confronting a communist revisionist led the author of the report to conclude that the radio staff was striking the wrong tone in its anti-communist messaging – Sereda's treatment of the national question might have seemed more in line with the agency's expectations for Soviet youth. Sereda criticized the Russification of

---

[1] Sereda is not named in the report but his identity can easily be established. See "Red Scientist Defects, Says Vienna Report," *The Deseret News*, 22 August 1961 and "Glimpses on World Outlook and on Ukrainian Related Topics by the Kind of Listener RL Attempts to Reach," BR # 35–61, 20 November 1961, RFE/RL, HIA, 530/2, 1–5. The interviewer "Mr. Diakovsky" was almost certainly Morris Diakowsky, a Ukrainian-Canadian aficionado of traditional Ukrainian music who worked at Radio Liberty in the period. See Geoffrey T. Hellman, "The Bandurist," *The New Yorker*, 27 September 1958.

language and culture in the Ukrainian republic; young Ukrainians were "very conscious of national identity," and those who succumbed to Russifying pressures were "neither good nor decent" people. Even here, however, Sereda's message was a mixed one. There was no "national or race hatred" in Ukraine, he insisted; instead, Ukraine was a "geographic and state concept" as much as an ethnic one, and local Russians felt themselves to belong to Ukraine as much as ethnic Ukrainians did. Above all, he asserted, "most intelligent Russians do not oppose Ukrainian independence," and the socialist future he anticipated would see the Ukrainian and Russian peoples living side by side in friendship.[2]

The defector Sereda's belief in a Ukrainian future that was both Soviet and national complicates views of ethnic nationalisms in the postwar period. It is indisputable that national thinking – if not specifically *nationalism* in the sense of aiming for an independent nation-state – took hold of growing numbers of educated Soviet citizens during the post-Stalin period.[3] This development is usually bracketed off from specifically Soviet identities and institutions. One line of analysis draws on influential theoreticians to connect national identities to processes of modernization such as education and mobility or, alternatively, to the unequal fruits these developments brought to different ethnic groups in the USSR.[4] Other works argue that Khrushchev's rule played a decisive role in activating national identities; de-Stalinization discredited communism, while radical policies in areas such as agriculture, religion, economic development, and urban construction generated nationalized responses throughout Soviet society.[5]

These two approaches provide critical contexts for the growing hold of national identity, while casting doubt on an earlier literature that drew a simplified picture of non-Russians in uniform opposition to a Russifying

[2] "Glimpses on World Outlook," 3–4.

[3] In common usage, nationalism refers to a doctrine that the nation and state should be coterminous. Ernest Gellner, *Nations and Nationalism* (Ithaca, NY: Cornell University Press, 1983), 6–7. I also use the term "cultural nationalism" as a way of distinguishing national expression in the cultural sphere from that which articulated explicitly political goals.

[4] For these perspectives, see Ronald Grigor Suny, *The Revenge of the Past: Nationalism, Revolution, and the Collapse of the Soviet Union* (Stanford University Press, 1993), 84–126 and Bohdan Krawchenko, *Social Change and National Consciousness in Twentieth-Century Ukraine* (New York: St. Martin's Press, 1985).

[5] See Yitzhak M. Brudny, *Reinventing Russia: Russian Nationalism and the Soviet State, 1953–1991* (Cambridge, MA: Harvard University Press, 1998); John B. Dunlop, *The Faces of Contemporary Russian Nationalism* (Princeton University Press, 1983), 175–76; and Peter J. S. Duncan, *Russian Messianism: Third Rome, Holy Revolution, Communism and After* (London: Routledge, 2000), 62–67. The best examination of de-Stalinization and Ukrainian politics is H. V. Kasianov, *Nezhodni: ukrains'ka intelihentsiia v rusi oporu 1960–80-kh rokiv* (Kyiv: "Lybid'," 1995), 1–46.

Soviet state. Yet neither perspective can explain the broader phenomenon of which Sereda was an example: the Soviet nationalist. Modernization might make some Ukrainians ethnically conscious. Indeed, the leaders of movements of cultural nationalism in Ukraine and elsewhere were, for the most part, beneficiaries of postwar modernization: students or young professionals with access to prestigious careers in the Soviet establishment. But as Sereda suggested, modernization was also compatible with "Russification" rather than Ukrainian identity. Moreover, the defector's belief in the nation as part of a reformed Soviet communism suggests the limits of accounts that connect nationalism to a discrediting of communism during the Khrushchev period. While Sereda's national communism was surely shaped by the politics of the Khrushchev era, it reflected a commitment to reforming Soviet socialism, not to rejecting it.

Despite the crucial insights on postwar Soviet nations in historical literature, a less global and more contingent approach is a necessity for understanding the emergence of national thinking among educated youth.[6] This chapter connects the rise of politicized national identities in Russia and Ukraine to the specific environment of postwar higher learning during the Khrushchev years. While the Russian and Ukrainian national projects were vastly different, three elements of the university environment in the period played a role in creating a student national revival among students in both contexts. First, the universities were nation-producing institutions, as they symbolized national accomplishments and trained professionals in disciplines concerned with studying national cultures and histories. Second, national thinking made sense in light of the status hierarchies of university life: "becoming national" offered a novel path to seek social prominence that was attractive to students at the margins of campus life, including uncultured former peasants and provincials, isolated eccentrics, and brainy loners. Finally, national identity emerged in close dialogue with the politics of the Thaw and the vision of a reformed socialism that figured so prominently in it. In these diverse ways, the specific contours of university life and student politics in the Khrushchev years produced individuals who were national-minded yet retained much of the worldview of their cohorts in the Soviet educated class.

---

[6] For a masterful account of the contingency of nation-building, see Timothy Snyder, *The Reconstruction of Nations: Poland, Ukraine, Lithuania, Belarus, 1569–1999* (New Haven, CT: Yale University Press, 2003).

Kyiv University: national in form and content

Few topics in Soviet history have undergone more thorough re-conceptualization in recent years than the national question. Following the original Marxist interpretation, Lenin and the party-state he created saw national consciousness as a screen for bourgeois class interests that sooner or later would have to be uprooted en route to communism. However, the Soviet project also found itself supporting Soviet nations. Understanding that nationalism was too powerful a force to be rejected out of hand, the early Soviet leaders tried to disarm its political implications by actively supporting Soviet nation-building: supporting and codifying languages, developing cultures, and promoting "national" cadres throughout the state and economy. During the conservative turn of the 1930s, Stalin curtailed these efforts on the suspicion that they were producing the nationalism they were intended to curb. While narrowing Soviet nationhood, however, Stalin also deepened it by introducing into Soviet discourse ethnic "primordialism," or a respect for the ancient roots and cultures of Soviet nations (and of the Russians most of all).[7] The crucial byproduct of the tangled history of interwar nationalities policies was the establishment of "institutionalized multi-ethnicity" as a permanent feature of Soviet statehood: the "thoroughgoing state-sponsored codification and institutionalization of nationhood and nationality exclusively on a sub-state rather than a state-wide level."[8] Rather than being elaborate window-dressing, the institutionalization of nations strengthened the national character of regional government structures and, more surprisingly, gave the ethnic nation some meaning in the minds of Soviet citizens. Sereda, for instance, thought that most Ukrainians accepted the national credentials of the Ukrainian Soviet Socialist Republic and even took pride in the republic's symbolic separate seat in the UN.[9]

At first glance, Ukrainian higher learning would seem a poor example of "institutionalized multi-ethnicity." Urban society in postwar Ukraine was traditionally Russian in language and culture, a deep-seated pattern upheld by historical precedent and the efforts of Ukrainian citizens to achieve social

---

[7] See Terry Martin, *The Affirmative Action Empire: Nations and Nationalism in the Soviet Union, 1923–1939* (Ithaca, NY: Cornell University Press, 2001); Serhy Yekelchyk, *Stalin's Empire of Memory: Russian–Ukrainian Relations in the Soviet Historical Imagination* (University of Toronto Press, 2004) and Yuri Slezkine, "The USSR as a Communal Apartment, or How a Socialist State Promoted Ethnic Particularism," *Slavic Review*, 53 (1994): 414–52.

[8] Rogers Brubaker, "Nationhood and the National Question in the Soviet Union and Post-Soviet Eurasia: An Institutional Account," *Theory and Society*, 23 (1994): 50.

[9] "Glimpses on World Outlook," 4.

mobility rather than by outright Russification from above.[10] Universities and other colleges in Ukraine helped to maintain the Russian character of urban areas. Most instruction was conducted in Russian, and this was especially true in the more prestigious physical and natural sciences.[11] In addition, ethnic Russians were disproportionately represented in both the student body and the teaching staff.[12] As a result, Ukrainian-speaking students from the peasantry quickly switched to speaking Russian as part of their transformation into city folk. This reflected and also contributed to the stigmatization of Ukrainian as an uncultured and peasant language; according to a KDU professor who administered language examinations, many students had a "dismissive" attitude toward studying Ukrainian language and culture.[13] By the end of the Khrushchev period, however, the university had been transformed: a significant part of the student body used Ukrainian as a medium of exchange, and national themes and ideas had gained a new prominence in student cultural activities.

One potential and perhaps natural source of national identity in Russified Kyiv was the Ukrainian West. In the territories Stalin had absorbed in 1939 and again after the war, Ukrainian was the dominant literary and spoken language – a position it would retain throughout the Soviet period despite the influx of outsiders and the Russocentric character of Sovietization after the war.[14] The Ukrainian West's sharp cultural differences from the rest of the country and its bitter experience of Soviet rule made for stronger ethnic identity among West Ukrainian youth relative to Easterners.[15] In the Khrushchev period, several influential young national-minded intellectuals

---

[10] For the interwar period, Peter A. Blitstein emphasizes that parents of non-Russians supported expansion of Russian-language education as a means to social mobility for their children. See "Stalin's Nations: Soviet Nationality Policy between Planning and Primordialism, 1936–1953" (Ph.D. diss., University of California, Berkeley, 1999), 13.

[11] "Glimpses on World Outlook," 6–7.

[12] According to a 1965 report of the Ukrainian minister of higher and specialized secondary education, only 61 percent of the students enrolled in the republic's eight universities were Ukrainian, while the figure for instructors was 56 percent. Both figures were significantly lower than the percentage of ethnic Ukrainians in the population of the republic. Kenneth C. Farmer, *Ukrainian Nationalism in the Post-Stalin Era: Myths, Symbols, and Ideology in Soviet Nationalities Policy* (The Hague and Boston: Martinus Nijhoff Publishers & Kluwer Boston, 1980), 141.

[13] TsDAHOU f. 1, op. 71, spr. 207, ark. 68–73.

[14] See William Jay Risch, *The Ukrainian West: Culture and the Fate of Empire in Soviet Lviv* (Cambridge, MA: Harvard University Press, 2011), 121–28 and Roman Szporluk, "The Soviet West – or Far Eastern Europe?" *East European Politics and Societies*, 5 (1991): 466–82. The national character of West Ukraine was in part Stalin's doing: the occupation of the territories by the Soviets, the Nazis, and the Soviets again during World War II provided the context for the elimination of longstanding Polish influence from the area. See Snyder, *The Reconstruction of Nations*, 154–78.

[15] Risch, *The Ukrainian West*, 179–219 and Kasianov, *Nezhodni*, 23–24.

in Kyiv hailed from West Ukraine, and their childhood experiences played an important role in shaping their thinking about the nation.[16] Nevertheless, the distinct ethnic identities of West Ukrainians cannot serve as a sufficient explanation for the revival of national identity in Kyiv or elsewhere in Central and Eastern Ukraine. West Ukraine remained a world apart for many young Ukrainians in Kyiv and other East Ukrainian cities, in part due to state policies that limited enrollment of West Ukrainians in colleges located in pre-1939 Ukraine.[17]

Surprisingly, East Ukrainian universities themselves provided a propitious context for thinking in nationally conscious terms. Of course, students in postwar Ukraine received an extremely limited and selective presentation of Ukrainian history through the curriculum. Nevertheless, even at the height of late Stalinist Russocentrism, a part of the student body did specialize in Ukrainian culture and history, both in the humanities departments at major universities and in institutes for training artistic cadres in the republic's capitals. Students at these institutions were the designated articulators of the Soviet Ukrainian culture of the future, and therefore had a vested interest in its fate. It was logical, then, that students in these disciplines came under suspicion during the battles against "bourgeois Ukrainian nationalism" that swept the republic during late Stalinism.[18] In 1952 and 1953, university party and security services arrested or expelled a number of students of the Ukrainian Division of the KDU Philology Department for demonstrating unhealthy nationalist deviations. At the center of the scandal was the West Ukrainian G. P. Voloshchuk, recently arrested by MGB, who was clearly an avid nationalist. Students recalled that, during a classroom discussion, he questioned the progressive nature of the seventeenth-century unification of Ukraine and Russia (a mythologized event that was widely touted in Soviet propaganda prior to the celebration of its anniversary in 1954).[19] This anti-Soviet nationalism was far from common among Kyiv students. And yet – as MGB and party overseers were shocked to discover – Voloshchuk was not denounced for his views by his East Ukrainian peers and was in fact quite popular among them (as one

[16] Cf. "My obyraly zhittia: Rozmova z Yevhenom Sverstyukom," in Bogumila Berdychowska and Olexandra Hnatiuk (eds.), *Bunt pokolinnia: Rozmovy z ukrainskimi intelektualamy* (Kyiv: Dukh i litera, 2004), 46–48.
[17] In 1953, only 2.3 percent of the youths admitted to higher-education establishments in Kyiv came from the "Western provinces." TsDAHOU f. 1, op. 71, spr. 105, ark. 89–103.
[18] See the report of the Student Division of the Ukrainian Komsomol TsK for 1948 in TsDAHOU f. 7, op. 6, spr. 2198, ark. 28.
[19] Ibid., ark. 26, 38.

put it, he was "a great boy, just a bit hot-headed").[20] Clearly, the strength of national identities among future Ukrainian specialists reflected the awkward position of the universities as conveyers of Ukrainian culture during late Stalinism.

The national character of the universities was only one factor in the rise of an Ukrainophile movement among students.[21] Many young Ukrainians in less specifically national institutions, such as Sereda's Polytechnic Institute, also developed national identities in the period. A second formative influence for the Ukrainian national revival was the paradoxical social and cultural logic of embracing Ukrainian nationality in postwar higher education. As discussed in Chapter 2, students from villages and provincial towns often felt out of place in colleges in the major cities. This social division was much starker in Ukraine than in Moscow or the Russian provinces. Ukrainian universities admitted large numbers of youths from worker and especially peasant backgrounds; if 4.5 percent of students admitted to MGU in 1952 listed "collective farmer" as their social origin, a corresponding figure in KDU was 28.2.[22] Ivan Drach, a Ukrainian writer born to a family of collective farmers, recalls of KDU that "the city youths were richer, better educated, and more elegantly dressed" and "slighted people" from the peasantry like him.[23] Youths from villages and provincial towns occupied a low position in the Soviet hierarchy of culture, and their automatic association with the Ukrainian language deepened this gap.

Paradoxically, it was precisely the stigmatization of the Ukrainian nation that made it an attractive basis for identity formation for some students at postwar universities. Ethnic Ukrainian students of lowly origins in the capital experienced a situation that Liah Greenfeld calls "status inconsistency," a "discrepancy between the possible and the existent, the frustrating apprehension of unfulfilled opportunity."[24] Studying in KDU brought lowly born youths close to the pinnacle of Soviet culture but also stigmatized them as cultural inferiors. Typically, Russification bridged this gap by providing a path to a more "cultured" identity, but plebeian ethnic Ukrainians might still feel that they would remain less cultured than the Russians and Russified

---

[20] Ibid., ll. 38, 32–33. At the same time, some students seem to have offered information for the investigation.

[21] I see "Ukrainophile" and "Russophile" as appropriate labels for the movements discussed here as both centered on an embrace of national culture rather than specific political agendas.

[22] The Kyiv figure is for 1953. These figures from reports on student admissions are in TsMAM f. 1609, op. 2, d. 361, l. 13; TsDAHOU f. 1, op. 71, spr. 105.

[23] Interview with Ivan Drach, Kyiv, 2005.

[24] Liah Greenfeld, *Nationalism: Five Roads to Modernity* (Cambridge, MA: Harvard University Press, 1992), 213.

urban folk – a logical concern given the importance of status markers for belonging to the intelligentsia. Status inconsistency was fertile soil for the formulation of Ukrainian national identity. Some young Ukrainians found in the nation a way to reverse their lowly social position by upsetting cultural and linguistic hierarchies. Rather than continuing the difficult struggle to adopt Russian culture, peasants' sons and daughters could define themselves as leading representatives of a Ukrainian culture, one that was equal to the more dominant Russian one and more native than it in the local context.[25]

As Eastern European history has often shown, raising a peasant culture to a viable ethnic nation is a difficult and contingent process. Some of the Ukrainian national revivalists could barely speak the language they had decided to champion – a serious matter given that, following European tradition, the nation can only appear ancient and eternal if its language becomes a medium for serious intellectual discourse.[26] Here the bold strategy of overturning national-cultural hierarchies received help from an unexpected quarter: the Soviet establishment itself. The national question was thrown open by Stalin's death. Led by Lavrentii Beria and Khrushchev, the collective leadership swiftly shifted nationalities policies, in the Ukrainian case by promoting "titular" cadres in the republic's party-state elites and curtailing the linguistic Russification of the recently acquired Western territories.[27] To many contemporaries, the Twentieth Party Congress also seemed to mark a principled rupture in the national question. The secret speech associated Stalin's cult of personality with "rude violations of the basic Leninist principles of the Soviet state's nationalities policies," specifically the mass ethnic deportations during World War II.[28] In the wake of the secret speech, a short-lived "Ukrainization of language, culture, education and personnel policy" took place.[29] While the

---

[25] It was not a coincidence that many of the prominent campus national activists came from villages and small towns. The list includes Ivan Drach, Viacheslav Chornovil, Valentyn Moroz, Vasyl Stus, Vasyl Symonenko, Ivan Svitlychny, Yevhen Sverstyuk, Vitalii Shevchuk and Lina Kostenko. Alla Hors'ka, who came from a family of Soviet *nomenklatura*, was the most notable exception to this trend. See the biographical sketches on the website "Dissident Movement in Ukraine" (www.khpg.org/archive/index.php), last accessed in May 2008.

[26] Krawchenko, *Social Change and National Consciousness*, 308. A classic comparative study of national movements and their attempt to pass the threshold of historicity is Miroslav Hroch, *Social Preconditions of National Revival in Europe: A Comparative Analysis of the Social Composition of Patriotic Groups Among the Smaller European Nations* (Cambridge University Press, 1985).

[27] Gerhard Simon, *Nationalism and Policy toward the Nationalities in the Soviet Union: From Totalitarian Dictatorship to Post-Stalinist Society*, trans. Karen Forster and Oswald Forster (Boulder, CO: Westview Press, 1991), 231–32.

[28] "O kul'te lichnosti i ego posledstviakh," in L. A. Kirshner and S. A. Prokhvatilova (eds.), *Svet i teni "velikogo desiatiletiia": N. S. Khrushchev i ego vremia* (Leningrad: Lenizdat, 1989), 84.

[29] Simon, *Nationalism and Policy toward the Nationalities*, 232.

phenomenon is poorly studied, it is clear that leading intellectuals and political elites in Ukraine anticipated – and, in some cases, perhaps agitated for – a return to the indigenization policies of the 1920s. An article in *Komunist Ukrainy*, the theoretical organ of the Ukrainian Communist Party, proclaimed that "the development of the national language, its introduction into all spheres of the republic's state, party and economic structure were questions of principle in Lenin's nationalities policy."[30]

Moscow quashed the notion that de-Stalinization spelled a return to "indigenization." But the increasing attention of Ukrainian elites to the national question did have tangible effects in Ukrainian public life, and they were nowhere more pronounced than at the flagship national university in the capital. Following the Twentieth Party Congress, KDU experienced an officially sponsored and deliberate policy of linguistic Ukrainization. Writing to her boyfriend in 1957, a first-year student at KDU commented that instruction at the university – with the notable exception of the ideological social science curriculum – was conducted in Ukrainian; she commented that many professors were lecturing in Ukrainian for the first time (and marring their lectures with Russianisms in the process!).[31] In the same period, use of Ukrainian also became the norm in the university's party and Komsomol organizations. In late 1956, the KDU vice-rector H. H. Vdovychenko chided an assembly of Komsomol activists for making speeches in Russian.[32] De-Stalinization provided a crucial spur to the nation by Ukrainizing public discourse, however incompletely.

The Thaw and the discovery of nationality

Higher education provided structures that facilitated national thinking in the form of national symbolism, the concentration of stigmatized peasants and workers, and experiments in Ukrainization. However, much of the language of national expression came from a different source: the Khrushchev Thaw. Even if it was centered in Moscow, the Thaw was a pan-Soviet rather than ethnically Russian phenomenon. The values proclaimed by its adherents – moral introspection, culture, openness – made it open to participation by non-Russian intellectuals. Virtually all young Ukrainian patriots of the period felt a strong connection to the cultural life of Moscow.

[30] H. Emel'ianenko, "Lenins'ki printsypy natsional'noi polityky KPRS," *Komunist Ukrainy*, no. 8 (1956): 58–59, cited in Krawchenko, *Social Change and National Consciousness*, 200.
[31] V. O. Shevchuk, *Na berezi chasu: Mii Kyiv. Vkhodyny: avtobiohrafichna opovid'-ese* (Kyiv: Vitae memoriae, 2002), 30, 104.
[32] DAKO f. 9912, op. 1, spr. 41, ark. 107.

The university graduate Svitlana Kyrychenko recalled that she and her friends in the late 1950s were "enraptured by the smallest democratic stirrings in the Soviet Union" and "assiduously read Russian journals" from Moscow and Leningrad.[33] More broadly, the articulation of nationalism in Kyiv emerged out of post-secret speech discussions of Soviet history. By bringing to light Stalin-era terror and clearing the name of some of its victims, the Twentieth Party Congress set in motion a campaign by Ukrainian intellectuals to redefine a *national* past. In the press and at public meetings in academic and creative institutions, intellectuals called for widening the approved canon of Ukrainian culture to include figures that had been discredited or repressed during the Stalin period.[34]

De-Stalinization provided the basis for a renewed Soviet-Ukrainian identity. The widely publicized "return to Leninist norms" seemed to extend to the national question: newspaper articles lauded Lenin's commitment to national self-determination and his struggle against "Russian chauvinists" in the Communist Party.[35] Indeed, the young intellectuals quickly developed their own version of Soviet-Ukrainian history, one in which a golden age of national communism in the 1920s fell to Stalin's Russifying dictatorship.[36] The lessons were clear: embracing Ukrainian nationality and furthering the revolutionary cause – namely, purging Marxism-Leninism of its Stalinist distortions – were mutually enriching commitments. In a recent interview, Ivan Drach reconstructed his thinking on the nexus between Ukrainian nationality and Soviet socialism in the following way: "I thought that was the way it had to be, that a true Leninist had to have a real national idea."[37] Here as elsewhere, the path to the nation led through Soviet ideas.

The Thaw also offered a means for overcoming the distortions of Stalinism: generating a culture that in this case was both Soviet and Ukrainian. As in Moscow, the Ukrainian Thaw benefitted from the coalescing of an officially tolerated Ukrainian-language cultural sphere centered on cultural associations which were relatively free of party-Komsomol control. The national purpose of the endeavor in KDU was implied by

---

[33] Svitlana Kyrychenko, "Uchyteli. 1957–1962 (uryvok zi spohadiv)," in Valerii Shevchuk et al. (eds.), *Dobrookyi: spohady pro Ivana Svitlychnoho* (Kyiv: Vydavnytstvo "Chas," 1998), 130; Leonid Hrabovs'ky, "Nezlamny dukh," ibid., 207; Interview with Yevhen Sverstyuk, Kyiv, July 2008.

[34] TsDAHOU f. 7, op. 13, spr. 1396, ark. 27. A number of writers called for the republication of works by the pre-revolutionary writers such as Oleksandr Oles', Vasyl Chumak, the communist Vasyl Blakytny, and the repressed Myroslav Irchan and Mykola Kulish. See the April 1956 informational note from the Kyiv Provincial Party Committee to Kyrychenko in TsDAHOU f. 1, op. 24, spr. 4256, ark. 11.

[35] H. Panikarsky, "Important Period in the Struggle for October," *Radians'ka Ukraina*, 7 May 1957, 3, republished in *Digest of the Soviet Ukrainian Press*, no. 1 (1957): 4–5.

[36] Interview with Iu. Iu. Onyshkiv, Kyiv, 2005.   [37] Interview with Ivan Drach, Kyiv, 2005.

the title of the "SICh" literary studio, named after the revolutionary Vasyl Chumak but also an underhanded reference to the Zaporizhzhian Cossacks, whose independence in the seventeenth century is a standard reference point for Ukrainian claims to historical statehood.[38] The Ukrainian cultural environment in Kyiv not only sustained spoken Ukrainian but made it *de rigueur* in some student circles. Moreover, it provided the milieu in which students could fashion themselves as national *intelligenty* – something that must have come much easier to students in the humanities preparing for careers in history or literary criticism than for others. The element of self-fashioning was captured by Valerii Shevchuk, a history student from a worker family in Zhytomyr. Shevchuk believed he and his friends were destined to do "great work" in the cause of Ukraine; they constituted an elite of creative ability devoted to overcoming a petty-bourgeois "gray mass" of humanity – exemplified, of course, by the Russified students in Kyiv.[39] The intellectual elitism of Thaw intellectuals proved a useful model for Ukrainians dreaming of a revived Ukraine.

Although the romantic nature of the Ukrainian national enterprise seems clear decades later, it is more fitting to stress its logic at the time. There seemed to be some basis for the widespread hope that the reform of the Soviet order would go hand in hand with a resurgence of Ukrainian language and culture. In the early 1960s there was a great deal of quiet cooperation between national activists and leaders of Ukrainian Komsomol organizations, the erstwhile representatives of ideological orthodoxy among youth. Komsomol leaders in the colleges and scientific institutes frequently provided cover for the national activists' poetry readings and discussions, and in some cases became converts to their cause.[40] Indeed, several of the leading national activists had themselves been party members or holders of responsible Komsomol positions. In 1960 the student Viacheslav Chornovil, who would become a leading dissident five years later, told his friends that they should "count on Komsomol," in which there were "wonderful boys and girls" who wanted a "transformation" of Soviet society. In fact, Chornovil boasted that he would become a leader of the Komsomol TsK one day![41] The official cultural establishment seemed to accept this newly nationalized intelligentsia; in the wake of Khrushchev's return to de-Stalinization at the Twenty-Second Party Congress in 1961,

[38] DAKO f. 158, op. 6, spr. 110, ark. 184.   [39] Shevchuk, *Na berezi chasu*, 63–64, 72–73, 78–79.
[40] See Natalka Chorna, "Nikoli nichoho ne treba boyatysia," in Shevchuk et al. (eds.), *Dobrookyi*, 122–26 and Viktor Malynko, "Talant. Krasa. Alla," in Oleksiy Zaretsky and Mykola Marychevsky (eds.), *Chervona tin kalyny: Lysty, spohady, statti* (Kyiv: Spalakh. LTD, 1996), 187.
[41] Les' Taniuk, *Tvory v 60-i tomakh. Tom IV: Schodennyky 1959–1960 rr.* (Kyiv: Al'terpres, 2004), 395–96.

the Union of Ukrainian Writers admitted several controversial young Ukrainian writers to its ranks, presumably with the agenda of pulling them closer to the party establishment.[42]

Nevertheless, the activists' goal of reviving national identity within a reformed Soviet socialism was fraught with tension from the beginning. Like national movements in other times and places, the Ukrainian activists set about establishing a national patrimony for which they would be keepers and articulators. The result was a slowly emerging set of conflicts between the Ukrainian activists and local representatives of party power over commonly accepted national symbols. At KDU, the young intellectuals clashed with party authorities over the nineteenth-century national poet Taras Shevchenko. Buoyed by official commemoration, the figure of Shevchenko enjoyed universal popularity in Soviet Ukraine; an American who spent a year at the university thought the cult of Shevchenko more substantial than that of Lenin.[43] Precisely because of his stature, Shevchenko became the object of conflicts over nationhood in Soviet Ukraine. National activists portrayed Shevchenko as a defender of the Ukrainian nation and victim of the Russian state, calling into question the official emphasis on the poet's credentials as a "revolutionary democrat" allied with progressive Russians.[44] At root, conflicts over the poet's image stemmed from a deeper issue than historical interpretation: whether young intellectuals, who saw themselves as the legitimate articulators of Ukrainian culture, should have the right to interpret national symbols independently of the party.

Precisely because of Shevchenko's established stature in Ukraine, national mobilization around the bard began innocuously. Starting in 1960, students in Kyiv organized independent commemorations of the poet's birth and death at the statue to Shevchenko that stood outside KDU, the university that bore his name. These meetings were public rehearsals of national identity at which students read Ukrainian poetry – the classics or their own works – and sang Ukrainian folk songs.[45] An early student-led commemoration actually earned the praise of the university newspaper as a triumph of Soviet patriotism and the

[42] See Farmer, *Ukrainian Nationalism in the Post-Stalin Era*, 97–98.
[43] "Interview with an American Student who Spent an Academic Year at the University of Kiev," BR # 8–63, 25 March 1963, RFE/RL, HIA, 530/5, 3.
[44] On the origins of the Shevchenko cult, see Yekelchyk, *Stalin's Empire of Memory*, 108–10.
[45] See Liudmila Alexeyeva, *Soviet Dissent: Contemporary Movements for National, Religious, and Human Rights* (Middletown, CT: Wesleyan University Press, 1985), 21–23.

"friendship of the peoples."[46] Nevertheless, the students gave the initiative a subtle oppositional push by commemorating the unrecognized date of 22 May when Shevchenko's body was brought from St. Petersburg to Ukraine.

Soon these rituals became caught up in the widening conflict between the national activists and the party. The curtailing of the Thaw following the Manezh Affair and popular unrest in 1962 – coupled with the resurgent activity of anti-Soviet nationalists in West Ukraine and other parts of the Soviet Western periphery – spurred Ukrainian authorities to take a harder line against nationalist activities in Kyiv.[47] Conflict over the interpretation of the poet exploded in 1964 during the official celebrations of the 150th anniversary of Shevchenko's birth, which many national-minded students boycotted. As part of the events, the deputy administrator of the KDU club commissioned a group of young activists to create a stained-glass window depicting the poet for the KDU entrance hall.[48] Their design "portrayed an angry Shevchenko embracing protectively a young girl who represented Ukraine," with the lines from Shevchenko: "I will exalt these small, mute slaves | I shall put the word on guard beside them."[49] Upon inspecting it, provincial party official V. A. Boychenko ordered that work on the window be halted; when the artists refused to comply, the work was "removed."[50] The destruction of the window quickly became a *cause célèbre* for Ukrainophile students, who interpreted the event as evidence that they were national intellectuals defending the nation against its slanderers. At a traditional yearly meeting of KDU Philology Department students with recent graduates in late March 1964, Pavlo Movchan, then a student at the Moscow Literature Institute, spoke out about the "tragic event" of the display's destruction, bemoaning that "people who [did] not understand real art" sat in judgment over true artists.[51] Movchan followed by reading his

---

[46] Shevchuk, *Na berezi chasu*, 136.
[47] See the informational note "on some causes of antisocial manifestations and crimes among youth" submitted by KGB USSR to the TsK in advance of the 1963 Moscow plenary meeting on ideological questions. RGANI f. 2, op. 1, d. 626, ll. 102–16 and P. Iu. Shelest, *Da ne sudimy budete: dnevnikovye zapisi, vospominaniia chlena Politbiuro TSK KPSS* (Moscow: Edition q, 1995), 175–77, 180–83.
[48] The artists were Alla Hors'ka, L. Semikina, P. Zalyvakha, H. Sevruk, and G. Zubchenko. DAKO f. 158, op. 6, spr. 110, ark. 28–29, 185.
[49] These details are from the Ukrainian-Canadian John Kolasky, who was studying in the university at the time. John Kolasky, *Two Years in Soviet Ukraine: A Canadian's Personal Account of Russian Oppression and the Growing Opposition* (Toronto: Peter Martin Associates, 1970), 93.
[50] DAKO f. 158, op. 6, spr. 110, ark. 28.
[51] TsDAHOU f. 1, op. 24, spr. 5904, ark. 36–37. A very similar account was given in a report by the Philology Department party secretary Ya. B. Biloshtan to the KDU Party Committee on 3 April 1964. DAKO f. 158, op. 6, spr. 100, ark. 182.

poem based on "Kateryna," Shevchenko's ballad depicting the evil of serfdom. To party officials, the hidden message was clear: the sufferings of the peasant girl were "still continuing today."[52]

Student commemorations of Shevchenko proved a highly effective mode of mobilization in Soviet conditions. Just a few months after the scandal over the university vestibule, the Ukrainophile students focused their efforts on extending their observance of the controversial celebration of 22 May mentioned above. Ignoring warnings from the party committee, they carried out a "torchlight parade" to the Shevchenko monument, creating a tense standoff between police and hundreds of young people who refused to disperse. This invented tradition repeated itself every year on the date until 1972, when a wave of arrests of national-minded intellectuals paralyzed the movement. The ability of the young intellectuals to appropriate public space year after year – despite yearly agitation and threats by the authorities – stood in contrast to an earlier episode that might be seen as a comparable action in Moscow: the Maiakovskii Square poetry readings discussed in Chapter 7.[53] The Kyiv students had the advantage of protesting in the name of an officially fêted cultural figure. At a discussion of the 1964 demonstration at the KDU Party Committee, V. P. Shevchuk, a standing member of the body, claimed that many of the event's participants had been unwitting protestors. "For four years in a row on 22 May, in an action organized by the provincial Komsomol Committee," he complained, students had "walked out and marked this date." In 1964, many of the participants had come out to the statue not because they had "some sort of intention," but because they understood the event to be "a tradition."[54] Whatever Shevchuk's motives in defending the students, the conceptual confusion he pointed to was a real one. The students' national traditions had arisen in dialogue with the official Shevchenko cult and gained legitimacy from it; moreover, the Komsomol activist's defense of the students was a reminder of the naïve Leninism that was prominent if far from universal in their ranks.

Perhaps most decisive was the very fact of "tradition," even if the students were clearly inventing one with their yearly gatherings. Unlike the Thaw project of Soviet cultural regeneration, the Ukrainian Thaw drew on the ethnic nation, an entity that came pre-packaged with an inspiring corpus of

---

[52] Ibid.
[53] For party responses to the yearly Shevchenko meetings, see TsDAHOU f. 1, op. 24, spr. 6060, ark. 105–6, 157–58.
[54] DAKO f. 158, op. 6, spr. 111, ark. 160.

national history.[55] As Chapter 7 argued, the Thaw suffered from an internal tension: while devoted to the intelligentsia cause of bringing culture to the masses, it also brought social division by interpreting "culture" in a maximalist and radical fashion. Of course, the national identity of many citizens of the Ukrainian Republic was anything but clear, despite all talk of ancient and primordial national feelings. Nevertheless, nationalism offered a trusted blueprint for transforming the people and a comforting sense that history was on their side – all of which was difficult to match in the more amorphous Thaw in Russia.

Russian problems

At first glance, Soviet socialism would seem to favor the Russian nation over non-Russian national projects of the USSR. The basic fact of institutionalized national identity that proved so important for the Ukrainian situation appeared all the more present in the Russian case. Late Stalinism had made expressions of Ukrainian nationalism ideologically suspect; in contrast, it cemented Russian nationalism as a key part of official discourse. The principle that the Russians had earned a special role in the Soviet state received a boost from victory in the Great Patriotic War; Stalin famously praised the Russians and their alleged faith in the Soviet state as the "decisive force which guaranteed victory over the enemy of humanity – fascism."[56] As explored in Chapter 1, postwar students were deeply affected by the patriotic mood of the war, if not always the excesses of chauvinism that accompanied the Cold War. Moreover, the expansion of literacy and mass media in the Soviet period brought Russian nationalism to wider parts of the population than ever before.[57]

The Russian character of Soviet ideology, however, was more appearance than reality. As Geoffrey Hosking has shown, even while promoting Russian feeling, the postwar Soviet state was careful to subsume it in a broader construct of Soviet patriotism.[58] As the state-carrying nation of the

---

[55] On historical purpose as critical to the appeal of the nation, see Benedict R. Anderson, *Imagined Communities: Reflections on the Origin and Spread of Nationalism* (London and New York: Verso, 1991), 9–38.

[56] See David Brandenberger, *National Bolshevism: Stalinist Mass Culture and the Formation of Modern Russian National Identity, 1931–1956* (Cambridge, MA: Harvard University Press, 2002), 116–239.

[57] This is a central theme in Brandenberger (ibid.)

[58] Geoffrey A. Hosking, *Rulers and Victims: The Russians in the Soviet Union* (Cambridge, MA: Harvard University Press, 2006).

USSR, Russia's national interests were thought to be synonymous with those of the international proletariat. In practice, the Russian nation paid dearly for its privileged position in the Soviet project. Along with other Soviet nations, Russia was in short supply of many of the raw materials that have proven central in constructing national identities in other European contexts: a full literary tradition, religion, and a connection to the traditional peasantry as a repository of national virtue. But the Russians also lacked the makeup of Soviet national statehood that served as a crutch for national movements in Ukraine and the other Union Republics. In Geoffrey Hosking's words, the Russians were "the orphans of the Soviet Union" who "had no Communist Party, no capital city, no Academy of Sciences, no national encyclopedia, no radio or television networks separate from those of the Soviet Union as a whole."[59]

Universities embodied this curious admixture of Soviet and Russian characteristics. They were widely understood as national institutions; for instance, it was stressed that MGU had played an historical "role in the development of Russian [*russkoi*] science."[60] Yet universities also represented the domestication of Russian ethnicity under Soviet conditions. The composition of the student bodies in elite universities reflected their ambivalent national character, as Chapter 2 showed: while Russians dominated the student body at Moscow and Leningrad Universities, the TsK made a determined effort to show that other nationalities were represented in at least token numbers.

The careful fusion of Russia and the USSR in Soviet ideology made independent Russian national mobilization almost impossible in the universities. It was precisely the state's credentials as a Russian entity that made it difficult to imagine – let alone try to bring about – a Russia independent of it. To be sure, an independent strain of national identity emerged in the 1950s with the well-studied "Village Prose" movement. As part of its urgent efforts to revive the impoverished countryside, the post-Stalin collective leadership condoned limited discussion of problems plaguing rural areas such as mismanagement and local-level corruption. Taking advantage of this opening, several writers exposed the dismal situation in the countryside and, more controversially, the decline of the Russian peasantry more generally.[61] As Nikolai Mitrokhin has shown, spearheading the national-minded part of

[59] Ibid., 80.
[60] "Rech' predsedatelia prezidiuma verkhovnogo soveta K. E. Voroshilova," *Moskovskii universitet*, 4 July 1955: 1.
[61] See Brudny, *Reinventing Russia*, 46–56 and Kathleen Parthet, *Russian Village Prose: The Radiant Past* (Princeton University Press, 1992).

this broad "Village Prose" movement was a specific cohort of postwar Soviet writers: veterans, often hailing from the villages and provincial towns, who developed distaste for the cosmopolitan world of the Moscow literary establishment during their college studies in the late Stalin period.[62]

A peasant-centered Russian identity, however, hardly fit the tenor of student life in the 1950s with its glorification of science and its cosmopolitanism. Russian nationalism as a political ideology was barely represented among the student opposition groups that formed after the secret speech, in sharp contrast to those of the working class.[63] Of course, activists of the Thaw were anything but indifferent about Russia; for instance, the best-known of the underground revolutionary organizations, the "Krasnopevtsev Group" centered at the MGU History Department, called their conspiratorial organization the "League of Russian Patriots." But the young university dissenters understood Russia in terms of the non-ethnic reference points of socialism and revolution rather than ethnicity.[64] The "Krasnopevtsev Group" found inspiration for their patriotism in the "revolutionary democrats" that figured prominently in Soviet renditions of nineteenth-century Russian history. Alternatively, the young Leningrad mathematician Revol't Pimenov found Russia in a glorious revolutionary tradition that lasted from 1870 to 1918, which the Bolsheviks had hijacked for their own ends.[65] For proponents of reform as well as their opponents, Russia's cause was that of socialism as a whole, and attempts to pry them apart seemed futile. It is in this sense that the nationalist literary critic Vadim Kozhinov claimed that no national question existed during his student years at MGU in the early 1950s.[66]

The dilemma posed by the interpenetration of Soviet and Russian shaped the political uses of Russian nationhood in the 1960s. A student movement of cultural nationalism took longer to arise than a Ukrainian one – but when it did, it was also more radical in its ideological message. There was logic to these differing trajectories. In Ukraine, the national cause emerged

[62] Nikolai Mitrokhin, *Russkaia partiia: dvizhenie russkikh natsionalistov v SSSR 1953–1985* (Moscow: Novoe literaturnoe obozrenie, 2003), 138–56.
[63] See the thorough discussion of political repressions involving Russian nationalism ibid., 49–53, 136–40, 169–77.
[64] See Lev Krasnopevtsev, "Osnovnye momenty razvitiia russkogo revoliutsionnogo dvizheniia v 1861–1905 godakh," *Karta*, no. 17 (1997): 57–64. Krasnopevtsev wrote a tract criticizing Bolshevism, but other members of the "League of Russian Patriots" seem to have remained Marxist-Leninists. Vladimir Men'shikov, "Mysli po povodu . . .," *Karta*, no. 17 (1997): 74.
[65] Arkhiv UFSB SPb arkh. no: P-81390, tom 4, ch. 2, ll. 374–75.
[66] Vadim Kozhinov, "Seiatel'," in Vadim Kozhinov and S. V. Marshkov, *Vadim Kozhinov: v interviu, besedakh, dialogakh i vospominaniiakh sovremennikov* (Moscow: Algoritm, 2004), 17.

in tandem with the broader agenda of reforming the Soviet order and therefore bore a strong connection to it. In contrast, a Russian national project had to oppose the Soviet idea in order to find separate articulation. As a result, it emerged as a clear alternative to the reformism and universalism of the Thaw. The small groups of students and recent graduates who embraced national culture in the early 1960s looked for inspiration to elements of the Russian old regime: conservative thought, the virtues of the peasantry, Russian Orthodoxy, anti-Semitism, and even monarchism. This position allowed them to reject the *national* credentials of the Soviet state – even if they were often proud of Russian accomplishments in World War II and sometimes the USSR's great power status.[67] Differing from the Ukrainian activists, the Russophiles opposed the Thaw, which they associated with socialist reformism, cosmopolitanism, deference to the West, and the Jews. In their view, all these characteristics made reformist intellectuals tragically distant from the *narod* and its true culture and spirituality.[68]

While the broader context of Russia's place in the USSR was crucial in shaping national identities, it does little to account for the more specific motivations of the Russophiles. Existing accounts of the Russian cultural and intellectual movement stress its "social and cultural roots."[69] Yitzhak Brudny has shown that the majority of Russian nationalists in the period were offspring of peasants and lower-class Russians from the provinces.[70] Yet rather than positing a natural relationship between peasant roots and national ideas – an approach that a modernist approach to nationalism would cast in doubt – it makes sense to stress the complicated paths by which young educated Russians arrived at politicized national identities. As in Ukraine, it was the experience of higher learning in the capitals that drove some lowly born youth to embrace the Russian cause. This was presumably the case for Sergei Kuniaev, an MGU student of simple provincial origins who recalled feeling out of place among his peers who hailed from privileged and educated backgrounds. In a diary entry written at an officer training camp in 1956, Kuniaev contrasted the simple and virtuous soldiers of worker and peasant origin with the self-satisfied university students who were training to be officers. He would "never again be satisfied with the insipid,

[67] See S. Iu. Kuniaev, *Poeziia, sud'ba, Rossia*, vol. 1 (Moscow: "Nash sovremennik," 2001), 40–41, 57–58.
[68] My understanding of the ideological contours of Russian nationalism in this period is heavily influenced by Mitrokhin, *Russkaia partiia*.
[69] Vladislav Zubok, *Zhivago's Children: The Last Russian Intelligentsia* (Cambridge, MA: Belknap Press, 2009), 241.
[70] See the data carefully assembled in Brudny, *Reinventing Russia*, 28–46, 35.

artificial intellectual dialogues" at the university, he noted. Taking up work at the Moscow journal *Znamia* (The Banner) at the end of the decade, Kuniaev fell in with a circle of ethnic Russian writers who devoted themselves to challenging what they saw as the domination of Moscow culture by Westernizers and Jews.[71] For Russians as for Ukrainians, then, politicized national identity was a way to overturn the social and cultural hierarchies that higher learning entrenched.

The common presentation of Russian nationalists as marginalized elements, moreover, has its limits in explaining the new movement. For one, the Russophiles' social and geographic origins were not uniform. The painter Il'ia Glazunov not only stemmed from the old nobility but internalized a decidedly non-Soviet vision of Russia from childhood, commenting in his diary in 1945 (at age fifteen) that he loved "Russian history, the Kremlin Walls, the great magnates (*boiare*)."[72] More importantly, the nationalist movement recruited heavily from the student circles of the Thaw. Kuniaev, noted above for his aversion to the intelligentsia milieu, was in fact deeply engaged in the intellectual scene at MGU, where he espoused the causes of cultural freedom, the struggle against bureaucracy, and a return to Leninism in campus debates. His path from cultural activism and socialism to chauvinistic nationalism – traversed by many other Russian nationalists – bore a kind of logic. Like the Ukrainian movement, Russian national activists appropriated the Thaw mission of bringing culture to the people. While a clear negation of the Thaw in ideological terms, the new Russian nationalism needs to be understood as an effort to find a new outlet for the Thaw *intelligent*.

The role of the intellectual life of the Thaw in the Russophile movement was particularly clear in the most militant group of young Russian nationalists. The All-Russian Social-Christian Union for the Liberation of the People (VSKhSON) was a conspiratorial political organization in Leningrad, uprooted by the KGB in 1968. The group was exceptional among the myriad underground parties of young intellectuals of the Khrushchev period for both its duration and its size; following tight conspiratorial practices, the Leningraders managed to recruit thirty members – all university graduates and students – and remain beyond the grasp of the KGB for four years. This is all the more remarkable given the group's uncompromisingly anti-socialist agenda. VSKhSON's program called for an armed overthrow of the Soviet

[71] Kuniaev, *Poeziia, sud'ba, Rossiia*, 71–75, 84, 110–22.
[72] L. E. Kolodnyi, *Liubov' i nenavist' Il'i Glazunova: dokumental'naia povest'* (Moscow: Golos, 1998), 51–85, 278.

order and the establishment of a "Social-Christian" order in its place. According to the group's program, communism was a totalitarian false religion that absorbed society into the state, and it could only be counteracted by a return to religious and national consciousness. The group called for the reorganization of Russia – importantly, standing alone without the other Soviet peoples – on a "Social-Christian" foundation. In their vision, Western-style representative democracy supervised by a clergy-dominated legislative chamber would replace the "reactionary and immoral" Soviet political system, while the individual and the traditional family would replace the "faceless Communist collective."[73]

The uncompromising agenda of VSKhSON did not obscure the organization's rootedness in Thaw culture. Like other members of the organization, Lev Borodin had been a fairly typical campus rebel of the 1950s: he was expelled from Irkutsk University in 1956 for forming a discussion circle devoted to generating "suggestions" for improving Komsomol.[74] By the time he entered intellectual circles in Leningrad in the early 1960s, Borodin and his friends had become disillusioned with the potential for reform within Marxism-Leninism: "absolutely no one" in his circle believed Khrushchev's promise that their generation would live to see communism, he recalled. Borodin's national and religious revivalism emerged at the end of a protracted search for a "third path" between capitalism and communism.[75] He and his comrades sought out a new faith in Western thinkers whose writings were then becoming available for the first time in the USSR in print or in *samizdat* editions: Hegel, Nietzsche, Heidegger, Sartre, and José Ortega y Gasset. But Borodin seems to have felt intuitively that these ideas were not global or total enough to replace Marxism-Leninism. He found his way out of this impasse in Russian nationalism and particularly its articulations in the experimental and spiritual turn-of-century Silver Age in Russian culture. When he read *Signposts* (*Vekhi*), the 1909 volume of essays written by former radicals which criticized the intelligentsia in the name of spirituality, morality, and personal freedom, Borodin felt that he had found the ground beneath his feet, namely "belief, Christianity, Orthodoxy, and Russia-Rus'."[76] As he explains, both as a socialist reformer and as a national revivalist he was driven by a thirst for all-encompassing truth that would

---

[73] The organization's program is reproduced in John B. Dunlop, *The New Russian Revolutionaries* (Belmont, MA: Nordland Pub. Co., 1976), 262–68.

[74] L. I. Borodin, *Bez vybora: avtobiograficheskoe povestvovanie* (Moscow: Molodaia gvardiia, 2003), 13–18, 49 and L. I. Borodin, "Vserossiiskii sotsial-khristianskii soiuz osvobozhdeniia naroda," *Veche*, no. 13 (1984): 169.

[75] Dunlop, *The New Russian Revolutionaries*, 276.   [76] Borodin, *Bez vybora*, 56, 60.

change the world. Against the backdrop of the crisis of socialist reformism, nationalism seemed to provide a fitting outlet for the culture-creating intellectual.

The intellectual background of Borodin and his comrades in reform socialism also informed the ideological vision of VSKhSON. Paradoxically given its traditionalist "Social-Christian" program, the group bore the imprint of ideas in wide circulation among young circles tied to the Thaw. It actually drew on an influential revisionist tract, Yugoslav dissident Milovan Djilas's *New Class*, by presenting communism as a screen for a bureaucratic ruling class. And while clearly breaking with communism, VSKhSON also rejected capitalism, going so far as to present the Soviet order as the "sickly offspring" of the exploitation and materialism of the capitalist system. One is even tempted to see an echo of socialist revisionist ideas in the group's espousal of creating a new and hazy category of "personalized" property in which labor and the means of production would merge.[77] And despite the anti-Semitic convictions of some of its leaders, VSKhSON also retained a trace of the cosmopolitanism of the Thaw. "Christian culture," according to its program, bore an "inherently supranational character which will play a decisive role in our era in the task of bringing peoples together into one pan-human family."[78] Clearly, the student Thaw had left an indelible mark on the Russian national groupings that sought to undo it.

Nationalist entrepreneurs and the end of the Thaw

Mobilizing around a non-Soviet Russia led the members of VSKhSON and other groups like it to the camps. Paradoxically, it brought other intellectuals to positions of influence in the Soviet cultural world. Despite their frequent anti-socialist thrust, many neo-Slavophiles found a degree of common ground with nationalist elements among post-Stalin party-state elites. A critical entrepreneur of the new nationalism in the halls of power was the painter Il'ia Glazunov. While a student of the Repin Leningrad Institute for Painting, Sculpture, and Architecture in the 1950s, Glazunov produced unorthodox if not explicitly nationalistic paintings: portraits of unknown old intellectuals, depictions of lonely couples against the background of a cold and unfeeling Leningrad, and illustrations meant to

---

[77] Dunlop, *The New Russian Revolutionaries*, 278.
[78] On anti-Semitism in the organization, see Bernard Karavatskii, "Vospominaniia uchastnika," in John B. Dunlop, *VSKhSON: Programma, sud, v tiur'makh i lageriakh* (Paris: YMCA-Press, 1975), 207.

accompany the works of Dostoevskii, which had not been published since the start of the Stalin period. Despite his unusual creative proclivities and his lack of interest in Komsomol affairs, Glazunov was wildly ambitious: a classmate recalled that Glazunov told him to "mark his word that he would be famous."[79] This came to pass sooner than expected. In 1956, Glazunov won an international art competition under the aegis of the international but Soviet-dominated Committee for Youth Organizations with a painting of the Czech communist Julius Fučík entitled, "A Poet in Prison." Soon thereafter, Komsomol officials organized an exhibition of his works in the Central Home of Workers of Art in Moscow – an unprecedented event for an artist still in his last year of study who did not yet have membership in the Artists' Union.

The young Glazunov's exhibition brought excitement and scandal. The Moscow party committee reported with consternation that a discussion of his work at the exhibition hall drew a thousand young spectators, from whom shouts were heard of "Glazunov is a fresh voice in painting!" and "we are sick of official art!"[80] Response was swift and harsh. After being excoriated at the party TsK with his academic advisor in attendance, Glazunov was allowed to graduate but given an unappealing distribution position as an art teacher. The experience of ostracism by the cultural establishment inspired Glazunov's transformation into a self-appointed apostle of the Russian idea. From the early 1960s, Glazunov cultivated an image as an embattled fighter for Russian interests in the de-nationalized cultural establishment, courting scandal by antics like placing the slogan "Russian for Russians" in a painting.[81] He also tried to mobilize support for his ideology of Russian rebirth among young intellectuals in the capital.[82] Unlike some other young nationalists of the period, Glazunov's conception of Russia did not draw on pride in Soviet accomplishments. Rather, he produced paintings on explicitly religious themes and flaunted monarchist ideas.[83] In 1963, a fellow nationalist was shocked to hear Glazunov refer to Lenin derisively as "Volod'ka" (the diminutive form of Vladimir) and "a Syphilitic" who headed a "gang that brought Russia immeasurable misfortune."[84]

And yet Glazunov was anything but an outcast. Ironically, the Russian activist found himself deeply enmeshed in the communist order he rejected. The exhibition had brought Glazunov fame and notoriety in Moscow society. In addition to enjoying the patronage of prominent nationalists

[79] Kolodnyi, *Liubov' i nenavist'*, 265.
[80] Although not fully referenced, this document is cited ibid., 335–36.   [81] Ibid., 388–89.
[82] Il'ia Glazunov, *Rossiia raspiataia* (Moscow: Olimp, 2004), 721.   [83] Ibid., 381–83.
[84] See the quotation from the diary of V. Desiatnikov in Mitrokhin, *Russkaia partiia*, 208–9.

in the creative elite, the enterprising Glazunov built political alliances within the central Komsomol apparat in Moscow. Under S. P. Pavlov, Komsomol sought to regain its position among youth by undertaking a battle against the inroads of "bourgeois ideology," an agenda that featured a cult of the Great Patriotic War and mass campaigns for "military-patriotic upbringing."[85] Indeed, the Komsomol took the army as a model for disciplining the students; at one function, Pavlov mused about the need to introduce uniforms for higher education students.[86] This chauvinist and anti-Western agenda led Pavlov and his team in the Komsomol leadership to cultivate ties with Russian nationalists in the cultural sphere. Of course, Russophile intellectuals and apparatchiks had very different agendas: the religious, anti-modernist, and ultimately anti-Soviet ideas of Russophiles like Glazunov could not but irk the chauvinistic and disciplinarian Komsomol leaders. But the groups could find common ground in Russian pride and hostility to the liberal intelligentsia, particularly to the young creative elites who were blamed for ensnaring Soviet youth in pessimism and unhealthy individualism. Association also yielded more practical benefits: the intellectuals could gain access to levers of power in the cultural establishment, while Youth League officials hoped to use the new movement to overcome their shrinking influence on educated youth.

An early engine of nationalist–apparat cooperation was "Homeland," a patriotic club founded by Glazunov in 1962 that brought together students in several Moscow institutes and established national-minded intellectuals. The club's "propaganda of Russian cultural and historical heritage," as they called it, soon brought Glazunov a devoted following. The club carried out trips to historical towns and monasteries and did volunteer restoration work at an historical site in Moscow. The group's most influential undertaking was an exhibition – located, notably, in the foyer of a hotel run by the Komsomol TsK – called "Poetry of the Russian Land" that featured displays of Russian costumes, coats of arms of Russian cities, and even *in situ* demonstrations of traditional music and crafts. Glazunov's invocation of a rich but neglected Russian cultural heritage caught the imagination of students in the capital, including Komsomol activists.[87] In the early

---

[85] The most thorough analysis of the "Pavlov Group" is Mitrokhin, *Russkaia partiia*, 241–47. See also Nina Tumarkin, *Lenin Lives! The Lenin Cult in Soviet Russia* (Cambridge, MA: Harvard University Press, 1983), 133–34.

[86] RGASPI-M f. 1, op. 5, d. 1097, ll. 90–91, 103.

[87] Glazunov, *Rossiia raspiataia*, 726–31. See the character references of several "Homeland" activists in RGASPI-M f. 1, op. 31, d. 181, ll. 36–41.

1960s, S. V. Petrova, a student at the MGU Philology Department, became an active member in "Homeland" after spending a summer collecting folklore in the Russian north on a curricular practicum. Petrova recalled being shocked by the state of Russian historical architecture that she witnessed: "icons were destroyed or shut up in barrels, there were garages inside churches."[88] Her intellectual discovery took place against a broader background discussed above: a desire for new values that gripped students who were both disillusioned with the period's reforms and discouraged that the "abstract discussions" of the Thaw seemed to have such a negligible impact on society.[89]

The "Homeland" Club episode was a fitting symbol of the entire Russian nationalist movement. Although the initiative enjoyed backing from the Komsomol establishment, it soon collided with established forces in the Soviet state. The accomplishments of the organization in preserving historical artifacts seem negligible: in 1965, the head of the Russian Museum alleged that "Homeland" activists were pilfering icons and other historical objects during their trips around the country.[90] Eventually, a narrower and more professional focus of restoring architectural objects came to dominate "Homeland" and Glazunov was removed from the organization – an outcome that he would blame on the machinations of the KGB but others see as a product of his megalomania.[91] Similarly, the courting of Russophile intellectuals by the Brezhnev party-state would eventually come under strain as the fundamentally different interests of the two groups became apparent.[92] With time it became clear that the party could not grant concessions substantial enough to contain a movement that was essentially anti-socialist. Nevertheless, the period of cooperation gave Russian nationalists a powerful hold in the cultural world of the final Soviet decades.

The influence of intellectuals with chauvinist, religious, anti-Semitic, and monarchist convictions would ensure a deep ideological division among Soviet intellectuals until the collapse of the USSR and indeed beyond. Nowhere were the disruptive implications of ethnic nationalism clearer than in the position of Jews in the educated classes. As Chapter 3 demonstrated, late Stalinist anti-Semitism had forced assimilated Jews

---

[88] Interview with S. V. Petrova, Moscow, 2004.
[89] Anatolii Ivanov, "Gavrilo Printsip naoborot," in L. V. Polikovskaia (ed.), *My predchuvstvie – predtecha –: ploshchad' Maiakovskogo, 1958–1965* (Moscow: "Zvenia," 1997), 174.
[90] See the letter from museum director V. A. Pushkarev to TsK Komsomol. RGASPI-M f. 1, op. 31, d. 181, ll. 29–32.
[91] Glazunov, *Rossiia raspiataia*, 743–49.
[92] For the broader context of this development, see Brudny, *Reinventing Russia*, 57–93.

to reconsider their origins but also deepened the association between Jewish and intelligentsia identities; both trends would develop under the different conditions of post-Stalinism. The initial post-Stalin years produced high hopes among the Jews; Stalin's death had brought an end to the Doctors' Plot and to secret police and party repressions of students deemed guilty of "Jewish bourgeois nationalism." Condemnation of the recent anti-Semitic campaigns was a constant refrain in the student discussions following the Twentieth Party Congress.[93] Despite the appearance of liberalizing trends, the Jews' tenuous place in the USSR became clear again. Hardening semi-formal *numerus clausus* policies in higher education and restrictions on some career paths – all of which was justified as an effort to level the playing field between the Jews and less modernized Soviet nationalities – created fears among highly educated Jews of downward social mobility.[94] At the same time, the ongoing void of specifically Jewish and Yiddish cultural outlets and the assault on Judaism as part of Khrushchev's anti-religious campaign deepened the sense that Jews were uniquely unprivileged among Soviet nations.[95] In this context, young Jews in the universities embraced the cultural Thaw with a passion. The imagined community of the culture-bearing and cosmopolitan intelligentsia seemed to offer young Jews a new basis for social identity within the Soviet project.[96]

Not surprisingly, the emergence of politicized ethnic nationalism within the intelligentsia milieu struck Jewish intellectuals and their sympathizers as apostasy. The anti-Semitic coloration of Russian cultural nationalism had deep roots beyond the careerist objectives sometimes stressed in the literature.[97] The prominence of Jews in Thaw circles seemed to confirm the nationalists' conviction that the "liberal" intelligentsia was fundamentally un-Russian. Resorting to anti-Semitism also proved useful in articulating an anti-Soviet Russian idea: ascribing a Jewish character to communism helped to mark it off from Russian traditions. For their part, the Ukrainian movement's relationship to Jews was more complex. Although anti-Semitism was widespread in West Ukrainian educated circles, socialist principles and ties to the Thaw made many Kyivan Ukrainophiles view

[93] RGASPI-M f. 1, op. 46, d. 191, ll. 5–7; ibid., d. 192, l. 146.
[94] Victor Zaslavsky and Robert J. Brym, *Soviet-Jewish Emigration and Soviet Nationality Policy* (New York: St. Martin's Press, 1983), 15–19.
[95] See Zvi Y. Gitelman, *A Century of Ambivalence: The Jews of Russia and the Soviet Union, 1881 to the Present* (Bloomington: Indiana University Press, 2001), 161–67.
[96] See Zubok, *Zhivago's Children*, 229–36.   [97] Zaslavsky and Brym, *Soviet-Jewish Emigration*, 111–12.

hostility to the Jews with distaste.[98] Regardless of its cosmopolitan strain, however, the rise of ethnic nationalism in Ukraine was hardly welcome to some Ukrainian Jews, especially given their longstanding connection to Russian language and culture.[99]

Faced with the growing national identification on all sides, some Jews joined their Russian and Ukrainian classmates in turning to their origins, sometimes for the first time: gathering outside the Moscow synagogue on the eve of the Jewish holidays, studying Jewish literature and folklore, and even trying to pepper their speech with Yiddish expressions.[100] Along with these signs of Jewish identity among educated youth came a desire to confront the Holocaust, which went against the Soviet narrative of common suffering in the Great Patriotic War. For instance, Jewish and non-Jewish youth met at the Babyn Yar ravine in 1966 to mark the twenty-fifth anniversary of the Nazis' wartime massacre there; speeches by writers Vladimir Nekrasov (a Russian Kyivan), Ivan Dziuba (a Ukrainian), and others condemned Soviet anti-Semitism and complained that no monument yet stood at the site.[101]

The re-emergence of Jewish consciousness among educated elites – which would crystallize in a movement for emigration in the 1970s – often constituted a sharp break in identities for the people involved. Many young Jews had a thoroughly secular outlook and had far less attachment to the world of their forebears than did the Russians or Ukrainians. In another sense, however, the Jewish trajectory in the post-Stalin period exemplified the broader fecundity of national ideas among postwar intellectual elites. Postwar national stirrings were the product of the social environment of higher learning during the Khrushchev period. Students' efforts to embrace and popularize their national heritage constituted a clear rejection of Soviet models of nationhood. And yet the universities offered students multiple resources needed for this undertaking. They trained specialists in national culture by providing specialized study of the stuff from which ethnic nationalism is forged: history, literature, folklore. They brought together different social worlds, inserting lower-class,

---

[98] On the persistence of anti-Semitism in Lviv, see Risch, *The Ukrainian West*, 166–67; TsDAHOU f. 7, op. 13, spr. 1397, ark. 43.

[99] An American exchange student who spent 1962 in Kyiv reported that most of the Jews he met spoke Russian at home. Notably, he added that he did not encounter signs of anti-Semitism among the students. "Interview with an American Student," 3.

[100] See "The Present Situation of Jews in the Soviet Union," BR # 28–61, 18 October 1961, RFE/RL, HIA, 530/2, 6.

[101] TsDAHOU f. 1, op. 24, spr. 6060, ark. 148–51.

rural, and provincial youth in an environment of cultural polish and relative privilege – one that some would reject by creating a separate national sphere of interaction with its own hierarchy of values. And the universities provided social space for the Thaw, the mission of overcoming Stalinism through culture which provided a template for cultural nationalism. In the case of nationalism as in other areas discussed in this book, the universities proved well positioned to underscore ambiguities in Soviet values and ideas.

Ernest Renan's famous comment that getting one's history wrong is essential in the making of a nation applies to the study of the Ukrainian and Russian intellectuals described here.[102] Looking back at the Soviet period, nationalist intellectuals in Moscow and Kyiv had little incentive to accentuate the close association of national thinking with Soviet ideas and institutions. A forging of selective national narratives on Soviet history has been influential in historical writing. In the wake of independence, Ukrainian historians favored the predictable narrative of the nation resisting an evil empire, understating the role of the Khrushchev Thaw and its brand of socialist reformism in spurring ethnic consciousness. For their part, nationalist Russian historians minimize the connections of national intellectuals to Soviet power structures as well as to the Thaw.[103] The students analyzed here stumbled upon many of their ideas in the milieu of higher education, which provided them with the building blocks for their ideas: an institutionalized discourse of nationhood, widespread social mobility into the educated classes, and the construct of a culture-giving intelligentsia. None of this made for particularly edifying national history, and the sources of national identity in the Soviet context have been partially obscured as a result.

---

[102] See Ernest Renan, "What is a Nation?" in Omar Dahbour and Micheline Ishay (eds.), *The Nationalism Reader* (Atlantic Highlands, NJ: Humanities Press, 1995), 143–56.

[103] Cf. Iu. Z. Danyliuk and Oleh Bazhan, *Opozytsiia v Ukraini: druha polovyna 50-kh–80-ti rr. XX st.* (Kyiv: Ridnyi krai, 2000). The nationalist historian Vadim Kozhinov criticizes the "intelligentsia" as out of touch with the people but excludes nationalists such as himself from this judgment. Vadim Kozhinov, *Rossiia vek XX: 1939–1964: opyt bespristrastnogo issledovaniia* (Moscow: Algoritm, 1999), 326–27.

Conclusion
Intellectuals and Soviet socialism

In 1959, Valerii Shevchuk, a KDU student and later a writer, composed an essay called "intelligence and education" (in Ukrainian, *intelligentnist' i osvita*). In it, Shevchuk pondered what the intelligentsia meant and what role it might play in the future. He started by describing intelligentsia as a social group of "cultural employees, engineers, doctors, educational workers," all, Shevchuk thought, members of Marx's "superstructure." Yet Shevchuk also thought that intelligentsia was a "moral" category, as its members held "ethical learning," "a developed individuality (*rozvynena individual'nist*)," and "a high level of consciousness."[1] This moral dimension made thinkers critically important to the construction of communism. In fact, Shevchuk argued that with the creation of a classless society and the passing of the historical stage of the dictatorship of the proletariat, "the understanding of *intelligent* will take on more of a moral meaning than a social one."[2]

Shevchuk's essay illustrates a fundamental development in postwar Soviet history: the entrenchment of the intelligentsia as an object of identification for middle-strata, professional citizens. Emerging from a war of unprecedented destruction, the Soviet system had to structure its institutions to pursue the interrupted task of world revolution. The shape of the future educated classes was universally understood to be a crucial question in this period of Soviet redefinition. As a result, the intelligentsia, an entity carrying rich associations in Russian and East European history, weighed on the minds of Shevchuk and countless other Soviet citizens.

---

[1] V. O. Shevchuk, *Na berezi chasu: Mii Kyiv. Vkhodyny: avtobiohrafichna opovid'-ese* (Kyiv: Vitae memoriae, 2002), 75–76.

[2] Ibid., 76. Notably, Shevchuk concluded that the dictatorship of the proletariat would soon become history at least a year before the party made the creation of an "all-people's state" official doctrine.

Lenin saw the old Russian intelligentsia as a group set to disappear en route to communism; Stalin rehabilitated the word but hollowed out its meaning by using it to categorize the ranks of subservient specialists his system had produced. Just how Soviet higher education sought to craft the Soviet intelligentsia, navigating this complicated past, is the subject of this book.

Shevchuk's musings suggest the widespread contestation that would accompany the project of making a postwar intelligentsia. As discussed in the introduction, scholarship has often argued that the intelligentsia was a well-defined group united by cohesive concerns of either class interests or civic engagement and autonomy from the state. This study questions this overall approach on two grounds. Rather than a unified societal group, the intelligentsia was a social construct, a constellation of ideas about the place of the holders of learning in society. Moreover, the meaning of the Soviet intelligentsia, despite its widespread appeal as symbol and myth, remained unfixed. Shevchuk's speculative musings about the intelligentsia were replayed, with varying results, in countless Soviet minds in the postwar years. Shevchuk offered many ideas about the Soviet intelligentsia that had wide circulation at the time: that it constituted a social category, that its consciousness was critical in creating communism, and that belonging to it gave one a special moral vision. Yet there was often no clarity about how to reconcile these different ideas or about their implications for identities or social and political behavior.

The universities were tasked with generating postwar intellectual elites – scientists, researchers, teachers, industrial specialists – and therefore had to navigate the multifaceted construct of the Soviet intelligentsia. Throughout the postwar period, university education served as a lightning rod for different ideas about the place of learning and those who practiced it in the Soviet project. One problem was the intertwining of social and moral meanings in notions of the Soviet intelligentsia that Shevchuk mentioned. In authoritative pronouncements on the subject, the Soviet state described intelligentsia as a group which devoted its superior knowledge and culture to the cause of mass enlightenment. At the same time, the intelligentsia was a construct that described and even legitimized social relationships. During the Stalin period, intelligentsia became a term for describing status-conscious educated strata. Indeed, although intelligentsia had universal ambitions, only certain kinds of people seemed to qualify for membership in it: those who possessed and practiced highly skilled, non-applied, and creative learning. Moreover, intelligentsia status was increasingly becoming a hereditary trait which Soviet professionals passed down to their offspring in the form of educational achievement and its cultural accoutrements.[3] Along with its awkward merging of communist mass enlightenment and social elitism, intelligentsia was a term laden with discordant historical baggage. The intelligentsia had been made, criticized, and remade at multiple points in Russian and Soviet history, providing postwar intellectual elites with a rich ideational heritage which they could draw on and question.

In its unstable social parameters and in its myriad historical ramifications, the Soviet intelligentsia appeared to postwar citizens as an entity that could be read and acted upon in different ways. Students, people preparing to enter the intelligentsia, were uniquely situated to experience its complications. As the book has argued, university life conveyed different messages about the intelligentsia. Owing to their prominence as strategic training grounds and as symbols of Soviet culture, universities accentuated intellectuals' duty to serve the state but also their considerable social status. They also had diverse temporal associations, pointing to the Soviet future but also celebrating Russian and non-Russian pasts. These traits of the universities shaped the everyday lives of postwar students in the late Stalin years. As Chapter 1 showed, universities directed postwar students to serve the wider society, but they also provided them with more immediate forms of social interaction that modified how this imperative was understood. The collectivist structure of student life brought Marxism-Leninism into the fabric of everyday social relationships but also provided outlets for sometimes de-centralizing group interests. And while students saw themselves as carriers of a cultural mission, the intellectual environment of the universities – and especially contact with professors of a pre-Stalin vintage, the old intelligentsia incarnate – encouraged localized and sometimes innovative interpretations of what the overarching goal meant. The university milieu was an important variable in all of these different situations, exposing the regimented and seemingly iron-clad system of higher education to unpredictable ideas and social influences.

The ideological agendas of the late Stalinist party-state only accentuated the unstable contours of the intelligentsia the universities sought to produce. In the late Stalin period, campaigns to discipline intellectuals and consolidate Marxism-Leninist ideology for the Cold War – whether by holding to account scholars seen as "kowtowing to the West" or by involving the party apparat more closely in scientific disputes – found a wide range

---

[3] On this point, see Dietrich Beyrau, *Intelligenz und Dissens: Die russischen Bildungsschichten in der Sowjetunion 1917–1985* (Göttingen: Vandenhoeck & Ruprecht, 1993), 11–12.

of responses in the universities. To varying degrees, party initiatives in all of these spheres found positive responses among students, and this should come as no surprise: for a conscious Soviet intellectual, it was clear, ideological imperatives and higher learning were indivisible. Yet late Stalinist campaignism in higher education also led to adverse reactions, especially when they brought about the abrupt overturning of scientific truths and academic hierarchies of the universities. Facing competing ideological messages and sensitive to the social status embedded in the universities, students not infrequently developed their own interpretations of where true knowledge and culture lay. Some held up the *victims* of postwar ideological campaigns in the universities – often, officially discredited but widely respected professors – as the true *intelligenty*. In a different manner, the Russocentric and anti-Semitic aspects of late Stalinism also accentuated the conceptual diversity of the intelligentsia. The prerogative of furthering historical Russian culture through forceful measures sometimes seemed to place in doubt the social position of intellectuals; it also seemed to contradict the doctrine of Soviet internationalism. In short, students found themselves pulled in different directions by their commitment to serve society and their social interests as members of university communities, all in the context of the intelligentsia's rich historical associations. As in the more everyday situations of university life, then, the tumult of Stalin's postwar ideological campaigns drew attention to intelligentsia but left its meaning open for interpretation.

The historical caesura of de-Stalinization complicated the intelligentsia question along with much else in the Soviet Union. The dethroning of Stalin threw into doubt ideological positions and interpretations of historical experiences that had seemed previously unquestionable. Perhaps inevitably given its historical resonances and association with societal leadership, the intelligentsia took on special meaning for some young educated citizens during a period of rampant confusion. Some students as well as professors saw the intelligentsia and its culture at the center of the post-Stalin situation: by reasserting its natural role as moral and intellectual guide, the intelligentsia would reunite a society emerging from Stalin's rule and create a perfected Soviet socialism. This book presents this appropriation of intelligentsia culture to confront the political dilemmas of post-Stalinism as the defining trait of "the Thaw," a term which historians have applied in many divergent ways.

Widespread student activism during the first phase of de-Stalinization showed how powerful the Thaw agenda was but it also refocused attention on seemingly intractable intelligentsia dilemmas. For a host of reasons, some students and faculty members rejected the attempt to make intelligentsia culture synonymous with the struggle against the cult of personality. The Thaw activists' claim to a broader societal and historical role alienated students who saw their goal as unquestioning service of the Soviet project, such as the MGU student who, when asked in a sociological survey what higher learning meant to him, stated his intention of being "a small screw in our society, one whose usefulness would be felt."[4] The Thaw activists, who took up protracted battles with party overseers over public space in the universities, were often less than sure about the nature of their goals as well. Whether engaged in independent cultural initiatives or penning revolutionary tracts, the student rebels of 1956 acted upon a diverse set of motives: a desire to protest the incomplete de-Stalinization of the country, an ongoing commitment to the Soviet project and its model of the culture-creating intelligentsia, and, in some cases, the social entitlement they felt as future members of the Soviet learned establishment.

As during the late Stalin period, the party-state destabilized student identities and the university communities as a whole through forceful intervention in higher learning. Already by Stalin's last years some party-state elites and faculty members became convinced that the universities' social elitism had produced students who were uncommitted to the Soviet project. These fears were surely exaggerated but not baseless. Chapter 2 shows that students' links to the broader Soviet society were indeed frequently characterized by conflict in the areas of admissions and postgraduate employment. Large parts of the university communities were attached to ostensibly meritocratic procedures in admissions and bristled at the inroads of non-academic principles in them, whether those spurred by ideological considerations or the less principled efforts of elites to place their children in prestigious institutions. Meanwhile, a statist system of postgraduate employment was often unable to satisfy the career ambitions and urban lifestyles of graduates in certain disciplines, encouraging some students to reinterpret or even neglect the demands made on them to serve the state.

Khrushchev tackled what he saw as the social malaise of the intelligentsia with his habitual gusto, rejecting the status quo in higher learning as a

---

[4] B. A. Grushin, *Chetyre zhizni Rossii v zerkale obshchestvennogo mneniia: ocherki massovogo soznaniia Rossii vo vremena Khrushcheva, Brezhneva, Gorbacheva, i El'tsina*, vol. 1 (Moscow: Progress-Traditsiia, 2001), 602, 210.

Stalin-era distortion and turning to the long-discarded model of creating an intelligentsia connected with the toiling masses. As discussed in Chapter 6, the return to policies of the Cultural Revolution destabilized university communities. It created a stark division between party demands and the social interests of educated society, if the latter are understood broadly to encompass the prestige of learned occupations, the passing of educational achievement to the offspring of educated elites, and the relatively scholastic and non-applied university education which facilitated these goals. Khrushchev's agenda of recreating a "toiling intelligentsia," as Stalin had once called it, proved elusive. Young people from educated backgrounds, their opportunities for further study placed in doubt, struggled to enter the universities, while newly promoted producers' and soldiers' academic and cultural disadvantages complicated their place in the university milieu. Soviet higher education had created the cultured intelligentsia and now, unhappy with the result, seemed unable to transform it. In this sense, the story of Khrushchev's attempt to reforge postwar higher learning demonstrated the tenacity of Stalin-era social and cultural structures.

The period of reforms had inadvertently clarified some questions: educated society would continue to dominate higher education, and the Soviet intelligentsia would continue to be a category expressing social elitism along with many other things. For increasing numbers of the university-trained educated class, the intelligentsia mission was tied to a specific style of life, one that featured urban living, the pursuit of learned professions, and the free transmission of educational opportunity across generations. For students entering its ranks, however, the intelligentsia remained as divisive as ever. The early 1960s saw the apogee of the Thaw, as parts of educated society and especially students sought to push forward an agenda of cleansing Soviet society of the "cult of personality and its consequences," however this was understood in practice. As Chapter 7 showed, the student Thaw carried the imprint of the intelligentsia milieu to which it belonged. To an extent not explored in the literature, social insularity complicated the Thaw. Widening contacts with the capitalist West caused similar problems, as they forced students to balance new sources of information and ideas with long-held convictions about the intelligentsia and its cultural and social functions. The national revivals that occurred in universities in the 1960s demonstrated the internal instability of the Thaw project, as Ukrainian and Russian students redirected intelligentsia culture to new ends. As Chapter 8 showed, the insertion of particularistic and tradition-oriented national movements challenged the universalistic and modernist assumptions of the Thaw from within, a fact that was particularly evident in the rise of an anti-Soviet and anti-Thaw Russophile movement.

At the end of the Khrushchev period, the intelligentsia remained an unstable entity. The social parameters of the intelligentsia were more pronounced than ever, and in fact gained recognition from the state. From the 1960s, Soviet propaganda embraced the intelligentsia's own view of its special social role by subtly reworking its vocabulary; rather than a census category as Stalin had defined it, intelligentsia now appeared as the highest phase of a Soviet civilizing process to which all Soviet citizens were expected to aspire.[5] In the universities, it was uncontroversial to stress the social markers of members of the intelligentsia, "active, creative thinking, widely learned" people who carried a "feeling of personal dignity and delicacy."[6] Clearly, far from being a group alienated from state and society as its pre-revolutionary predecessor had been, the intelligentsia was a commonly accepted part of mature Soviet society.[7] At the same time, the meaning of intelligentsia for political action was anything but clear, and this fact would continue to haunt the Soviet project in its final decades.

Looking forward

This study has focused on the late Stalin and Khrushchev years, the period when the expansion of higher learning, in the context of rapid political change, made the intelligentsia both an ideal and a problem for Soviet society and state. The intelligentsia pictured here, and specifically the political and social tensions that attended that construct, would shape the Brezhnev period, when the first secretary's former protégés pursued a domestic agenda of maintaining stability and avoiding disruptive experiments. Despite the stabilizing general trajectory of Soviet history after 1964, both graduates of the universities and the new cohorts of youth that entered them continued to struggle to define the intelligentsia's place in society.

[5] Stephen Lovell, *The Russian Reading Revolution: Print Culture in the Soviet and Post-Soviet Eras* (New York: St. Martin's Press, 2000), 18.

[6] I. Parfenov, "Student universiteta – intelligent prezhde vsego," *Leninskii put'*, 1 August 1968: 2.

[7] Indeed, by the late Soviet period, older forms of Bolshevik anti-intellectualism appeared hopelessly anachronistic to educated society. A popular 1973 comedic film featured a scientist who conducts mysterious experiments in his apartment and is taunted by a simple-minded neighbor: "a miserable *intelligent*! And the people had the stupidity to educate you!" (in Russian, *intelligent neschasntyi. Vyuchili vas na svoiu golovu*). This scene would hardly have seemed funny twenty years earlier. Leonid Gaidai, *Ivan Vasil'evich meniaet professiiu* (Mosfil'm, 1973).

The end of Khrushchevism solidified the universities' position as preserves of intelligentsia privilege. When practitioners of the new discipline of Soviet sociology turned to studying higher learning, they discovered patterns of stable inequality. Students of intelligentsia origins were over-represented in all areas of higher learning, particularly in institutions offering training in the pure sciences and humanities such as the universities.[8] To be sure, the Brezhnev regime did not abandon the goal of inserting toilers into the intelligentsia, as the remnants of Khrushchev's admissions reforms ensured a small stream of working citizens and former servicemen into the universities.[9] Nevertheless, the failure of the Second Cultural Revolution deepened the association of universities with the hereditary intelligentsia and urban society. In 1968, a student at the Odessa Polytechnic Institute conveyed the social insularity of his own milieu in a lengthy report to the KGB. Students dubbed their classmates from rural areas "collective farmers," he reported, while the perception that the overwhelming majority of student communists were demobilized soldiers led students to associate party membership itself with "insufficient mental development."[10] While bitter about party privileges – a fact of Soviet life that was increasingly visible during the Brezhnev years – many students of intelligentsia origins saw their own social privilege as a natural outcome of intellectual abilities. And as before, students fought to maintain intelligentsia status whenever state institutions failed to recognize it, for instance by contesting distribution placements far from the city or low in prestige. Indeed, social grievances among the young intelligentsia grew in the period, as professional salaries fell to a level frequently below those of manual laborers and social mobility as a whole slowed along with decreasing rates of economic growth in the 1970s.[11]

---

[8] George Avis, "The Sociology of Soviet Higher Education: A Review of Recent Empirical Research," in Bohdan Horasymiw (ed.), *Education and the Mass Media in the Soviet Union and Eastern Europe* (New York: Praeger, 1976), 45–50.

[9] Indeed, in the 1970s, the student body across the USSR became more socially diverse, in part because of the revival of the old Bolshevik institution of "workers' colleges." S. V. Volkov, *Intellektual'nyi sloi v sovetskom obshchestve* (St. Petersburg: Fond "Razvitie," Institut nauchnoi informatsii po obshchestvennym naukam RAN, 1999), 57–59.

[10] "'Otchuzhdennoe ot partii sostoianie': KGB SSSR o nastroeniiakh uchashchikhsia i studenchestva, 1968–1976 g.g.," *Istoricheskii arkhiv*, no. 1 (1994): 177, 182, 184.

[11] See David Ruffley, *Children of Victory: Young Specialists and the Evolution of Soviet Society* (Westport, CT and London: Praeger, 2003), 32–42 and Vladimir Shlapentokh, "Attitudes and Behavior of Soviet Youth in the 1970s and 1980s: The Mysterious Variable in Soviet Politics," in Richard G. Braungart and Margaret M. Braungart (eds.), *Research in Political Sociology*, vol. 2 (Greenwich, CT: JAI Press, 1986), 199–224.

In the political sphere, the post-Khrushchev situation was much more contentious. In its immediate wake, many students and other Soviet citizens met the leader's ouster in 1965 with relief and satisfaction.[12] As an American who studied in Leningrad put it, students thought an "uncultured boor" had been "replaced by somewhat more suitable symbols of modern society" – if hardly inspiring ones – in the form of "technocrats" and "colorless bureaucrats."[13] Nevertheless, the eviction of Khrushchev signaled an admission that promises of imminent communist construction had come to naught. As an MGU student complained at a public meeting, "Khrushchev said we would soon overtake America and live under Communism. The leadership has been wrong so many times that now it's hard to believe anything."[14] Moreover, the circumstances surrounding the change in leadership – a palace coup poorly covered up as a voluntary retirement – made the new political leadership appear cynical and self-serving. Adding to the unsavory impression of Khrushchev's removal was the abruptly changed tone in party circles, as officials who had only recently given the first secretary fulsome praise now condemned him. One student in Novosibirsk asked publicly with regard to the powerful provincial party secretary F. S. Goriachev, "when was he honest, when he glorified Khrushchev or now?"[15]

More remarkable than such frank talk was the fact that it occurred in public spaces and often went unpunished. In the Brezhnev years, party authorities pursued a policy of containing rather than uprooting signs of "ideological wavering" in the universities. Indeed, party and Komsomol bodies allowed and even oversaw the formation of discussion clubs and initiatives over which they had incomplete control. M. I. Zhuravleva, responsible for student questions in TsK Komsomol, explained the more permissive line succinctly. There was "nothing criminal" in instances when students strayed from the party line in public discussions, she argued, and a distinction had to be made between truly "hostile elements" (who needed to be silenced) and those who are simply "poorly informed" (who should be

---

[12] For the expression of extreme hostility to Khrushchev voiced by different social groups, see public meetings of various kinds designated with explaining the change in leadership in RGANI f. 5, op. 31, d. 233, ll. 214–29.

[13] "Some Attitudes of Soviet Students in Moscow and Leningrad," BR # 76-65, 17 December 1965, RFE/RL, HIA, 531/2, 4.

[14] William Taubman, *The View from Lenin Hills: Soviet Youth in Ferment* (New York: Coward-McCann, 1967), 13.

[15] Mikhail Shilovskii, "Istoriia universitetskogo vol'nodumiia: chast' 1: do 1968 goda (po arkhivnym materialam," *Nauka v Sibiri*, nos. 1–2 (1998), www.nsc.ru/HBC/hbc.phtml?31+80+1 (accessed 20 September 2012).

brought over to correct positions through debate).[16] Underpinning this approach was the pragmatic view that debate in the universities was inevitable in any case. As Zhuravleva said of students on a different occasion, presumably with a tone of regret, "here we are forced to deal with the thinking part of youth that reads literature and ponders things every day."[17] Although policies toward students stiffened following the Czechoslovakian crisis of 1968, the loosening of repressive policies seems to have continued through the Brezhnev years. The KGB maintained an active agenda in higher education, but usually continued the late-Khrushchev approach of relying on putatively "educational" ("prophylactic") measures, such as talks and warnings, rather than arrests.[18] Less ideological sensitive agencies of control in higher education weakened far more; a recent discussion suggests that dormitory officials in the late 1960s demanded only a ritualistic fulfillment of rules and overlooked students' "obviously fictitious" explanations for infringements, ones that might have carried serious consequences in previous years.[19]

The more calibrated policing of speech in the universities went along with a widening of opportunities in the universities' cultural sphere in the Brezhnev years. A case in point was the consolidation of a student theater movement. Exploiting the advantage of their amateur status, some student troupes continued the Thaw agenda by undertaking veiled social criticism of Stalinism, anti-Semitism, and ideological orthodoxy in their work.[20] The well-known troupes in the capital, the MGU Student Theater and MGU's Our Home Studio, were centers for *intelligentnost'* in its Thaw manifestation, stressing honesty and the ethos of "spiritual togetherness" that united the actors with their no doubt predominantly intelligentsia audiences.[21] Striking in this context was the role of the party and Komsomol in promoting Student Theater. A 1965 "All-Union Festival of Student

[16] RGASPI-M f. 1, op. 5, d. 1096, ll. 111–12.   [17] Ibid., d. 802, ll. 109–10.
[18] On this change in KGB practices in the period more broadly, see Julie Elkner, "The Changing Face of Repression under Khrushchev," in Melanie Ilič and Jeremy Smith (eds.), *Soviet State and Society Under Nikita Khrushchev* (London: Routledge, 2009), 153–56 and V. A. Kozlov, *Mass Uprisings in the USSR: Protest and Rebellion in the Post-Stalin Years*, trans. and ed. Elaine McClarnand MacKinnon (Armonk, NY: M. E. Sharpe, 2002), 308.
[19] Sergei Korolev, "The Student Dormitory in the 'Period of Stagnation': The Erosion of Regulatory Processes," *Russian Social Science Review*, 45 (2004): 83.
[20] See Susan Costanzo, "Amateur Theatres and Amateur Publics in the Russian Republic, 1958–71," *The Slavonic and East European Review*, 86 (2008): 372–94 and Bella Ostromoukhova, "Le Dégel et les troupes amateur: Changements politiques et activités artistiques des étudiants, 1953–1970," *Cahiers du Monde Russe et Soviétique*, 47 (2006): 303–26.
[21] M. L. Kniazeva et al., *200 let plus 20. Kniga o studencheskom teatre Moskovskogo universiteta* (Moscow: Iskusstvo, 1979), 4–6, 18.

Theater" was sponsored by Komsomol TsK but its jury of well-known actors and performers in fact allowed considerable creative license to the students.[22] Nor should Komsomol sponsorship of the Thaw come as a surprise. For both students and Komsomol leaders, amateur theater was to be a serious affair, a fight against "philistinism" and spiritual emptiness pursued in the name of an enlightened social consciousness and "civic spirit" or *grazhdanstvennost'*, even if students often read these goals differently than Komsomol leaders.[23] The Student Theater was evidence that the Brezhnev regime offered substantial (if fragile) outlets for the ongoing expression of the Thaw project in culture – all of which ran contrary to the fears of re-Stalinization that many intellectuals at the time nurtured.

The growing scope for student cultural and political expression in the universities in the late 1960s – and, in subdued form, after the conservative turn sparked by the Czechoslovak Crisis of 1968 – should not obscure the ongoing ambivalence of intelligentsia thinking. Among students, the category of intelligentsia produced wide divergences in viewpoints. This became evident at the relatively un-policed "disputes" and discussions that were a widespread fixture of student life in the 1960s. At KDU, a "discussion club" at the Philosophy Department organized a discussion called "Ideals and Idols" which the Komsomol organizers envisioned as an attack on religion. Instead, the event turned into a wide-ranging debate about what constituted current-day "philistinism" (*meshchanstvo*), a term that was the traditional antipode of the intelligentsia's consciousness. The orthodox position proposed by Komsomol activists, that philistinism was the product of "youth without ideals" who kept apart from public life, did not convince many of the participants. Some defended philistinism on principle, while others commented that "the contemporary philistine" often keeps abreast of current affairs and even takes part in them (an argument that was surely a subtle attack on party bureaucracy).[24] Talking about the intelligentsia proved just as controversial in the scientific hub of Novosibirsk, where the president of the café-club "Under the Integral" – a virtually autonomous institution that brought together young scientists and students – held a dispute "on the sluggishness of the intelligentsia." The organizer, A. I. Burshtein, gave a speech rebuking young scientists for

---

[22] The list of prizes established for the troupes shows how far the competition strayed from typical Komsomol endeavors: the Maiakovskii prize for "civic spirit," the Il'f and Petrov prize for best humor, and a prize for "original development of a topic." RGASPI-M f. 1, op. 46, d. 382, ll. 1–5.

[23] See the discussion in Susan Costanzo, "The Emergence of Alternative Culture: Amateur Studio-Theaters in Moscow and Leningrad, 1957–1984" (Ph.D. diss., Northwestern University, 1994), 66–67.

[24] RGASPI-M f. 1, op. 5, d. 1096, ll. 100–15.

lacking "responsibility for the fate of society," an articulation of a discourse of civic duty that was prominent among the nascent human rights movement of the period.[25] However, a colleague fired back that "everyone should take care of his own business," by which presumably he meant devoting oneself fully to science (he added that he fulfilled his civic duty by voting against all in the single-candidate elections to local Soviets).[26] Clearly, intelligentsia remained an eagerly coveted but disruptive term, one that tended to embroil students and others in endless debates.

Intelligentsia dilemmas also vexed the organized movements of intellectual dissent that emerged in the 1960s. Despite the relative permissiveness of university life in these years, the post-Khrushchev leadership initiated a crackdown on critical intellectuals in Russia and Ukraine, arresting the Muscovite writers Andrei Siniavskii and Yulii Daniel for publishing their works in the West while pursuing a more thorough round-up of Ukrainian college-educated nationalists in Ukraine, mostly from the Western territories. These repressions brought about spiraling conflict, as intellectuals in Moscow and Kyiv expressed solidarity with those already arrested and became targeted for party or judicial repressions themselves.[27] The opposition movements that emerged from this process in the short term – a nationalist movement in Ukraine and a movement for human rights in Moscow – were closely tied to university life. The leaders of these movements had experienced the student Thaw in Moscow, Kyiv, Lviv, or elsewhere and were shaped by its ideas. At least in part, the embrace of an ideology of human rights was an outgrowth of the morally charged defense of intellectual integrity that had been a mainstay of university politics.[28] In addition, university communities and students in particular furnished many of the movements' supporters. Pockets of students across the country voiced

---

[25] Stephen Bittner, *The Many Lives of Khrushchev's Thaw: Experience and Memory in Moscow's Arbat* (Ithaca, NY: Cornell University Press, 2008), 174–210.

[26] A. G. Borzenkov, *Molodezh' i politika: vozmozhnosti i predely studencheskoi samodeiatel'nosti na vostoke Rossii, 1961–1991 gg.*, vol. 2 (Novosibirsk: Novosibirskii gosudarstvennyi universitet, 2002), 21–22.

[27] See Liudmila Alexeyeva, *Soviet Dissent: Contemporary Movements for National, Religious, and Human Rights* (Middletown, CT: Wesleyan University Press, 1985), 21–59, 267–317 and H. V. Kasianov, *Nezhodni: ukrainska intelihentsiia v rusi oporu 1960–80-kh rokiv* (Kyiv: "Lybid," 1995).

[28] See Marshall S. Shatz, *Soviet Dissent in Historical Perspective* (Cambridge University Press, 1980), 126. Indeed, the human rights activists' distinctive strategy of calling on the Soviet state to obey its own laws was first formulated by students during de-Stalinization. Notable were Ernst Orlovskii and Revol't Pimenov, who embraced the notion of "legal methods of struggle" against the Soviet state. Revol't Pimenov, *Vospominaniia* (Moscow: Informatsionno-ekspertnaia gruppa "Panorama," 1996), 70–75. See also Benjamin Nathans, "The Dictatorship of Reason: Aleksandr Vol'pin and the Idea of Rights under 'Developed Socialism'," *Slavic Review*, 4 (2007): 630–63.

support of the dissenters, reading the recent arrests as a campaign against the Soviet – or, for some, the Ukrainian – intelligentsia.[29]

Movements of intellectual dissent would nevertheless stumble on the constellation of issues that might be dubbed the "intelligentsia question." For several reasons, large parts of educated society in the universities and beyond them opposed the new embrace of clear opposition to the state. Some students at MGU played a large role in the organization of the "glasnost'" meeting of 1965 to demand an open trial for the writers Siniavskii and Daniel, but others belonged to the ranks of anti-demonstrators as well (this is not to mention the great many who remained indifferent to the undertaking).[30] Indeed, some intellectuals in the capital blamed Siniavskii and Daniel for derailing the Thaw and "the achievements of the Soviet intelligentsia" by publishing abroad.[31] For many, the dissidents' reliance on Western media to broadcast their message into the USSR made their activities appear distasteful if not treasonous.[32] By undertaking actions that set them apart from (and even outside) the single system by which everyone lived, dissenters seemed to be rebuking the rest for cowardice and conformity. Finally, the national question plagued movements of dissent in Moscow and Kyiv. In the Ukrainian case, the steadfastly Russian character of many urban centers in the republic automatically limited the scope of the dissidents' appeal. In Russia, the emergence of Russophilism in the 1960s and its support in official circles divided the oppositional intelligentsia into mutually hostile national and liberal camps. Not surprisingly, this fundamental divide found expression in a debate about what constituted the true intelligentsia. If Andrei Sakharov invoked the role of a progressive intelligentsia in creating a rational, scientific, and universalistic future, Aleksandr Solzhenitsyn famously branded Soviet intellectuals (and liberals among

---

[29] See sources on student groups in Donetsk and Odessa in TsDAHOU f. 1, op. 24, spr. 6313, ark. 3–6, and ibid., f. 1, op. 24, spr. 6060, ark. 153–57. See also S. I. Zhuk, *Rock and Roll in the Rocket City: The West, Identity, and Ideology in Soviet Dniepropetrovsk, 1960–1985* (Washington, DC: Woodrow Wilson Center Press, 2010), 29–52.

[30] D. I. Zubarev and A. U. Daniel, *5 Dekabria 1965 goda v vospominaniiakh uchastnikov sobytii, materialakh samizdata, publikatsiiakh zarubezhnoi pressy i v dokumentakh partiinykh i komsomol'skikh organizatsii i zapiskakh komiteta gosudarstvennoi bezopasnosti v Tsk KPSS* (Moscow: Obshchestvo "Memorial," 2005), 47, 69, 77–79, 91, 107–10. An American graduate student at MGU at the time did not notice widespread student interest in the trial. "Life at MGU – Comments of an American Student," BR # 72–66, 7 November 1966, RFE/RL, HIA, 531/4, 5.

[31] Nina Voronel', *Bez prikras: vospominaniia* (Moscow: Zakharov, 2003), 144–45.

[32] For one expression of this distrust, see Donald J. Raleigh (ed.), *Russia's Sputnik Generation: Soviet Baby Boomers Talk about their Lives* (Bloomington: Indiana University Press, 2006), 47.

them) a self-serving, cynical, and fundamentally non-national "semi-educated estate."[33]

Despite its kaleidoscopic nature – or perhaps because of it – the Soviet intelligentsia played an important role in the collapse of the Soviet system in the 1980s. Unexpectedly for Western onlookers, a group of reformist bureaucrats had risen within the Brezhnev-period party *nomenklatura*, individuals who managed to balance commitment to communism with the intelligentsia's self-image as a progressive force in society.[34] The patron of these party intellectuals, Mikhail Gorbachev, derived his respect for intellectuals from his student years at MGU in the first half of the 1950s.[35] When Gorbachev became the leader of the crisis-ridden superpower in 1985, he set about courting reformist intellectuals to serve as foot soldiers in a bold campaign to revitalize socialism. After a few frustrating years of piecemeal reforms, he turned to a radical agenda of *glasnost'* or openness, the spurring of public debate in order to drive thoroughgoing political and economic reforms. *Glasnost'* was clearly informed by the Thaw agenda of creating progress and moral values through public discussion and culture. Gorbachev's propaganda chief and ideological linchpin Aleksandr Iakovlev once described perestroika as "the intellectualization of society"; the opening up of the long-shackled public sphere to free expression and debate would, he clearly believed, bring the moral and spiritual values held by the intelligentsia to the people as a whole.[36] Alternatively, one could think of Gorbachev's agenda as an intellectualization of socialism itself, an injection of the intelligentsia's superior consciousness – perhaps the closest

---

[33] See Andrei Sakharov et al., "A Reformist Plan for Democratization," in Stephen Cohen (ed.), *An End to Silence: Uncensored Opinion in the Soviet Union: From Roy Medvedev's Underground Magazine "Political Diary"* (New York: Norton, 1982), 322 and Alexander Solzhenitsyn, "The Smatterers," in A. I. Solzhenitsyn et al., *From under the Rubble*, trans. A. M. Brock (Boston: Little, Brown, 1975), 242.

[34] Work on this cohort includes Robert D. English, *Russia and the Idea of the West: Gorbachev, Intellectuals, and the End of the Cold War* (New York: Columbia University Press, 2000) and Roger Markwick, "Catalyst of Historiography, Marxism and Dissidence: The Sector of Methodology, Institute of History, Soviet Academy of Sciences, 1964–68," *Europe-Asia Studies*, 46 (1994): 579–96. For a broader account of the "vitality and creativity" of intellectual life during the Brezhnev period, see Mark Sandle, "A Triumph of Ideological Hairdressing? Intellectual Life in the Brezhnev Era Reconsidered," in Edwin Bacon and Mark Sandle (eds.), *Brezhnev Reconsidered* (Houndmills, Basingstoke: Palgrave Macmillan, 2002), 154.

[35] Although Gorbachev has repeatedly stressed the impact of university life on his personality, he has provided few details about what form it took. See Mikhail Sergeevich Gorbachev, *Memoirs* (New York: Doubleday, 1996), 42 and Mikhail Sergeevich Gorbachev and Zděnek Mlynář, *Conversations with Gorbachev: On Perestroika, the Prague Spring, and the Crossroads of Socialism* (New York: Columbia University Press, 2002), 22–23.

[36] Aleksandr Iakovlev, "Perestroika or the 'Death of Socialism,'" in Stephen F. Cohen and Katrina van den Heuvel (eds.), *Voices of Glasnost: Interviews with Gorbachev's Reformers* (New York: Norton, 1989), 64.

thing to revolutionary enthusiasm after the long period of stagnation – into the feeble body of the Soviet order.[37]

The attempt to draw on the intelligentsia to rebuild socialism ran into insurmountable problems. Not surprisingly, mistrust between dissidents and leaders of the communist system plagued the new alliance from the start. More broadly, Gorbachev's *glasnost'* exposed the inherent divisions of postwar Soviet intellectual life. The potential for journalists, professors, and the like to make unsettling and demoralizing revelations about Soviet society and history was endless, and they plunged into the task of exposing truths with admirable gusto. If open discussion modeled on intellectual discourse had failed to produce a common political outlook among postwar intellectuals, how could it be expected to solve the crises of state socialism? The political inadequacy of the "intellectualization of society" was particularly clear in the national question, where *glasnost'* provided convenient cover for mobilization around previously unthinkable demands for autonomy in non-Russian republics and then by Russians as well.[38] The result was that facilitating public debate led to the "ideological self-destruction" of communism rather than to its salvation.[39]

Gorbachev's motives will continue to perplex scholars for generations: how could a product of the communist apparat be so naïve as to believe that intellectual discussion and democratization would save it? One part of an explanation for this puzzle is surely a distinctive peculiarity of late Soviet society: the conviction among large numbers of people that learning and science were the true source of moral values and progress, and that, accordingly, the most educated citizens were society's true leaders. This faith in the intelligentsia was a product of postwar higher learning, when the ascendancy of university life in the Cold War – in the context of frequently tumultuous policies imposed by party leaders – enhanced the status of thinkers of all stripes and raised crucial questions about their place in Soviet society. The rootedness of the intelligentsia in the historical conditions of postwar Sovietism became apparent after 1991, when the Soviet state disappeared from the map. Educated elites overwhelmed by acute socio-economic crisis would cling to *intelligentnost'* as a form of social identity.[40] At the same time, the loss of the Soviet state's exaggerated respect

---

[37] The moral vocabulary of perestroika is discussed in Archie Brown, *Seven Years that Changed the World: Perestroika in Perspective* (New York: Oxford University Press, 2007), 109.

[38] Ronald Grigor Suny, *The Revenge of the Past: Nationalism, Revolution, and the Collapse of the Soviet Union* (Stanford University Press, 1993), 127–62.

[39] Stephen Kotkin, *Armageddon Averted: The Soviet Collapse, 1970–2000* (Oxford University Press, 2001), 67.

[40] Jennifer Patico, *Consumption and Social Change in a Post-Soviet Middle Class* (Washington, DC: Woodrow Wilson Center Press, 2008), 48–49.

for intellectuals – but also its despotic oversight of them – placed in doubt the very category of intelligentsia. The startling new situation inspired soul-searching and even some nostalgia for the old regime among educated post-Soviet citizens.[41] To the end, the intelligentsia was fundamentally Soviet, a product of postwar socialism's unsustainable love–hate relationship with the life of the mind.

[41] See A. Siniavskii, *The Russian Intelligentsia*, trans. Lynn Visson (New York: Columbia University Press, 1997); Masha Gessen, *Dead Again: The Russian Intelligentsia after Communism* (London and New York: Verso, 1997).

A note on oral history interviews

During research trips to Moscow and Saratov in 2003–4 and Kyiv and St. Petersburg in 2005 I conducted, recorded, and transcribed forty nine interviews with a total of forty four people who were students or faculty in the postwar years. In the text, I have assigned pseudonyms to all of my interview subjects to protect their identities, making exceptions only in cases where published sources would allow the reader to establish an individual's identity. I provide below a complete list of interview subjects which excludes two people who asked for total anonymity. I began each interview by presenting subjects with a form explaining my proposed method of citation, to which they gave oral consent.

Alibastrova, Albina Anatol'evna
Avrus, Anatolii Il'ich
Azef, Vitalii Samuilovich
Beletskii, Mikhail Ivanovich
Burmistrovich, Il'ia
Butuzov, Valentin F.
Chichik, Natalia L'vovna
Dedkova, Tamara Fedorovna
Del'tsov, Lev Sergeevich
Drach, Ivan Fedorovich
Gerlin, Valeria Mikhailovna
Gluzman, Semen Fishelevich
Gorina, Liudmila Vasil'evna
Iankov, Vadim Anatol'evich
Iskhizov, Mikhail Davydovich
Ivanova, Natalia Borisovna
Khakhaev, Sergei Dmitrievich

Lavut, Aleksandr Pavlovich
Letuvet, Pavel
Linnik, Viktor Alekseevich
Litvinenko, Sergei Fillipovich and spouse
Loginov, Aleksandr Sergeevich
Maslova, Valentina
Petrova, Nina Konstantinovna
Podugol'nikova, Olga Andreevna
Pokhil, Grigorii Pavlovich
Pokrovsky, Natalia I.
Seleznev, Viktor Makarovich
Shikhanovich, Iurii
Simonov, Iurii Gavrilovich
Smorgunova, Elena Mikhailovna
Solokhin, Nikolai Dmitrievich
Taniuk, Leonid (Les') Stepanovych
Tikhomirov, Vladimir Mikhailovich

Krasnopevtsev, Lev Nikolaevich
Kristy, Irina
Kudriavtsev, Valerii Borisovich
Larkov, Sergei

Tolochko, Petro Petrovych
Verblovskaia, Irena
Zvereva, Iulia Ivanovna

Bibliography

PRIMARY SOURCES
Archival materials

I provide the name of each archive in which I worked, organized alphabetically. In citing documentation for Russian archives I follow the convention of *fond, opis', delo, list* ("collection, subgroup within a collection, file, leaf"); for Ukrainian archives, the terms are *fond, opys', sprava, arkush*. I provide information on fondy from which I cite material; in the case of especially large fondy, I list opisi as well. For the sake of brevity, I provide shortened or simplified titles of different sections of the archives. References to Radio Free Europe/Radio Liberty corporate records accessed at the Hoover Institution Archive include document title, document number (BR conveys "Background Report"), date, box and folder numbers (for instance, 592/3).

Derzhavnyi arkhiv mista Kyiva (DAK)
f. R-1246: Kyiv State University

Derzhavnyi arkhiv Kyivs'koi oblasti (DAKO)
f. 1, op. 16, 20, 22: KPU, City of Kyiv
f. 158: KPU, Kyiv State University
f. 9912: LKSMU, Kyiv State University

Dom Russkogo zarubezh'ia imeni Aleksandra Solzhenitsyna (DRZ)
f. 1, op. 1, d. R-472: N. K. Shor

Gosudarstvennyi arkhiv noveishei istorii Saratovskoi oblasti (GANISO)
f. 35: KPSS, Saratov State University
f. 594: KPSS, Saratov Province
f. 652: VLKSM, Saratov University

f. 3234: VLKSM, Kirov District
f. 4529: VLKSM, Saratov City

Gosudarstvennyi arkhiv Rossiiskoi federatsii (GARF)

f. 605-R: RSFSR Ministry of Higher and Secondary Specialized Education
f. 8131: USSR Public Prosecutor's Office
f. 9396: USSR Ministry of Higher Education

Gosudarstvennyi arkhiv Saratovskoi oblasti (GASO)

f. 332: Saratov State University

Hoover Institution Archives (HIA)

Radio Free Europe/Radio Liberty corporate records, Background Reports, Boxes
529–31

*Nauchno-informatsionnyi tsentr "Memorial" v Sankt-Peterburge
(NITs "Memorial" SPb)*

Holdings from Archive of the Administration of the Federal Security Service
for St. Petersburg and Leningrad Province (Arkhiv upravleniia federal'noi
sluzhby bezopasnosti po Sankt-Peterburgu i Leningradskoi oblasti) (cited at
Arkhiv UFSB SPb)
arkh. no.: P-66655 (counter-revolutionary group "Kolokol")
arkh. no.: P-66655 (counter-revolutionary group led by M. M. Molostvov)
arkh. no.: P-81390 (counter-revolutionary group led by Revol't Pimenov)
M. M. Molostvov Papers

Rossiiskii gosudarstvennyi arkhiv noveishei istorii (RGANI)

f. 2: TsK KPSS Plenary Meetings
f. 5: TsK KPSS Apparat
    op. 17: Division of Science and Culture
    op. 35, 37: Division of Science and Higher Education Establishments
f. 13: Bureau, TsK KPSS po RSFSR
f. 89: Trial of the Communist Party

Rossiiskii gosudarstvennyi arkhiv sotsial'no-politicheskoi istorii (RGASPI)

f. 17: TsK KPSS
    op. 125: Division of Agitation and Propaganda
    op. 133: Division of Literature, Science and Higher Education Establishments

Rossiiskii gosudarstvennyi arkhiv sotsial'no-politicheskoi istorii – molodezhnyi arkhiv (RGASPI-M)

f. 1: TsK VLKSM
  op. 6: Division of Komsomol Organizations
  op. 31: General Division
  op. 32: Division of Agitation and Propaganda
  op. 46: Division for Student Youth

Tsentr dokumentatsii "Narodnyi arkhiv" (TsDNA)

f. 314: T. P. Mazur

Tsentral'nyi arkhiv obshchestvenno-politicheskoi istorii Moskvy (TsAOPIM)

f. 4 KPSS, Moscow City
  op. 80: Division of Propaganda and Agitation, Science and Culture
  op. 113: MGK KPSS, Division of Science and Culture
  op. 100, 102, 105: MGK KPSS
f. 478: KPSS, Moscow State University
f. 635: MGK VLKSM
f. 5463: VLKSM, Lenin Pedagogical Institute
f. 6083: VLKSM, Moscow State University
f. 7063: Central School of the Young Communist League

Tsentral'nyi derzhavnyi arkhiv hromads'kykh ob'iednan' Ukrainy (TsDAHOU)

f. 1: TsK KPU
  op. 24: Special Sector
  op. 71: Division of Science and Higher Education Establishments
f. 7: TsK LKSMU
  op. 6: Division of Student Youth and Propaganda and Agitation
  op. 13: Special Sector
  op. 17: Division of Komsomol Organizations

Tsentral'nyi derzhavnyi arkhiv vyshchykh orhaniv vlady ta upravlinnia Ukrainy (TsDAVO)

f. 4621: Ukrainian SSR Ministry of Higher and Secondary Specialized Education

Tsentral'nyi munitsipal'nyi arkhiv Moskvy (TsMAM)

f. 1609: Moscow State University
f. 26: Moscow Committee of Unions of Employees of Education, Higher Education and Science

Newspapers and periodicals

Current Digest of the Soviet Press *(CDSP)*
Digest of the Soviet Ukrainian Press
Komsomol'skaia Pravda
Kuranty
Literaturnaia gazeta
The Deseret News *(Salt Lake City)*
The New Yorker
Ukrainskyi visnyk *(Paris and Baltimore)*
Vestnik vysshei shkoly *(VVSh)*
(Ministry of Higher Education USSR)

Molodoi tselinnik na studencheskoi stroike
Moskovskii universitet
Molodoi Stalinets *(Saratov University)*
MSOshnik *(Moscow)*
Sovety: fakty, sobytiia *(Saratov)*
Voprosy Istorii Estestvoznaniia i tekhniki *(VIET)*
Za radians'ki kadry *(Kyiv University)*

Memoirs, literary works, and published source collections

Aimermakher, K. et al. (eds.), *Doklad N. S. Khrushcheva o kul'te lichnosti Stalina na XX s'ezde KPSS: dokumenty* (Moscow: ROSSPEN, 2002).

Alexeyeva, Ludmila and Paul Goldberg, *The Thaw Generation: Coming of Age in the Post-Stalin Era* (Boston: Little, Brown, 1990).

Altshuler, Mordechai et al. (eds.), *Sovetskie evrei pishut Il'e Erenburgu: 1943–1966* (Jerusalem: Yad Vashem, 1993).

Arbatov, Georgi, *The System: An Insider's Life in Soviet Politics* (New York: Random House, 1993).

Artisevich, V. A., *Odinakovykh sudeb ne byvaet: vospominaniia* (Saratov: Izdatel'stvo Saratovskogo universiteta, 2009).

Azadovskii, M. K. et al., *Perepiska: 1944–1954* (Moscow: Novoe literaturnoe obozrenie, 1998).

Azef, Vitalii, "'Taina' 42-ei komnaty: odnazhdy v Khrushchevskuiu 'ottepel'," *Sovety: fakty, sobytiia*, 28 April 1991: 3.

Bakaev, N. T., *Na mekhmat kto popal … Ivan, ne pomniashii rodstvo i potomok Chingis-Khan* (Moscow: Knizhnyi dom "Moskovskii universitet," 2000).

Baron, Samuel H. and Cathy A. Frierson (eds.), *Adventures in Russian Historical Research: Reminiscences of American Scholars from the Cold War to the Present* (Armonk, NY: M. E. Sharpe, 2003).

Baturina, Iu. Iu., "Organizatsionnye izmeneniia v uchebnom protsesse vysshykh uchebnykh zavedenii v 1956–1965 godakh (na primere nizhnego povolzh'ia)," *Vestnik Cheliabinskogo gosudarstvennogo universiteta*, 179, no. 41, "Istoriia," 100–101, www.lib.csu.ru/vch/179/017.pdf (accessed 9 July 2012).

Belkin, V. I., "Protiv Stalina pri Staline (zametki uchastnika i ochevidtsa). Pis'mo A. Zhigulinu," in I. A. Mazus (ed.), *"Poka svobodoiu gorim …" (o molodezhnom antistalinskom dvizhenii kontsa 40-kh – nachala 50-kh godov)* (Moscow: Nezavisimoe izdatel'stvo "Pik," 2004).

Belova, A. D. et al. (eds.), *My – matematiki s leninskikh gor* (Moscow: Fortuna Limited, 2003).

Berestov, V. D., "Shef (glava iz knigi vospominanii)," *Etnograficheskoe obozrenie*, no. 1 (1997): 58–70.

Berg, Raissa L., *Acquired Traits: Memoirs of a Geneticist from the Soviet Union*, trans. David Lowe (New York: Viking, 1988).

Bernshtein, S. B., *Zigzagi pamiati: vospominaniia, dnevnikovye zapisi* (Moscow: Institut slavianovedeniia RAN, 2002).

Bikkenin, N. B., "Stseny obshchestvennoi i chastnoi zhizni: 'moi universitety'," *Svobodnaia mysl'*, 3 (2001): 75–88.

Bocharov, A. G., "Vstrechi s Iuriem Trifonovym: vospominaniia," *Literaturnoe obozrenie*, nos. 1–2 (1994): 80–5.

Bogachaevskaia, K. P. (ed.), "Iu. G. Oksman v Saratove: pis'ma 1947–1957," *Voprosy literatury*, no. 5 (1993): 240–56.

Bogomolov, A. N. and T. L. Kandelaki, *Leonid Samuilovich Leibenzon* (Moscow: Nauka, 1991).

Borodin, L. I., *Bez vybora: avtobiograficheskoe povestvovanie* (Moscow: Molodaia gvardiia, 2003).

"Vserossiiskii sotsial-khristianskii soiuz osvobozhdeniia naroda," *Veche*, no. 13 (1984), 164–75.

Bovin, Aleksandr, *XX vek kak zhizn'* (Moscow: Zakharov, 2003).

Britashinskii, Vladimir, "Studencheskoe poeticheskoe dvizhenie v Leningrade v nachale ottepeli," *Novoe literaturnoe obozrenie*, no. 14 (1995): 167–80.

Bukovsky, Vladimir, *To Build a Castle: My Life as a Dissenter* (New York: Viking Press, 1979).

Burtin, Iu. G., *Ispoved' shestidesiatnika* (Moscow: Progress-Traditsiia, 2003).

(ed. and comp.), "Studencheskoe brozhenie v SSSR (konets 1956 g.)," *Voprosy istorii*, 1 (1997): 3–23.

Callaghan, Tim, "Studying the Students: Between Conformity and Dissent," *Survey*, no. 33 (1960): 12–19.

Chauncey, Henry, "Interviews with Soviet Educators on Recent Developments and the Current Status of Education in the U.S.S.R.: Report of Visit to the Soviet Union Sponsored by the United States Office of Education under the Auspices of the US–USSR Cultural Exchange Agreement for 1964–65" (May 1965).

"'Chelovek, okonchivshii universitet s otlichiem, v zhizni mozhet etogo otlichiia ne poluchit': Vystuplenie N. S. Khrushcheva na vypuske fizicheskogo fakul'teta Moskovskogo gosudarstvennogo universiteta imeni M. V. Lomonosova 20 ianvaria 1959 g.," *Istochnik*, 6 (2003): 97–101.

Cohen, Stephen, "The Stalin Question since Stalin," in Stephen Cohen (ed.), *An End to Silence: Uncensored Opinion in the Soviet Union: From Roy Medvedev's Underground Magazine "Political Diary"* (New York: Norton, 1982), 22–50.

Cohen, Stephen F. and Katrina van den Heuvel (eds.), *Voices of Glasnost: Interviews with Gorbachev's Reformers* (New York: Norton, 1989).

Dedkov, Igor', *Dnevnik 1953–1994* (Moscow: Progress-Pleiada, 2005).

"'Delo' molodykh istorikov (1957–1958 gg.)," *Voprosy istorii*, no. 4 (1994): 106–35.

Dmitriev, S. S., "Iz dnevnikov Sergeia Sergeevicha Dmitrieva," *Otechestvennaia istoriia*, no. 3 (1999): 142–69.

Dudintsev, Vladimir, *Not by Bread Alone*, trans. Edith Bone (New York: Dutton, 1957).

Dunlop, John B., *VSKhSON: Programma, sud, v tiur'makh i lageriakh* (Paris: YMCA-Press, 1975).

Dziuba, Ivan and M. H. Zhulyns'kyi, *Spohady i rozdumy na finishnii priamii* (Kyiv: Vydavnytstvo "Krynytsia," 2004).

Friese, H. G., "Student Life in a Soviet University," in George L. Kline (ed.), *Soviet Education* (New York: Columbia University Press, 1957), 53–78.

Fursenko, A. A. et al. (eds.), *Prezidium TsK KPSS 1954–1964, Tom 1: Chernovye protokol'nye zapisi zasedanii. Stenogrammy* (Moscow: ROSSPEN, 2004).

Galkin, I. S., *Zapiski rektora Moskovskogo universiteta* (Izdatel'stvo Moskovskogo universiteta, 2004).

Ganelin, R. Sh., *Sovetskie istoriki: o chem oni govorili mezhdu soboi: stranitsy vospominanii o 1940-kh–1970-kh godakh* (St. Petersburg: "Nestor-Istoriia," 2004).

Gaponov, Iu. V., "Otryvki iz nenapisannogo: 'iznachalie'," *VIET*, 1 (2001): 213–34.

et al., "Studencheskie vystupleniia 1953 goda na fizfake MGU kak sotsial'noe ekho atomnogo proekta," in V. P. Vizgin (ed.), *Istoriia sovetskogo atomnogo proekta: dokumenty, vospominaniia, issledovaniia* (Moscow: Ianus-K, 1998), www.russcience.euro.ru/papers/gkkozap.htm (accessed 2 October 2013).

Gidoni, Aleksandr, *Solntse idet s zapada: kniga vospominanii* (Toronto: Sovremennik, 1980).

Ginetsinskaia, T. A., "Biofak Leningradskogo universiteta posle sessii VASKhNIL," in M. G. Iaroshevskii (ed.), *Repressirovannaia nauka* (Leningrad: Nauka, Leningradskoe otdelenie, 1991), 115–25.

Glazunov, Il'ia, *Rossiia raspiataia* (Moscow: Olimp, 2004).

Gorbachev, Mikhail Sergeevich, *Memoirs* (New York: Doubleday, 1996).

and Zdeněk Mlynář, *Conversations with Gorbachev: On Perestroika, the Prague Spring, and the Crossroads of Socialism* (New York: Columbia University Press, 2002).

Gorbacheva, Raisa Maksimovna and G. V. Priakhin, *I Hope: Reminiscences and Reflections* (New York: HarperCollins Publishers, 1991).

Graham, Loren R., *Moscow Stories* (Bloomington: Indiana University Press, 2006).

Guseev, M. V. et al. (eds.), *Avtoportrety pokoleniia biologov MGU: vypuskniki biofaka MGU o biofake, ob uchiteliakh, o sebe, 1950–2000* (Moscow: Izdatel'stvo MGU, 2000).

Gutnova, E. V., *Perezhitoe* (Moscow: ROSSPEN, 2001).

Iakovlev, A. N., *Omut' pamiati* (Moscow: "Vagrius," 2000).

Il'chenko, E. V., *Akademik I. G. Petrovskii – rektor Moskovskogo universiteta* (Moscow: Izdatel'stvo Moskovskogo universiteta, 2001).

Iofe, V. V., *Granitsy smysla: stat'i, vystupleniia, esse* (Saint-Petersburg: Memorial, 2002).

Ioslovich, Il'ia, "Universitet i iashchik," *Den' i noch'*, no. 3 (2010), "Megalit: Evraziiskii zhurnal'nyi portal," www.promegalit.ru/publics.php?id=1638 (accessed 23 September 2012).

Ivanova, Lia, *Iz moego proshlogo: ocherki-razmyshleniia* (Saratov: [published by author], 2003).

Kara-Murza, Sergei, '*Sovok' vspominaet* (Moscow: Algoritm, 2002).

Karpov, L. I. and V. A. Severtsev (eds.), *Vysshaia shkola: osnovnye postanovleniia, prikazy i instruktsii* (Moscow: Sovetskaia nauka, 1957), translated as *Higher School: Main Decrees, Orders, and Instructions*, 4 vols. (New York, U.S. Joint Publications Research Service, 1959).

Khrushchev, N. S., *An Account to the Party and the People: Report of the C.C. C.P.S.U. to the 22nd Party Congress of the Party, October 17, 1961* (Moscow: Foreign Languages Publishing House, 1961).

Kirshner, L. A. and S. A. Prokhvatilova (eds.), *Svet i teni "velikogo desiatiletiia": N. S. Khrushchev i ego vremia* (Leningrad: Lenizdat, 1989).

Kniazeva, M. L. et al., *200 let plus 20: kniga o studencheskom teatre Moskovskogo universiteta* (Moscow: Iskusstvo, 1979).

Kolasky, John, *Two Years in Soviet Ukraine: A Canadian's Personal Account of Russian Oppression and the Growing Opposition* (Toronto: Peter Martin Associates, 1970).

Kolodnyi, L. E., *Liubov' i nenavist' Il'i Glazunova: dokumental'naia povest'* (Moscow: Golos, 1998).

Kopylov, G. I., "Evgenii Stromynkin," *VIET*, 2 (1998): 96–122.

Kostyrchenko, G. V. (ed. and comp.), *Gosudarstvennyi antisemitizm v SSSR: ot nachala do kul'minatsii, 1938–1953* (Moscow: "Mezhdunarodnyi fond "Demokratiia," 2005).

Kovaleva, Svetlana, *Ty pomnish, fizfak?* (Moscow: Pomatur, 2003).

Kovnator, R. A., *Nikolai Kallinikovich Gudzii: k 70-letiiu so dnia rozhdeniia i 45-letiiu nauchno-pedagogicheskoi deiatel'nosti* (Moscow: Izdatel'stvo Moskovskogo universiteta, 1957).

Kozhinov, Vadim and S. V. Marshkov, *Vadim Kozhinov: v interviu, besedakh, dialogakh i vospominaniiakh sovremennikov* (Moscow: Algoritm, 2004).

Kozlov, V. A. et al. (eds.), *Kramola: Inakomyslie v SSSR pri Khrushcheve i Brezhneve, 1953–1982 gg.: rassekrechennye dokumenty Verkhovnogo suda i Prokuratury SSSR* (Moscow: "Materik," 2005).

___ and S. I. Mironenko (eds.), *58–10: nadzornye proizvodstva prokuratury SSSR po delam ob antisovetskoi agitatsii i propagande: annatirovannyi katalog, mart 1953–1991* (Moscow: Mezhdunarodnyi fond "Demokratiia," 1999).

Krasnopevtsev, Lev, "Osnovnye momenty razvitiia russkogo revoliutsionnogo dvizheniia v 1861–1905 godakh," *Karta*, no. 17 (1997): 57–64.

Kuniaev, S. Iu., *Poeziia, sud'ba, Rossia*, vol. 1 (Moscow: "Nash sovremennik," 2001).

Kuznetsov, Vladimir, *Istoriia odnoi kompanii* (Moscow: Izdanie avtora, 1995).

Lakshin, Vladimir, *Golosa i litsa* (Moscow: Geleos, 2004).

Lektorskii, V. A. (ed.), *Kak eto bylo: Vospominaniia i razmyshleniia* (Moscow: ROSSPEN, 2010).

Lenin, Vladimir, *Collected Works*, 4th English edn., 45 vols. (Moscow: Progress Publishers, 1965).

Liubarskii, Kronid, *"Kronid": izbrannye stat'i K. Liubarskogo* (Moscow: Rossiiskii gos. gumanitarnyi universitet, 2001).

Lur'e, L. Ia. and Irina Maliarova (eds.), *1956 god: seredina veka* (St. Petersburg: Neva, 2007).

Lur'e, V. F. (ed.), *Fol'klor i kul'turnaia sreda GULAGA* (St. Petersburg: Sovmestnoe izdanie Fonda "Za razvitie i vyzhivanie chelovechestva" i Izdatel'stva "Kraia Moskvy," 1994).

Manevich, Eleanor D., *Such Were the Times: A Personal View of the Lysenko Era in the USSR* (Northampton, MA: Pittenbruach Press, 1990).

Maslova, Valentina, *Paralleli i meridiany: povest' o shestidesiatykh*, vol. 2 (Saratov: "Sokol," 2002), 20.

Mihajlov, Mihajlo, *Moscow Summer, 1964: A Traveler's Notebook* (New York: Farrar, Straus and Giroux, 1965).

Mitsel, Mikhail (ed. and comp.), *Evrei Ukrainy v 1943–1953 gg.: ocherki dokumentirovannoi istorii* (Kyiv: Dukh i litera, 2004).

Molostvov, M. M., "Revizionizm – 58 (iz vospominanii)," in N. G. Okhotin et al. (eds.), *Zven'ia: istoricheskii al'manakh*, vol. 1 (Moscow: Progress, 1991), 577–92.

"My obraly zhittia: Rozmova z Yevhenom Sverstyukom," in Bogumila Berdychowska and Olexandra Hnatiuk (eds.), *Bunt pokolinnia: rozmovy z ukrains'kimi intelektualamy* (Kyiv: Dukh i litera, 2004), 33–90.

"'My sobralis' dlia togo, chtoby iskrenne vyskazat' svoi mysli' (K istorii vstrech N. S. Khrushcheva s tvorcheskoi intelligentsiei v 1962 i 1963 gg.), *Izvestiia TsK KPSS*, no. 11 (1990): 205–17.

Motroshilova, N. V., "Pamiati professora," *Voprosy filosofii*, no. 5 (1988): 67–70.

Nadzhafov, D. G. and Z. S. Belousova (eds.), *Stalin i kosmopolitizm: dokumenty agitpropa TsK KPSS, 1945–1953* (Moscow: Materik, 2005).

Nalepin, A. L. (ed.), *Filologicheskii fakul'tet MGU, 1950–1955: zhizn' iubileinogo vypuska: vospominaniia, dokumenty, materialy* (Moscow: Rossiiskii fond kul'tury "Rossiiskii arkhiv," 2003).

Nekrich, Aleksandr M., *Forsake Fear: Memoirs of an Historian* (Boston: Unwin Hyman, 1991).

O rabote komsomol'skykh organizatsii vysshykh uchebnykh zavedenii: postanovlenie IX plenuma TsK VLKSM (Moscow: Izdatel'stvo TsK VLKSM Molodaia gvardiia, 1952).

Osipov, V. N., "Ploshchad' Maiakovskogo, stat'ia 70-ia," *Grani*, 80 (1971): 107–62.

"'Otchuzhdennoe ot partii sostoianie': KGB SSSR o nastroeniiakh uchashchikhsia i studenchestva, 1968–1976 g.g.," *Istoricheskii arkhiv*, no. 1 (1994): 175–207.

Ozhegov, S. I., *Slovar' russkogo iazyka: okolo 57, 000 slov* (Moscow: Russkii iazyk, 1989).

Paneiakh, V. M., *Tvorchestvo i sud'ba istorika: Boris Aleksandrovich Romanov* (St. Petersburg: DBulanin, 2000).

Pavlova, Ekaterina, "Delo sestr Liapunovykh," *Znanie-sila*, 8 (1998), www.znanie-sila.ru/online/issue_177.html (accessed 12 January 2010).

Piatigorskii, Aleksandr and Vadim Sadovskii, "Kak my izuchali filosofiu: Moskovskii universitet, 50-e gody," *Svobodnaia mysl'*, 2 (1993): 42–54.

Pimenov, R. I., *Vospominaniia* (Moscow: Informatsionno-ekspertnaia gruppa "Panorama," 1996).

Plimak, E. G., *Na voine i posle voiny: zapiski veterana* (Moscow: Izdatel'stvo "ves' mir," 2005).

Plyushch, Leonid, *History's Carnival: A Dissident's Autobiography*, ed. and trans. Marco Carynnyk (New York: Harcourt Brace Jovanovich, 1979).

Polikovskaia, L. V. (ed.), *My predchuvstvie – predtecha: ploshchad' Maiakovskogo, 1958–1965* (Moscow, "Zvenia," 1997).

Pozner, Vladimir, *Parting with Illusions: The Extraordinary Life and Controversial Views of the Soviet Union's Leading Commentator* (New York: Atlantic Monthly Press, 1990).

Pravila priema i programmy priemnykh ekzamenov dlia postupaiushchikh v vysschie uchebnye zavedeniia SSSR (Moscow: "Sovetskaia nauka," 1957).

Raleigh, Donald J. (ed.), *Russia's Sputnik Generation: Soviet Baby Boomers Talk about their Lives* (Bloomington: Indiana University Press, 2006).

Reifman, P. S., "Dela davno minuvshikh dnei," *Vyshgorod*, 3 (1998): 16–35.

Robert, David, "Moscow State University," *Survey*, no. 51 (1964): 24–31.

Ronkin, Valerii, *Na smenu dekabriam prikhodiat ianvari: vospominaniia byvshego brigadmil'tsa i podpol'shchika, a pozzhe-politzakliuchennogo i dissidenta* (Moscow: "Zvenia," 2003).

Sakharov, Andrei et al., "A Reformist Plan for Democratization," in Stephen Cohen (ed.), *An End to Silence: Uncensored Opinion in the Soviet Union: From Roy Medvedev's Underground Magazine "Political Diary"* (New York: Norton, 1982), 317–27.

Sergeev, E. M., *Moskovskii universitet – vzgliad skvoz' gody* (Moscow: Izdatel'stvo Moskovskogo universiteta, 1992).

Shakhnazarov, G. Kh., *S vozhdiami i bez nikh* (Moscow: "Vagrius," 2001).

Shcheglov, Mark, *Na poldoroge: slovo o russkoi literature* (Moscow: Progress-Pleiada, 2001).

et al., *Studencheskie tetradi* (Moscow: Izdatel'stvo "Sovetskaia Rossiia," 1973).

Shelest, P. Iu., *Da ne sudimy budete: dnevnikovye zapisi, vospominaniia chlena Politbiuro TSK KPSS* (Moscow: Edition q, 1995).

Shevchuk, V. O., *Na berezi chasu: Mii Kyiv. Vkhodyny: avtobiohrafichna opovid'-ese* (Kyiv: Vitae memoriae, 2002).

Shevtsova, N. S. (ed.), *XXII s'ezd Kommunisticheskoi partii sovetskogo soiuza – s'ezd stroitelei kommunizma; lektsii dlia studentov gosudarstvennykh universitetov* (Izdatel'stvo Moskovskogo universiteta, 1963).

Shilovskii, Mikhail, "Istoriia universitetskogo vol'nodumiia: chast' 1: do 1968 goda (po arkhivnym materialam)," *Nauka v Sibiri*, nos. 1–2 (1998), www.nsc.ru/HBC/hbc.phtml?31+80+1 (accessed 20 September 2012).

Shishkinskaia, N. A., "K 100-letiiu Sergeia Spiridonovicha Khokhlova," *Vavilovskii zhurnal genetiki i selektsii*, 1 (2011), www.bionet.nsc.ru/vogis/pict_pdf/2011/ 15_1/17.pdf (accessed 27 May 2012).

Shlapentokh, Vladimir, "A Sociological Portrait of a Russian Intelligent: My Friend Felix Raskolnikov," *Johnson's Russian List*, no. 85, 1 May 2008, www.cdi.org/ russia/johnson/2008-85-40.cfm (accessed 22 March 2009).

Siegelbaum, Lewis and Andrei Sokolov, *Stalinism as a Way of Life: A Narrative in Documents* (New Haven, CT: Yale University Press, 2000).

Siniavskii, Andrei, *The Russian Intelligentsia*, trans. Lynn Visson (New York: Columbia University Press, 1997).

Sirotnina, O. B., *Zhizn' vopreki, ili ia schastlivyi chelovek: vospominaniia* (Saratov: Izdatel'stvo Saratovskogo universiteta, 2009).

Smirnov, V. P., "Anatolii Vasil'evich Ado: chelovek, prepodavatel', uchenyi (1928–1995)," *Novaia i noveishaia istoria*, no. 1 (1997): 184–209.

Solokhin, Nikolai, "Podsnezhniki 'ottepeli,'" in V. Dolinin and B. Ivanov (eds.), *Samizdat: po materialam konferentsii "30 let nezavisimoi pechati. 1950–80 gody" Sankt-Peterburg, 25–27 aprelia 1992 g.* (St. Petersburg: Nauchno-informatsionnyi tsentr "Memorial," 1993), 22–31.

Solzhenitsyn, Alexander, "The Smatterers," in A. I. Solzhenitsyn et al., *From under the Rubble*, trans. A. M. Brock (Boston: Little, Brown, 1975).

"Speech Delivered by Ivan Svitlychnyi in Memory of Vasyl Symonenko (Kyiv Medical Institute, 1963)," *Ukrainian Herald: Underground Magazine from Ukraine*, Issue IV (Munich: ABN press bureau, 1972), 108–12.

Stalin, I. V., "O proekte konstitutsii soiuza SSSR," in Robert H. McNeal (ed.), *Sochineniia*, 3 vols. (Stanford, CA: The Hoover Institution on War, Revolution, and Peace, Stanford University).

Svirskii, G. Ts., "Zdravstvui, universitet! Roman," *Oktiabr'*, nos. 1 and 2 (1952): 4–107 and 8–124.

Taniuk, Les', *Tvory v 60-i tomakh. Tom IV: Schodennyky 1959–1960 rr.* (Kyiv: Al'terpres, 2004).

Taranov, Evgenii (ed.), "'Raskachaem leninskie gory': iz istorii 'vol'nodumstva' v Moskovskom uiversitete (1955–1956)," *Svobodnaia mysl'*, no. 10 (1993): 94–103.

Taubman, William, *The View from Lenin Hills: Soviet Youth in Ferment* (New York: Coward-McCann, 1967).

Trifonov, Iu. V., *Students: A Novel* (Moscow: Foreign Languages Publishing House, 1953).

Ustav vsesoiuznogo leninskogo kommunisticheskogo soiuza molodezhi (Moscow: Molodaia gvardiia, 1957).

Vail', Boris, *Osobo opasnyi* (London: Overseas Publications Interchange, 1980).

Voevodin, V. V. (ed.), *Neuzheli iubilei? Ne veriu!* (Moscow: NIVTs MGU, 2004).

Volokonskii, V., "Komsomol'skaia gruppa," *Komsomol'skaia rabota v vuze* (Moscow: Molodaia gvardiia, 1953), 37–44.

Voronel', Nina, *Bez prikras: vospominaniia* (Moscow: Zakharov, 2003).

Vorontsov, N. N., "Sobytiia kontsa 40-kh gg. v biologii: vzgliad iunnata," *Voprosy istorii estestvoznanii i tekhniki*, 1 (2001): 216–19.

"Vospitanie istoriko-arkhivnogo instituta-Kazakhstantsev," *Otechestvennye arkhivy*, no. 4 (2002): 60–70.

Yevtushenko, Yevgeny, *A Precocious Autobiography*, trans. Andrew R. MacAndrew (London: Collins and Harvill, 1963).

Zakharova, L. G. et al. (eds.), *P. A. Zaionchkovskii 1904–1983 gg.: Stat'i, publicatsii, i vospominaniia o nem* (Moscow: ROSSPEN, 1998).

Zaretsky, Oleksiy and Mykola Marychevsky (eds.), *Chervona tin kalyny: Lysty, spohady, statti* (Kyiv: Spalakh. LTD, 1996).

Zasurskii, Ia. N. (ed.), *Polveka na Mokhovoi (1947–1997)* (Moscow: Moskovskii gos. universitet im. M. V. Lomonosova, Fakul'tet zhurnalistiki, 1997).

Zhdanov, Andrei Aleksandrovich, *Essays on Literature, Philosophy, and Music* (New York: International Publishers, 1950).

Zhigulin, Anatolii, *Chernye kamni: avtobiograficheskaia povest'* (Moscow: "Sovremennik," 1990).

Zhylenko, Iryna, "Homo feriens," *Suchasnist'*, no. 10 (1997): 16–36.

Zubarev, D. I. and A. U. Daniel, *5 Dekabria 1965 goda v vospominaniiakh uchastnikov sobytii, materialakh samizdata, publikatsiiakh zarubezhnoi pressy i v dokumentakh partiinykh i komsomol'skikh organizatsii i zapiskakh komiteta gosudarstvennoi bezopasnosti v Tsk KPSS* (Moscow: Obshchestvo "Memorial," 2005).

Zubkova, Elena et al. (eds.), *Sovetskaia zhizn', 1945–1953* (Moscow: ROSSPEN, 2003).

Secondary sources

Adams, Mark B., "Biology in the Soviet Academy of Sciences, 1953–1965: A Case Study in Soviet Science Policy," in John R. Thomas and Ursula M. Kruse-Vaucienne (eds.), *Soviet Science and Technology: Domestic and Foreign Perspectives: Based on a Workshop Held at Airlie House, Virginia, on November 18–21, 1976* (Washington, DC: Published for the National Science Foundation by the George Washington University, 1977), 161–88.

"Science, Ideology, and Structure: The Kol'tsov Institute, 1900–1970," in Linda L. Lubrano and Susan Gross Solomon (eds.), *The Social Context of Soviet Science* (Boulder, CO: Westview Press, 1980), 173–204.

Aksiutin, Iurii, "Popular Responses to Khrushchev," in William Taubman et al. (eds.), *Nikita Khrushchev* (New Haven, CT: Yale University Press, 2000), 177–209.

Alexeyeva, Liudmila, *Soviet Dissent: Contemporary Movements for National, Religious, and Human Rights* (Middletown, CT: Wesleyan University Press, 1985).

Altshuler, Mordechai, "Antisemitism in Ukraine Toward the End of the Second World War," *Jews in Eastern Europe*, 3 (1993): 40–81.

Anderson, Benedict R., *Imagined Communities: Reflections on the Origin and Spread of Nationalism* (London and New York: Verso, 1991).

Andreev, A. V., *Fiziki ne shutiat: stranitsy sotsial'noi istorii nauchno-issledovatel'skogo instituta fiziki pri MGU (1922–1954 gg.)* (Moscow: Progress-Traditsiia, 2000).

Andrews, James T., *Science for the Masses: The Bolshevik State, Public Science, and the Popular Imagination in Soviet Russia, 1917–1934* (College Station, TX: Texas A & M University Press, 2003).

Avis, George, "The Sociology of Soviet Higher Education: A Review of Recent Empirical Research," in Bohdan Horasymiw (ed.), *Education and the Mass Media in the Soviet Union and Eastern Europe* (New York: Praeger, 1976), 39–64.

Avrus, A. I., *Istoriia rossiiskikh universitetov: kurs lektsii* (Saratov: Kollezdh, 1998).

Azadovskii, Konstantin and Boris Egorov, "From Anti-Westernism to Anti-Semitism," *Journal of Cold War Studies*, 4 (2002): 66–80.

Babiracki, Patryk, "Imperial Heresies: Polish Students in the Soviet Union, 1948–1957," *Ab Imperio*, 4 (2007): 199–236.

Bassin, Mark et al. (eds.), *Space, Place, and Power in Modern Russia: Essays in the New Spatial History* (DeKalb: Northern Illinois University Press, 2010).

Batygin, Gennadii and Inna Deviatko, "The Case of Professor Z. Ia. Beletskii," *Russian Studies in Philosophy*, 33 (2010): 73–96.

Bauman, Zygmunt, "Legislators and Interpreters: Culture as the Ideology of Intellectuals," in Chris Jenks (ed.), *Culture: Critical Concepts in Sociology* (New York: Routledge, 2002), 316–36.

Bel'chikov, Iu. A., "K istorii slov intelligentsia, intelligent," in M. V. Liapon et al. (eds.), *Filologicheskii sbornik: k 100-letiiu so dnia rozhdeniia akademika V. V. Vinogradova* (Moscow: Institut russkogo iazyka im. V. V. Vinogradova, 1995), 62–69.

Bereday, George Z. F., "Class Tensions in Soviet Education," in George Z. F. Bereday and Jaan Pennar (eds.), *The Politics of Soviet Education* (Westport, CT: Greenwood Press, 1976), 164–74.

Berel'kovskii, I. V., *Sovetskaia nauchno-pedagogicheskaia intelligentsiia i ideologiia totalitarizma v kontse 1920-k–nachale 1950-kh gg: bor'ba s inakomysliem: po materialam Nizhegorodskoi gubernii-Gor'kovskoi oblasti* (Moscow: MGGU, 2007).

Bergman, Jay, "Soviet Dissidents on the Russian Intelligentsia, 1956–1985: The Search for a Usable Past," *Russian Review*, 51 (1992): 16–35.

Berkhoff, Karel C., *Harvest of Despair: Life and Death in Ukraine under Nazi Rule* (Cambridge, MA: Belknap Press of Harvard University Press, 2004).

Berlin, Isaiah, *Russian Thinkers* (New York: Viking Press, 1978).

Beyrau, Dietrich, *Intelligenz und Dissens: die russischen Bildungsschichten in der Sowjetunion 1917–1985* (Göttingen: Vandenhoeck & Ruprecht, 1993).

Bittner, Stephen, *The Many Lives of Khrushchev's Thaw: Experience and Memory in Moscow's Arbat* (Ithaca, NY: Cornell University Press, 2008).

Blitstein, Peter A., "Stalin's Nations: Soviet Nationality Policy between Planning and Primordialism, 1936–1953" (Ph.D. diss., University of California, Berkeley, 1999).

Boobbyer, Philip, *Conscience, Dissent and Reform in Soviet Russia* (London and New York: Routledge, 2005).

Borzenkov, A. G., *Molodezh' i politika: vozmozhnosti i predely studencheskoi samo-deiatel'nosti na vostoke Rossii, 1961–1991 gg.*, 2 vols. (Novosibirsk: Novosibirskii gos. universitet, 2002).

Boterbloem, Kees, *The Life and Times of Andrei Zhdanov, 1896–1948* (Montreal: McGill-Queen's University Press, 2004).

Bourdieu, Pierre, *Distinction: A Social Critique of the Judgement of Taste* (Cambridge, MA: Harvard University Press, 1984).

The State Nobility: Elite Schools in the Field of Power, trans. Lauretta C. Clough (Stanford University Press, 1996).

Bowen, James, *Soviet Education: Anton Makarenko and the Years of Experiment* (Madison: University of Wisconsin Press, 1965).

Boym, Svetlana, *Common Places: Mythologies of Everyday Life in Russia* (Cambridge, MA: Harvard University Press, 1994).

Bradatan, Costica and Serguei Alex. Oushakine, *In Marx's Shadow: Knowledge, Power, and Intellectuals in Eastern Europe and Russia* (Lanham: Lexington Books, 2010).

Brandenberger, David, *National Bolshevism: Stalinist Mass Culture and the Formation of Modern Russian National Identity, 1931–1956* (Cambridge, MA: Harvard University Press, 2002).

"Stalin's Last Crime? Recent Scholarship on Postwar Soviet Antisemitism and the Doctor's Plot," *Kritika*, 6 (2005): 187–204.

Brooks, Jeffrey, *Thank You, Comrade Stalin! Soviet Public Culture from Revolution to Cold War* (Princeton University Press, 1999).

Brower, Daniel R., *Training the Nihilists: Education and Radicalism in Tsarist Russia* (Ithaca, NY: Cornell University Press, 1975).

Brown, Archie, *Seven Years that Changed the World: Perestroika in Perspective* (New York: Oxford University Press, 2007).

Brubaker, Rogers, "Nationhood and the National Question in the Soviet Union and Post-Soviet Eurasia: An Institutional Account," *Theory and Society*, 23 (1994): 47–78.

Brudny, Yitzhak M., *Reinventing Russia: Russian Nationalism and the Soviet State, 1953–1991* (Cambridge, MA: Harvard University Press, 1998).

Buchli, Victor, *An Archaeology of Socialism* (Oxford: Berg, 1999).

Churchward, L. G., *The Soviet Intelligentsia: An Essay on the Social Structure and Roles of Soviet Intellectuals during the 1960s* (London and Boston: Routledge & Kegan Paul, 1973).

Clark, Katerina, *The Soviet Novel: History as Ritual* (Bloomington: Indiana University Press, 2000).

Colton, Timothy J., *Moscow: Governing the Socialist Metropolis* (Cambridge, MA: Belknap Press of Harvard University Press, 1995).

Condee, Nancy, "Cultural Codes of the Thaw," in William Taubman et al. (eds.), *Nikita Khrushchev* (New Haven, CT: Yale University Press, 2000), 160–76.

Connelly, John, *Captive University: The Sovietization of East German, Czech and Polish Higher Education, 1945–1956* (Chapel Hill: University of North Carolina Press, 2000).

Connelly, John and Michael Grüttner (eds.), *Universities under Dictatorship* (University Park, PA: Pennsylvania State University Press, 2005).

Cooper, Julian, "The Military and Higher Education in the USSR," *Annals of the American Academy of Political and Social Science*, 502 (1989): 108–19.

Costanzo, Susan, "Amateur Theatres and Amateur Publics in the Russian Republic, 1958–71," *The Slavonic and East European Review*, 86 (2008): 372–94.

"The Emergence of Alternative Culture: Amateur Studio-Theaters in Moscow and Leningrad, 1957–1984" (Ph.D. diss., Northwestern University, 1994), 66–67.

Coumel, Laurent, "L'appareil du parti et la réforme scolaire de 1958: Un cas d'opposition à Hruščev," *Cahiers du Monde Russe et Soviétique*, 47 (2006): 173–94.

"The Scientist, the Pedagogue and the Party Official: Interest Groups, Public Opinion and Decision-making in the 1958 Education Reform," in Melanie Ilič and Jeremy Smith (eds.), *Soviet State and Society under Nikita Khrushchev* (London: Routledge, 2009), 66–85.

Cummings, Richard H., *Cold War Radio: The Dangerous History of American Broadcasting in Europe, 1950–1989* (Jefferson, NC: McFarland & Co., 2009).

Danyliuk, Iu. Z. and Oleh Bazhan, *Opozytsiia v Ukraini: druha polovyna 50-kh–80-ti rr. XX st.* (Kyiv: Ridnyi krai, 2000).

David-Fox, Michael, "The Assault on the Universities and the Dynamics of Stalin's 'Great Break,' 1928–1932," in Michael David-Fox and György Péteri (eds.), *Academia in Upheaval: Origins, Transfers, and Transformations of the Communist Academic Regime in Russia and East Central Europe* (Westport, CT: Bergin & Garvey, 2000), 73–104.

Revolution of the Mind: Higher Learning among the Bolsheviks, 1918–1929 (Ithaca, NY: Cornell University Press, 1997).

De Witt, Nicholas, *Education and Professional Employment in the USSR* (Washington, DC: National Science Foundation, 1961).

Dobrenko, E. A., *The Making of the State Reader: Social and Aesthetic Contexts of the Reception of Soviet Literature*, trans. Jesse M. Savage (Stanford University Press, 1997).

Dobson, Miriam, *Khrushchev's Cold Summer: Gulag Returnees, Crime, and the Fate of Reform after Stalin* (Ithaca, NY: Cornell University Press, 2009).

"The Post-Stalin Era: De-Stalinization, Daily Life, and Dissent," *Kritika*, 12 (2011): 905–24.

Duncan, Peter J. S., *Russian Messianism: Third Rome, Holy Revolution, Communism and After* (London: Routledge, 2000).

Dunham, Vera S., *In Stalin's Time: Middleclass Values in Soviet Fiction*, enlarged and updated edn. (Durham, NC: Duke University Press, 1990).

Dunlop, John B., *The Faces of Contemporary Russian Nationalism* (Princeton University Press, 1983).

The New Russian Revolutionaries (Belmont, MA: Nordland Pub. Co., 1976).

Duskin, J. Eric, *Stalinist Reconstruction and the Confirmation of a New Elite, 1945–1953* (Houndmills, Basingstoke and New York: Palgrave, 2001).

Edele, Mark, "More Than Just Stalinists: The Political Sentiments of Victors, 1945–1953," in Juliane Fürst (ed.), *Late Stalinist Russia: Society between Reconstruction and Reinvention* (London and New York: Routledge, 2006), 167–91.

"Soviet Society, Social Structure, and Everyday Life: Major Frameworks Reconsidered," *Kritika*, 8 (2007): 349–73.

"Soviet Veterans as an Entitlement Group, 1945–1955," *Slavic Review*, 65 (2006): 111–37.

"Strange Young Men in Stalin's Moscow: The Birth and Life of the Stiliagi, 1945–1953," *Jahrbücher für Geschichte Osteuropas*, 50 (2002): 37–61.

Elkner, Julie, "The Changing Face of Repression under Khrushchev," in Melanie Ilič and Jeremy Smith (eds.), *Soviet State and Society Under Nikita Khrushchev* (London: Routledge, 2009), 142–61.

Engerman, David C., *Know Your Enemy: The Rise and Fall of America's Soviet Experts* (Oxford University Press, 2009).

English, Robert D., *Russia and the Idea of the West: Gorbachev, Intellectuals, and the End of the Cold War* (New York: Columbia University Press, 2000).

Farmer, Kenneth C., *Ukrainian Nationalism in the Post-Stalin Era: Myths, Symbols, and Ideology in Soviet Nationalities Policy* (The Hague and Boston: Martinus Nijhoff Publishers and Kluwer Boston, 1980).

Fateev, A. V., *Obraz vraga v sovetskoi propagande: 1945–1954 gg.* (Moscow: Rossiiskaia akademiia nauk, Institut rossiiskoi istorii, 1999).

Field, Deborah A., *Private Life and Communist Morality in Khrushchev's Russia* (New York: Peter Lang Publishing, 2007).

Filtzer, Donald A., *The Hazards of Urban Life in Late Stalinist Russia: Health, Hygiene, and Living Standards, 1943–1953* (Cambridge University Press, 2010).

Finkel, Stuart, *On the Ideological Front: The Russian Intelligentsia and the Making of the Soviet Public Sphere* (New Haven, CT: Yale University Press, 2007).

Fitzpatrick, Sheila, "Ascribing Class: The Constitution of Social Identity in Soviet Russia," in Sheila Fitzpatrick (ed.), *Stalinism: New Directions* (London and New York: Routledge, 2000).

The Cultural Front: Power and Culture in Revolutionary Russia (Ithaca, NY: Cornell University Press, 1992).

Education and Social Mobility in the USSR, 1921–1934 (Cambridge University Press, 1979).

Everyday Stalinism: Ordinary Life in Extraordinary Times: Soviet Russia in the 1930s (New York: Oxford University Press, 2000).

"Postwar Soviet Society: The Return to Normalcy, 1945–1953," in Susan J. Linz (ed.), *The Impact of World War II on the Soviet Union* (Totowa, NJ: Rowman & Allanheld, 1985).

"Signals from Below: Soviet Letters of Denunciation of the 1930s," *The Journal of Modern History*, 68 (1996): 831–66.

Fleurs, Loretta Dawn, "Education Reform in Moscow Secondary Schools, 1958–1964" (Ph.D. diss., Princeton University, 1999).

Fürst, Juliane, "Friends in Private, Friends in Public: The Phenomenon of the Kompania among Soviet Youth in the 1950s and 1960s," in Lewis H. Siegelbaum (ed.), *Borders of Socialism: Private Spheres of Soviet Russia* (New York: Palgrave Macmillan, 2006), 229–50.

"Prisoners of the Soviet Self? Political Youth Opposition in Late Stalinism," *Europe-Asia Studies*, 54 (2002): 353–75.

Stalin's Last Generation: Soviet Post-War Youth and the Emergence of Mature Socialism (Oxford University Press, 2010).

(ed.), *Late Stalinist Russia: Society between Reconstruction and Reinvention* (London: Routledge, 2006).

Gella, Alexander, "The Life and Death of the Polish Intelligentsia," *Slavic Review*, 30 (1971): 1–27.

Gerovitch, Slava, *From Newspeak to Cyberspeak: A History of Soviet Cybernetics* (Cambridge, MA: MIT Press, 2002).

"'New Soviet Man' Inside Machine: Human Engineering, Spacecraft Design, and the Construction of Communism," *Osiris*, 22 (2007): 135–57.

Gessen, Masha, *Dead Again: The Russian Intelligentsia after Communism* (London and New York: Verso, 1997).

Gilburd, Eleonory, "Picasso in Thaw Culture," *Cahiers du Monde Russe et Soviétique*, 47 (2006): 65–108.

"To See Paris and Die: Western Culture in the Soviet Union, 1950's, and 1960's" (Ph.D. diss., University of California, Berkeley, 2010).

Gitelman, Zvi Y., *A Century of Ambivalence: The Jews of Russia and the Soviet Union, 1881 to the Present* (Bloomington: Indiana University Press, 2001).

Gorlizki, Yoram, "Policing Post-Stalin Society: The Militsiia and Public Order under Khrushchev," *Cahiers Du Monde Russe et Soviétique*, 44 (2003): 465–80.

Gorlizki, Yoram and Oleg Khlevniuk, *Cold Peace: Stalin and the Soviet Ruling Circle, 1945–53* (New York: Oxford University Press, 2004).

Gorsuch, Anne E., *All This Is Your World: Soviet Tourism at Home and Abroad After Stalin* (Oxford University Press, 2011).

Youth in Revolutionary Russia: Enthusiasts, Bohemians, Delinquents (Bloomington: Indiana University Press, 2000).

Graham, Loren R., *Science in Russia and the Soviet Union: A Short History* (Cambridge University Press, 1993).

Green, Anna and Kathleen Troup, *The Houses of History: A Critical Reader in Twentieth-Century History and Theory* (New York University Press, 1999).

Greenfeld, Liah, *Nationalism: Five Roads to Modernity* (Cambridge, MA: Harvard University Press, 1992).

Gross, Jan Tomasz, *Revolution from Abroad: The Soviet Conquest of Poland's Western Ukraine and Western Belorussia* (Princeton University Press, 2002).

Grushin, B. A., *Chetyre zhizni Rossii v zerkale obshchestvennogo mneniia: ocherki massovogo soznaniia Rossii vo vremena Khrushcheva, Brezhneva, Gorbacheva, i El'tsina*, 4 vols. (Moscow: Progress-Traditsiia, 2001).

Haimson, Leopold H., "Three Generations of the Soviet Intelligentsia," in Howard W. Winger (ed.), *Iron Curtains and Scholarship: The Exchange of Knowledge in a Divided World: Papers Presented before the Twenty-third Annual Conference of the Graduate Library School of the University of Chicago, July 7–9, 1958* (University of Chicago, Graduate Library School, 1958), 28–43.

Halfin, Igal, *From Darkness to Light: Class, Consciousness, and Salvation in Revolutionary Russia* (University of Pittsburgh Press, 2000).

Hall, Karl, "The Schooling of Lev Landau: The European Context of Postrevolutionary Soviet Theoretical Physics," *Osiris*, 23 (2008): 230–59.

Harding, Neil, *Lenin's Political Thought: Theory and Practice in the Democratic and Socialist Revolutions* (Chicago: Haymarket Books, 2009).

Heinzen, James, "A 'Campaign Spasm': Graft and the Limits of the 'Campaign' against Bribery after the Great Patriotic War," in Juliane Fürst (ed.), *Late Stalinist Russia: Society between Reconstruction and Reinvention* (London: Routledge, 2006), 123–41.

Hellbeck, Jochen, "Fashioning the Stalinist Soul: The Diary of Stepan Podlubnyi (1931–1939)," *Jahrbücher für Geschichte Osteuropas*, 44 (1996): 344–73.
    Revolution on my Mind: Writing a Diary under Stalin (Cambridge, MA: Harvard University Press, 2006).

Hessler, Julie, "A Postwar Perestroika? Toward a History of Private Enterprise in the USSR," *Slavic Review*, 57 (1998): 516–42.
    "Death of an African Student in Moscow: Race, Politics, and the Cold War," *Cahiers du Monde Russe et Soviétique*, 47 (2006): 33–64.

Hixson, Walter L., *Parting the Curtain: Propaganda, Culture, and the Cold War, 1945–1961* (New York: St. Martin's Press, 1997).

Hoffmann, David L., *Stalinist Values: The Cultural Norms of Soviet Modernity, 1917–1941* (Ithaca, NY: Cornell University Press, 2003).
    "Was There a 'Great Retreat' from Soviet Socialism? Stalinist Culture Reconsidered," *Kritika*, 5 (2004): 651–74.

Hooper, Cynthia, "A Darker 'Big Deal': Concealing Party Corruption, 1945–1953," in Juliane Fürst (ed.), *Late Stalinist Russia: Society between Reconstruction and Reinvention* (London: Routledge, 2006), 142–64.

Hopf, Ted, *Social Construction of International Politics: Identities and Foreign Policies, Moscow, 1955 and 1999* (Ithaca, NY: Cornell University Press, 2002).

Horowitz, Helen Lefkowitz, *Campus Life: Undergraduate Cultures from the End of the Eighteenth Century to the Present* (New York: A. A. Knopf, distributed by Random House, 1987).

Horton, Andrew (ed.), *Inside Soviet Film Satire: Laughter with a Lash* (Cambridge University Press, 1993).

Hosking, Geoffrey A., *The First Socialist Society: A History of the Soviet Union from Within*, 2nd edn. (Cambridge, MA: Harvard University Press, 1992).
    Rulers and Victims: The Russians in the Soviet Union (Cambridge, MA: Harvard University Press, 2006).

Hroch, Miroslav, *Social Preconditions of National Revival in Europe: A Comparative Analysis of the Social Composition of Patriotic Groups Among the Smaller European Nations* (Cambridge University Press, 1985).

Inkeles, Alex and Raymond A. Bauer, *The Soviet Citizen: Daily Life in a Totalitarian Society* (New York: Atheneum, 1968).

Jarausch, Konrad, "The Old 'New History of Education': A German Reconsideration," *History of Education Quarterly*, 26 (1986): 225–41.

Jones, Polly, 'From the Secret Speech to the Burial of Stalin: Real and Ideal Responses to De-Stalinization," in Polly Jones (ed.), *The Dilemmas of De-Stalinization: Negotiating Cultural and Social Change in the Khrushchev Era* (London: Routledge, 2006), 41–63.

"From Stalinism to Post-Stalinism: De-Mythologising Stalin, 1953–56," in Harold Shukman (ed.), *Redefining Stalinism* (London and Portland, OR: Frank Cass, 2003), 127–48.

"Memories of Terror or Terrorizing Memories? Terror, Trauma and Survival in Soviet Culture of the Thaw," *Slavonic and East European Review*, 86 (2008): 346–71.

"Revisions, Revisionism, or Dissent? Stalinist History and 'Stalinist' Historians in the Thaw," unpublished manuscript.

Joravsky, David, *The Lysenko Affair* (Cambridge, MA: Harvard University Press, 1970).

Josephson, Paul R., "Atomic-Powered Communism: Nuclear Culture in the Postwar USSR," *Slavic Review*, 55 (1996): 297–324.

New Atlantis Revisited: Akademgorodok, the Siberian City of Science (Princeton University Press, 1997).

"Rockets, Reactors, and Soviet Culture," in Loren R. Graham (ed.), *Science and the Soviet Social Order* (Cambridge, MA: Harvard University Press, 1990), 168–94.

"Stalinism and Science: Physics and Philosophical Disputes in the USSR, 1930–1955," in Michael David-Fox and György Péteri (eds.), *Academia in Upheaval: Origins, Transfers, and Transformations of the Communist Academic Regime in Russia and East Central Europe* (Westport, CT: Bergin & Garvey, 2000), 105–40.

Kasianov, H. V., *Nezhodni: ukrains'ka intelihentsiia v rusi oporu 1960–80-kh rokiv* (Kyiv: "Lybid," 1995).

Kassof, Allen H., "Scholarly Exchanges and the Collapse of Communism," *The Soviet and Post-Soviet Review*, 22 (1995): 263–74.

Kassow, Samuel D., *Students, Professors, and the State in Tsarist Russia* (Berkeley: University of California Press, 1989).

Keep, John, "Sergei Sergeevich Dmitriev and his Diary," *Kritika*, 4 (2003): 709–33.

Kelly, Catriona, "Kul'turnost' in the Soviet Union: Ideal and Reality," in Geoffrey A. Hosking and Robert Service (eds.), *Reinterpreting Russia* (London: Arnold, 1999), 198–214.

Refining Russia: Advice Literature, Polite Culture, and Gender from Catherine to Yeltsin (Oxford University Press, 2001).

Kharkhordin, Oleg, *The Collective and the Individual in Russia: A Study of Practices* (Berkeley: University of California Press, 1999).

Kiselev, G. I., "Moscow State University Physics Alumni and the Soviet Atomic Project," *Physics – Uspekhi*, 48 (2005): 1343–56.

Klier, John, *Russians, Jews, and the Pogroms of 1881–1882* (Cambridge University Press, 2011).

Knight, Nathaniel, "Was the Intelligentsia Part of the Nation? Visions of Society in Post-Emancipation Russia," *Kritika*, 7 (2006): 733–58.

Kojevnikov, Alexei, "The Phenomenon of Soviet Science," *Osiris*, 23 (2008): 115–35.

Konecny, Peter, *Builders and Deserters: Students, State, and Community in Leningrad, 1917–1941* (Montreal and Ithaca: McGill-Queen's University Press, 1999).

"Library Hooligans and Others: Law, Order, and Student Culture in Leningrad, 1924–1938," *Journal of Social History*, 30 (1996): 97–128.

Korolev, Sergei, "The Student Dormitory in the 'Period of Stagnation': The Erosion of Regulatory Processes," *Russian Social Science Review*, 45 (2004): 77–93.

Kostyrchenko, G. V., *Stalin protiv "kosmopolitov": vlast' i evreiskaia intelligentsiia v SSSR* (Moscow: ROSSPEN, 2009).

Tainaia politika Stalina: vlast' i antisemitizm (Moscow: "Mezhdunarodnye otnosheniia," 2003).

V plenu u krasnogo faraona: politicheskie presledovaniia evreev v SSSR v poslednee stalinskoe desiatiletie: dokumental'noe issledovanie (Moscow: "Mezhdunarodnye otnosheniia," 1994).

Kotkin, Stephen, *Armageddon Averted: The Soviet Collapse, 1970–2000* (Oxford University Press, 2001).

Magnetic Mountain: Stalinism as a Civilization (Berkeley: University of California Press, 1995).

Kozhinov, Vadim, *Rossiia vek XX: 1939–1964: opyt bespristrastnogo issledovaniia* (Moscow: Algoritm, 1999).

Kozlov, Denis, "I Have Not Read, But I Will Say': Soviet Literary Audiences and Changing Ideas of Social Membership, 1958–66," *Kritika*, 7 (2006): 557–97.

"Naming the Social Evil: The Readers of *Novyi mir* and Vladimir Dudintsev's *Not by Bread Alone*, 1956–59 and Beyond," in Polly Jones (ed.), *The Dilemmas of De-Stalinization: Negotiating Cultural and Social Change in the Khrushchev Era* (London: Routledge, 2006), 80–98.

The Readers of Novyi Mir: Coming to Terms with the Stalinist Past (Cambridge, MA: Harvard University Press, 2013).

Kozlov, V. A., *Mass Uprisings in the USSR: Protest and Rebellion in the Post-Stalin Years*, trans. and ed. Elaine McClarnand MacKinnon (Armonk, NY: M. E. Sharpe, 2002).

Kozovoi, Andrei, "Eye to Eye with the 'Main Enemy': Soviet Youth Travel to the United States," *Ab Imperio*, 2 (2011): 221–37.

Koivunen, Pia, "The 1957 Moscow Youth Festival: Propagating a New, Peaceful Image of the Soviet Union," in Melanie Ilič and Jeremy Smith (eds.), *Soviet State and Society under Nikita Khrushchev* (London: Routledge, 2009), 46–65.

Krawchenko, Bohdan, *Social Change and National Consciousness in Twentieth-Century Ukraine* (New York: St. Martin's Press, 1985).

Krementsov, N. L., *Stalinist Science* (Princeton University Press, 1997).

Kuchment, Mark, "Bridging the Two Cultures: The Emergence of Scientific Prose," in Loren R. Graham (ed.), *Science and the Soviet Social Order* (Cambridge, MA: Harvard University Press, 1990), 325–40.

Kulavig, Erik, *Dissent in the Years of Khrushchev: Ten Stories about Disobedient Russians* (New York: Palgrave, 2002).

Kuromiya, Hiroaki, "'Political Youth Opposition in Late Stalinism': Evidence and Conjecture," *Europe-Asia Studies*, 55 (2003): 631–38.

Kuzovkin, Gennadii, "Partiino-komsomol'skie presledovaniia po politicheskim motivam v period rannei 'ottepeli'," in L. S. Ereminaia and E. B. Zhemkova (eds.), *Korni travy: sbornik stat'ei molodykh istorikov* (Moscow: "Zvenia," 1996), 88–125.

Lahusen, Thomas, *How Life Writes the Book: Real Socialism and Socialist Realism in Stalin's Russia* (Ithaca, NY: Cornell University Press, 1997).

Lenoe, Matthew E., "In Defense of Timasheff's Great Retreat," *Kritika*, 5 (2004): 721–30.

Livschiz, Ann, "Children's Lives after Zoia's Death: Order, Emotions, and Heroism in Children's Lives and Literature in the Post-War Soviet Union," in Juliane Fürst (ed.), *Late Stalinist Russia: Society between Reconstruction and Reinvention* (London and New York: Routledge, 2006), 192–208.

Loewenstein, Karl E., "Re-Emergence of Public Opinion in the Soviet Union: Khrushchev and Responses to the Secret Speech," *Europe-Asia Studies*, 58 (2006): 1329–45.

Lovell, Stephen, *The Russian Reading Revolution: Print Culture in the Soviet and Post-Soviet Eras* (New York: St. Martin's Press, 2000).

Summerfolk: A History of the Dacha, 1710–2000 (Ithaca, NY: Cornell University Press, 2003).

Lygo, Emily, "The Need for New Voices: Writers' Union Policy towards Young Writers, 1953–64," in Polly Jones (ed.), *The Dilemmas of De-Stalinization: Negotiating Cultural and Social Change in the Khrushchev Era* (London: Routledge, 2006), 193–208.

Magnusdottir, Rosa, "The Myth of 'Amerika' and Soviet Socialism: Perceptions and Realities in the Postwar Soviet Union," *The Soviet and Post-Soviet Review*, 31 (2004): 291–307.

Manchester, Laurie, "Harbingers of Modernity, Bearers of Tradition: Popovichi as a Model Intelligentsia Self in Revolutionary Russia," *Jahrbücher für Geschichte Osteuropas*, 20 (2002): 321–44.

Manley, Rebecca, *To the Tashkent Station: Evacuation and Survival in the Soviet Union at War* (Ithaca, NY: Cornell University Press, 2009).

Markwick, Roger, "Catalyst of Historiography, Marxism and Dissidence: The Sector of Methodology, Institute of History, Soviet Academy of Sciences, 1964–68," *Europe-Asia Studies*, 46 (1994): 579–96.

Martin, Terry, *The Affirmative Action Empire: Nations and Nationalism in the Soviet Union, 1923–1939* (Ithaca, NY: Cornell University Press, 2001).

Matthews, Mervyn, *Class and Society in Soviet Russia* (New York: Walker, 1972).

Education in the Soviet Union: Policies and Institutions since Stalin (London and Boston: Allen & Unwin, 1982).

McCauley, Martin, *Khrushchev and the Development of Soviet Agriculture: The Virgin Land Programme 1953–1964* (London: Macmillan, in association with the School of Slavonic and East European Studies, University of London, 1976).

McClelland, James C., *Autocrats and Academics: Education, Culture, and Society in Tsarist Russia* (University of Chicago Press, 1979).

"Bolshevik Approaches to Higher Education, 1917–1921," *Slavic Review*, 30 (1971): 818–31.

"Proletarianizing the Student Body: The Soviet Experience during the New Economic Policy," *Past and Present*, 80 (1978): 122–46.

McMillan, Priscilla Johnson, *Khrushchev and the Arts: The Politics of Soviet Culture, 1962–1964* (Cambridge, MA: MIT Press, 1965).

Medvedev, Roy A., and Zhores A. Medvedev, *Khrushchev: The Years in Power* (New York: Columbia University Press, 1976).

Medvedev, Zhores A., *The Rise and Fall of T. D. Lysenko*, trans. I. Michael Lerner (New York: Columbia University Press, 1969).

Merridale, Catherine, *Night of Stone: Death and Memory in Twentieth Century Russia* (New York: Viking, 2001).

Mikkonen, Simo, "Stealing the Monopoly of Knowledge? Soviet Reactions to Cold War Broadcasting," *Kritika*, 11 (2010): 771–805.

Miłosz, Czesław, *The Captive Mind* (New York: Vintage International, 1990).

Mitrokhin, Nikolai, *Russkaia partiia: dvizhenie russkikh natsionalistov v SSSR 1953–1985* (Moscow: Novoe literaturnoe obozrenie, 2003).

Morrissey, Susan, *Heralds of Revolution: Russian Students and the Mythology of Radicalism* (Oxford University Press, 1998).

Nathans, Benjamin, "The Dictatorship of Reason: Aleksandr Vol'pin and the Idea of Rights under 'Developed Socialism'," *Slavic Review*, 4 (2007): 630–63.

Nelson, Michael, *War of the Black Heavens: The Battles of Western Broadcasting in the Cold War* (Syracuse University Press, 1997).

Nilsson, Nils Åke, "Soviet Student Slang," *Scando-Slavica*, 6 (1960): 113–23.

Ostromoukhova, Bella, "Le Dégel et les troupes amateur: Changements politiques et activités artistiques des étudiants, 1953–1970," *Cahiers du Monde Russe et Soviétique*, 47 (2006): 303–26.

Oushakine, Serguei A., "The Terrifying Mimicry of Samizdat," *Public Culture*, 13 (2001): 191–214.

Papovian, Elena, "Primenenie stat'i 58–10 UK RSFSR v 1957–1958 gg.: po materialam verkhovnego suda i prokuratury SSSR v GARF," in L. S. Ereminaia and E. B. Zhemkova (eds.), *Korni travy: sbornik stat'ei molodykh istorikov* (Moscow, "Zvenia," 1996).

Parsons, Talcott, "The Strange Case of Academic Organization," *The Journal of Higher Education*, 42 (1971): 486–95.

Parthet, Kathleen, *Russian Village Prose: The Radiant Past* (Princeton University Press, 1992).

Patico, Jennifer, *Consumption and Social Change in a Post-Soviet Middle Class* (Washington, DC: Woodrow Wilson Center Press, 2008).

Péteri, György, "The Communist Idea of the University: An Essay Inspired by the Hungarian Experience," in John Connelly and Michael Grüttner (eds.), *Universities under Dictatorship* (University Park: Pennsylvania State University Press, 2005), 139–66.

Petrone, Karen, *Life Has Become More Joyous, Comrades: Celebrations in the Time of Stalin* (Bloomington: Indiana University Press, 2000).

Peukert, Detlev, *Inside Nazi Germany: Conformity, Opposition and Racism in Everyday Life* (New Haven, CT: Yale University Press, 1987).

Pinkus, Benjamin, *The Soviet Government and the Jews, 1948–1967: A Documented Study* (Cambridge University Press, 2008).

Pinner, Frank A., "Student Trade Unionism in France, Belgium, and Holland: Anticipatory Socialization and Role Seeking," *Sociology of Education*, 37 (1964): 177–99.

Pipes, Richard (ed.), *The Russian Intelligentsia* (New York: Columbia University Press, 1961).

Platt, Kevin M. F. and David Brandenberger, *Epic Revisionism: Russian History and Literature as Stalinist Propaganda* (Madison: University of Wisconsin Press, 2006).

Pohl, Michaela, "The Virgin Lands between Memory and Forgetting: People and Transformation in the Soviet Union, 1954–1960" (Ph.D. diss., Indiana University, 1999).

Pollock, Ethan, "Stalin as the Coryphaeus of Science: Ideology and Knowledge in the Post-War Years," in Sarah Davies and James R. Harris (eds.), *Stalin: A New History* (Cambridge University Press, 2005), 271–88.

Stalin and the Soviet Science Wars (Princeton University Press, 2006).

Pyzhikov, A. V., *Khrushchevskaia ottepel', 1953–1964* (Moscow: OLMA-PRESS, 2002).

"Reformirovanie sistemy obrazovaniia v SSSR v period 'ottepeli' (1953–1964 gg.)," *Voprosy Istorii*, 9 (2000): 95–104.

"Sources of Dissidence: Soviet Youth after the Twentieth Party Congress," *Russian Social Science Review*, 45 (2004): 66–79.

Raleigh, Donald J., *Soviet Baby Boomers: An Oral History of Russia's Cold War Generation* (Oxford University Press, 2012).

Read, Christopher, *Culture and Power in Revolutionary Russia: The Intelligentsia and the Transition from Tsarism to Communism* (Houndmills, Basingstoke: Macmillan, 1990).

Reid, Susan, "Cold War in the Kitchen: Gender and De-Stalinization of Consumer Taste in the Soviet Union under Khrushchev," *Slavic Review*, 61 (2002): 211–52.

"Destalinization and Taste, 1953–1963," *Journal of Design History*, 10 (1997): 177–201.

"In the Name of the People: The Manège Affair Revisited," *Kritika*, 6 (2005): 673–716.

"Who Will Beat Whom? Soviet Popular Reception of the American National Exhibition in Moscow, 1959," *Kritika*, 9 (2008): 855–904.

Renan, Ernest, "What is a Nation?" in Omar Dahbour and Micheline Ishay (eds.), *The Nationalism Reader* (Atlantic Highlands, NJ: Humanities Press, 1995), 143–56.

Reyman, Karl and Herman Singer, "The Origins and Significance of East European Revisionism," in Leopold Labedz (ed.), *Revisionism: Essays on the History of Marxist Ideas* (Plainview, NY: Books for Libraries Press, 1974), 215–22.

Richmond, Yale, *Cultural Exchange and the Cold War: Raising the Iron Curtain* (University Park: Pennsylvania State University Press, 2003).

Ringer, Fritz K., *Education and Society in Modern Europe* (Bloomington: Indiana University Press, 1979).

Risch, William Jay, *The Ukrainian West: Culture and the Fate of Empire in Soviet Lviv* (Cambridge, MA: Harvard University Press, 2011).

Roth-Ey, Kristin, "'Loose Girls' on the Loose: Sex, Propaganda, and the 1957 Youth Festival," in Susan E. Reid and Melanie Ilič (eds.), *Women in the Khrushchev Era* (Houndmills, Basingstoke and New York: Palgrave Macmillan, 2004), 75–95.

Moscow Prime Time: How the Soviet Union Built the Media Empire that Lost the Cultural Cold War (Ithaca, NY: Cornell University Press, 2011).

Rozhdestvenskii, S. D., "Materialy istorii samodeiatel'nykh ob'edinenii v SSSR posle 1945 goda," *Pamiat': istoricheskii sbornik*, 5 (1981): 226–86.

Rudakov, B. N., *Mnogo let proneslos' . . . o veteranakh Moskovskogo universiteta* (Moscow: Izdatel'stvo MGU, 1995).

Ruffley, David, *Children of Victory: Young Specialists and the Evolution of Soviet Society* (Westport, CT and London: Praeger, 2003).

Rutkevich, M. N. and F. R. Filippov, "Social Sources of Recruitment of the Intelligentsia," in Murray Yanowitch and Wesley A. Fisher (eds.), *Social Stratification and Mobility in the USSR* (White Plains, NY: International Arts and Sciences Press, 1973), 241–74.

Sandle, Mark, "A Triumph of Ideological Hairdressing? Intellectual Life in the Brezhnev Era Reconsidered," in Edwin Bacon and Mark Sandle (eds.), *Brezhnev Reconsidered* (Houndmills, Basingstoke: Palgrave Macmillan, 2002), 135–64.

Schattenberg, Susanne, "'Democracy' or 'Despotism'? How the Secret Speech was Translated into Everyday Life," in Polly Jones (ed.), *The Dilemmas of De-Stalinization: Negotiating Cultural and Social Change in the Khrushchev Era* (London: Routledge, 2006), 64–79.

Schwartz, Joseph, "The Young Communist League (1954–1962): A Study of Group Cooperation and Conflict in Soviet Society" (Ph.D. diss., Indiana University, 1965).

Seleznev, Viktor, *Kto vybiraet svobodu. Saratov: khronika inakomysliia, 1920–1980-e gody* (Borisoglebsk: "Poliarnaia zvezda," 2010).

"Saratov: khronika inakomysliia" (unpublished manuscript).

Shapoval, Iurii, *Ukraina XX stolittia: osobi ta podii v kontektsi vazhkoi istorii* (Kyiv: "Heneza," 2001).

Shatz, Marshall S., *Soviet Dissent in Historical Perspective* (Cambridge University Press, 1980).

Shils, Edward, "The Intellectuals and the Powers: Some Perspectives for Comparative Analysis," *Comparative Studies in Society and History*, 1 (1958): 5–22.

Shlapentokh, Vladimir, "Attitudes and Behavior of Soviet Youth in the 1970s and 1980s: The Mysterious Variable in Soviet Politics," in Richard G. Braungart and Margaret M. Braungart (eds.), *Research in Political Sociology*, vol. 2 (Greenwich, CT: JAI Press, 1986), 199–224.

Soviet Intellectuals and Political Power: The Post-Stalin Era (Princeton University Press, 1990).

Shternshis, Anna, *Soviet and Kosher: Jewish Popular Culture in the Soviet Union, 1923–1939* (Bloomington: Indiana University Press, 2006).

Siddiqi, Asif A., *The Red Rockets' Glare: Spaceflight, and the Soviet Imagination, 1857–1957* (Cambridge University Press, 2010).

Siegelbaum, Lewis H. (ed.), *Borders of Socialism: Private Spheres of Soviet Russia* (New York: Palgrave Macmillan, 2006).

Silina, L. V., *Nastroeniia sovetskogo studenchestva, 1945–1964* (Moscow: Russkii mir, 2004).

Simon, Gerhard, *Nationalism and Policy toward the Nationalities in the Soviet Union: From Totalitarian Dictatorship to Post-Stalinist Society*, trans. Karen Forster and Oswald Forster (Boulder, CO: Westview Press, 1991).

Slezkine, Yuri, *The Jewish Century* (Princeton University Press, 2004).

"The USSR as a Communal Apartment, or How a Socialist State Promoted Ethnic Particularism," *Slavic Review*, 53 (1994): 414–52.

Smith, Kathleen E., "'Acts Incompatible with the Title of Komsomol': Studying Genetics in the Age of Lysenko," a paper presented at the 2009 Association for Slavic, East European, and Eurasian Studies National Convention in Boston.

"A New Generation of Political Prisoners: 'Anti-Soviet' Students, 1956–1957," *The Soviet and Post-Soviet Review*, 32 (2005): 191–208.

Snyder, Timothy, *The Reconstruction of Nations: Poland, Ukraine, Lithuania, Belarus, 1569–1999* (New Haven, CT: Yale University Press, 2003).

Soifer, Valerii, *Vlast' i nauka: razgrom kommunistami genetiki v SSSR* (Moscow: Izdatel'stvo "CheRo," 2002).

Solnick, Stephen, *Stealing the State: Control and Collapse in Soviet Institutions* (Cambridge, MA: Harvard University Press, 1998).

Sonin, A. S., "'Delo' Zhebraka i Dubinina," *Voprosy istorii estestvoznaniia i tekhniki*, 1 (2000): 34–68.

Starr, Frederick, *Red and Hot: The Fate of Jazz in the Soviet Union 1917–1991* (New York: Limelight editions, 1994).

Suny, Ronald Grigor, *The Revenge of the Past: Nationalism, Revolution, and the Collapse of the Soviet Union* (Stanford University Press, 1993).

Suri, Jeremi, *Power and Protest: Global Revolution and the Rise of Détente* (Cambridge, MA: Harvard University Press, 2003).

Swafford, Michael, "Perceptions of Social Status in the USSR," in James R. Millar (ed.), *Politics, Work, and Daily Life in the USSR: A Survey of Former Soviet Citizens* (Cambridge University Press, 1987), 279–300.

Szelenyi, Ivan and Bill Martin, "The Three Waves of New Class Theories," *Theory and Society*, 17 (1988): 645–67.

Szporluk, Roman, *Communism and Nationalism: Karl Marx versus Friedrich List* (New York: Oxford University Press, 1988).

"The Soviet West – or Far Eastern Europe?" *East European Politics and Societies*, 5 (1991): 466–82.

Taubman, William, *Khrushchev: The Man and His Era* (New York: Norton, 2003).

et al. (eds.), *Nikita Khrushchev* (New Haven, CT: Yale University Press, 2000).

Titov, Alexander, "The 1961 Party Programme and the Fate of Khrushchev's Reforms," in Melanie Ilič and Jeremy Smith (eds.), *Soviet State and Society under Nikita Khrushchev* (London: Routledge, 2009), 8–25.

Tolz, Vladimir with Julie Corwin, "Soviet Reactions to Foreign Broadcasting in the 1950s," in A. Ross Johnson and R. Eugene Parta (eds.), *Cold War Broadcasting: Impact on the Soviet Union and Eastern Europe: A Collection of Studies and Documents* (Budapest: Central European University Press, 2010), 277–98.

Tomoff, Kirill, *Creative Union: The Professional Organization of Soviet Composers, 1939–1953* (Ithaca, NY: Cornell University Press, 2006).

Tromly, Benjamin, "Brother or Other? East European Students in Soviet Higher Education Establishments, 1948–1956," forthcoming in *European History Quarterly*.

"Intelligentsia Self-Fashioning in the Postwar Soviet Union: Revol't Pimenov's Political Struggle, 1949–1957," *Kritika*, 13 (2012): 151–76.

"Re-imagining the Soviet Intelligentsia: Student Politics and University Life, 1948–1964" (Ph.D. diss., Harvard University, 2007).

"The Rise and Decline of Soviet Patriotism: University Students in Khrushchev-Era Russia and Ukraine," *Nationalities Papers*, 37 (2009): 299–326.

Tsipursky, Gleb, *Having Fun in the Thaw Youth Initiative Clubs in the Post-Stalin Years* (University of Pittsburgh Press, 2012).

"Integration, Celebration, and Challenge: Soviet Youth and Elections, 1953–1968," in Ralph Jessen et al. (eds.), *Voting for Hitler and Stalin Elections under 20th Century Dictatorships* (Frankfurt: Campus Verlag, 2011), 81–102.

Tumarkin, Nina, *Lenin Lives! The Lenin Cult in Soviet Russia* (Cambridge, MA: Harvard University Press, 1983).

Turner, Frank M., "Newman's University and Ours," in John Henry Newman, *The Idea of a University* (New Haven, CT: Yale University Press, 1996), 282–301.

Urban, Michael, "Regime and Politics in the Pre-Political Period," in Michael Urban et al. (eds.), *The Rebirth of Politics in Russia* (Cambridge University Press, 1997).

Vail', Petr and Aleksandr Genis, *60-e: mir sovetskogo cheloveka* (Moscow: "Novoe literaturnoe obozrenie," 1996).

Vihavainen, Timo, *The Inner Adversary: The Struggle against Philistinism as the Moral Mission of the Russian Intelligentsia* (Washington, DC: New Academia Publishing, 2006).

Volkov, S. V., *Intellektual'nyi sloi v sovetskom obshchestve* (St. Petersburg: Fond "Razvitie," Institut nauchnoi informatsii po obshchestvennym naukam RAN, 1999).

Volkov, Vadim, "The Concept of Kul'turnost': Notes on the Soviet Civilizing Process," in Sheila Fitzpatrick (ed.), *Stalinism: New Directions* (London: Routledge, 1999), 210–30.

Von Geldern, James, "The Centre and the Periphery: Cultural and Social Geography in the Mass Culture of the 1930s," in Ronald G. Suny (ed.), *The Structure of Soviet History: Essays and Documents* (New York: Oxford University Press, 2002), 177–88.

Voslensky, Mikhail, *Nomenklatura: The Soviet Ruling Class*, trans. Eric Mosbacher (London: Bodley Head, 1984).

Walker, Barbara, *Maximilian Voloshin and the Russian Literary Circle: Culture and Survival in Revolutionary Times* (Bloomington: Indiana University Press, 2005).

"On Reading Soviet Memoirs: A History of the 'Contemporaries' Genre as an Institution of Russian Intelligentsia Culture from the 1790s to the 1970s." *The Russian Review*, 59 (2002): 327–52.

Weber, Max, "Class, Status, Party," in H. H. Gerth and C. Wright Mills (eds.), *From Max Weber: Essays in Sociology* (New York: Oxford University Press, 1958), 180–95.

Weiner, Amir, "The Empires Pay a Visit: Gulag Returnees, East European Rebellions, and Soviet Frontier Politics," *The Journal of Modern History*, 78 (2006): 333–76.

"The Making of a Dominant Myth: The Second World War and the Construction of Political Identities within the Soviet Polity," *Russian Review*, 55 (1996): 638–60.

Making Sense of War: The Second World War and the Fate of the Bolshevik Revolution (Princeton University Press, 2001).

Weiner, Douglas R., *A Little Corner of Freedom: Russian Nature Protection from Stalin to Gorbachev* (Berkeley: University of California Press, 1999).

Woll, Josephine, *Invented Truth: Soviet Reality and the Literary Imagination of Iurii Trifonov* (Durham, NC: Duke University Press, 1991).

Yekelchyk, Serhy, "Celebrating the Soviet Present: The Zhdanovshchina Campaign in Ukrainian Literature and the Arts, 1946–1948," in Donald J. Raleigh (ed.), *Provincial Landscapes: Local Dimensions of Soviet Power, 1917–1953* (University of Pittsburgh Press, 2001), 255–75.

"The Civic Duty to Hate: Stalinist Citizenship as Political Practice and Civic Emotion (Kiev, 1943–53)," *Kritika*, 7 (2006): 529–56.

Stalin's Empire of Memory: Russian–Ukrainian Relations in the Soviet Historical Imagination (University of Toronto Press, 2004).

Yurchak, Alexei, *Everything was Forever, until it was No More: The Last Soviet Generation* (Princeton University Press, 2006).

Zaslavsky, Victor and Robert J. Brym, *Soviet-Jewish Emigration and Soviet Nationality Policy* (New York: St. Martin's Press, 1983).

Zemskov, V. N., "Repatriatsiia sovetskikh grazhdan i ikh dal'neishaia sud'ba," *Sotsiologicheskie issledovaniia*, 5 (1995), at *Vtoraia mirovaia voina, Velikaia Otechestvennaia voina*, www.pseudology.org/Pobeda/Repatriacia1944_1956. htm (accessed 5 February 2012).

Zezina, M. R., *Sovetskaia khudozhestvennaia intelligentsiia i vlast' v 1950-e–60-e gody* (Moscow: Dialog MGU, 1999).

Zhuk, Sergei I., *Rock and Roll in the Rocket City: The West, Identity, and Ideology in Soviet Dniepropetrovsk, 1960–1985* (Washington, DC: Woodrow Wilson Center Press, 2010).

Zubkova, Elena, *Obshchestvo i reformy* (Moscow: Rossiia molodaia, 1993).

Poslevoennoe sovetskoe obshchestvo: politika i povsednevnost', 1945–1953 (Moscow: ROSSPEN, 1999).

Zubok, Vladislav, *A Failed Empire: The Soviet Union in the Cold War from Stalin to Gorbachev* (Chapel Hill: University of North Carolina Press, 2007).

Zhivago's Children: The Last Russian Intelligentsia (Cambridge, MA: Belknap Press, 2009).

Index

Printed in Great Britain
by Amazon

79755425R00176